TEXT AND CONTEXT
FRANK COULSON, SERIES EDITOR

READING OVID in MEDIEVAL WALES

PAUL RUSSELL

THE OHIO STATE UNIVERSITY PRESS | COLUMBUS

Library of Congress Cataloging-in-Publication Data
Names: Russell, Paul, 1956 February 23– author.
Title: Reading Ovid in medieval Wales / Paul Russell.
Other titles: Text and context (Columbus, Ohio)
Description: Columbus : The Ohio State University Press, [2017] | Series: Text and context |
    Includes bibliographical references and index.
Identifiers: LCCN 2016051359 | ISBN 9780814213223 (cloth ; : alk. paper) | ISBN 0814213227 (cloth ;
    : alk. paper)
Subjects: LCSH: Ovid, 43 B.C.–17 A.D. or 18 A.D. Ars amatoria. | Ovid, 43 B.C.–17 A.D. or 18 A.D.—
    Language—Glossaries, vocabularies, etc. | Welsh language—To 1100—Glossaries, vocabularies,
    etc. | Ovid, 43 B.C.–17 A.D. or 18 A.D.—Criticism and interpretation. | Love poetry, Latin—History
    and criticism. | Manuscripts, Medieval—Wales.
Classification: LCC PA6519.A8 R87 2017 | DDC 871/.01—dc23
LC record available at https://lccn.loc.gov/2016051359

Cover design by Martyn Schmoll
Text design by Juliet Williams
Type set in Charis and Gill Sans

Cover image: *P. Ouidii Nasonis libri de tristibus.* Venice, 1511, fol. 58v.

9 8 7 6 5 4 3 2 1

In memoriam matris meae

CONTENTS

ILLUSTRATIONS

TABLES

FIGURES

MANUSCRIPT SIGLA

Note: This list is not exhaustive but includes the glossed manuscripts which are discussed in this volume.

A	London, British Library Additional 14086 (ca. 1100)
A_b	London, British Library, Additional 21169 (s. xiii)
B	Bern, Burgerbibliothek 478 (s. xii/xiii)
b	Bamberg Msc. Class. 30 (M. V.18) (s. ix)
H	London, British Library, Additional 49369 (olim Holkham 322) (s. xiii)
O	Oxford, Bodleian Library, Auct. F. 4. 32 (s. ix)
O_b	Oxford, Bodleian Library, Canon. Class. 1 (s. xiii)
O_g	Oxford, Bodleian Library, Canon. Class. 18 (s. xv *inc.*)
Ox. 1	See O (for this usage, see p. 25).
Ox. 2	Oxford, Bodleian Library, 572 (for this usage, see p. 25).
o	Oxford, Bodleian Library, Rawlinson Q d. 19 (s. xiii)
P_a	Paris BN Latin 7993 (s. xiii)
P_f	Paris BN Latin 8430 (s. xiii)
p_2	Paris BN Latin 15155 (excerpts) (s. xiii)
R	Paris, BN Latin 7311 (Regius) (s. xi)
S_a	St Gall, Stiftsbibliothek, 821 (s. xi)
Y	Berlin, Staatsbibliothek, Hamilton 471 (s. xi)
W	Perpignan, Bibliothèque municipale, 19 (olim Bibliothèque munici-pale, 10) (s. xiv)

ABBREVIATIONS

Note: The abbreviations of the titles of texts are explained by short titles; the full details can be found in the Bibliography. Old Welsh words from the text under discussion are printed in bold throughout.

AA	Ovid, *Ars amatoria*
Angers	Angers MS 477; a text of Bede on time containing glosses in Latin, Old Breton and Old Welsh (*EGOW* xiv; Fleuriot and Evans, *Dictionary/Dictionnaire*, I. 8–11)
BAV	Bibliotheca Apostolica Vaticana
BBCS	*Bulletin of the Board of Celtic Studies*
BL	British Library, London
BN	Bibliothèque Nationale, Paris
ByT (Cleo)	*Brut y Brenhinedd: Cotton Cleopatra Version* (ed. Parry).
ByT (RB)	*Brut y Tywysogyon . . . Red Book of Hergest Version* (ed. and trans. Jones)
ByT (Pen. 20)	*Brut y Tywysogyon, Peniarth MS. 20* (ed. Jones); trans. in *Brut y Tywysogyon . . . Peniarth MS. 20 Version* (trans. Jones)
CBMLC	Corpus of British Medieval Library Catalogues
CBT I	*Gwaith Meilyr Brydydd* (ed. Williams et al.).
CBT II	*Gwaith Llywelyn Fardd I ac Eraill* (ed. Bramley et al.)
CBT IV	*Gwaith Cynddelw Brydydd Mawr* II (ed. Jones and Owen)
CBT VII	*Gwaith Bleddyn Fardd a Beirdd Eraill* (ed. Andrews et al.)
CCCC	Corpus Christi College, Cambridge
CDG	*Cerddi Dafydd ap Gwilym* (ed. Johnston et al.)
CMCS	*Cambridge Medieval Celtic Studies* 1–25; *Cambrian Medieval Celtic Studies* 26—
CUL	Cambridge University Library

CYSDT	*Cywyddau Ymryson Syr Dafydd Trefor* (ed. Ifans).
De raris fabulis	Oxford, Bodleian Library, 572, fol. 41v–47r; a colloquy text (*Early Scholastic Colloquies* (ed. Stevenson), 1–11)
DGA	*Selections from Dafydd ap Gwilym: Apocrypha* (ed. Helen Fulton)
DIL	*Dictionary of the Irish Language* (ed. Quin et al.).
DMLBS	*Dictionary of Medieval Latin from British Sources* (ed. Latham, et al.)
DN	*Poetical Works of Dafydd Nanmor* (ed. Roberts and Williams)
EGOW	Falileyev. *Etymological Glossary*
GDB	*Gwaith Dafydd Bach* (ed. Daniel)
GDE	*Gwaith Dafydd Epynt* (ed. Thomas)
GDG	*Gwaith Dafydd ap Gwilym* (ed. Parry)
GDLlF	*Gwaith Dafydd Llwyd* (ed. Richards)
GGG	*Gwaith Guto'r Glyn* (ed. Willams and Williams)
GGM	*Gwaith Gwerful Mechain* (ed. Howells)
GHD	*Gwaith Hywel Dafi* (ed. Lake)
GIF	*Gwaith Iorwerth Fynglwyd* (ed. Jones and Rowlands)
GIG	*Gwaith Iolo Goch* (ed. Johnston)
GILlF	*Gwaith Ieuan ap Llywelyn Fychan* ((ed. Bryant-Quinn)
GIRh	*Gwaith Ieuan ap Rhydderch* (ed. Daniel)
gl.	glossed by
GLGC	*Gwaith Lewis Glyn Cothi* (ed. Johnston)
GLM	*Gwaith Lewys Morgannwg* (ed. Lake)
GLl	*Gwaith Llawdden* (ed. Daniel)
GLlG	*Gwaith Llywelyn ap Gutun* (ed. Daniel)
GLlGMH	*Gwaith Llywelyn Goch ap Meurig Hen* (ed. Johnston)
GMRh	*Gwaith Maredudd ap Rhys* (ed. Roberts)
GMW	Evans, *A Grammar of Middle Welsh*
GO	*L'oeuvre poétique de Gutun Owain* (ed. Bachellery)
GP	*Gramadegau'r Penceirddiaid* (ed. Williams and Jones)
GPB	*Gwaith Prydydd Breuan* (ed. Edwards)
GPC	*Geiriadur Prifysgol Cymru* (ed. Thomas, et al.)
GRB	*Gwaith Rhys Brydydd a Rhisiart ap Rhys* (ed. Williams and Rowlands)
GRhGE	*Gwaith Rhys Goch Eryri* (ed. Evans)
GSDT	*Gwaith Syr Dafydd Trefor* (ed. Ifans)
GSH	*Gwaith Siôn ap Hywel ap Llywelyn Fychan* (ed. Lake)
GSRh	*Gwaith Sefnyn, et al.* (ed. Jones and Rheinallt)
GST	*Gwaith Siôn Tudur* (ed. Roberts)
GTA	*Gwaith Tudur Aled* (ed. Jones)
HGK	*Historia Gruffud vab Kenan* (ed. Evans)
HRB	*Geoffrey of Monmouth*, The History of the Kings of Britain (ed. Reeve, trans. Wright)

ID	*Casgliad o Waith Ieuan Deulwyn* (ed. Williams)
IGE[1]	*Cywyddau Iolo Goch ac Eraill,* 1st edn (ed. Lewis, Roberts, and Williams)
IGE[2]	*Cywyddau Iolo Goch ac Eraill,* 2nd edn (ed. Lewis, Roberts, and Williams)
IRHT	Institut de Recherche et de l'Histoire des Textes, Paris
Mart. Cap.	The text of Martianus Capella preserved in CCCC 153 which is glossed in Latin and Old Welsh (*EGOW* xvi)
Met.	Ovid, *Metamorphoses*
MPW	*A Medieval Prince of Wales* (trans. Evans) (English translation of *HGK*)
MW	Middle Welsh
MnW	Modern Welsh
NLW	National Library of Wales, Aberystwyth
NLWJ	*National Library of Wales Journal*
OCT	Oxford Classical Texts
ODNB	*Oxford Dictionary of National Biography,* ed. Matthew, Harrison et al.)
OW	Old Welsh
PRO	Public Records Office (now The National Archives)
SDR	*Chwedlau Seith Doethon Rufein* (ed. Lewis)
S. C.	Madan and Craster. *A Summary Catalogue of Western Manuscripts*
SG	*Y Seint Greal* (ed. Williams)
UCL	University College London
VGC	*Vita Griffini filii Conani* (ed. Russell)
VVB	Loth, *Vocabulaire vieux-breton*
YT	*Ystoria Taliesin* (ed. Ford)
ZCP	*Zeitschrift für celtische Philologie*

ACKNOWLEDGMENTS

This year marks the two thousandth anniversary of Ovid's death in Tomis. It is fitting that this volume should appear now and that its focus is both the earliest surviving manuscript fragment of his work and its reception some eight hundred years later in medieval Wales at the other end of the former empire.

A work like this incurs a vast number of debts. Much time has been spent in libraries, and I am grateful to the librarians at the Bodleian Library, the British Library, the Cambridge University Library, the Library of the Royal Society of Physicians, the National Library of Wales in Aberystwyth, and the libraries of St John's College and Trinity College, Cambridge, for their help. At an early stage Ted Kenney, the editor of the Oxford Classical Text of Ovid's amatory works, very kindly lent me his collection of photographs of manuscripts, which has saved me an immense amount of time in working out which manuscripts I needed to see. Likewise, the apparently bottomless collection of microfilms (and extraordinarily helpful staff) at the IRHT in Paris also helped to shorten my task. The following libraries kindly granted me permission to publish images from their collections and helped me track down elusive material: the Bodleian Libraries, the British Library, the Staatsbibliothek Berlin (with particular thanks to Robert Giel), the Médiathèque municipale in Perpignan (especially Marie-Andrée Calafat), the Stiftsbibliothek St Gall, and University College London (especially Dan Mitchell).

The individual debts amassed are considerable and, *inter alios,* I am grateful to the following people for placing their expertise at my disposal in many ways: Gareth Bevan, Rachel Bond, Mary Clapinson, Charlene Eska, Georgia Henley, Pierre-Yves Lambert, Karianne Lemmen, Rosalind Love, Silva Nurmio, Elena Parina, Erich Poppe, Michael Reeve,

Simon Rodway, Peter Schrijver, Richard Sharpe, and Patrick Sims-Williams. Maredudd ap Huw, Alderik Blom, Thomas Charles-Edwards, Barry Lewis, and Silva Nurmio have read parts or all of this work in draft and have saved me from much confusion and error, as did the thoughtful and extremely help-ful comments of two anonymous readers. Over the last several years papers based on various sections of this book have been presented in Cambridge, the Dublin Institute for Advanced Studies, the École Pratique des Hautes Études in Paris, NUI Galway, Northwestern University, Oxford, UCLA, and the Uni-versity of Connecticut. On two occasions the members of the workshop on Datblygiad yr Iaith Gymraeg—Development of the Welsh Language (funded by the British Academy)—have had excerpts of this material presented to them. I am grateful to the audiences on all of these occasions for their feedback and stamina.

The Department of Anglo-Saxon, Norse, and Celtic in Cambridge kindly covered the costs of reproducing the images in this book, and thanks go to Myriah Williams for her help in processing them. When presented with the proposal for this book, Frank Coulson at The Ohio State University greeted it with enthusiasm, and I am grateful for his support and willingness to give it a home in his Text and Context series. Eugene O'Connor and the staff at The Ohio State University Press have been extremely helpful in turning this into a book. I am, as ever, grateful to my family for their support.

The last few years have also been a period of losses. I first encountered the Old Welsh glosses to *Ars amatoria* I in classes taught by the late D. Ellis Evans, the Jesus Professor of Celtic in Oxford when I was a fledgling graduate stu-dent; the detailed notes I amassed under his instruction underlie the Welsh aspects of this work. The late Anna Morpurgo Davies, Oxford professor of comparative philology, taught me to think and argue; although she claimed to know nothing of Celtic, she could always ask the most penetrating questions. Finally, and most importantly, as we were growing up, my mother taught us the value of hard work; this work which she will never see is dedicated to her memory. But since she always regarded the end of one thing as the beginning of the next, she would have been quietly pleased but would have wanted to know what the next book was about.

1

INTRODUCTION

Qui sine commento rimaris scripta Maronis
Inmunis nuclei solo de cortice rodis

You who investigate the writings of Virgil without a commentary are gnawing only at the outer bark of an untouched core

—Egbert of Liège, *The Well-Laden Ship*[1]

lthough these lines refer to Virgil, the same sentiment—that commentary and gloss were vital to the understanding of such texts—permeated medieval thinking about other classical texts as well. The fourth part of Oxford, Bodleian Library, Auct. F. 4. 32 (*S. C.* 2176), contains a ninth-century copy of Ovid's *Ars amatoria*, Book I, parts of which are heavily glossed in Latin and Old Welsh. It is a text which has been more mentioned in passing than studied in detail and consequently has remained marginal to the several scholarly fields in which it should figure. Classicists interested in the textual transmission of Ovid's love poetry have acknowledged its early date but have noted its sometimes inferior text and fragmentary nature and have not unreasonably ignored its glosses. Most medievalists, whose expertise tends more naturally to be Latinate than Celtic, have pointed to its significance as a forerunner of the commentary tradition of the *Aetas Ovidiana* and moved on.[2] Celticists have plundered it for its vernacular glosses, added them to the meagre store of evidence for the oldest stages of the Brittonic languages, and ignored the Latin glosses completely. Palaeographers have observed that it is a good example of early Welsh minuscule (occasionally noting the two finely drawn ornamental letters), argued about whether Dunstan

---

1. Egbert of Liège, *The Well-Laden Ship,* ed. Babcock, ll. 923–4; cf. Black, "Teaching Techniques," 246.
2. An honourable exception is Hexter, *Ovid and Medieval Schooling,* 26–41.

copied the final page, and wondered vaguely why a copy of Ovid's *Ars amatoria* should find itself in such august company in Glastonbury (where it was eventually bound together with the other sections of the current compilation). Scholars of medieval Welsh interested in the frequent references to *Ofydd* in fourteenth- and fifteenth-century Welsh poetry have occasionally noted the presence of an Ovid manuscript in ninth-century south Wales. But no one working in these disparate fields has stopped to look at all these aspects of the text in any significant detail, nor attempted to tie it into what is known about these various fields. This is a text, however, which stands at the intersection of all these areas and deserves to be better known by scholars working in these fields. This is what this volume sets out to do.

At its core, this volume presents an edition of the text including all the glosses and annotation with a full commentary on the glosses. The surrounding discussion examines the various contexts in which the text should be considered. It is argued that the glossed text of *Ars amatoria* I preserved in this manuscript represents an important outlier of the early glossing tradition on Ovid which developed into the fully fledged commentary tradition seen from the eleventh century onwards. Comparison with other glossed manuscripts, such as St Gall Stiftsbibliothek 812 (S_a), BL Additional 14086 (A), and Perpignan Bibliothèque municipale 19 (W), suggests that the Latin glosses and commentary were added cumulatively and that the Old Welsh vernacular glosses only constitute the last of many layers of glosses.[3] It is also argued that at least one layer of the Latin glosses must have been added in a Celtic context (perhaps with some Irish influence) as they show distinctively Celtic features in the Latin or in the glossing technique.[4] The Old Welsh glosses are also examined in the context of the Brittonic and Old Irish glossing tradition; it is shown that they are consistent with the glossing techniques in the other parts of this and other manuscripts and are part of the vibrant and productive vernacular glossing tradition in early medieval Britain, Ireland, and on the Continent.[5] The cumulative glossing in this manuscript (and especially the later phases of it) had the prime purpose of teaching learners what they needed to know to read Latin verse, and this is why it concentrates on the features where Latin verse differs from prose. As such, the teaching techniques can be usefully compared with other texts from Celtic-speaking areas which operate at a more basic pedagogical level (such as the colloquy text preserved in Oxford, Bodleian Library, 572, fols. 41v–47r). Such is the density of the glossing in certain parts of the text that it is even possible to gain a sense of how a running commentary on the text might go, how it might have been used in a

---

3. See Chapter 3.
4. See 76–78.
5. See 8–12.

classroom, and what was important for a teacher to get across to his pupils. It was clearly not an issue that most glosses were in Latin but that some were in Welsh; it was all grist to the mill in terms of teaching the text. As a postscript, the later life of Ovid's love poetry in medieval Wales is considered both in terms of continuity (or the lack of it) from the ninth century and also in its own right as possible evidence for the Ovidian tradition in later medieval Wales.[6]

The remainder of this introductory chapter briefly considers some of the broader contextual aspects while maintaining the focus on our text: the later Ovidian commentary tradition, the practice of glossing texts in Brittonic languages, and the context of the manuscript in which our text is preserved.

THE OVIDIAN COMMENTARY TRADITION

Quia etsi auctor Ouidius idem in quibusdam opusculis suis, id est Fastorum, de Ponto, de Nuce et in aliis utcumque tolerandus esset, quis eum de amore croccitantem, in diuersis epistolis euagantem, si sanum sapiat, toleret?[7]

Conrad of Hirsau's anxiety, expressed in his *Dialogus super auctores*, about Ovid "croaking on about love" clearly had a sufficient resonance with the composers of *accessus* to these texts that they felt the need to justify why Ovid's love poetry should still figure as part of their compendia. The fact that the *Remedia amoris*, a text which takes a step back from the three books of *Ars amatoria*, became the most common of the amatory works in such collections may be significant, but it does raise interesting questions as to how and why a fragment of the *Ars* survived into the ninth century in Wales.

This is not the place for a full survey of the great flourishing of scholarship on the *Aetas Ovidiana* and the growth of the Ovidian commentary tradition, and what follows in this section takes our text of Ovid, *Ars amatoria* I, as its focus and attempts to embed it further into the context of the scholarship on the medieval Ovid than has been done previously.[8] As observed above, this

---

6. See Chapter 6.

7. *Accessus ad auctores,* ed. Huygens, p. 114 (ll. 1332–35): "Even if the author, Ovid, should be tolerated up to a point in some of those works of his, such as the *Fasti,* his *Epistulae ex Ponto,* the *Nux,* and the others, who in their right mind would tolerate him croaking on about love, digressing disgracefully in various letters?" (my translation); also in *Dialogo sugli autori,* ed. Marchionni, ll. 1189–93. Cf. also Munk Olsen, "*Accessus*"; Whitbread, "Conrad of Hirsau."

8. In doing so, I recognize that it covers some of the same ground as the opening chapters of Hexter, *Ovid and Medieval Schooling.* Recent general studies include Ward, "The Classics in the Classroom"; Knappe, "Manuscript Evidence of the Teaching of the Language Arts"; Lendinara, "Instructional Manuscripts in England"; also Riché, *Écoles et enseignement.* Although Ovid is not discussed in detail, Reynolds, *Medieval Reading* is an important contribution.

version with its glossing (in whichever language) has remained on the sidelines. It typically figures in the introduction to volumes of collected essays or in the introductory remarks of the requisite medieval chapter within such volumes, and tends to be the subject of overgeneralization or underspecification—which only serves to highlight the necessity of a full discussion of this manuscript in all its various contexts.[9] Richmond, for example, notes that it contains "glosses of an elementary nature, explaining in Latin or Welsh even quite simple words, and features of life in the classical period that were no longer familiar."[10] All this is correct and unobjectionable but implying that they were not very interesting, or at least less interesting than what was to follow in the later commentaries. It is certainly a striking feature of the glossing (both Latin and Welsh) that it is most densely concentrated on two key passages—the arcades, colonnades, and law courts in and around the forum (ll. 56–90) and a military triumph (ll. 175–224)—and not on, as one might suppose, the more titillating episodes in the book. Clark's introduction to a recent collection of essays on medieval Ovid follows a similar train of thought; he is descriptively correct that Ovid was "a point of reference for those beginning to grasp Latin grammar, syntax and vocabulary" and that "a deeper engagement with the ethical Ovid was encouraged by the pre-occupations of twelfth-century masters with conceptions of the self and self-expression."[11] But, when we bring this text more fully into the picture and examine it in detail, it is not so obvious that it predates "the change of emphasis in the schoolroom, from reading Ovid as a source for grammatical and rhetorical paradigms to recognition of its value as a stimulus for moral, ethical and philosophical reflections."[12] The "change of emphasis" is less clear-cut. Hexter, for example, has alluded to the moralizing elements in the longer marginal comments in our text, and indeed it may be hinted at in at least one Old Welsh gloss.[13] Moreover, Clark's description of the Ovid manuscript makes several assumptions which at best remain to be verified:

The so-called "Dunstan classbook" (Oxford, Bodl. Auct. MS F 4 32), passed through other hands before reaching Benedictine Glastonbury, but perhaps

---

9. Clark, "Introduction"; id., "Ovid in the Monasteries"; Dimmick, "Ovid in the Middle Ages"; Fyler, "The Medieval Ovid"; Hexter, "Ovid in the Middle Ages"; Richmond, "Manuscript Traditions"; Robathan, "Ovid in the Middle Ages," 192–93; cf. also Alton and Wormell, "Ovid in the Medieval Schoolroom," 25; McKinley, "Manuscripts of Ovid in England," 56. Indispensable are Coulson and Roy, *Incipitarium,* and Coulson, "Addenda and Corrigenda."

10. Richmond, "Manuscript Traditions," 448; cf. also Hexter, *Ovid and Medieval Schooling,* 34.

11. Clark, "Introduction," 8–9 and 11 respectively; note, however, that Clark is simply mistaken in stating that O contains a text of the *Heroides* and that the glosses are in Old English.

12. Clark, "Introduction," 13.

13. Hexter, *Ovid and Medieval Schooling,* 40–41; at l. 138 *nota* is glossed by Old Welsh **cared** "sin, blemish"; but cf. the discussion below, 84, 174–75.

it was principally the monks there, indeed Dunstan himself, who prepared its partial copy of the *Ars amatoria* for study. It was these same masters, and their *discipuli*, who formed the foundations of Ovid criticism, which grew incrementally from the forms of interlinear and marginal gloss that cluster in the Dunstan classbook, to the concise *accessus* found in the eleventh-century anthology of introductions to the curriculum authors, into fully formed commentaries. [14]

Given the Welsh content of this manuscript—and indeed the fact that the Welsh glossing is, apart from a handful of later glosses in the early pages, the final layer of glossing[15]—it is unlikely that the manuscript was "prepared" as a teaching text in Glastonbury.[16] Moreover, while as a type of text it could be argued to represent the forerunner to the more complex later *accessus* and commentaries, it will be argued below that this version with its vernacular glosses is very much an outlier rather than a forerunner; better examples of forerunners would be versions like S_a (the St Gall fragment of *AA* I) or *W* (Perpignan 19).[17] Another contention of what follows is that the glossing on our text is the product of accumulated layers of glossing, some of which is shared by other Continental manuscripts and only the last of which is in the vernacular.

However, it is certainly the case that an interest in language is to the fore, as Hexter has observed:

> The *Ars Amatoria,* or at least half of its first book, was used for educational purposes in the ninth century, when it was first written and glossed. . . . The primary function of the glosses was to facilitate the reading and comprehension of Ovid's text. The particular form and focus of many of the glosses lead to the conclusion that the master was keen to improve students' Latin, especially their grasp of grammar and command of vocabulary.[18]

He goes on to comment that:

> Much more time and energy were invested in working through the text and dealing with the kinds of questions the *glosulae* addressed. From this it seems

---

14. Clark, "Ovid in the Monasteries," 178.

15. See below, 39–41.

16. Clark's discussion of the manuscript, especially with its concentration on Dunstan and assumption that most of glossing took place at Glastonbury, follows on from Irvine's discussion (*The Making of Textual Culture,* 407–9, 411); as will emerge from what follows, this cannot be right.

17. For discussion, see below, 92–95 and 107–11.

18. Hexter, "Sex Education," 305. The comment that only the first half is glossed is misleading as there is a later batch of glosses as well (ll. 620–52) and his comment also implies intention; it is argued below that the patchy nature of the glossing is best explained by a broken exemplar (48–55).

clear to me that reading the *Ars Amatoria* (and other works of Ovid) in the schools was largely a means to an end: learning Latin and commanding the diction of Roman poetry that were clearly important constituents of high medieval Latin school culture and tools for acculturation and advancement.[19]

Similarly, an earlier remark by Hexter (relating to a different Ovidian text) about rapid changes of addressee being "dizzying," and therefore badly in need of glossing, is well taken and directly applicable to our text.[20] In the episode about a mistress and her servant (ll. 351–98) and the Pasiphaë episode (ll. 289–326), where multiple individuals are involved, and with at least two being of the same gender (which means that even pronouns can be ambiguous), the glossing is consequently preoccupied with ensuring we know who is who in any given line.

As "tools for acculturation and advancement," a detailed control and high-level competence in Latin verse would not have been simply the polish but a fundamental accomplishment and absolutely necessary for those seeking to grasp the nuance of sophisticated Latin discourse.[21] These issues in relation to Ovid are not so different from those discussed by Lapidge and Wieland and others for the early medieval period as to whether glossed texts were for classroom use or private study.[22] Presumably copies of such texts were not so common that any text could function only in one way. Moreover, whether we are talking about the complexity, subtlety, and nuance of Ovidian verse or sophisticated biblical and patristic exegesis, the point could easily, and often crucially, turn on whether a particular nominal form was understood as dative singular or ablative singular, as a genitive singular or nominative plural, or a verb as an indicative or subjunctive; in some instances the forms might be identical or the difference might lie in a single vowel. Given the vagaries of manuscript transmission, such variation, together with the concomitant exegetical risk, was inherent in every manuscript copy, and so it is hardly surprising that what seems like very elementary glossing was a vital prerequisite to more advanced exegesis.[23] In other words, detailed control of Latin verse is implicit in the later commentaries, and what we see in our text is that type of teaching relatively uncluttered by the accumulation of later comment.

---

19. Hexter, "Sex Education," 314.

20. Hexter, "Sex Education," 301, where he is referring to the opening lines of *Ars amatoria* III.

21. We may recall, for example, the clever Ovidian-style verses circulating among Alcuin and his friends.

22. Lapidge, "The Study of Latin Texts"; Wieland, "The Glossed Manuscript."

23. It is worth pointing out that scattered through O, and not just in the glossed sections, there are about a dozen instances of what might be collation readings which would suggest that on occasions our copy shared a desk with another copy of the same text; see below, 70–72.

There are often interesting sidelights and stimulating ideas to be derived from thinking about scholars' work on the later tradition even in work which does not directly relate to our text. For example, following on the theme of the preceding paragraph, Coulson's discussion of how William of Orléans taught the *Metamorphoses* is strikingly similar to what might be said of parts of the glossing strategy in O; in his exposition of *Met.* 2.689 "William is careful to guide his reader through a word-by-word exposition of the text, scrupulously underlining the connections between the constituent parts."[24] William was clearly under no illusions that the students could do this for themselves and it emphasizes the importance of the basic type of glossing that is the bread and butter of our text. In our text, mutatis mutandis, "scrupulous underlining of the connections" is mapped out, especially in the opening lines, by the detailed use of construe marks to mark the bigger building blocks of the line.[25] Smaller links are often provided by simple glosses which repeat a verb or a noun from the preceding lines in order to show that a noun or verb has to be understood in the next line too.[26] Even in sixteenth-century Paris, Blair has noted that the teacher "probably began his lessons on Ovid and other poets by providing a word-by-word paraphrase of each verse. . . . The commentary was clearly the focus of the lesson."[27]

Another stimulating case is that of Woods's work on the *Poetria nova*, which offers interesting parallels when thinking about how Ovid might be of use in the classroom;[28] both have to do with teaching verse and no doubt students several centuries apart would have been confused by the same things and cluttered their texts with the same or similar glosses as an aid to construing them. Woods quotes a marginal comment in a copy of *Poetria nova*:

Correxi textum ut potui; glosas pueriles quas scriptor apposuit teduit me abradere.[29]

---

24. Coulson, "Ovid's *Metamorphoses*," 58.

25. For construe marks in our text, see below, 64–67; for a more general discussion, see Robinson, "Syntactical Glosses"; Korhammer, "Mittelalterliche Konstruktionshilfen"; Blom, *Glossing the Psalms*.

26. For example, cf. l. 126 where *multas* is glossed by *puellas*, picking up the *puellae* of the preceding line; in l. 31 *este* is glossed *pro estote* to indicate that it is imperative, and then in the next line *queque* is glossed *.i. estote* to show that the force of the verb is carried over into the next line. For discussion, see below, 160.

27. Blair, "Lectures," 131–32; for other useful work in this area, see Black, "Teaching Techniques"; Alton, "The Medieval Commentators"; Coulson, "The Vulgate Commentary"; Engelbrecht, *Filologie in der Dertiende Eeuw*; id., "Carmina Pieridum"; id., "Fulco, Arnulf and William"; Ganz, "Conclusion"; Hexter, "Medieval Articulations"; id., "Ovid's Transformation"; McGregor, "Ovid at School"; Tarrant, "The *Narrationes* of Lactantius"; Ward, "From Marginal Gloss to *Catena* Commentary."

28. Woods, *Classroom Commentaries*; ead., *An Early Commentary*.

29. Woods, *Classroom Commentaries*, 50 (from Padua, Biblioteca universitaria, 505, fol. iiv): "I have corrected the text as much as possible; it wearied me to erase the puerile glosses that the

A similar sentiment may well have flickered through the mind of a monk of Glastonbury before he reminded himself how useful the glosses are.

THE BRITTONIC GLOSSING TRADITION

The evidence for the earliest stages of the insular Celtic languages (i.e. Old Irish, Old Welsh, Old Cornish, and Old Breton) almost entirely consists of glosses on Latin texts.[30] Although the same manuscripts occasionally have vernacular verse in their margins, by far the majority of the evidence is in the form of glosses. The Latin texts which are glossed range from biblical and patristic texts (e.g. Psalms, Pauline epistles), learned texts (e.g. Priscian, Martianus Capella, Bede's chronological texts), and historical texts (e.g. Bede, Orosius) to literary texts (such as the Ovid discussed in this volume). The glosses can be described generically as educational in purpose, but within that broad definition there are one-word lexical glosses, larger explanatory glosses, and long contextualizing commentary on the Latin text. Moreover, almost in all cases the texts also contain substantial amounts of glossing and commentary in Latin as well; in fact, the vernacular glossing is always proportionally only a small part of the learned commentary on these texts.

Scholarly work began on most of these glosses in the mid-nineteenth century with the publication of the first edition of Zeuss's *Grammatica Celtica* in 1853.[31] For Old Irish, the standard edition has been, and still is, for most purposes Stokes's and Strachan's *Thesaurus Palaeohibernicus* of 1901–3.[32] After Zeuss, the Brittonic glosses were republished piecemeal by Stokes and others in the late nineteenth century, including glosses discovered since Zeuss's grammar. For many of these collections of glosses, and especially the Old Welsh ones, Stokes' editions have remained standard with additional discussion of specific glosses carried out in the subject journals.[33] For Old Welsh,

---

scribe put in." The glossing of a vocative *papa* with *tu* (Angers, BM 523) can be compared with the glossing of vocatives in our text where in Latin we find *uō* (for *uocatiuus*) and in Old Welsh by **a** (corresponding to the more usual *o* in Latin texts); see ibid., 53, n. 19.

30. For a brief overview, see Dumville, "A *Thesaurus Palaeoanglicus*?," 61–65. This section concentrates on glossing in Brittonic languages, with occasional comments about glossing in Old Irish. Such discussions would also benefit from a comparison with glossing in Germanic languages; for an excellent example of this approach, see Blom, *Glossing the Psalms.*

31. A second edition, edited by Ebel, followed in 1871 after Zeuss's death.

32. For a useful and up-to-date bibliographical survey of Old Irish glossing, see Bronner, *Verzeichnis*; for recent work, see also n. 33 below.

33. See, for example, Stokes, "Cambrica"; id., "Die Glossen und Verse"; id., "The Old Welsh Glosses in Juvencus;" id., "The Old-Welsh Glosses on Martianus Capella." On the Martianus Capella glosses, see Bishop, "The Corpus Martianus Capella," and now, on the Old Welsh glosses, Lemmen, "The Old-Welsh Glosses on Martianus Capella." On their discovery by Bradshaw, see Russell, "'Grilling in Calcutta.'" For further bibliography, see Falileyev, *EGOW*.

Falileyev's *Etymological Glossary,* and his recent publication of a selection of glosses, has made the material more accessible even if it has not moved the subject forward very far.[34] That said, while Old Irish had its *Thesaurus Palaeohibernicus,* the equivalent for the Brittonic languages is lacking.[35]

One weakness of all the scholarship has always been that it focused on the Celtic glossing, provided relatively short ranges of the Latin text being glossed, and rarely, if ever, discussed the majority of the glosses in the manuscript—namely, the Latin ones. For example, although the *Thesaurus Palaeohibernicus* remains the fullest collection of the Old Irish glosses, no attention is paid to the Latin glossing and relatively little Latin context is provided for the Old Irish ones. More recently, Hofman's edition of the first five books of the St Gall Priscian (St Gall, Stiftsbibliothek 903) edited all the glosses;[36] and the recent online edition has extended Hofman's work for the whole text.[37] For the Brittonic material, the series of publications by McKee, who edited and discussed all the glossing and commentary in the Cambridge Juvencus (CUL, Ff. 4. 42), was a significant landmark;[38] most of the glossing and commentary is in Latin but there are significant amounts in Old Welsh and Old Irish.[39] The value of this edition, apart from its completeness, is that the glossing and commentary were added by a number of scribes and their stints and contributions can in most cases be clearly distinguished. It is possible, therefore, to get a sense of what individual scribes were doing—for example, one or two scribes were translating (or, indeed, partially translating) glosses from Old Irish into Old Welsh.[40] For many glossed manuscripts, the surviving manuscript is often a fair copy in one, maybe two, hands copying text and glosses together; such is the case for the Ovid text discussed in this volume. The effect is that in such manuscripts it is less easy to see what a particular scribe is doing, and that makes the survival of a manuscript like the Juvencus with its multiple hands all the more important.

---

34. *EGOW;* Falileyev, *Le Vieux-Gallois;* id., *Llawlyfr Hen Gymraeg.*

35. See Dumville, "A *Thesaurus Palaeoanglicus?*," 71–73.

36. Hofman, *The Sankt Gall Priscian Commentary.*

37. *St Gall Priscian Glosses* (ed. Hofman and Moran). This may be contrasted with the online edition of the Old Irish Milan glosses which only deals with the Old Irish ones: *Dictionary of the Old Irish Glosses* (ed. Stifter and Griffith), or the print dictionary of the Würzburg glosses: Kavanagh (ed. Wodtko), *Lexicon,* which likewise only deals with Old Irish.

38. *Juvencus Codex Cantabrigiensis Ff.4.22* (ed. McKee); ead., McKee, *The Cambridge Juvencus Manuscript;* ead., "Scribes and Glosses from Dark Age Wales." The poems preserved in the top margins of several pages have been edited by Stokes, "Die Glossen und Verse" and "The Old Welsh Glosses in Juvencus"; I. Williams, "The Juvencus Poems"; Watkins, "Englynion y Juvencus"; and Haycock, *Blodeugerdd,* 3–16.

39. For an earlier, excellent overview, see Lapidge, "Latin Learning in Dark Age Wales."

40. Harvey, "The Cambridge Juvencus Glosses"; Russell, "*An habes linguam Latinam?,*" 206–14; cf. also Russell, "Teaching between the Lines", 145–48.

While much of the work on Old Welsh was, as noted above, carried out in the late nineteenth and early twentieth centuries, work on Old Breton, where there are significantly more glosses than in Welsh, continued more energetically throughout the twentieth century. The groundwork of Zeuss and Stokes was carried on by Fleuriot and more recently by Lambert. Fleuriot's *Dictionnaire* was an important landmark in Old Breton studies as it gathered all the glosses into one volume, though in a dictionary format without edited texts;[41] the price paid for that compression was a reduction in context. More recent work, much of it by Lambert, has tackled the Old Breton (and Old Welsh and Old Irish) glosses from a different perspective, focusing on detail and context; the effect has been at times to reduce what we formerly thought of as Old Breton glosses into rather more banal Latin ones. In other cases, by paying close attention to the relationship between the lemma and the gloss (and in some cases reidentifying the lemma), interesting features of the glossing process have emerged, such as the identification of a medieval methodology for glossing grammatical features.[42] Another approach which has been developed is to compare similar glossing techniques across several collections, e.g. looking at the glossing of Priscian or Bede in several different manuscripts;[43] as a result, we gain a clear sense that vernacular glossing in Celtic languages, whether Brittonic or Goidelic, had much in common. Indeed, in some instances, such as the Cambridge Juvencus and elsewhere, there is evidence that not only might glosses have been copied from one copy to another but they might well have been translated from one vernacular language into another.[44] As will emerge from what follows in this volume, the close reading and understanding of how glosses work in their context can lead to interesting discoveries and re-evaluations, not least because the glosses are often triggered by very local pedagogical concerns within a line or two of the lemma and gloss.[45]

On the other hand, as will also be seen, it is crucial that the broader pedagogical context is taken into account. A particularly interesting manuscript in this context is Oxford, Bodleian Library 572, fols. 41v–47r, a colloquy

---

41. Fleuriot and Evans, *Dictionnaire.*

42. Lambert, "Les gloses grammaticales brittoniques"; id., "Vieux-gallois *nou, nom, inno.*" For the importance of the application of *philologie* as well as *linguistique* to these glosses, see id., "'Thirty' and 'Sixty' in Brittonic," 29.

43. Cf. Lambert, "Les commentaires celtiques, I"; id., "Les commentaires celtiques, II"; id., "Les gloses du manuscrit BN Lat. 10290"; id., "Les gloses en vieux breton"; id., "Notes"; id., "Rencontres culturelles"; id., "La typologie."

44. See, for example, Lambert, "Old Irish *gláoṡnáthe*"; Bauer, "Parallel Old Irish and Old Breton Glosses"; cf. also Dumville, "A *Thesaurus Palaeoanglicus*?," 68–70.

45. See below, 55–57.

conventionally entitled *De raris fabulis*.[46] As we have it, the text is glossed in Old Welsh and Old Cornish, but there is also another, earlier layer of glossing which has been embedded in the main text, a process no doubt aided by the nature of the text itself, a colloquy designed to teach students Latin vocabulary and basic grammar and syntax, and as such containing lists of words for substitution into sentences. A few more vernacular words absorbed into the text would hardly have been noticed. The glosses on Ovid's *Ars amatoria* discussed below represent a step up from basic vocabulary learning as, it is argued below, they are part of the process of learning how to read Latin verse. It would be very easy to imagine that students grappling with the glossed text of Ovid might have been learning the basics from a text book like *De raris fabulis* a year or so earlier. Once they had cut their teeth on the Ovid, they might well have moved on to the significantly more challenging exegetical glossing and commentary of the Juvencus manuscript.[47] That kind of pedagogical trajectory may be implied by a passage from *De raris fabulis* where a *princeps sacerdotum,* clearly some kind of senior priest, admits that his control of Latin is rather less complete than he might wish, and in the process reveals the anxiety common to all second-language learners that their knowledge is far more passive than active:

Et episcopus dicit ad principem sacerdotum, "An habes Latinam linguam?"

"Etiam, uel utique; non tam bene sapio, quia non multum legi, sed tamen fui inter scolasticos et audiui lectores docentesque predicantesque atque illam mirabiliter die et nocte meditantes atque dicentes et obsonium facientes. Unde et ego ex illis aliquid, quanquam sum paruus ingenio, longua tamen meditatione pauca fona, .i. uoces uel uerba, recognosco, sed etiam haec regulariter respondere non possum. Ignoro enim regulas grammaticorum nec exempla poetarum."[48]

---

46. *Early Scholastic Colloquies,* ed. Stevenson, 1–11; *De raris rabulis* (ed. Gwara) (but note Lapidge's warning about the latter edition in Lapidge, "Colloquial Latin," 410, n. 7); on its vocabulary, see Harvey, "Cambro-Romance?"

47. For discussion, see Russell, "Teaching between the Lines," 135–40.

48. *Early Scholastic Colloquies* (ed. Stevenson), 10 (§ 26); *De raris fabulis* (ed. Gwara), 30–31 (§ 23): "And the bishop says to the leader of the priests, 'Do you have Latin?' 'Yes, or indeed; I do not know it very well, as I have not read much, but I have been among scholars and I have heard readers teaching and preaching and wondrously meditating day and night and speaking and disputing. As a result, then, although I am of little talent, nevertheless by long study I recognize a few words, i.e. sounds or words, but even these I cannot regularly get right. For I am ignorant of the rules of the grammarians, nor do I know the examples of the poets.'" (my translation). Cf. Russell, "*An habes linguam Latinam?*," 202–3. One problematic phrase here is *obsonium facientes*: if we follow DMLBS, s.v. *obsonium* "feast" (based presumably on *obsōnāre* "dine"), the phrase would presumably mean something like "talking over dinner"; Gwara's translation, "performing mass," is derived from that. However, I would be inclined to take the noun as *obsŏnium,* from *obsŏnāre* "dispute, quarrel."

The last sentence is disarmingly honest as to where he sees his weaknesses. In fact, *De raris fabulis* by itself would not help with either of these two aspects; it is not a grammar book, nor is it concerned with poetry. Presumably it would have been used in conjunction with other aids, such as some of the more basic grammars derived from Donatus which were in use in Britain and Ireland at this period, simplified so that they were accessible to speakers of languages which were not derived from Latin.[49] The *exempla poetarum* may well refer to the examples quoted by the grammarians, such as Donatus and Priscian, which would have been an essential stepping stone to tackling continuous verse, such as the Ovid and eventually the Juvencus. That Ovid's love poetry seems to have been a set text for teaching purposes is striking and even more so if we are to assume that much, if not all, of this teaching took place in a monastic context, and especially if we take heed of Conrad of Hirsau's anxieties about Ovid's love poetry. On the other hand, it may be that beggars could not be choosers and this was the only text available. That said, Porter has drawn attention to some scurrilous and obscene content in the colloquies discussed above and argued that this was an excellent way of getting students to use Latin in an informal context, and it is not impossible that the Ovid might have been used in a similar way to concentrate their minds on Latin verse.[50] However, one interesting point about the glossing on the Ovid is that it is mainly concerned with Latinity and the explanation of features of Roman culture; it does not dwell on the amatory content.[51] On the other hand, if we were to take one passage of *De raris fabulis* seriously, it may be that the students needed no lessons in love:

"Audi, uxor pulcherrima. Ueni huc cito, et osculare mé et pone manus tua<s> circa collum meum."
  "Ó puella optima, da mihi osculum."[52]

OXFORD, BODLEIAN LIBRARY, AUCTARIUM F. 4. 32

The text of Ovid which forms the subject of this volume is preserved as the final section of this composite manuscript.[53] The make-up of the manuscript is as follows:

---

49. On such grammars, see Law, *Early Insular Grammarians.*
50. Porter, "The Latin Syllabus," 478; cf. also Russell, "Teaching between the Lines," 138–40.
51. For discussion of the spread of glossing and comment across the text, see 48–55.
52. *Early Scholastic Colloquies* (ed. Stevenson), § 10, p. 4 (*De raris fabulis* [ed. Gwara], § 11): "'Listen, most beautiful wife. Come here quickly, and kiss me and put your hands around my neck.' 'O fine girl, give me a kiss'" (my translation).
53. For discussion of this manuscript, see Madan and Craster, *Summary* Catalogue, II.1, no. 2176; Bodden, "Study"; Budny, "'St Dunstan's Classbook'"; cf. also Gneuss, "Dunstan and Hrabanus

I   fols. 1–9: Eutyches, *Ars de uerbo* (fragment); glossed in Old Breton.

II   fols. 10–18: Old English homily added after Dunstan's time

III fols. 19–36: the *Liber Commonei* (Book of Commoneus), the oldest part of the manuscript (early ninth century), was described as "the patriarch of all Welsh books known" by Bradshaw.[54] Its wide range of unusual texts includes scientific and astronomical materials, and displays rare evidence for knowledge of Greek. In several sections, it also contains many Old Welsh glosses, some of which may have been taken from the exemplar; but it also has Irish links, particularly in the name Commoneus, perhaps a form of *Cummianus,* Old Irish *Cuimíne* or *Cumméne* in the colophon at the bottom of fol. 19r *Finit opus in domino e thei quiri altisimo meo patre commoneo scriptum simul ac magistro.*[55] Its subsections are as follows:

fol. 20r Text on number; alphabet of Nemnivus; two sections on date of Easter;

fol. 20v Table on course of moon through the zodiac;

fol. 21r Pascal table for years 817–827;

fol. 21v *Questio* on Colossians 2:14;

fol. 22r Computistic tract;

fol. 23r Weights and measures tract (with Old Welsh glosses and commentary);

fol. 24r Minor Prophets (Greek and Latin); and

fol. 28r Lessons and canticles for the Easter vigil (Latin and Greek).

IV fols. 37–47: Ovid, *Ars amatoria* I; one of the oldest surviving manuscript fragments, and the only evidence that the text was known in early medieval Britain; glossed in Latin and Old Welsh.

The different sections of this manuscript have been described and discussed inter alios by Hunt, Bodden, and Budny.[56] It has been argued by Hunt that the Celtic sections of the manuscript (I, III, and IV) were in Glastonbury

---

Maurus." A facsimile of the whole manuscript is *Saint Dunstan's Classbook* (ed. Hunt); digital images of the whole manuscripts are available on the *Early Manuscripts at Oxford University* website. I do not at this point delve into the earlier pre-nineteenth-century scholarship on this manuscript. The earlier history of the final section is discussed below, 16–29, and many aspects of that discussion relate to the whole manuscript.

54. Ellis, "De *Artis amatoriae* Ovidianae codice Oxoniensi," 426. Note that the outer leaf of this gathering has been reversed; see Budny, "'St Dunstan's Classbook,'" 105, 110.

55. The translation is uncertain and the text may be corrupt; for example, I wonder whether *in domino e thei quiri* is a corruption of *in nomine thei quiri* "in the name of the Lord God." However, it seems to mean something like "The work ends . . . written for my father and teacher, Commoneus" (Williams, "Notes on Nennius," 393; cf. Bradshaw, *Collected Papers,* 456; *Saint Dunstan's Classbook* (ed. Hunt), xi; Budny, "'St Dunstan's Classbook,'" 113–14; Breen, "The Liturgical Material," 153). Hence the traditional title for the book, *Liber Commonei.*

56. *Saint Dunstan's Classbook* (ed. Hunt), v–xiii; Bodden, "Study"; Budny, "'St Dunstan's Classbook,'" 105–15.

by the second half of the tenth century, and that sections III and IV may been together at this point.[57] All three sections contain additions by what Hunt calls "Hand D," which is thought to be that of St Dunstan; notably, the fragment of Eutyches, which starts in fol. 1v has the famous image of St Dunstan kneeling at the feet of Christ on the recto. That the Eutyches was separate at this stage is suggested by the fact that the 1247–48 library catalogue of Glastonbury (preserved as Cambridge, Trinity College, R 5. 33) refers to *Duo libri Euticis de uerbo uetustiss<imi>* as a separate item.[58] Section II of the manuscript, the Old English Finding of the True Cross, dates to the second half of the eleventh century and must therefore have been a later arrival;[59] it has now been edited by Bodden and will not be discussed further here.[60] As for when the sections were united into one composite volume, it was certainly bound together before 1601 when Thomas Allen gave it to the Bodleian Library, and Hunt has suggested that it may not have been until the late fifteenth or early sixteenth century when the dispute between Glastonbury and Canterbury was revived over the possession the body of St Dunstan.[61]

The fragment of Eutyches's *De uerbo* is of particular significance as it has been glossed in Latin and Old Breton. Written "in Caroline minuscule of the middle or third quarter of the ninth century," both text and glosses are in the same hand.[62] It is likely that the manuscript is of Breton or northern French origin and presumably reached Glastonbury soon after it was copied perhaps via Cornwall.[63] The Old Breton glosses were edited by Zeuss and Stokes and have been absorbed into the standard collections of Brittonic glosses.[64] The main text contributed to the standard edition by Keil and the new edition by Sarginson, but the Latin glosses and commentary remain to be edited; and they have certainly not been integrated into thinking about the Old Breton glosses, or indeed vice versa.[65]

---

57. *Saint Dunstan's Classbook* (ed. Hunt), xiv–xv.

58. Budny, "'St Dunstan's Classbook,'" 124; *English Benedictine Libraries* (ed. Sharpe et al.), 206 (B39.312).

59. Bodden, "Study"; Budny, "'St Dunstan's Classbook,'" 123–26; *Saint Dunstan's Classbook* (ed. Hunt), vii; Ker, *Catalogue*, 355; Gneuss and Lapidge, *Anglo-Saxon Manuscripts*, 432.

60. *The Old English Finding of the True Cross* (ed. Bodden); on this section of the manuscript, cf. also Budny, "'St Dunstan's Classbook,'" 109–10.

61. *Saint Dunstan's Classbook* (ed. Hunt), xvi–xvii; Budny, "'St Dunstan's Classbook,'" 125; cf. also Watson, "Thomas Allen," 293–94, 310.

62. Budny, "'St Dunstan's Classbook,'" 105.

63. Madan and Craster, *Summary Catalogue* II.1, 244, seem to assume for no obvious reason that the Eutyches fragment ended up in Wales before going to Glastonbury.

64. Zeuss, *Grammatica Celtica*, 1076–81 (1st ed.), 1052–54 (2nd ed.); Stokes, "Cambrica," 232–34; cf. also Fleuriot and Evans, *Dictionnaire*, esp. 5.

65. *Grammatici Latini* (ed. Keil), V.447–88 (the text of this fragment ends on 460.36); Sarginson, "Edition"; our manuscript is noted at cx where she notes that "much of the Old Breton tends to gloss Latin words of a less savoury nature"; though my sensitivities may be different, it is not clear that this is the case. Cf. also Jeudy, "Les manuscrits."

Section III is a very interesting miscellany of texts written mainly in "a rapid, skilled and unembellished Welsh minuscule" of the early ninth century, which, following Bradshaw, has usually been called *Liber Commonei*.[66] The various subdivisions of this section have been set out above. Some of them have been examined in detail; for example, the so-called Alphabet of Nemnivus has been examined by Derolez and Williams;[67] the Calculus of Victorius of Aquitaine and its associated heavy glossing in Latin and Old Welsh have recently been re-edited by Lambert;[68] and the set of biblical and liturgical lessons and canticles in both Greek and Latin has received detailed discussion from Breen.[69] Both Budny and Breen have been at pains to point out the significant Irish element in the contents of this section.[70] Although useful progress has been made on various sections, there are significant gaps in the scholarship which need to be filled with an overarching study.[71]

Section IV, the final part of this composite manuscript, is the subject of the rest of this volume. It is clear from the above brief survey that essentially there have been three strands of scholarship—classical, Celtic, and medieval—and only rarely and intermittently have they intersected. What follows endeavours to bring these strands together and to direct attention at this manuscript for its own sake rather than as a staging post to something else.

---

66. Budny, "'St Dunstan's Classbook,'" 114; Bradshaw, *Collected Papers*, 455–56; on this section generally, see also *Saint Dunstan's Classbook* (ed. Hunt), vii–xii; Budny, "'St Dunstan's Classbook,'" 110–14; Bodden, "Study," 107–97.

67. Derolez, *Runica manuscripta*, 157–59; Williams, "Notes on Nennius."

68. Lambert, "Old Welsh glosses"; for earlier studies and discussions, see Williams, "Glosau Rhydychen: Mesurau a Phwysau"; Thurneysen, "Notes"; Lewis, "Glosau Rhydychen"; Lambert, "'Thirty' and 'Sixty' in Brittonic" 37–43. On the main text, see Friedlein, "Der Calculus des Victorius," 72–76, and "Victori Calculus."

69. Breen, "Liturgical Material."

70. For possible Irish aspects of section IV, see below 85–88.

71. The computistic material, for example, is in need of a fuller study; cf. the comments in Warntjes, *The Munich Computus*, xci–xciii (and n. 248), clxiii, 169, 237, 339–40 (21v); lxxi (and n. 180), clxii (n. 485), clxv–clvi, 248–49, 333–36 (22r–v); id., "Irische Komputistik," 16–17.

2

OVID, *ARS AMATORIA*, BOOK I

he fourth and final section of Oxford, Bodleian Library MS, Auct. F. 4. 32, fols. 37r–47r (s. ix), contains a glossed text of Ovid, *Ars amatoria*, Book I.[1]

PREVIOUS SCHOLARSHIP

The Main Text of *Ars amatoria*

The main text (allocated the siglum O by editors of Ovid) has figured in most of the early-modern and modern editions of Ovid's love poetry, even though its significance is reduced since it only contains *Ars amatoria* I. The earliest use of O as a witness was by Nicolaus Heinsius who collated the text in the Bodleian Library, Oxford, in late July–August 1641 and published the readings in his 1661 edition.[2] None of the distinctive

---

1. Unless otherwise indicated, references to the manuscripts and text of *Ars amatoria* use the sigla, edition, and line numbering of Kenney's second edition (1994).

2. "Nicolaus Heinsius Dan. filius Hollandus" was admitted as a reader on 27 July 1641 (Oxford, Bodleian Library, Library Records e. 533, fol. 172v); according to Philip, *Bodleian Library*, 35, he was the last of "a steady stream of young men who came from Dutch universities to work under John Prideaux." Cf. Blok, *Nicolaas Heinsius*, 21; also *Adversariorum libri* (ed. Burman) IV, I.5; and Kenney, "Manuscript Tradition," 2, n. 3. On Heinsius's Ovid manuscripts and collations, see Munari, "Codici Heinsiani"; id., "Manoscritti Ovidiani"; Lenz,

readings of O appear in any earlier edition that I have seen.[3] Three years later, in a letter to Johann Friedrich Gronovius, Heinsius noted (in the context of lamenting that he had mislaid his collation) that it was worth all the other manuscripts he had used put together:

> Et jam ad Artem Amatoriam perveneram, cujus liber primus Oxoniae olim a me cum longe optimo ac veterrimo codice collatus. Quae excerpta dum inter schedas meas quaero sive neglegentia mea alicubi seposita, sive, quod potius existimem, ab amicorum aliquo mihi sublecta, certe hactenus non inventa, ecce sororis supervernit [*sic*] morbus, qui omnem mihi de Ovidio meo cognationem prorsus excussit. Idque eo magis, quod aegerrime jacturam excerptorum istorum ferrem, quae reliquorum omnium manuscriptorum, quibus usus sum, instar mihi erat.[4]

In a letter to Patrick Young in 1656 in which he described it as a *codex singularis plane* "a clearly outstanding volume," he also expressed the wish that someone could be found to collate it *cum vulgatis editionibus* and to copy the glosses.[5] That the manuscript he was referring to was in fact O is confirmed in another letter to Gronovius in 1657 where he quotes a reading unique to O:

> Nisi quod unus Oxoniensis literis Longobardicis scriptus secundo versu *mandari* pro *mandatis* exhibet.[6]

"Die Wiedergewinnung"; Boese, "Zu den Ovidkollationen"; Reeve, "Heinsius' Manuscripts of Ovid," and "Heinsius' Manuscripts of Ovid: A Supplement." On Heinsius more generally, see Kenney, *The Classical Text,* 57–63, and on his textual criticism, Tarrant, "Nicolaus Heinsius."

3. Distinctive readings include the following (the readings of earlier editions are given in brackets): l. 76 *Syro* (*uiro*); l. 201 . . . *uincantur* . . . *uincantur* . . . (. . . *uincuntur* . . . *uincantur* . . .); l. 255 *Bais* (*uelis*); l. 352 *molliat* (*molliet*); l. 438 *nuncia* (*conscia*), l. 482 *uenient* (*ueniunt*); by "distinctive," I mean readings that are all in O but some of which are shared by a scattering of other manuscripts such that they are most likely to derive from O. I have seen a good selection of earlier editions (in reverse chronological order): Bersman (1582; on this date and the confusion between Bersman's editions, see Reeve, "Heinsius' Manuscripts of Ovid: a Supplement," 77), the three Aldine editions (1533, 1515, 1503), Paris (1529), Merula (1494), Accursius and Superchius (1489), Rubeus (pre-1474).

4. *Sylloges epistolarum . . . Tomi Quinque* (ed. Burman), III.125 (written at Leiden in 1644): "And now I had come to the *Ars amatoria*, the first book of which was collated by me with by far the best and oldest manuscript. While I was searching for these collations among my papers which either through my own negligence had been put somewhere else, or, what I think more likely, had been borrowed by one of my friends, but at any rate so far they remain undiscovered, behold the illness of my sister drove any thought of my Ovid straight out of my head. All the more so, since I was very upset by the loss of those collations which were the equal of all the other manuscripts I had used put together" (my translation).

5. Oxford, Bodleian Library, Smith 75 (Letters to Patrick Smith), pp. 153–54 (letter CLXXIV (written at Leiden on 13 June 1656)).

6. *Sylloges epistolarum . . . Tomi Quinque* (ed. Burman), III.370: "Except for that one in Oxford written in Lombard script which has *mandari* for *mandatis* in the second line of the couplet" (my translation); cf. *AA* I.588: *mandari* O, *mandatis* cett. For the tendency to describe the insular Welsh minuscule script as Lombard, see Loew, *Beneventan Script,* 28, n. 1(b).

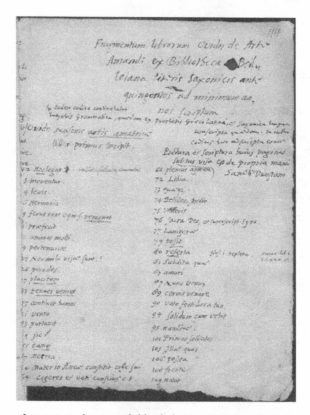

Plate 2.1. Berlin, Staatsbibliothek, Diez MS B Sant. 148e, fol. 14r

Happily, he must have recovered his collation, as two versions have been preserved in the Berlin Staatsbibliothek in the Diez collection:[7] his original collation is Diez MS B Sant. 148e, fols. 114r–15v, the heading of which reads (Plate 2.1):

> Fragmentum librorum Ovidii de Arte Amandi ex Bibliotheca Bodleiana literis Saxonicis ante quingentos ad minimum annos scriptum.[8] In eodem codice continebatur Eutychis Grammatica, quaedam ex prophetis Graeco Latina, et Saxonica lingua conscripta quaedam. In initio codicis haec adscripta erant:

---

7. Boese, "Zu den Ovidkollationen," 169; for descriptions, see Winter, *Die europäischen Hand-schriften*, I.20 and II.16–17 respectively (see also Plates 2.1 and 2.2a–c).

8. As can be seen from Plate 2.1, the first sentence is set in display script centred at the top of the page; the subsequent text is added as a sprawling note beneath.

Plate 2.2a. Berlin, Staatsbibliothek, Diez
MS qu. 1071, p. 206

Pictura et scriptura huius paginae subtus visa est de propria manu Sancti
Dunstani.[9]

He subsequently copied the collation into an interleaved copy of his father's
1629 edition of Ovid (now Diez MS quart. 1071 (part of Boese's "Verzeich-
nis III"); Plates 2.2a and 2.2b), where this manuscript is designated "O" and
its readings have been added on both the text and on the interleaved page as
part of the cumulative process of adding readings from various manuscripts.
On the blank pages at the beginning of this copy, Heinsius added notes on

---

9. "A fragment of the books of Ovid on the Art of Love from the Bodleian Library written in
Saxon script at least five hundred years previously. In the same codex are contained the Grammar
of Eutyches, some Graeco-Latin texts on the prophets, and some texts written in Old English. At the
beginning of the codex the following has been written: an image with writing beneath on the page
which seems to be in St Dunstan's own hand" (my translation).

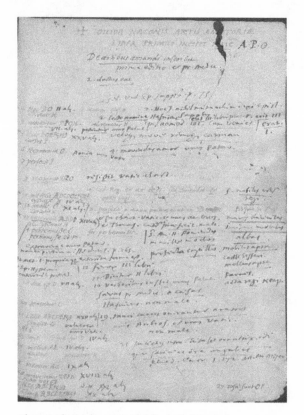

Plate 2.2b. Berlin, Staatsbibliothek, Diez MS qu. 1071,
leaf facing p. 206

each of the manuscripts in which O is described with a shortened version of
the heading in Diez MS B Sant. 148e (Plate 2.2c):[10]

O. Oxoniensis Bodleianus veterrimus[11] codex litteris Longobardicis scriptus in
quo liber primus tantum extabat et Eutychis Grammatica et alia quaedam. Ini-
tio [sic] codicis haec adscripta: Pictura et scriptura huius paginae subtus visa
est de propria manu S.[ti] Dunstani.[12]

---

10. Diez MS qu. 1071, third unfoliated leaf at the beginning of the volume. I am grateful to
Robert Giel for kindly tracking down these notes at the beginning of the volume.

11. *Bodleianus veterrimus* is added above the line.

12. *Pictura . . . Dunstani* is underlined. "O. Oxford, Bodleian Library, a very old codex written in
Lombard script in which only the first book survives, and the Grammar of Eutyches and some other
texts. At the beginning of the codex the following has been written: an image with writing beneath
on the page which seems to be in St Dunstan's own hand" (my translation). For the text, see Boese,
"Zu den Ovidkollationen," 169.

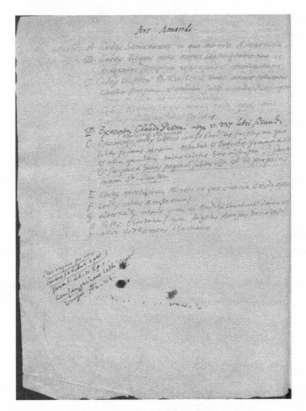

Plate 2.2c. Berlin, Staatsbibliothek, Diez MS qu. 1071,
third unfoliated leaf at the beginning of the volume

The description of the script in the latter as *litteris Longobardicis* (changed
from *literis Saxonicis*) matches his description in the letter to Patrick Young in
1656 and the second letter to Gronovius in 1657.[13] Heinsius went on to report
the significant readings of O in the notes to his various editions from 1661
onwards in which the text is variously referred to as "Oxoniensis," "fragmen-
tum veterrimum Oxoniense," "Bodlejanum fragmentum," and "fragmentum
Oxoniense Bodleijanae Bibliothecae."[14]

---

13. Both noted above, 17.

14. See, for example, the notes in Heinsius's 1661 and 1664 editions to *AA* I, lines 76, 170,
428, 438, 482, 662, 727, 761, etc.; his notes were then reported in eighteenth- and nineteenth-
century editions where the notes of previous scholars were collated; see, for example, those of
Cnippingius (1760) Burman (1727), Bentley (1825), etc. Cf. also Ellis, "De *Artis amatoriae* Ovidianae
codice Oxoniensi," 425: "Notus fuit codex Heinsio apud quem modo Bodleianus, modo fragmentum
Oxoniense uocatur" [The volume was known to Heinsius who sometimes called it "the Bodleian"
and sometimes "the Oxford fragment"].

O belongs to the older α-group (to use Kenney's term to distinguish it from a later β-group), alongside R, S$_a$, b, and Y, and so its readings figure in the apparatus of all modern editions (see Figure 2.1 for a stemma).[15] The earliest discussion and the first collation of the manuscript after Heinsius was carried out in 1881 by Ellis, who quoted the view of Henry Bradshaw on the date and significance of this text:

> The Ovid you mention in the Bodleian Library is one of the standing authorities for what is called Old Welsh. I am afraid to place it earlier that the latter half of the IXth century. The writing and ornamentation both resemble very strongly the Augustine written by Johannes son of Sulgen in the monastery of St. Paternus in Cardiganshire between 1080 and 1090, but the Ovid cannot possibly be so late as that. It seems to have passed out of Welsh hands into Dunstan's possession at Glastonbury in the Xth century. . . . [But] the Ovid in the Bodleian MS. is more like that of some of the later IXth century documents written in the margins of the Gospel of Telian [*sic*; *recte* Teliau], when a somewhat different and more set style of writing had come in; so perhaps the nearest phrase [*sic*; *recte* phase] for the date of the Ovid would be *late* mid-IXth or late-IXth century.[16]

Since then, it has figured in all the main discussions and in the introductions to the standard editions.[17] That said, it has never been of central importance partly because it contains only Book I but also because relatively rarely can it be shown to preserve the reading of α.[18] Moreover, with the relatively recent realization that Y is one of the *antiquiores*, subsequent editions may well take even less notice of O.[19]

---

15. For discussion, see Kenney, "Manuscript Tradition," "Notes on Ovid: II," 241–54; Tafel, "Die Überlieferungsgeschichte"; Goold, "*Amatoria Critica*," 60–68; with summary discussions in Tarrant, "Ovid," 259–62, and Richmond, "Manuscript Traditions," 459–62. Y was a late addition to this group, as for many years it was thought to be later in date; see Munari, *Il Codice Hamilton 471*, and Kenney, "First thoughts." The important arguments of McKie, "Ovid's *Amores*," have no direct impact on our discussion of O; on whether β is a legitimate group with a single archetype, see Kenney, "Manuscript Tradition," 9; id., *The Classical Text*, 134; McKie, "Ovid's *Amores*," 231–38; *P. Ovidius Naso. Carmina amatoria*, ed. Ramírez de Verger, cxlviii–clxv; Ovid, *Ars amatoria*, Book 3, ed. Gibson, 44.

16. Ellis, "De *Artis amatoriae* Ovidianae codice Oxoniensi," 425–27 (Ellis's italics but my suggested corrections). On Bradshaw's contribution to the scholarship on this text, see below, 25–28. For corrections to Ellis' collation, see Kenney, "Manuscript Tradition," 2, n. 2. The "Gospel of Telian [*sic*]" is now Lichfield Cathedral Library, MS 1 (the Lichfield Gospels); the "Augustine written by Johannes son of Sulgen" is now Cambridge, Corpus Christi College, MS 199.

17. See the discussions cited in n. 15 above, and, for example, the introductions to the editions by Kenney, Bornecque, Hollis, and Ramírez de Verger; Ramírez de Verger and Socas; etc.

18. For discussion of the stemma of *AA*, see Kenney, "Manuscript Tradition," 14–15; Tarrant, "Ovid," 261.

19. Kenney's second (1994) edition incorporates Y into the apparatus as does the edition of Ramírez de Verger; Hollis' edition of Book I takes little account of Y (see xx–xxi).

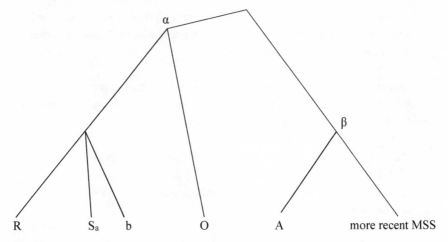

Figure 2.1. Stemma of the manuscripts of Ovid, *Ars amatoria* I (based on Kenney, "The Manuscript Tradition," 14; with Kenney I have hesitated to include Y though it clearly belongs to the α-group)

The Welsh Glossing

Most scholarship on the Ovidian text barely notes the glosses. Sixty-one years after Heinsius's visit to Oxford, between September 1702 and February 1702/3, Humfrey Wanley, whose prime interests lay in the palaeography of Anglo-Saxon manuscripts, had an exchange of letters with his friend, the Welsh antiquary, philologist, botanist, and palaeontologist, Edward Lhuyd.[20] Although their exchange focused on the Old Welsh entries in the Lichfield Gospels, which Wanley had on loan from the cathedral in 1701–2, he also drew Lhuyd's attention to some early British manuscripts in the Bodleian Library, one of which is our manuscript, then carrying the shelf mark NE D. 2. 19.[21] Three years later, Wanley published a description in his catalogue of Anglo-Saxon manuscripts and described this section of the manuscript as follows:

20. On this correspondence, see Sharpe, "In Quest of Pictish Manuscripts," 157–58. On these early phases of Welsh scholarhip, see Roberts, "Edward Lhuyd a Darganfod Hen Gymraeg"; id., "Discovery of Old Welsh," esp. 763–69; id., "Translating Old Welsh."

21. Wanley to Lhuyd, dated at London 14 September 1702 (Oxford, Bodleian Library, Ashmole 1817B, fols. 197r–198v; Heyworth, *Letters of Humfrey Wanley,* 188–92 (no. 88)), and dated at London 29 January 1702/3 (Bodleian Library, Ashmole 1817B, fols. 201r–202v; Heyworth, *Letters of Humfrey Wanley,* 207–11 (no. 95)). Lhuyd to Wanley, dated at Oxford 21 September 1702 (BL, MS Harley 3780 (now 3777), fols. 96–97; unpublished but cited by Roberts, "Discovery of Old Welsh," 764), and 8 February 1702/3 (Harley 3780 (now 3777), fol. 100; "Letter I" (ed. anon.); Gunther, *Life and Letters,* 495–97 (no. 253)). There is a conversion-table for the seventeenth-century shelf marks in Madan and Craster, *Summary Catalogue,* I.57–58. I am grateful to Richard Sharpe for help in disentangling this correspondence.

... praeter Ovidii Nasonis Artis Amatoriae librum primum, litteris Saxonicis antiquioribus scriptum, in quo etiam, aliqua plurima verba Brittonice occurrunt glossata, ut videre est, fols. 37, etc.[22]

Five years later, in 1707, the Ovid with its Welsh glosses was listed second in Lhuyd's list of Welsh manuscripts in his *Archaeologia Britannica* (though he did note that some of the glosses were in Latin):

The second (to retain its own title) is inscrib'd *Ovidii Nasonis Artis Amatoriae Lib. Primus* and is probably, tho' it be the small British character, as old as the first [sc. the Lichfield Gospels]. Some words have their British interpretations superscrib'd

	(funiou		olin		loinou
As	(vittae	—	rota	—	frutices
	(legit		amlais		crichet
	(oculis	—	dimissa	—	ruga

The old fragment is bound with various others and is preserv'd in the Bodley Library, NE. D. 2.19. All the words superscrib'd (which may be understood of the other Ancient Latin Manuscripts written by the *Britans*) are not *British*, but sometimes other Latin words for better explanation.[23]

Lhuyd went on to describe the Celtic language of these glosses as

Loegrian British, in some measure yet retained in Cornwal, which I gather partly from the Elegance of the Hand and partly from some Terms as *mor liaus* many, much; *caiauc*, A book (probably from the Latin *Codice*); *guarim*, a Play; *guardi*, A scene, etc. not to insist on the Plural Termination of Nouns in *ou*, as *loinou*, Bushes; *funiou*, Fillets; which was constant among the *Cornish* as well as the *Armoric British* and never used (that we know of) in Wales.[24]

---

22. Wanley, *Librorum vett. Septentrionalium . . . catalogus*, 63: ". . . except for the first book of the *Ars amatoria* of Ovidius Naso, written in Saxon script, in which many words occur also glossed in Brittonic, as can be seen on fol. 37, etc." (my translation).

23. Lhuyd, *Archaeologia Britannica*, 226. Lhuyd added a cross reference in the manuscript itself in the top margin of fol. 37r; see below, 41–43. For the quoted text and glosses: *vittae* : **funiou** (l. 31), *rota* : **olin** (l. 40), *frutices* : **loinou** (l. 47), *oculis* : *legit* (l. 109: recte *elegit*), *dimissa* : **amlais** (l. 153), *ruga* : **criched** (l. 240). Lhuyd read the last gloss in error as **crichet**. The gloss on *oculis*, which he uses as an example, is in fact Latin *elegit*; see below, 170–71, for details.

24. Lhuyd, *Archaeologia Britannica*, 226; for the glosses, see **mor liaus** (l. 176), **caiauc** (l. 167; not from Latin *codex*), **guaroimaou** (l. 89; from which Lhuyd extracted *guarim*), **guarai** (l. 106; misread as *guardi*, or **guaroiou** (l. 133)); **loinou** and **funiou** as in n. 23 above.

In fact, all these are Welsh; the -**auc** of **caiauc** is diagnostically Welsh (it would be -*oc* in Old Cornish or Breton), and the -*ou* plural preserved in Cornish and Breton is also attested in Old Welsh and is the ancestor of the Middle Welsh plural marker -*eu* (Modern Welsh -*au*).[25]

To judge from the reference by Johann Kaspar Zeuss in the Introduction to his *Grammatica Celtica* of 1853 (the earliest modern grammar of the Celtic languages), Wanley's report seems to have been the source of Zeuss's awareness of the manuscript.[26] Between 5 and 11 October 1844 Zeuss was transcribing manuscripts in London and Oxford.[27] He is recorded as having seen Bodleian 572 and Auct. F. 4. 32 on 10 October 1844 and it must have been then that he transcribed the glosses in F. 4. 32.[28] His edition and discussion of the Old Welsh glosses (but not the Latin ones) first brought them into the ambit of Celtic philological scholarship and they have figured ever since in all the standard discussions and grammars of the Celtic and Brittonic languages and in all the collections of glosses.[29] Zeuss seems also to be the person who christened this manuscript "Oxoniensis Prior" (often abbreviated as "Ox. 1"), the name by which it has been known by Celticists ("Oxoniensis Posterior" ("Ox. 2") being Oxford, Bodleian Library, 572, fols. 41v–47r).[30]

While scholarship on these glosses as a body of evidence started early (by Celtic standards), with a few additions we are still reliant on the nineteenth-century scholarship; after Zeuss the only edition of the Old Welsh glosses in this text was that of Whitley Stokes in 1861, though, unlike much of Stokes's later philological work, it was not a significant advance on Zeuss but for the addition

---

25. On Old Welsh -**auc** beside Old Cornish and Old Breton -*oc*, see Russell, "An habes linguam Latinam?," 205–6; for the development of the plural marker -*ou* into Middle Welsh -*eu*, see Jackson, *Language and History*, 370. For examples of Old Welsh plurals in -**ou** in the glosses on the Ovid text edited below, see Notes to ll. 31, 47, 69, 71, 76, 79, 82, 89, 103, 133, 138, 163, 179, 183, 188, 191, 249, 320, 332, and 633.

26. Zeuss, *Grammatica Celtica*, xxxviii (1st ed.), xxvi–xxvii (2nd ed.): "Wanley Catalogue MS anglo-sax 2.63"; the Old Welsh glosses are printed at 1081–89 (2nd ed., 1054–59). Another early report is that of Hersart de la Villemarqué, "Rapport," 241–44, at 243, who at one point criticizes Zeuss—"On regrette toutefois qu'il n'ait pas toujours exactement suivi le manuscrit"—and gives the example of **guaroimaou** glossing *theathris* (l. 81), but in doing so perpetrates several transcription errors of his own and is incorrect in his claim that the reading is *guaromaou*.

27. Stokes, Review, 200–201; Ó Cróinín, "The Reception of Johann Kaspar Zeuss's *Grammatica Celtica*," 85 (and the references cited there). The scholarship on Zeuss is considerable; the essays in *Johann Kaspar Zeuss* (ed. Hablitzel and Stifter) are a good starting point.

28. Oxford, Bodleian Library Records, e 570, fol. 83r.

29. Pedersen, *Vergleichende Grammatik*, I.13 (where glosses are mentioned as a genre of evidence, but the Ovid is not mentioned specifically (nor are sources discussed at all in Lewis and Pedersen, *Concise Comparative Celtic Grammar*), though Old Welsh examples from the Ovid are cited throughout both volumes); Jackson, *Language and History*, 53–54; VVB 22 and *passim* (note that *breton* in its title here means "Brittonic," not "Breton"); EGOW, xvi and passim; Falileyev, *Le Vieux-Gallois*, 78–81 (a selection of Ovid glosses); cf. id., *Llawlyfr Hen Gymraeg*, 21.

30. This is how it is referred to in most early editions of the Welsh glosses, e.g. Stokes, "Cambrica," etc. and still used in, e.g., EGOW.

of three extra glosses.[31] It was one of Stokes's earliest forays into Old Welsh and his working practices at this stage in his career are unclear. We know that his later work on other collections of Old Welsh and Old Breton glosses (when he was working as a lawyer in India[32]) was based on transcriptions made by Henry Bradshaw, whose work was mainly carried out while he was Cambridge University librarian (1867–89).[33] Bradshaw's views on this manuscript have been published on a number of occasions.[34] In addition, his notes and transcriptions of the glosses are preserved among his Celtic papers (CUL, Add. 6245, fols. 556–72 (sheets of mainly unbound lined foolscap written only on the recto)). As with other sections of this collection, his focus is on the vernacular glossing; he produces lists of the glosses sorted alphabetically (557, 570 (draft)), by parts of speech (568), and in textual order (571 and 572), but at the core (558–67) is a transcription of the text and all the Welsh glosses (and any adjacent Latin ones). In other sets of notes, we see him experimenting with different ways of laying out the text and gloss, but here (and this may be an indication of a relatively late date for this transcription) he unhesitatingly knows how he is going to do it.[35] We take his transcription of ll. 31–32 as an example:

Este[a] procul vittæ[1] tenues insigne[b] pudoris
Queque[c] tegis medio[2] instita[3] longa pedes.

[a] este pro estote   [1] a mein funiou
[b] signum   [2] or garr
[c] .i. estote   [3] a hir etem

---

31. Stokes, "Cambrica," 234–37 (corr. 292–93); cf. also Stokes, "Die Glossen und Verse in dem Codex des Juvencus," 421; Stokes, "The Old-Welsh Glosses on Juvencus," 415. On these different editions, see Russell, "'Grilling in Calcutta,'" 159–60 (to which should be added Stokes, "The Old-Welsh Glosses on Martianus Capella").

32. For biographical details, see McKitterick, "Bradshaw," and the essays in The Tripartite Life of Whitley Stokes (ed. Boyle and Russell).

33. Russell, "'Grilling in Calcutta.'"

34. Cf. his letter quoted by Ellis, "De Artis Amatoriae Ovidianae codice Oxoniensi," 425–27 noted above, 22; cf. also Bradshaw, Collected Papers, 283–84, 455–58. Bradshaw did not publish prolifically but was very generous with transcriptions and notes; one recipient was Ellis, and Stokes benefited enormously in his later work on Old Welsh and Breton. Much of Bradshaw's best work remains unpublished in letters in scholarly archives and among his own papers in the Cambridge University Library. For details, see Owen, "Henry Bradshaw and his correspondents"; Russell, "'Grilling in Calcutta,'" 144–48.

35. The lines transcribed by Bradshaw in Add. 6425, fols. 558–67 are as follows (* indicates that there is no Welsh gloss but that there is something of interest in the line, such as an interesting initial): 1–2, 31–32, 35–36, 39–40, 47–48, 65–66, 69–82, 87–90, 103–14, 121–22, 125–30, 133–38, 141–42, 149–54, 163–64, 167–68, 175–84, 187–88, 191–92, 197–98, 201–2, 207–14, 223–24, 233–34, 239–40, 249–52, 271–72, 301–6, 309–10, 319–20, 325–28, 331–34, 367–70, *399–40, *585–86, 627–28, 633–34, *745–46. For his experimentation with different layouts for text and gloss, see Add. 6425, fols. 269–83 (Eutyches), 369–420 ("Liber Canonum" in Orléans, Bibliothèque municipale 221 (formerly (and in Bradshaw's time) 193)).

The text is transcribed by couplet and the glosses listed underneath in two columns, the Latin in the left column is keyed to the text by superscript letters and the Welsh in the right by numbers. An important consequence of this approach is that Latin glosses which do not share a couplet with a Welsh gloss are not transcribed. The papers are unfortunately not dated. We know that Bradshaw had borrowed the manuscript from the Bodleian Library early in 1872 as there is a postcard from H. O. Coxe, Bodley's Librarian, in March of that year bearing a brusque request for its return.[36] His transcription must predate 1876, when Ebel published three glosses which Bradshaw had passed on to him, glosses missed by both Zeuss and Stokes. It is reasonable then to assume that it dates to 1872.[37] Bradshaw's working notebooks are also preserved for the later part of his career, but they do not survive for the 1860s (if they ever existed).[38] Generally the better documented part of his career is after he became University Librarian until his death in 1889. But he was already in correspondence with Stokes in the early 1860s and the letters give no indication that their acquaintance is recent.[39] It is therefore possible that Bradshaw, even at that early period, was the source of Stokes's transcriptions. However, Stokes's publication of the Ovid glosses (along with other Old Welsh glosses from Oxford and Cambridge) predates his twenty-year spell in India, and it would have been possible for him to have made the transcriptions himself, were it not for the fact that in a letter to Bradshaw in 1882 (on his final return from India) Stokes proudly announced that he had just made his first visit to the Bodleian Library.[40]

More headway can be made by considering Stokes's working patterns later in life, especially during his years in India (1862–82), when Bradshaw supplied the transcriptions as the basis of the edition and Stokes provided the detailed philological commentary. Typically, he would have printed in India (often at Simla) what was effectively a proof copy and sent it to various colleagues, such as John Rhŷs, Hermann Ebel, and others; comments from them would be incorporated in the final published version.[41] However, his 1861 edition of the Old Welsh glosses in Ovid and of the Old Breton ones in the Eutyches earlier

---

36. CUL, Add. 8916/A72/77; Bradshaw, *Collected Papers*, 455–56; Russell, "'Grilling in Calcutta,'" 159–60.

37. Ebel, "Miscellanea," 374n, where he notes that "Der ausserdem mehrere lesarten berichtigt und folgende glossen neu entdeckt hat . . ." (where the referent in the main text is Bradshaw).

38. CUL, Add. 4545–67.

39. CUL, Add. 8916/A60/7, 10 (in which Stokes grumbles at Bradshaw for failing to turn up in London with several Cambridge manuscripts for him to examine); Add. 8916/A62/6. On Bradshaw's correspondents and correspondence, see Owen, "Henry Bradshaw."

40. CUL Add. 8916/A82/128 (1 June 1882).

41. Copies of these "proofs" are preserved among the papers of various scholars, some of whose responses can be found pasted into Stokes's copy of Zeuss kept in the Stokes Archive at University College London, Special Collections (for shelf marks, see Russell, "'Grilling in Calcutta,'" 147, n. 16).

in the same compilation are very different;[42] there are very few philological notes, little Latin context (less than Bradshaw would supply for later editions), and none of the Latin glosses. For example, for the section quoted above from Bradshaw's notes, in Stokes's edition we are simply given the following:

> 37[a] *a mein funiou* gl. vittae tenues [voc. pl.]
>
> *orgarn* gl. medio
>
> a hir etem gl. instita longa[43]

In fact, what we are given is rather less than that offered by Zeuss, who often provided quite lengthy notes in Latin. At the beginning of the section Stokes acknowledges Zeuss's "description of the MS. and an admirable commentary on these glosses."[44] On that basis it would be reasonable to suppose that Stokes had simply reproduced Zeuss's readings. For the most part it appears that this is what he did, but there is evidence of some further input. Where Zeuss read **trudou** (l. 129), Stokes read **grudou** perhaps incorporating a suggestion that Zeuss makes in his note. He also included three glosses missed by Zeuss: **lo** glossing *ipsa* (l. 78), **termisceticion** glossing *sollicita* (l. 101), and **nepun** glossing *qua* (l. 127).[45] For each of these a little more context and comment is supplied, presumably on the grounds that they were lacking in Zeuss. Moreover, that these were later additions to Stokes's edition (perhaps at proof stage) is strongly suggested by the fact that, as an *Anhang* to the 1865 German version of his discussion of the glosses on the Cambridge Juvencus manuscript (CUL, Ff. 4. 42), he printed the additions noted above.[46] Several stages, therefore, can be deduced in the development of Stokes's edition:

(a) a list of the glosses and lemmata (based on Zeuss);

(b) the change of **trudou** to **grudou**, probably following Zeuss's suggestion in his notes;

---

42. Note that at this period the glosses on the Eutyches were thought to be Old Welsh too and it was only later work by Bradshaw that separated Old Welsh and Old Breton. It is thought that the term Old Breton was invented by Bradshaw; see Lambert, "La situation linguistique de la Bretagne."

43. Stokes, "Cambrica," 234.

44. Stokes, "Cambrica," 232n.

45. For the last two, but not the first, Stokes indicates that it was missed by Zeuss (235). For discussion of these glosses see below, 48, 101, 166. All three glosses were added by Ebel in the second edition of *Grammatica Celtica* (1871), but at this stage of course, probably in the late 1850s, Stokes was using the first edition. In fact, it is likely that **lo** is not Old Welsh for "calf" but the Latin name *Io* (see Bodden, "Study," 220–21; Hexter, *Ovid and Medieval Schooling*, 39, n. 75; Lambert, "Les gloses grammaticales," 292; Bradshaw's transcription also has *Io*), and the gloss on *qua* is, as it stands, **nepun** *puella*, though it is likely that *puella* was added first, above but just to the right, and then **nepun** added over *qua* (see Notes below, 173).

46. Stokes, "Die Glossen und Verse," 421; by 1873 he had realized (or had it pointed out to him) that Old Irish *tairmesc* was not cognate with **termisceticion**, and he published a retraction of that detail (Stokes, "The Old-Welsh Glosses on Juvencus," 415).

(c) addition of the extra glosses (perhaps at proof stage at the suggestion of other scholars).

It seems unlikely that he saw the manuscript before 1861; if he had done so, it is likely that he would have noted at least some of the three glosses, **penitra** (39v2 (l. 182)), **ir cretuis** (41v3 (l. 327)), **hi ataned** (45v2 (l. 627)) which Ebel published from Bradshaw's transcription and added to the second edition of *Grammatica Celtica* in 1871.[47]

Despite its drawbacks, it is worth pointing out that Stokes's edition remains the most recent attempt to publish all the Old Welsh glosses from this manuscript in textual order. There have been discussions of individual glosses and some additions to, and subtractions from, the dossier.[48] They have also been incorporated into more general discussions of glossing in Celtic languages;[49] and also more recently have featured in discussions of literacy, manuscript culture, and educational practice in early medieval Wales and Britain.[50] The most recent discussions of the body of glosses are those of Bodden and Hexter, both of whom consider all the glossing, Latin and Welsh. Their work will be discussed in the next section.[51]

The Latin Glossing

Although Lhuyd reported that there were Latin glosses in the manuscript (and indeed even thought one of them was Welsh), they were ignored by Zeuss and only minimally noted in Ellis's collation:

---

47. Ebel, "Miscellanea," 374n; it is argued below, 78–79, 180, that **penitra** glossing *tractat* is in fact to be read as Latin *peius tra*, and is perhaps a collation gloss, the glossator having encountered a worse reading elsewhere, *tratat* for *tractat*. It is possible that Bradshaw (and Stokes) may already have come to the same conclusion, and that is why it was not included.

48. The three added by Ebel noted above; Williams, "Glosau Rhydychen a Chaergrawnt," 113–15 (adding **ledit** (l. 112 (38v6))); Lewis, "Nodiadau cymysg," 203 (on **arpeteticion** (l. 73 (38r4))); Dumville, "A *Thesaurus Palaeoanglicus?*," 71–73 (adding **cant** (l. 102 (38r33)), which seems to have eluded most earlier scholars (see below, 67–68 and n. 168), though Bradshaw transcribed it); see also below, 83, where a gloss **ir** (l. 142) is identified. For some doubts over other glosses, see below, 83–84. For further early discussion, see also Rhŷs, "Die kymrischen Glossen zu Oxford," 230–35, 466–67; Williams, "Glosau Rhydychen" (a selection of Old Welsh glosses from Oxford manuscripts is listed and discussed in alphabetical order). For more general collections of Brittonic glosses, see *VVB*; *EGOW*; Falileyev, *Le Vieux-Gallois*, 78–81, contains *inter alia* a discussion of some of the Old Welsh glosses in Ovid (cf. also id., *Llawlyfr Hen Gymraeg*, 21). Note also that Whitley Stokes's copy of *VVB* (UCL Stokes's Collection 114.f.10) contains annotations and corrections; these are recorded in the Notes to relevant items (see, for example, 80n205, 83n222).

49. See, for example, Lambert, "Les gloses grammaticales"; id., "La typologie."

50. Sims-Williams, "The Uses of Writing," esp. 22–24; Charles-Edwards, "The Use of the Book in Wales," 400–402; id., *Wales and the Britons*, 643–50; McKee, "Script in Wales, Scotland and Cornwall," 167–68; ead., "The Circulation of Books Between England and Celtic Realms," 341.

51. Bodden, "Study," 198–246; Hexter, *Ovid and Medieval Schooling*, 26–42.

Prius dimidium libelli glossas habet modo inter lineas modo in margine. Ple-
raeque Latinae sunt; quaedam veteri Gualliae dialecto conscriptae, unde ad
philologiam Celticam non leuis momenti sunt.[52]

Bradshaw transcribed some of the Latin glosses, but, as noted above, only
where they were in the same couplet as an Old Welsh gloss.[53] They are noted
in a somewhat dismissive and confused way by Boutemy in his notices on
A (probably the oldest and most significant of the *recentiores*): "Celui d'Oxford
n'offre que des gloses interlinéaires dénuées d'originalité";[54] and "L'autre,
l'*Oxoniensis*, ne renferme que des gloses, dont les plus intéressantes sont
encore celles en anglo-saxon [*sic*], qui constituent un document précieux pour
l'histoire de cette langue."[55] But for all practical purposes Celticists (and most
classicists) have been almost completely unaware of the presence of Latin
glosses except insofar as they can confuse the identification of Old Welsh
ones.[56] Hunt's 1961 facsimile was probably an important catalyst in bring-
ing the full range of glossing to the attention of scholars.[57] Even so, the Latin
glossing did not receive any serious attention until the late 1970s when they
were discussed by Bodden in her dissertation and studied independently by
Hexter as part of the introductory section to his work on the later Ovidian
commentaries.[58] But for neither, as so often with this text, were the Ovid text
and its glossing their prime concern; for Bodden, the focus was the second
part of the manuscript, the Old English sermon (fols. 10–18), and even Hex-
ter regarded this text of Ovid as preliminary to his central concern, the later
commentaries.

---

52. Ellis, "De *Artis amatoriae* Ovidianae codice Oxoniensi," 427: "The first half of the book has
glosses, some interlinear, some marginal. Most are Latin; some are written in an old dialect of
Welsh, and as a result are of no small importance for Celtic philology" (my translation). Ellis goes
on to point out several omissions and errors made by Zeuss (427, n. 1), while perpetrating some of
his own.

53. See above, 26–28.

54. Boutemy, "Un manuscript inconnu," 272.

55. Boutemy, "Une copie de l'*Ars amatoria*," 98. There is no Old English in this section of the
manuscript except for one later note on fol. 47v, for which see *Saint Dunstan's Classbook* (ed. Hunt),
xiii, and below 41. For a similar error, see Clark, "Introduction," 8, noted above, 4n11.

56. There have been exceptions: Lindsay provided a transcription of fol. 40r (*Early Welsh Script*,
56 (and Plate XI)); Dumville also acknowledged the presence of Latin glosses in this manuscript and
was the first to point out that some of the Latin glosses must have been composed by a speaker of
a Celtic language (Dumville, "A *Thesaurus Palaeoanglicus*?," 71–73, 75–76 (the latter being an exper-
imental transcription of fol. 38r); id., "Notes on Celtic Latin," 286–88); for further discussion, see
below, 76–77. For cases where there is confusion or doubt as to whether a gloss is Latin or Old
Welsh, see below, 83–84.

57. *Saint Dunstan's Classbook* (ed. Hunt).

58. Bodden, "Study," 198–246; Hexter, *Ovid and Medieval Schooling*, 26–42. Hexter became aware
of Bodden's work only at a late stage; see ibid., 301 (Addenda), and so their work can effectively be
treated as two independent discussions.

Even so, both make extremely useful contributions, though neither presents all the data. Bodden printed a complete list of the old Welsh glosses in her thesis and made the first attempt to classify them by function;[59] she noted rightly that the focus of the glossing is on the nominal declension and especially where confusion could arise, e.g. first declension -*a* and second declension -*a* (neut. pl.), or in different declensional forms of the same word with a concentration on any potential confusion among the oblique cases. One possible explanation of this, she suggests, may be that the glosses may have ultimately derived from lists of *differentiae* (as in Isidore's *De differentiis verborum* and *De differentiis rerum*), a view she had developed in relation to the Eutyches fragment earlier in the manuscript.[60] She likewise classified the Latin glosses, distinguishing between lexical, grammatical, syntactical, metaphorical, exegetical, directional glosses, glosses which refer or clarify, etc.[61] In addition to drawing attention to the use of construe marks to aid comprehension of the broader structures, she also notes that the list of Latin glosses she provides was "meant to be representative, not complete."[62] Even so, an important aspect of her work is that it looked beyond the text of Ovid to what we might learn from comparing the glosses in this manuscript with those in other Ovid manuscripts.

Hexter's discussion again takes into account both sets of glosses and they are subjected to a similar functional analysis.[63] However, he bases his discussion on the work of Schwarz and uses the fine-grained system of classifying glosses developed by him for analysing the vernacular glosses on a text of Priscian's *Institutiones grammaticae* in Wolfenbüttel, Herzog August Bibliothek, Guelf. 50 Weissenburg.[64] While admitting his total reliance on the work of Zeuss and Stokes for the Old Welsh glosses, Hexter analyses all the glosses according to Schwarz's scheme. However, although it is clear that he must have transcribed the Latin glosses, no transcriptions are provided, although several examples are given in the text and notes.[65] He also has some very interesting things to say about some of the longer marginal comments in Latin that contain hints of the moralizing tendency which will emerge more strongly in the later commentary tradition.[66]

---

59. Bodden, "Study," 222–26, 229–31 respectively.
60. Bodden, "Study," 233, 43–98 respectively; nothing in the following discussion offers any corroboration for this view.
61. Bodden, "Study," 234.
62. Bodden, "Study," 243.
63. Hexter, *Ovid and Medieval Schooling*, 35–39; for summary of his analysis, see below, 56.
64. Schwarz, "Glossen als Texte"; Hexter, *Ovid and Medieval Schooling*, 30–33.
65. Hexter, *Ovid and Medieval Schooling*, 36–39.
66. Hexter, *Ovid and Medieval Schooling*, 40–41.

Between them, Bodden and Hexter made important headway, and their suggestions and proposals are pursued in greater detail below. On the other hand, important aspects have been missed or downplayed; notably, neither seems to have realised that in the Old Welsh glosses prepositions were being used to indicate the case of the Latin lemma.[67] In other words, they provide some useful starting points for thinking about this text, but their directions of travel were such that, reasonably enough, they did not develop their thinking beyond what was necessary for their purposes.

OXFORD, BODLEIAN LIBRARY MS, AUCT. F. 4. 32, FOLS. 37R–47R: THE MAIN TEXT

Facsimile Images

Selected images of the manuscript have been available from the late nineteenth century in the collections of Chatelain, Ellis, Maunde-Thompson, et al., all of whom were concerned mainly with the classical and palaeographical context.[68] Lindsay printed an image of fol. 40r in his study of medieval Welsh palaeography.[69] More recently, the complete text was presented in Hunt's facsimile, and digital images are now available on the *Early Manuscripts in Oxford* website.[70]

Page Layout

In contrast to the preceding sections of this manuscript, but like all other surviving Ovid manuscripts, the Ovid has a relatively spacious feel about it as the text is written as a single column in metrical lines (see Plate 2.3).[71]

---

67. For discussion, see below, 60–61.

68. *Paléographie des classiques latins* (ed. Chatelain), II, pl. XCIII.2; *XII Facsimiles from Latin MSS.* (ed. Ellis), pl. 1 (39v); *XX Facsimiles from Latin MSS.* (ed. Ellis), pl. 1 (38r); *Specimens of Latin Palaeography* (ed. Ellis), Pl. 8 (38r); *New Palaeographical Society* (ed. Maunde Thompson et al.), Pl. 82b (37r); Pl. 81and 82a are from other parts of the same manuscript.

69. Lindsay, *Early Welsh Script*, 56 (and Pl. XI (fol. 40r)).

70. *Saint Dunstan's Classbook* (ed. Hunt), xii–xiii (notes), fols. 37r–47r.; *Early Manuscripts in Oxford*, http://image.ox.ac.uk/show?collection=bodleian&manuscript=msauctf432 (consulted 24 September 2014); cf. Huws, *Medieval Welsh Manuscripts*, pl. 2 (facing 5). For a full list of images from this part of the manuscript, see Gneuss and Lapidge, *Anglo-Saxon Manuscripts*, 431.

71. In many larger Ovid manuscripts, especially the *Opera omnia*, the text is arranged in two columns; cf., for example, the Ovid fragment in St Gall, Stiftsbibliothek, 821, 94–96 (see Chapter 3, Plate 3.1). Earlier manuscripts tend to be smaller with a single column of text, e.g. (in addition to O) R, S_a, Y, and A; for images of Y, see Munari, *Il codice Hamilton 471*, pl. 1–6 (after 85).

Ingue meo nullu carmine crimen erit.

P rincipio quod amare uelis reperire labora,
qui noua nc primu miles in arma uenis.
Proximus huic labor est placitam exorare puellam;
tertius ut longuo tempore duret amor.
hic modus, hec nostro signabitur area curru,
hec erit admissa meta terenda rota.

Dum licet et loris passim potes ire solutis
elige cui dicas tu mihi sola places.
Hec tibi non tenues uenies delapsa per auras,
querenda est oculis apta puella tuis.
Scit bene uenator ceruus ubi retia tendat,
scit bene qui frendens uallem moretur aper.
Aucupibus noti frutices; qui sustinet hamos
nouit que multo pisce natentur aque.
Tu quoq; materiam longuo qui queris amori,
ante frequens quo sit disce puella loco.
Non ego quaerentem uento dare uela iubebo,
nec tibi ut inuenias longua terenda uia est.
Andromedon Perseus nigris portauit ab Indis,
rapta Phrygio Grecia puella uiro.
Tot tibi tamque dabit formosas roma puellas,
hec habet ut dicas quicquid in orbe fuit.
Gargara quot segetes, habet metina racemos,
aequore quot pisces frunde teguntur aues,
quot celum stellas, tot habet tua roma puellas,
mater in ethere desedit urbe sua.
Seu caput uis pinni et adhuc crescentibus annis,
ante oculos ueniet uera puella tuos.
Siue cupis iuuenem, iuuenes tibi mille placebunt,
cogeris et uoti nescius ipse tui.
Seu te forte iuuat sera et sapientior etas,
hoc quoq; crede mihi plenius agmen erit.
Tu modo Pompeia latus spatiare sub umbra
cum sol herculei terga leonis adit.
Aut ubi muneribus nati sua munera mater

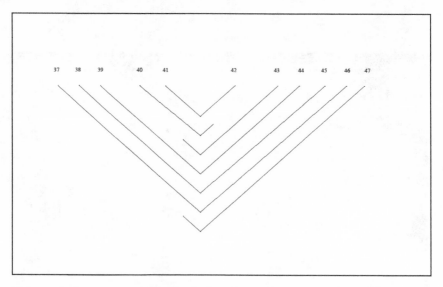

Figure 2.2. The current quiring of Oxford, Bodleian Library, Auct. F. 4. 32, fols. 37–47 (based on Budny, "St Dunstan's Classbook," p. 108, Figure 11, c. 1)

The folios are approx. 250mm × 170mm with a text box of 210–220mm × 100–110mm depending on the number of lines on the page. Hunt observes that "there is no sign of pricking having been used to guide ruling, which appears to have been done after folding on the rectos one at a time."[72] On the surviving bifolios, fols. 37/46, 38/45, 39/44, 41/42, the distance between the two text boxes varies by as much as 11mm.[73] Each bifolio was certainly ruled separately but may well have been ruled before folding, as the variation in the width of the margins is proportional: wide margins on the first half of the bifolio corresponding to narrow ones on the second. We have no idea how much might have been trimmed off the quire to make it fit the rest of the book when the different sections were compiled.

Generally, the effect of the dry-point ruling of the pages is that on the recto the leaves have been ruled and then folded so that the lines start about a centimetre in from the gutter, thus leaving a generous but uneven right-hand margin (uneven because the metrical lines are of different lengths); on the other hand, the verso has the spacious margin on the left with the lines of text starting several centimetres in from the edge of the page. Consequently, on the verso the text seems to be in the centre of the page with

---

72. *Saint Dunstan's Classbook* (ed. Hunt), xii.
73. For the collation of this quire, see below, 55.

Table 2.1. Number of lines per page in
fols. 37–47

folio	recto/verso
37	34 (hand A) / 36
38	37/37
39	37/35
40 (singleton)	36/36
41	37/37
42	38 (hand A/B) / 38
43 (singleton)	33/33
44	37/39
45	39/39
46	39 / 41 (hand C)
47 (singleton)	26 (hand D)

plenty of space around the main text. As such it resembles many of the other medieval manuscripts of Ovid's love poetry.[74] As we shall see, in addition to the interlinear glossing there is some marginal annotation and commentary, but they do little to reduce the open feeling of the pages.

Collation

The quiring of this section of the manuscript has been discussed by Budny.[75] Figure 2.2 shows the current quire structure. Fols. 40, 43 and 47 are singletons. The number of lines of text per page shows some variation even on the recto and verso of the same folio (Table 2.1): the opening page, fol. 37r has thirty-four lines but on fols. 37v–42 it varies between thirty-five and thirty-eight; fol. 43 (a singleton) contains thirty-three lines of text on each page; fol. 44r has thirty-seven; fols. 44v–46r contain thirty-nine lines on each page; fol. 46v has forty-one, and the last fol. 47r has twenty-six lines of text.

---

74. Compare, for example, R and A, though the heavy glossing and commentary on the small page of the latter rather reduces the effect.

75. Budny, "'St Dunstan's Classbook,'" 115; the upper diagram on 108 (Fig. 11.1) is redrawn here as Figure 2.2; the earlier form of the quiring proposed by Budny (and illustrated in the lower diagram on the same page (Fig. 11.2)) is discussed below, 52–55 (with Figure 2.5).

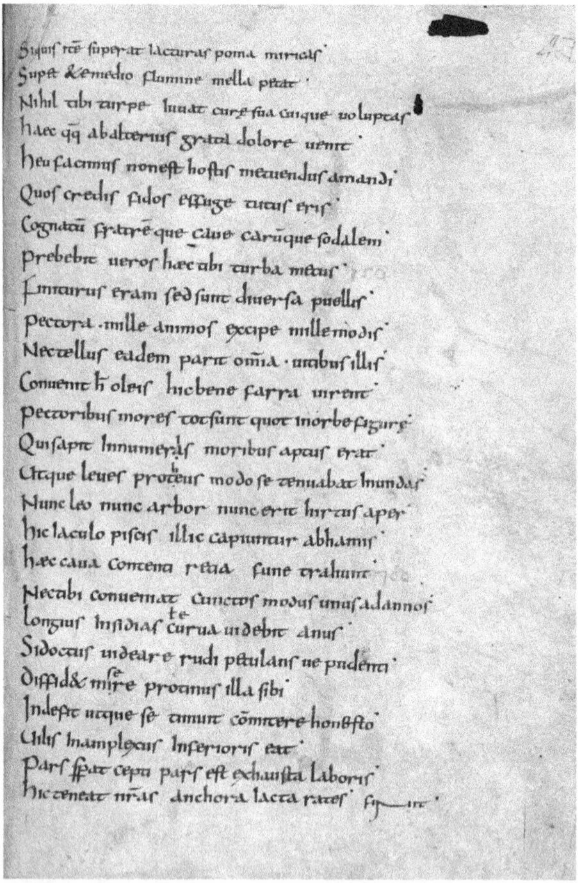

Plate 2.4. Oxford, Bodleian Library, Auct. F. 4. 32, fol. 47r

Scribes

The number of scribes involved in copying the Ovid has been a matter of uncertainty. Budny thought that "the original portion, folios 37–46, was written by a single Welsh scribe," but that another scribe, thought to be St Dunstan, added the last twenty-six lines on fol. 47r (Plate 2.4).[76] However, it is also pretty clear that fol. 46v was copied by a different scribe from the preceding part of the manuscript (Plate 2.5). In other words, the last two pages of the text were copied by two different scribes, each filling exactly a page (though varying hugely in the number of lines: forty-one lines on fols. 46v and 26

76. Ibid., 115.

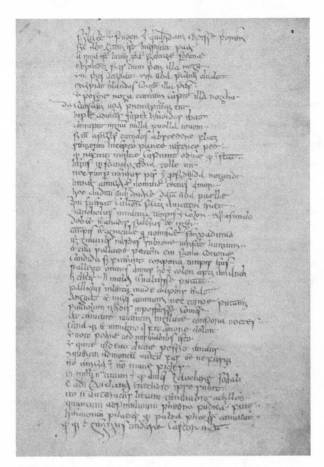

Plate 2.5. Oxford, Bodleian Library, Auct. F. 4. 32, fol. 46v

lines on fol. 47r). It had been thought that the main part of the text (fols. 37r–46r) was the work of one scribe, although some unease can be detected among scholars that this might not be the case. Ellis was, as far as I can tell, the first to think that there was more than one scribe involved; he suggested that the change came at the beginning of fol. 42r (l. 362), but his observation was then largely ignored (see Plates 2.6 and 2.7).[77] Madan and Craster likewise suggested a change of scribe but located it a folio later: "ll. 286–439

77. Ellis, "De *Artis amatoriae*," 427 : "vv. 1–361 [i.e. fols 37–41] pulchrior et exactior manus exaravit; 362–746 [i.e. fols 42–46] similes plerumque exhibent formas litterarum, sed minus diligenter nec tam nitide ac perspicue figuratas" (my additions in square brackets) [ll. 1–361 were written by a finer, more precise hand; ll. 362–746 display for the most part similar letter forms, but they are less carefully and not so cleanly and clearly drawn (my translation)].

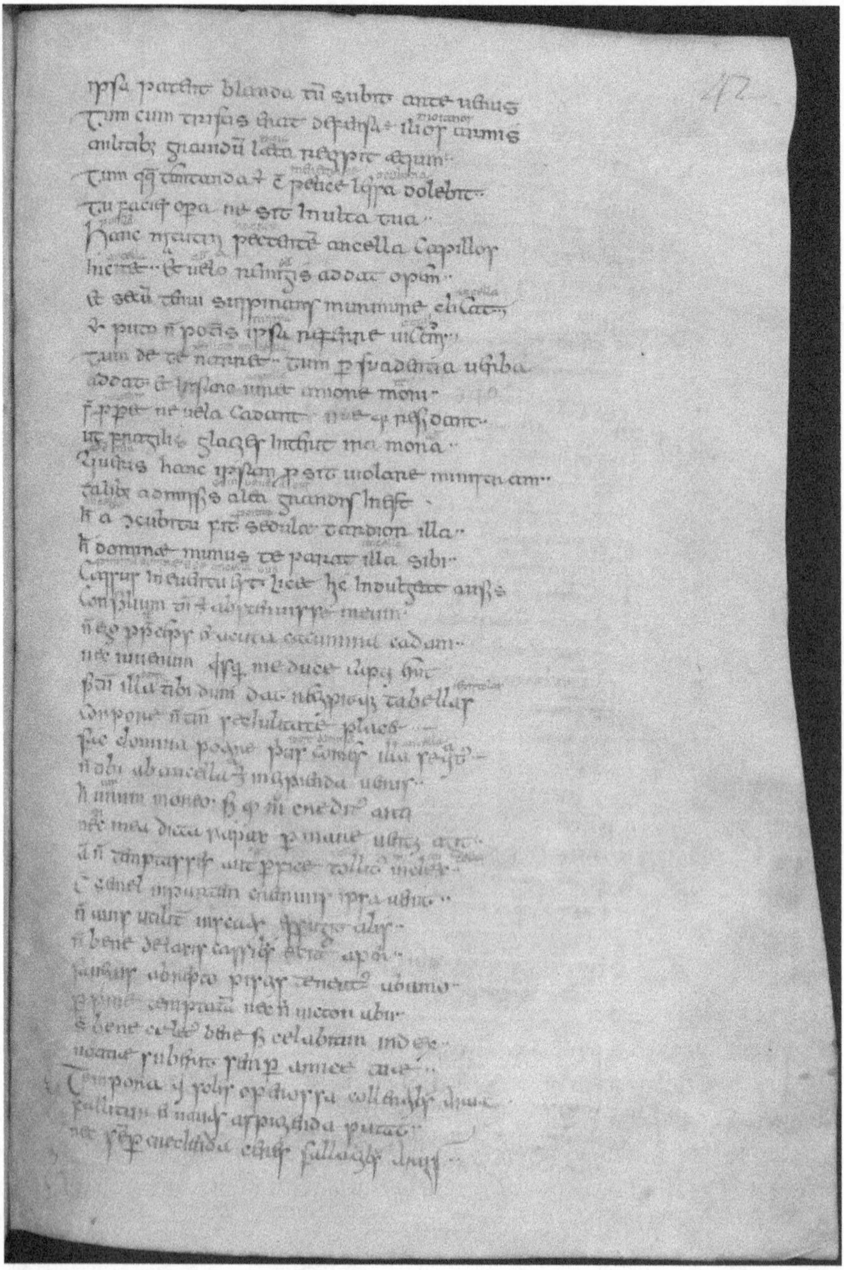

Plate 2.6. Oxford, Bodleian Library, Auct. F. 4. 32, fol. 42r

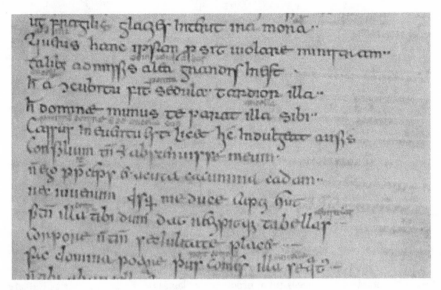

Plate 2.7. Oxford, Bodleian Library, Auct. F. 4. 32, fol. 42r13–24 (showing change of hand at the line beginning *Consilium* . . . (1. 19)

(fols. 41–2) and ll. 440–746 (fols. 43–6) are in two different but contemporary hands."[78] Lindsay made no mention of the scribe(s) of this section of the manuscript, nor did Hunt, although he noted that the script was "very variable."[79] More recently, a change in hand has been observed by Bodden, Conway, and Charles-Edwards at l. 380 (42r18) and in what follows that division is followed.[80] As discussed below, the glosses and marginal notes were copied along with the main text by the same scribes; thus for the two scribes who copy glosses, we have evidence for both their main-text hand and how they wrote glosses and commentary. The main text, then, and most of the glossing and marginal notes were written by four scribes as follows, with a later fifth scribe adding three glosses to the first few lines of the first page (fols. 37r):

> Scribe A: 37r1–42r18 (ll. 1–379) but copying glosses as far as 42r28 (l. 389). He wrote in a very accomplished and even form of Welsh minuscule. He also wrote the great majority of the glosses and commentary.[81] There is no significant

78. Madan and Craster, *Summary Catalogue*, II. 244: no indication is given as to whether they think the scribe of ll. 1–285 (fols. 37–40) is the same scribe as on fols. 41–42 or not.

79. Lindsay, *Early Welsh Script*, 8; *Saint Dunstan's Classbook* (ed. Hunt), xii.

80. Bodden, "Study," 203 (with discussion on 203–10); Conway, "Towards a Cultural Context," 15; Charles-Edwards, "The Use of the Book in Wales," 400–401; id., *Wales and the Britons*, 644–45. Note that for Bodden "the second scribe begins at l. 379," while for the others he began a line later.

81. For discussion, see below.

difference in his glossing hand except for size, but we might note that, while he used the full range of standard abbreviations in copying Latin glosses, he only occasionally used abbreviations when copying Old Welsh. The one exception is **apthou** glossing *sacra* (38r7 (l. 76)) for **aperthou** "offerings," a form which he used without any abbreviation eight lines earlier, **di aperthou** (37v37 (l. 69)), to gloss *muneribus*, and in the singular, **aperth**, to gloss *uictima* (41v10 (l. 334));[82] even here, strictly speaking he is not using an abbreviation as there is no mark for the *er*, but it looks as if the intention had been to abbreviate the *er*.[83] The glosses generally seem to be written in a lighter-coloured ink. This may be a function of the size of the letters, but, if the distinction is real, then it follows that the glosses were not copied pari passu with the main text but added subsequently.[84]

Scribe B: 42r19–46r end (ll. 380–704). Although his hand is very similar to that of scribe A, his line of text is generally more uneven (Plate 2.7); while both scribes A and B "hang" their lower-case letters from the ruled line, scribe A is notably more successful at producing a clean line of text than scribe B (Plate 2.7 comparing 42r13–14 (scribe A) with 42r19–24 (scribe B)). Some letter forms are also diagnostic. While scribe A does use the insular form of *s*, he also frequently uses the *s*-form, while scribe B is wedded firmly to the insular form with only occasional use of the *s*-form; furthermore, where he does use the latter form it is very upright with the tail ending level with the curve above, while the tail of scribe A's *s* ends underneath the rest of the letter, thus giving his *s*'s an appearance of a backwards tilt (cf. 42r8 (l. 369) *suspirans* (scribe A) : 42r34 (l. 397) *sed* (scribe B)). Scribe A's *g* is very perpendicular with the tail sitting under the top, while the tail of scribe B's *g* runs well under the next letter (cf. 42r13 (l. 374) *glacies* (scribe A): 42r30 (l. 392) *effugit* (scribe B)). They form the letter *a* in very different ways: scribe A's *a* is very round, while scribe B produces a much more angular form (cf. 42r13 (l. 374) *glacies* (scribe A): 42r20 (l. 381) *acuta* (scribe B)). Their abbreviations of *est* are markedly different: scribe A has a comma or dot above the line but a dot below the line, while scribe B has a comma above and below (cf. 42r2 (l. 363) (scribe A): 42r25 (l. 386) (scribe B)). Similarly, hand A uses the usual abbreviation for *-us* in *-ibus* (like a subscript 3), while hand B writes *-bs* with a superscript *v* (compare 41v8 (l. 332) *ingunibus* [sic] with 42r31 (l. 392) *cassibus*).

On the basis of these distinctive features, it appears that the glosses on 42r19–28 (ll. 380–89) on the main text copied by scribe B were copied by hand A. Two of the diagnostic features noted above can be highlighted: the

---

82. On the use of *di* to mark a dative, see below, 60–61.

83. For a particularly problematic instance of an abbreviation, see below on *peius tra* (read in the past as *penitra*), 78–79.

84. For further discussion on the glossing, see below.

form of the gloss *ancella* (with two round *a*s) is identical at 42r17 (l. 378) and
18 (l. 379) (scribe A) and at 42r 24 (l. 285) (where the main text is copied by
scribe B). In addition *nec* (42r27 (l. 388)) is glossed by *si* by scribe A with his
distinctive form of *s*. This has the important consequence that scribes A and
B must have been collaborating on this section of text. On the other hand, the
later batch of glosses at 45r33–45v26 (ll. 620–52), where the main text is still
being copied by scribe B, seems also to have been copied by scribe B.[85]

Scribe C: 46v (ll. 705–46 (Plate 2.5)). This is a distinctively curly and ornate version
of Welsh minuscule with exuberant ascenders and descenders; the scribe con-
tributed one page of text only (forty-one lines in total).

Scribe D: 47r (747–72 (plate 4)). The last twenty-eight lines of the text were copied
on 47r by a distinctive hand writing in a form of Anglo-Caroline. It has been
suggested that this may be the hand of St Dunstan himself.[86]

In addition, another scribe, scribe E, subsequently added three glosses to the
first few lines of 37r (Plate 2.8): *.i. ueloces* glossing *citae* (37r4 (l. 3)), *nomen
deae* glossing *uenus* (37r8 (l. 7)), and *proprium nomen* glossing *automedon* (37r9
(l. 8)). All three glosses are in a much darker ink and in two of them a distinc-
tive abbreviation, *nm̃*, is used for *nomen*, which differs from the abbreviation
nō used in the rest of the glosses (as at 37v20 (l. 53)).[87] The mode of reference
to a proper name is also different: typically a name is marked by the standard
abbreviation for *pro* (e.g. 37r11 (l. 12)), but in this case the abbreviation is *p̃ro*
(e.g. 37r9 (l. 8)).[88] In addition, at 39r34 (l. 175) *quod* is glossed by *.i. id* in a very
similar hand and darker ink; although it is difficult to be sure, this may be
another intervention by the same scribe.

To complete the dossier of scribal activity on these folios, in the eleventh
century scribe F copied onto 47v (the additional leaf at the end) two lines of
Old English to which another scribe (scribe G) added another brief clause.[89] The
text is a very brief extract from the so-called Penitential of Pseudo-Egberht:
*her segð hu se halga apostol Paulus lærð ælcum mæssepreoste þe godes folce to lare
byð gesett* [scribe F adds: *þæt he beo pær*] "here it says how the holy apostle Paul
teaches every mass-priest who is established to teach God's people" [*scribe
F adds*: that he is a man].[90] At the bottom of the folio a note reads *In custodia
fratris h. langley*, who has been identified with Henry Langley, a junior monk

85. For discussion, see below 52–55, 200–202.

86. See *Saint Dunstan's Classbook* (ed. Hunt), xii–xiii; Budny, "'St Dunstan's Classbook,'" 115.

87. For *nm̃*, see Lindsay, *Notae Latinae,* 140.

88. For *p̃ro*, see Lindsay, *Notae Latinae,* 196.

89. For the dating and discussion, see *Saint Dunstan's Classbook* (ed. Hunt), xiii.

90. See *Die altenglische Version* (ed. Raith), III.15; cf. *The Ancient Laws and Institutes* (ed. Thorpe),
II.202.

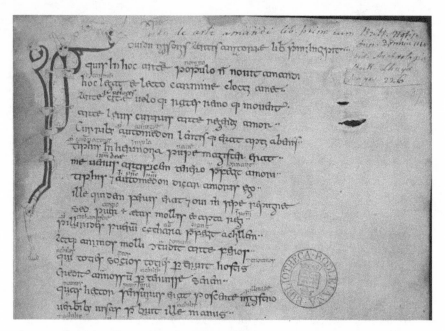

Plate 2.8. Oxford, Bodleian Library, Auct. F. 4. 32, fol. 37r1–16 (*AA* I.1–16); showing the notes in the top margin, the penned initial, glossing by scribe E on ll. 3, 7, and 8, and construe marks throughout

at Glastonbury in 1456.[91] Finally, a reference was added at the top of the first folio (fol. 37r; see Plate 2.8) to Lhuyd's note on the manuscript in *Archaeologia Britannica: Ovidii de arte amandi lib. prim. cum Britt. notis. | Anno Domini 1161| vid. Archaeologia | Britt. Lhuyd | page 226.*

This note is more problematic than it appears. It may be in two hands: *Ovidii . . . 1161* is perhaps in the hand of Edward Lhuyd but, even if it is not, it was written by someone who could identify the glosses as Brittonic; the second part, containing a reference to the *Archaeologica Britannica* may have been added later, and certainly after 1707.[92] The first part is written over Gerard Langbaine's foliation which was probably added in the 1630s or 1640s when he was active in the library.[93] More puzzling is the date of 1161. The

---

91. *Saint Dunstan's Classbook* (ed. Hunt), xv.

92. A similar note, in the same two hands (if that is correct), is found at the top of fol. 2r at the beginning of the fragment of Eutyches: *Eutex de declinationibus discernendis cum notis cambro-brittanicis. vid. Lhuyd, Archae. pag. 226.*

93. On Langbaine, see Hegarty, 'Langbaine.' For Langbaine as the foliator, see *Saint Dunstan's Classbook* (ed. Hunt), xvii. Langbaine's notes on the manuscript are at Oxford, Bodleian Library, Langbaine 5, 386–90; there is no indication of when these notes were written, nor is the date of the manuscript mentioned. His notes formed the basis for the entry in the 1697 catalogue, Bernard,

only way that I can see to make sense of this very precise date is to assume that whoever wrote it was aware of Nicolaus Heinsius's observation, which he added at the top of his collation (and is noted above), dating the script to *ante quingentos ad minimum annos* "at least five hundred years previously."[94] Heinsius collated the manuscript in 1641 and produced a new edition in 1661. If my theory is correct, then the countback is from the latter date. If so, the calculation relates to the edition and cannot therefore have been by Langbaine, who died in 1658. The dating also makes it less likely that the note was written by Lhuyd; in the discussion in the *Archaeologica Britannica,* our manuscript is placed second in the list and is dated in relation to the first manuscript: "It is probably . . . as old as the first."[95] The first manuscript in his list is the Lichfield Gospels (confusingly also labelled the "Landaf Gospels" by Lhuyd), which he describes as possibly being "eleven hundred years standing," and he goes on to suggest that the Old Welsh glosses in it "are of about 900 years standing."[96] It is unlikely then that he would have thought that the manuscript was written in 1161. Another problem is that, if the connection with Heinsius is correct, it relates to the 1661 published edition even though nowhere in that edition (and I have checked different printings) is there a reference to the manuscript being at least five hundred years old. Even so, the date at the top of the manuscript is striking and it is difficult to see how it is unrelated to Heinsius's comment. However, it remains unclear how that knowledge was retained in the Bodleian long enough for it to be added to the top of fol. 37r.

Why the last two scribes appear to copy very precise sections of text, scribe C exactly one page with scribe D completing the text again in a page, remains a puzzle. Although Budny did not recognize a different scribe on fol. 46v (our scribe C), she did suggest that it was characteristic of scribe D, identified as St Dunstan, to supply extra leaves and the final sections of texts, as here and also at the end of the *Liber Commonei* (36r).[97] However, she was not inclined to see the additions as repairing damage but rather as evidence for the scribe engaging in editing and cutting down; her suggestion is that our quire originally ended at l. 746 and that the last few lines of the book began the next quire which continued with the other books of the *Ars amatoria*; then,

---

et al., *Catalogi librorum,* 114 (2176.19), where similarly no date is given. However, we do know that Langbaine wrote to Ussher about the manuscript on 21 June 1650 and sent him a copy of the so-called alphabet of Nemnivus on fol. 20r (*The Life of . . . James Ussher* (ed. Parr), 551–53; *The Correspondence of James Ussher 1600-1656* (ed. Boran), III.975–77 (letter 561) and Appendix 2 (1172); it is possible, then, that his other notes on the manuscript are of a similar date.

94. On his collation, see the discussion above, 16–21.
95. Lhuyd, *Archaeologica Britannica,* 226.
96. Lhuyd, *Archaeologica Britannica,* 226.
97. Budny, "'St Dunstan's Classbook,'" 118–22.

for whatever reason, perhaps as a form of censorship, the ending of Book I was copied onto a single leaf and added to our quire.[98] However, if fol. 46v was copied by a different scribe, as proposed above, that means that two scribes were involved. Whatever we are to think about the end of the *Liber Commonei*, the simplest explanation of what went on at the end of the Ovid is that we have to do with some kind of loss. Perhaps originally the quire ended with a single leaf which contained the end of *Ars amatoria*, Book I, and possibly the beginning of Book II; that final leaf was lost and subsequently recopied from another copy. Or, as a variant on that theory, the text continued onto the original verso of the final folio but the next quire was missing, and so the final folio was recopied so that it simply contained the end of the first book and omitted the beginning of the next book. The change of scribe on 46v may simply be because there was a change of scribe at that point, just as there was at 42r19, and that scribe originally continued copying the text beyond 46v. Thus, if scribe D made any choice, it may simply have been to copy to the end of Book I and no further. If we suppose damage to the final leaf, then there may have been another copy of the *Ars amatoria* available to be copied. But, if we think in terms of a scribe wishing to end tidily at the end of the first book, we need not imagine that there was another copy to hand. In support of the latter, no textual study of *Ars amatoria* I has drawn attention to any variation in the textual relationships of these last sixty-nine lines; if, then, they were copied from a different text, that text must have been very closely related to the original exemplar; perhaps the final leaf was damaged but not illegible and was simply recopied. Questions remain about his final scribal stint, but, since they do not contain any glosses (though there is the occasional collation gloss[99]), they will not affect the subsequent discussion.

One other feature of the main text is worth noting: the latter part of the text shows possible signs of dictation in the form of a number of instances of variants which are unlikely to have arisen through miscopying but could easily have been caused by mishearing.[100] They occur particularly frequently in the part of the text copied by scribe B, and include the following:[101] regular -nd- for -nt-, e.g. *contendam* (42v24) for *contentam* (l. 425), *amandum* (45v7)

---

98. Budny, "'St Dunstan's Classbook,'" 108 and 122 (censorship). However, if censorship were involved, it is not clear why any effort would be made to preserve the first book. This is an issue we shall need to come back to when we have gained a greater understanding of the context in which texts of Ovid were transmitted and circulating in medieval Britain.

99. For example, 47r14 (l. 760) *innumeras* corrected to *innumeris*; 47r15 (l. 761) *h* added above the *t* of *proteus*; 47r20 (l. 766) *curua: uel e* added above; 47r22 (l. 768) *misere:* the *se* added above. See below, 70–72, 201–2.

100. On the kinds of errors perpetrated through mishearing and dictation, see Russell, "Revisiting the 'Welsh Dictator,'" 48–53, and references cited there.

101. The first version is the manuscript reading, the second from the edition of the text by Kenney.

for *amantum* (l. 633), *uiolendi* (45v27) for *violenti* (l. 653), *adamanda* (45v33) for *adamanta* (l. 659), *rogandi* (46v15) for *roganti* (l. 719), *amandi* (46v25, 47r5) for *amanti* (ll. 729, 751);[102] -*b/u*- confusions, e.g. *libia* (38r3) for *liuia* (l. 72);[103] and more specifically, *credita mens speculo* (41r20) for *crede tamen speculo* (l. 307), *atque* (43r32) for *ecce* (l. 543), *sibi bellatore* (43v9) for *siue illa toro* (l. 487), *uacuans illis spatiosa* (43v13) for *uacuis illi spatiosa* (l. 491), *locare* (43v22) for *loquare* (l. 500), *incedit* (fol. 45v26) for *inquit et* (l. 652). There is no textual evidence to encourage us to suppose that scribe B was using a different exemplar and we have to assume that these were a feature of this part of the exemplar and reflect an earlier layer of the textual history of this text.

Decoration

The only two decorated initials are at the beginning of the text at 37r1 (l. 1) where the first word, *SI*, is highly decorated, and at 37v2 (l. 35) where the *P* of *Principio* is again decorated in the same way but less elaborately (see Plates 2.8 and 2.3 respectively). There is no other decoration in the manuscript. Both initials are in black ink and the only colour is to be found on fol. 39v15–16 where the capital *C*s at the beginning of the lines have been filled in green (see Plate 2.10 below). The initials have been discussed by Pächt and Alexander, who see the forms of these initials as intermediate between the beasts of the Barberini Gospels (BAV, Barb. Lat. 570) and those in tenth- and eleventh-century Anglo-Saxon manuscripts and use the location of the manuscript at Glastonbury to account for the link.[104] Bodden compared the initials with those found in Bern, Burgerbibliothek 671 (the so-called Bern Gospels which also contain two acrostic poems to Alfred).[105] She supplements the discussion of the initials by arguing that there are similarities also in the "frill ornamentation" of several letters, especially on capital *T*s at the beginning of a line (e.g. 44v37, 43v2) and also both manuscripts contain a sign invoking Christ at the top of the first page above the title. She concludes by suggesting that

---

102. Another crux may turn on the variation: *petenda* (38v8) perhaps for *petente* (l. 114) (Kenney, "Notes on Ovid: II," 242–43; Gould, "*Amatoria critica*," 60–61).

103. Cf. *obidius dicit* glossing *pelicibus* (41r34 (l. 321)).

104. Alexander, *Insular Manuscripts*, 87 (no. 71), and Plate 333; Pächt and Alexander, *Illuminated Manuscripts*, III.3, and Plate I.17; cf. also Wormald, "Decorated Initials," 112–13, and Plate III.8 (mistakenly labelled Hatton 60); Rickert, *Painting in Britain*, 53, n. 5. Both Pächt and Alexander describe the manuscript as containing Old Welsh glosses with no mention of the Latin glosses, even though almost all the glosses in the images they reproduce are in Latin. See also Gameson, "Book Decoration."

105. Bodden, "Study," 210–19; for the Bern Gospels, see Lindsay, *Early Welsh Script*, 10–16 (who suggests a Cornish rather than a Welsh origin), and Plates IV and V; for images, see also Homburger, *Die illustrierten Handschriften*, pl. 52 and 58.

both were produced in the same scriptorium. Graham has drawn attention to similarities with the decoration in the manuscripts associated with Sulien and his family in Llanbadarn in the late eleventh century.[106] More recently, Edwards has described the initials as follows: "The opening 'SI' (fol. 37r) is quite complex . . . the strokes of the letters terminating and being bound together by delicately drawn animal heads, some with lappets or biting jaws, some with feline features; one snaps at a mouse."[107] She goes on to compare these animal heads with the stylised animal heads in CCCC 153 (Martianus Capella, *De nuptiis*, with Latin and Old Welsh glosses) and to suggest that "they are best paralleled in Southumbrian manuscripts of the late eighth and early ninth centuries."[108] The proposed connections between these manuscripts are tantalizing and unsurprisingly bring our manuscript into a Welsh milieu.

OXFORD, BODLEIAN LIBRARY MS, AUCT. F. 4. 32, FOLS. 37R–47R: THE GLOSSES AND MARGINAL ANNOTATIONS

All the glosses and marginal notes (except for the three, perhaps four, noted above) seem to have been copied by the same scribes who copied the main text. Further evidence that the glosses were copied comes in two forms: first, there are a few glosses which can only be understood on the basis of a copying error; for example, *satirbane* (fol. 40v9 (l. 259)) glossed by *ciuitatis* is a case where a copying error was perpetrated in the main text, though the gloss seems to have been copied accurately; the result is that the gloss becomes meaningless in the context.[109] Other glossed manuscripts of Ovid's *Ars amatoria* have the correct reading, *suburban(a)e*, to which a gloss *ciuitatis* (or perhaps another case form) would give tolerable sense. The confusion can only have arisen if the gloss was copied along with the main text by a scribe who misread the *suburban(a)e* of his exemplar as *satirbane*.

There is no distinction in terms of ink colour or position between the Latin and Old Welsh glosses; both are written in slightly lighter-coloured ink than the main text and both occur interlinearly and marginally. In other words, the Old Welsh glosses were copied along with the Latin ones from an earlier exemplar. In this respect, our text more resembles the text and glosses in *De raris fabulis* (Oxford, Bodleian Library, 572, fols. 41v–47r (s. x²) glossed in Latin, Old Welsh, and Old Cornish), where all the glosses were copied from

---

106. Graham, "The Poetic, Scribal, and Artistic Work of Ieuan ap Sulien," 249–50 and Plate 8.
107. Edwards, "The Decoration of the Earliest Welsh Manuscripts," 246 (and Plate 9.2).
108. Ibid.
109. On the form of the gloss, see the Notes, l. 259.

an earlier exemplar *pari passu* with the main text, than the glossing and commentary in the Juvencus manuscript (Cambridge, University Library MS, Ff. 4. 42) where we can distinguish the individual contributions of different scribes who added different layers of glosses and commentary to the manuscript.[110] However, the parallel with *De raris fabulis* is not exact: a copying error at 40r34–35 (ll. 249–50) where a long interlinear gloss is partially copied in the wrong place and then fully copied in the right place (one line further down) strongly suggests that scribe A at least was copying a section of the main text and then going back and adding the relevant glosses, but in this case he started at the wrong line.[111] Scribe A also added glosses to the first ten lines of scribe B's stint and that may be because the latter had a differing copying habit, perhaps copying more of the main text before adding the glosses. The general consequence, then, is that in our manuscript palaeography does not generally permit us to discern different layers of glosses, or whether they might differ in terms of chronology and origin, though we can usually work out which language they are. But, as we shall see, there are other ways of prising apart some of the layers of glossing.[112]

There is, however, evidence for the reworking and layering of glosses during the final stages of copying, some of which suggests that Welsh speakers were involved. We may take three examples illustrating different stages of the process. At 39r4 (l. 147) *eburnis* is confusingly glossed by *dentes r eliphantis*: it seems that *r* was first written over the *-rn-*, perhaps to indicate that it should be read as *eburis* "of ivory." Subsequently, *dentes . . . eliphantis* was added, one word either side of *r*. This gloss, then, is the consequence of two stages of glossing, though it is not clear how late in the glossing process this occurred.

Another gloss may be the result of merging an Old Welsh gloss with a Latin one. At 39v18 (l. 198) *ab inuito* (sc. *parente*) "from an unwilling (parent)" is glossed by **or guordiminntius** (the *-us* separated from the rest of the word by a descender from the line above): **o** marks the word as glossing an ablative, **r** is the article, and **guordiminnt** (modern Welsh *gorddyfynt*) means "displeasure, opposition."[113] As a gloss on *de inuito,* this would seem to be fine, but the scholarship is remarkably reticent about the final *-ius;*[114] while it could be

---

110. For an example of a gloss in *De raris fabulis* copied literally *pari passu,* see Russell, "An habes linguam Latinam?," 200–204. On the copy of Juvencus in CUL Ff. 4. 42, see McKee, *The Cambridge Juvencus Manuscript*; ead., "Scribes and Glosses from Dark Age Wales"; Russell, "An habes linguam Latinam?," 206–14.

111. See Notes to ll. 249–50 for details.

112. See Chapter 3 below.

113. On the use of Old Welsh prepositions to mark the case of the Latin lemma, see below, 60–61.

114. No comment is made in *VVB*; *EGOW,* s.v. *guordiminntius,* simple notes that "the *-ius* is thus left unexplained."

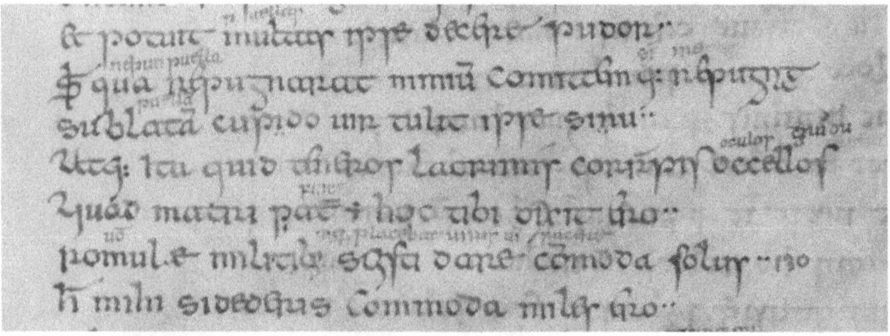

Plate 2.9. Oxford, Bodleian Library, Auct. F. 4. 32, fol. 38v21–26

the Old Welsh adjectival suffix -us, that leaves the -i- unexplained. One possibility is that we have to do with a merger between the Old Welsh gloss and a Latin gloss ius on regna (the word following ab inuito), intended to indicate that regna was that to which the heir was entitled.[115] The two glosses were subsequently merged in copying. It is possible that the error was encouraged by a scribe thinking that it contained the Latin grammatical term diminutiuus; such a gloss would make no sense in the context, but it is perhaps a useful indicator of the kind of thing the scribe was expecting to encounter among the glosses on this text. If this is right, it also provides evidence that the Old Welsh glosses were copied from an earlier version as **or guordiminntius** looks all of a piece in our version.

The final example involves the reworking of an Old Welsh gloss. At 38v23 (l. 129) occellos is glossed by both Latin oculos and Old Welsh **grudou** "cheeks" in the right margin (Plate 2.9). In this context (l. 129), "quid teneros lacrimis corrumpis occellos?" "'Why do you spoil your pretty eyes with tears?,'" the Latin gloss oculos "eyes" is perfectly to the point, but in **grudou** "cheeks" the Welsh offers an alternative reading indicating what might be spoilt by tears. However, the Old Welsh gloss has been overwritten and corrected: the original gloss was **tru** "alas!" which was changed to **grudou** by the change of **t**- to **g**-, and the addition of the plural ending -**ou** and a -**d**- above. It follows from the last example that at least one scribe could adjust and rewrite an Old Welsh gloss. That is more likely to be happening in Wales than at Glastonbury and a further confirmation that the main text of our manuscript was not copied at Glastonbury but in Wales.

One curious feature of the glossing in this manuscript is that it stops and then starts again. The Latin and Old Welsh glosses have exactly the same

---

115. I am grateful to an anonymous reviewer for this suggestion.

distribution, but it is uneven: they are found between 37r1 and 42r28 (ll. 1–389) and then again in a short batch from 45r33 to 45v26 (ll. 620–52). Between these batches of glosses and annotation—that is, between 42r29 and 45v27 and then from 45v27 to the end—there is no annotation apart from the occasional gloss which seems to have arisen from collation with another manuscript.[116] It has been suggested, or at least hinted at, that the restriction of the glossing to the first part of the text was in some sense deliberate: "Perhaps it was principally the monks there (sc. at Glastonbury), indeed Dunstan himself, who prepared its partial copy of *Ars amatoria* for study";[117] "The *Ars amatoria,* or at least the half of its first book was used for educational purposes."[118] The implication is that the partial glossing was at some point a deliberate choice as this text was regarded as a set text. This does, of course, ignore the later batch of glosses spread over thirty-three lines (ll. 620–52), a range which seems random in that it does not correspond to an identifiable and distinct episode in Ovid's text. It is also worth adding that of all the glossed manuscripts of Ovid I have inspected this is the only one where the glossing is discontinuous.[119] In what follows, other scenarios are explored and in particular the possibility that we have the surviving remains of a more fully glossed version of the text.

It should be noted at the outset that there seems to be some difference in the density of glosses in the two sections: in ll. 1–389 the ratio is 524 glosses : 389 lines (= 1.35 glosses/line); in ll. 623–52 there are 24 glosses : 30 lines (= 0.80 glosses/line); moreover, within the first 389 lines the glossing is uneven in that certain passages are much more heavily glossed than others. Figures 2.3 and 2.4 present the data graphically for the pages of the manuscript containing glosses (hence fol. 45r–v is represented by a separate dot). Figure 2.3 shows the number of glosses (Latin and Old Welsh separately) by page, and it can be seen that, although the variation in the numbers of line per page is not huge, some peaks of glossing are apparent. Figure 2.4 presents the same data calculated by the average number of glosses per line per page, and shows all the glosses together and then also the Latin and Old Welsh glosses separately. The two peaks (fols. 38r and 39v) where the glossing gets close to an average of two glosses per line are even more noticeable; in fact, for some parts of those pages the combined Latin and Old Welsh glossing can exceed three glosses per line, as in the first dozen or so lines of fol. 38r (ll. 70–82). An important point to note is that this distribution is visible in both the Latin and Old Welsh glosses; it is not the effect of particularly heavy Latin or Old Welsh glossing on a particular passage. It appears, rather, that the concentration of glossing

---

116. For a list and discussion of these collation glosses, see below 70–72.
117. Clark, "Ovid in the Monasteries," 178.
118. Hexter, "Sex Education," 305.
119. For further discussion of other Ovid manuscripts, see below 89–119.

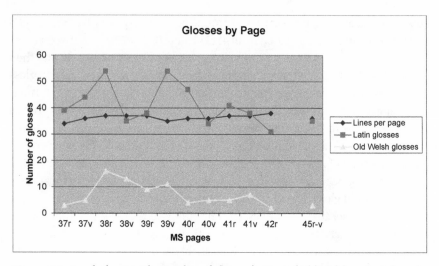

Figure 2.3. Graph showing the number of glosses (Latin and Old Welsh separately and together) per page

has to do with subject matter, and focuses on two of the most Roman sections, the description of the arcades and temples of Rome (37v–38r (ll. 65–90) and the predicted triumph of Gaius Caesar on his return from defeating the Parthians (39r–v (ll. 175–92)).[120] A third minor "hump" is the episode of Pasiphaë and the bull (41r–v (ll. 300–35)), but this has more to do with the allusiveness and complexity of the language where there is heavy pronominal usage and a greater need to mark who is who; the increase in the density in the glossing here is consequently in the Latin glossing and not the Old Welsh.

What is more puzzling is why the glossing stops and then makes a brief reappearance for thirty-two lines at ll. 620–52. The lighter glossing in the later batch is to be expected in that it is relatively common for the first part of a text to be heavily glossed and the later parts to be more lightly glossed, if at all. But typically we would expect the glossing gradually to tail off, but in this case it stops abruptly at 42r28, and then reappears just as abruptly at 45r33. Given that these lines contain much the same proportion of Latin and Old Welsh glosses as in the first 389 lines, it is worth exploring whether what we have is a broken copy of a more fully glossed text. If the glossing had been continuous, the reduction in density in the latter part of the poem is more or less what we might have expected. It may be, therefore, that the gap in the glossing is due to factors other than scribal inertia. As noted above, it appears that the glossing of the first few lines of scribe B's main text was done by scribe A. That

---

120. The nature of the glossing is considered below, 55–88, 163–68, 178–81, 192–95.

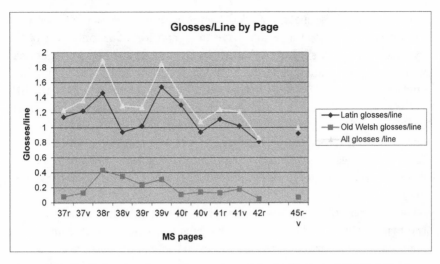

Figure 2.4. Graph showing the average number of glosses (Latin and Old Welsh separately and together) per line by page

the glossing stopped there and was then resumed by scribe B on fol. 45r is presumably because there were no glosses in the exemplar between lines 389 and 620 of the poem; when he reached l. 620 the glosses then resumed for the next thirty-three lines. It is unclear whether the fact that the glosses lasted for thirty-three lines is significant; it may perhaps be indicative of the number of lines per page in the exemplar but, since our text is not glossed on every line, it is probably no more than a useful guide to its minimum length.[121]

In effect, all this does is to push the puzzle back into the ancestor manuscripts. As noted above, other, but not all, manuscripts of Ovid's *Ars amatoria* also carry substantial glossing and marginal annotation, often much more than in our manuscript, but there is no other extant version which has the kind of patchy glossing found here;[122] a manuscript is glossed and annotated throughout, or it is heavily glossed at the beginning but there is a gradual reduction in the frequency of glossing, or it is not glossed at all. It would follow, then, that somewhere in the recent textual tradition of our manuscript something out of the ordinary occurred. We know anyway that something drastic must have happened since it is unlikely that our copy of *Ars amatoria,* Book I, travelled alone in the manuscript tradition; all other surviving manuscript copies which preserve more than small fragments or selections of lines contain all three books of the poem and are often part of a complete

---

121. As suggested by Charles-Edwards, *Wales and the Britons,* 645, who does not pursue the point further.

122. For further discussion, see 89–119 below.

collection of Ovid's amatory works. Even if we had a complete glossed copy of *Ars amatoria,* Book I, it would have to be considered as only part of the usual whole. Budny suggested that originally most of our text was contained in a single quire ending at 46r (at l. 746) and that the end of the book was in another quire "with Book II or other texts."[123] As she later observes, the title at the beginning (fol. 37r) would lead us to assume the existence of the whole of the *Ars.*[124] She went on to argue that the last few lines were then copied onto a single leaf (perhaps by Dunstan himself) and attached to the end of the first quire. However, none of that explains the change of hand on 46r nor the distribution of the glosses, even if it offers one possible solution to why we only have Book I.

With regard to the unglossed part of our text, one likely possibility is that the manuscript was damaged and the gaps filled from another unglossed manuscript. One particular feature of these Ovid manuscripts may help us to develop this hypothesis. Because the text is always copied by metrical line, we know how many lines of manuscript text are missing, and how many lines of text had to be copied overall. Book I of the *Ars amatoria,* as preserved in the Glastonbury manuscript, has a total of 770 lines of text;[125] the breakdown of these figures is as follows:

ll. 1–389:   389 lines of glossed text
ll. 390–619:   230 lines of unglossed text,
ll. 620–52:   33 lines of glossed text
ll. 653–770:   118 lines of unglossed text.

If we were to assume that the thirty-three lines of glossed text (45r33–45v26 (ll. 620–52)) represent the maximum number of lines on a page, and that a page ruled for thirty-three lines might also occasionally have thirty-two lines of text, these figures start looking very significant.[126] The 770 lines of a full text would fit into twenty-four pages (or twelve folios) with the last eleven lines in page 24 (thus leaving room for the beginning of Book II). If the twelve folios were made up of two quires, each of three folded bifolios, lines 1–389 (the first main glossed section of the text) would fit exactly into the first quire

---

123. Budny, "'St Dunstan's Classbook,'" 108 (Fig. 11(c)).

124. Ibid., 122

125. As do all the standard editions; however, the OCT edition by Kenney numbers them 1–772, while the Budé edition by Bornecque numbers them 1–770. In fact, the texts are identical, but Kenney allows two extra lines (ll. 395–96) for a couplet which he excises. The recent Teubner edition (ed. Ramírez de Verger) prints all 772 lines.

126. Note incidentally that Kenney suggests that the archetype of Ovid's amatory works may have had 25 lines per page ("Manuscript Tradition," 24); the discussion here relates to the immediate archetype of O.

assuming that five pages had thirty-three lines and seven had thirty-two (as in Figure 2.5: Phase I). Assuming a similar variation between thirty-three and thirty-two lines in the second quire, the short passage of glossed text at ll. 620–52 would on this hypothesis be page 16, the verso of folio 10, in the second quire, and, perhaps significantly for its survival, part of the central bifolio of the quire. The last 118 lines of the book would have filled the last two folios ending on line 23 of the final page, leaving room for the beginning of Book II. Now, if the second quire was damaged or lost with only one folio surviving (one half of the central bifolio), and only one side of that folio legible, we can account for the distribution of the glossed text by assuming that text was copied from an unglossed exemplar to fill the gaps (Figure 2.5: Phase II). After the loss of the rest of the quire, folio 10, containing the single surviving page of thirty-three lines from quire 2, may well have been attached to the end of the preceding quire (Figure 2.5: Phase III). This is an attractive way of explaining why only one side of it was legible, even if it requires that the folio was mistakenly attached the wrong way round, with the result that it was the original recto that became worn and illegible.[127]

The above account is, of course, hypothetical, but, on the assumption of a maximum of thirty-three lines per page (with occasional pages with thirty-two lines), we can make sense of the line-numbers at which the changes in the nature of the text occur. It is tempting to connect the fact that somewhere in the recent history of our manuscript something drastic happened to the central part of our text with the obvious replacement of text at the end of the manuscript where scribes C and D probably recopied text. However, this latter recopying is clearly more recent and presumably took place at Glastonbury, while the damage discussed in the preceding paragraph almost certainly occurred one or two removes further back in the tradition though still post-dating the addition of Old Welsh glosses to the manuscript. If so, some interesting conclusions emerge.

Our text seems to have had a more chequered recent history than has perhaps been realized, but its travails reveal some interesting features about the transmission of the text within Wales. If we assume that the Old Welsh glosses can only have been added to the text in Wales (or at the widest western Britain), there must have been a tradition of copying the text of *Ars amatoria,* glosses and all, in Britain.[128] Since somewhere in its recent textual history

---

127. For a similar inversion of a (bi)folio in the previous quire, the *Liber Commonei,* see Budny, "'St Dunstan's Classbook,'" 110; there the outer bifolium was turned inside out and bound the wrong way round.

128. It is worth noting that we may have a hint of a previous stage in the Old Welsh glossing; the diphthong /ui/ is spelt in two different ways: up to l. 150 as **oi** and as **ui** from then on (see below, 156). It is possible that this reflects the work of two different scribes as the variation does not correspond to the two stints of scribal activity in this manuscript.

Phase I: Complete glossed text of Ovid, *Ars Amatoria,* Book I

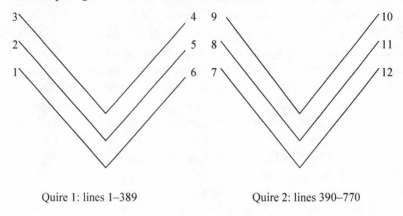

Quire 1: lines 1–389   Quire 2: lines 390–770

Phase II: Damaged glossed text of Ovid, *Ars Amatoria,* Book I (dotted lines = lost folios)

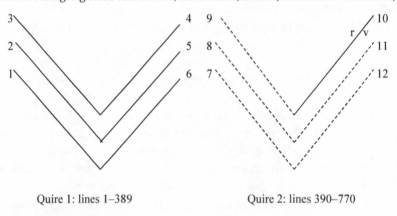

Quire 1: lines 1–389   Quire 2: lines 390–770

Phase III: Surviving glossed text of Ovid, *Ars Amatoria,* Book I: Quire 1: lines 1–389, 620–52 (folio 10 mistakenly reversed)

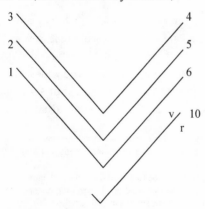

Figure 2.5. Hypothetical quiring of the exemplar of Ovid, *Ars amatoria,* Book I

it appears to have sustained significant damage and that damage could be repaired by copying text from an unglossed copy, it follows that there was at least more than one copy of Ovid's Ars amatoria, Book I, available in Wales— one glossed and one unglossed. Furthermore, when the text reached Glastonbury, another (or perhaps the same) unglossed copy was available to fill in the end of the book when that either became damaged or a tidy-minded scribe chose only to copy Book I. We might also surmise something further about this unglossed copy of Ars amatoria, Book I: expanding on what was noted above, no textual study of Ars amatoria I has drawn attention to any significant change in the textual relationship either of ll. 390–619 or of the last sixty-nine lines with regard to the readings of other manuscripts. If so, then, it would follow that the unglossed exemplar for those sections must have been very closely related to the original exemplar, perhaps a copy of it before it was damaged, but a clean copy without any glosses.

The scenario depicted here has the merit of attempting to account for several features of the glossing which have hitherto remained unexplained: in particular, why the glossing stops abruptly, starts, and stops again just as abruptly. The starting point was the later batch of glosses over thirty-three lines. If we take that as a guide to the number of lines on a manuscript page, then some progress can be made. The exact circumstances of what happened at the end of the manuscript are unclear and, since they happened rather later, are unrelated to whatever misadventures the central part of the manuscript suffered.

The Nature of the Glossing

This section begins by considering features common to the Latin and Old Welsh glossing and then moves on to discuss language-specific features. The most detailed classification of the glosses on this text is that of Hexter who modelled his analysis on that of Schwarz.[129] The analysis is very fine grained and useful as far as it goes in allowing us to see the main concerns of the glossator(s). A summary version of Hexter's classification is presented in Table 2.2.[130] I have not attempted to adjust his figures to take into account changes in the analysis of particular glosses, as they provide a sufficiently

---

129. Hexter, *Ovid and Medieval Schooling*, 35–39; Schwarz, "Glossen als Texte"; note also the very detailed classification used in Hofman, *The Sankt Gall Priscian Commentary*, I.40–95; cf. the very useful discussion of glossing in the Lambeth Psalter by O'Neill, "Latin Learning," 151–55. On classifying glosses, see also Blom, *Glossing the* Psalms.

130. I have not included Hexter's category II.4 (construe marks) as to my mind they are difficult to assess and count, and also provide a different category of information; for discussion of construe-marks, see below, 64–67.

Table 2.2. Summary of Hexter's classification of the glosses (from Hexter, *Ovid and Medieval Schooling*, 36–39, omitting III.4 Construe marks; cf. 37, n. 69, for an explanation of the distinction between II.1 and II.2)

Type	Latin	Old Welsh
I Replacement		
1. Grammatical replacement	10	1
2. Synonym/translation	90	55
3. Explanatory replacement	56	17
II Identification		
1. Identification as and of a proper name	13	0
2. Identification simply as a proper name	4	0
3. Identification of case, part of speech, etc.	49	0
III Explanation		
1. Supplied	62	8
2. Expansion of thought	24	7
3. Supplied to (e.g. adjective to noun, nominal reference to a pronoun, etc.)	75	1

precise guide for our purposes; the overall principle of such classifications, however, presents larger problems than can be resolved by minor tinkering. Such classification tends to be a major preoccupation for those working on glossed texts partly because it allows one to compare the pattern of glossing on different texts, but it has its drawbacks and is in the end only part of the story. It can provide a useful snapshot of the types of glossing on a particular manuscript, but some classifications are so detailed and fine grained that it becomes impossible to compare them with others which have used slightly different principles of classification; in many respects a more broad-brush approach would make comparison easier. Moreover, in a manuscript like ours where the glossing has built up over time through collation with other versions, it provides no indication of how those layers have accumulated and how at any point in that process of accumulation the glosses might have been used. Moreover, a major interest in this manuscript (and in others) is how the glosses work with the text and with each other in the local context of a five- or ten-line passage, and how they work alongside construe marks. These more local preoccupations of the glossators are not so amenable to this kind of classification but are just as important as a way of assessing the nature of the glossing. In addition, more context-specific study allows us to explain, in some instances at least, why one word is glossed and another is not; it often comes down to a difficulty arising either from the conjunction of two words in a particular line or in adjacent lines or alternatively because, due to Ovid's allusive style, a word has to be understood from somewhere in the preceding lines.

A further drawback that emerges from this particular application of classification is that sometimes glosses are doing more than one thing at a time, being both grammatical and lexical. When we consider the data in Table 2.2, it is clear that some types of glossing, such as "replacement" or certain types of "explanation," can be carried out in either Latin or Old Welsh. Other types, such as "classification" and "explanation" type 3, it appears, can only be performed in Latin. Thus, identification with a proper name, supplying the noun to which a pronoun refers, etc. can only sensibly be done in Latin. Similarly, identifying cases by their Latin terms should be a Latin-specific activity. However, glossators in Brittonic languages, which lack declension, devised a way of indicating the case of the Latin lemma by using Brittonic prepositions, o "from" marking ablative, etc.[131] In such glosses rarely does the preposition have a semantic contribution to make; it is simply marking case. In other words, the Old Welsh column for category II.3 should probably not be zero but nineteen.

In short, then, such tidy classifications, useful though they are in some respects in giving a general overview, do not satisfactorily capture the subtlety and multifaceted nature of such glossing.

(a) The Glossing of Latin Verse

It was suggested above that the glossing of this copy of Ovid's *Ars amatoria*, and in other manuscripts, might be considered in the light of Latin pedagogy. Comparison with other glossed and annotated versions of Ovid's poem indicate that our text is particularly heavily glossed with grammatical annotation both in Latin and in Old Welsh. Other texts from western Britain may usefully be compared. For example, we might compare our text with the fragment of Eutyches's *De uerbo*, by chance bound into the same manuscript as the Ovid, where the glosses, both in Latin and Old Breton, are unsurprisingly concerned

---

131. See below, 60–61, for further discussion.

with verbs.[132] The colloquy text known as *De raris fabulis,* which seems to have come from Cornwall and dates to a slightly later period than our Ovid, seems preoccupied with teaching pupils the basics of Latin and especially, in relation to vocabulary, with teaching them about nouns, though it has to be said there is a subtle increase in the level of difficulty in verbal morphology and syntax in later sections;[133] but crucially in that text the greater focus tends to be on developing vocabulary, not morphology.[134] We have already noted the striking passage in the *De raris fabulis* where a *princeps sacerdotum* laments the poor quality of his Latin; he explains why he cannot speak accurate Latin: *Ignoro enim regulas grammaticorum nec exempla poetarum* "For I am ignorant of the rules of the grammarians nor do I know the examples of the poets."[135] As noted above, it is likely that the *exempla poetarum* refer primarily to the examples from Virgil and other poets used in the grammars of Priscian and Donatus, grammars which, as Vivien Law has pointed out, were singularly unhelpful for the teaching of Latin to non-native speakers of Latin-derived languages.[136] However, at a later stage of the pedagogical process, the ability to parse and read Latin verse was also required for texts such as Juvencus's metrical version of the Gospels, and CUL, Ff. 4. 42, provides a fine example of such a text heavily glossed in Latin, Old Welsh, and Old Irish.[137]

Latin verse presented particular problems for the learner, and Ovid's verse more than most. In addition to the general allusiveness of his verse, the range of reference, and the assumption that the reader knows exactly what is going on and so can identify the referents of all the pronouns, the language itself provided many grammatical challenges.

---

132. Fols. 2r–9v; on these glosses, see Stokes, "Cambrica," 232–34. The glossing on this manuscript is partly lexical (especially in the case of the Old Breton glosses); much of the other commentary seems to be derived from the standard commentaries on Eutyches.

133. *Early Scholastic Colloquies* (ed. Stevenson), 1–11; *De raris fabulis* (ed. Gwara); Lapidge, "Colloquial Latin"; Russell, "*An habes linguam Latinam?,*" 200–204; id., "Teaching Between the Lines," 135–40.

134. There are a few instances where the student is required to change the case of a noun from the nominative to the accusative, but nothing more sophisticated than that; see Russell, "*An habes linguam Latinam?,*" 200–206 (and the bibliography cited there).

135. *Early Scholastic Colloquies* (ed. Stevenson), 10 (§ 26); *De raris fabulis* (ed. Gwara), 30–31 (§ 23); cf. Russell, "*An habes linguam Latinam?,*" 202–3. For the full passage, see above, 11.

136. Law, *Insular Latin Grammarians,* 53–80, 106–7. See also above, 12. Note that earlier in the same text a student asks to read a book and, when asked what kind of book, goes to say "*Uolo legere canonicum librum, uel euangelium uel librum gramaticum, .i. Donaticum*" "'I wish to read a book of canon law, or a gospel, or a book of grammar, i.e. the one by Donatus'" (*Early Scholastic Colloquies,* (ed. Stevenson), 3 (§ 6); *De raris fabulis* (ed. Gwara), 8–9 (§ 7)). (*Liber) Donaticus* may perhaps have already become a generic term for any grammar book (and in some languages, into which it was borrowed, it was eventually to become the term for any kind of primer; for further discussion, see below, 226–29).

137. On the importance of Latin verse, see above, 12; cf. Russell, "Teaching Between the Lines," 145–48. On the Cambridge Juvencus, see 9n38 above.

Table 2.3. The number of glosses noting grammatical features

Gloss (or Old Welsh equivalent)	Latin	Old Welsh	Total
ab*latiuus*	14	11 (**o(r)**)	25
datiuus	11	5 (**di(r)**)	16
[*priuatiuus*	2]		2
genitiuus	1	1 (**nom**)	2
uocatiuus	16*	2 (**a**)	18
ut (marking subordination)	11		11
ad*uerbum*	2		2
imperatiuus	1		1
infinitiuum	1		1
interiectio	1		1
inter(r)ogatiuus	2		2
proprium (nomen)	10		10
optatiuus	1		1
	(73)	(19)	(92)

*including one case of Latin *a* and one of *o*

As a starting point, Table 2.3 shows the number of glosses noting gram-matical and syntactical features of Ovid's Latin. It is immediately obvious that the focus and preoccupation of the glossators is nominal morphology, and in particular the morphology of the oblique cases, and is aimed at distin-guishing, for example, all the different cases which might be marked by final -*e*.[138] Latin verse did not always distinguish clearly, especially in adjectives, between dative and ablative singulars in the third declension, which in prose would usually be clearly marked with a dative in -*i* and an ablative in -*e* (with still further variation in the ablative singular of *i*-stem nouns). In addition, it was also necessary to distinguish them from vocative singulars and adverbs in -*e*. Further confusion would have been caused since the orthography of the manuscript often spells classical Latin -*ae* as -*e*, and so genitive singulars and nominative plurals of first declension nouns would also have been implicated. Vocatives, too, presented problems: such is the nature of Ovid's verse that

---

138. This point is made by Bodden, "Study," 227–28, though she underestimates the range of the grammatical comment by failing to grasp the use of Old Welsh prepositions to indicate cases (see 60–61).

he could switch into apostrophe unpredictably and without warning;[139] since vocatives only have a distinct case ending in the singular of second declension masculine nouns, again -e, and also would have been less familiar from any prose the readers might have already encountered, it is no wonder then that *uō* as a gloss appears fourteen times. Moreover, Latin verse tends, rather more than prose, to rely on the oblique cases to mark relationships which in prose would more usually be marked by prepositions, and so the ambiguity of some case endings becomes even more critical. Significantly, there are only two finite verbs glossed in the whole of our text:[140] *uenare* glossed by Old Welsh **helghati** (38r20 (l. 89)), *ortabere* by Old Welsh **nerthiti** (39v27 (l. 207)); both involve a poetical ending, the second singular deponent ending -re as opposed to the usual prose ending in -ris, significantly another ending in -e to confuse the unwary pupil, and an ending which could additionally be confused with an infinitive.

A good proportion of the Old Welsh glossing (nineteen out of some eighty glosses) is at least in part concerned with case marking. Of all the vernacular non-Romance languages of northern Europe, Brittonic languages are notable for having lost case distinctions at a very early period and so speakers of these languages would have been at a particular disadvantage in construing Latin cases in that they could not match the cases with anything in their own languages. Accordingly, a system had been devised (common to glossing in all the Brittonic languages) for marking cases in glosses by using prepositions:[141] **a** (or **ha**) for vocative, e.g. fol. 39r36 (l. 179) **ha arcibrenou** glossing *sepulti*;[142] **di** "to" for dative, e.g. fol. 39v22 (l. 203) **di litau** glossing *latio*; **o** "from" for ablative, e.g. fol. 40r8 (l. 223) **o corsenn** glossing *harundine*; in addition, **nom**, the origin of which is unclear, was used for genitive, e.g. fol. 38r8 (l. 77) **nom ir bleuporthetic** glossing *lanigerae*.[143] In these cases the preposition has no semantic force: **di litau** is not to be understood as "to Brittany" or **o corsenn** as "from a reed," but simple "Brittany (dative)," "a reed (ablative)," etc.[144] Such glosses, therefore, are both lexical and grammatical at the same time. Old Welsh glosses can also mark definiteness, something not explicit in the

---

139. Cf. also the occasional textual crux which turns on reading -es or -et, -is or -it, eris or erit, e.g. l. 588.

140. Oddly, Bodden, "Study," 231, remarks that no verbs are glossed.

141. For discussion and examples from other manuscripts, see Lambert, "Les gloses grammaticales"; id., "Vieux-gallois *nou, nom, inno*."

142. Both VVB 28, and EGOW 1, describe this **a** as "exclamative," but it is simply intended to mark a vocative.

143. The reading *lanigerae* (in contrast to *linigerae* or *niligenae*) is restricted to O and A among the *antiquiores* but is very common among the *recentiores*; one is tempted to think that this is a cold-weather reading originating in northern Europe. On **nom**, see Lambert, "Vieux gallois *nou, nom, inno*."

144. On Old Welsh **litau** "Brittany" (Modern Welsh *Llydaw*) as a gloss on *Latium*, see 86.

Latin, but not indefiniteness; Welsh has a definite article, **ir** (or **r** after prepositions ending in a vowel, e.g. **or, dir**) but not an indefinite article, and the former appears where the Latin noun is most naturally understood as definite: thus, l. 80, *flammaque in arguto sepe referta foro* "the flame (sc. of love) is often found in the noisy forum," where *foro* refers to *the* Roman forum, and *arguto* is consequently glossed by Old Welsh **in ir guorunhetic** "in the noisy—"

More nuanced grammatical distinctions can also be marked. While datives can be marked in Latin by *dā* or by the Old Welsh preposition **di**, subtler distinctions may be needed. This is particularly the case in distinguishing "the dative of advantage" and "the dative of disadvantage." The Old Welsh preposition **di** "to" clearly prioritizes the former, but there are instances where a sense of "away from, disadvantage" has to be distinguished. At fol. 38r16 (l. 85) *diserto* is glossed *priuatiuus,* as is *niso* (fol. 41v7 (l. 331)), and in both cases a "privative" dative is involved. Strikingly, *priuatiuus* figures as a gloss on the same words in another glossed manuscript of Ovid, suggesting that this usage derives from further back in the tradition.[145] Such glosses are relatively rare elsewhere:[146] BAV Latinus 296 (Orosius), a manuscript of Breton provenance (copied at the command of Liosmonocus and containing twenty Old Breton glosses) has three examples of the gloss *.i. datiuus priuatiuus* (e.g. 55v2, on *Octauio tribuno plebe[s] obsistenti demit imperium* (cf. also fols. 66v2 and 72v)).[147] Another term for the same type of dative is *datiuus fraudatiuus* which is attested twice in the Cambridge Juvencus and also in the vernacular Old Irish term *diupartach*.[148] Lambert has suggested that the marking of these nuances and subdivisions of case usage may be a feature of Celtic glossing; if so, the examples in our manuscript may be a relatively late layer of glossing in this manuscript.[149]

A similar usage may be observable in the Latin glossing as well. There are two examples where nouns in the ablative (or at least the glossator thought they were ablatives) which are glossed by prepositions. At fol. 39r22 (l. 165) *illa* is glossed by *in*; since prepositionless case forms is one of the features of poetical Latin, it is not surprising that prepositions might be added, and here it is glossing *illa* to show that it goes with *harena* "in that arena, on that sand." In this instance the addition of a preposition makes good sense of the Latin.

---

145. See below, 110.

146. They may well be less rare than we think, but work on the Latin glossing of Celtic manuscripts (as opposed to the vernacular glossing) is still in its infancy.

147. I am grateful to Pierre-Yves Lambert for providing me with these examples.

148. See Lambert, "'Fraudatiuus'"; the form found twice in the Juvencus manuscript, *dā fraud/atius,* had long been thought to be Old Welsh (cf. McKee, *The Cambridge Juvencus Manuscript,* 485).

149. For other possible Celtic features, see below, 76–78. Note that neither of these terms is listed in Schad, *Lexicon,* which again is suggestive of a more localized practice.

The second example, however, makes less sense; fol. 37v18 (l. 51), has *uento* glossed by *cum* "with" even though *uento* has to be dative after *uela dare*. The gloss is almost certainly an error, but in this case it is difficult to see what sense *cum* might have, and it is possible that the glossator was using *cum* simply to mark case just as **o** would be in Old Welsh.

Another form of glossing with preposition is, as far as I am aware, unique to this manuscript. As discussed below, accusatives are generally not glossed but the relationship of objective accusatives to a verb can be indicated by construe marks.[150] However, there are several accusatives in our manuscript which are glossed simply by *per*. In all cases, they either cannot be, or need not be construed as, objects but rather they have another function. At 40r8 (l. 223) *hic est eufrates precinctus harundine frontem* "here is the Euphrates edged by reeds with respect to its frontage," the last word, an accusative of respect, is glossed by *per*. A particularly clear example is at 45v21–22 (ll. 647–48) where two accusatives are marked by *per*: *dicitur egiptus caruisse iuuantibus arua* (gl. *per*) | *imbribus atque annos* (gl. *per*) *sicca fuisse nouem* "Egypt is said to have lacked rains to help the fields and to have been dry for nine years." The latter *per* marks an accusative of duration of time, but, while it might be thought that the former, *arua*, is the object of the participle *iuuantibus*, it is probably being understood as an accusative of respect, thus "rains helping with respect to the fields." At 40v27 (l. 278) the second half of the line in O is corrupt: *faemina iam partes* (gl. *per*) *blanda rogansque cogat;*[151] even so, it is clear that *partes* is not the object of a verb. In short, it looks as if *per* was being used to mark non-objective accusatives. It might just be possible in some of these instances to understand *per* as "throughout," but it is not easy to do so in all of them. In other words, could this be an extension of the Brittonic use of prepositions to mark cases in a more Latinate context?[152] If so, such glossing may belong to a relatively late phase of Latin glossing, one which may have been in Wales itself.[153]

So far the discussion has concentrated on nouns, but pronouns could cause difficulties. For example, the tendency in verse to use a dative pronoun to mark the agent with a passive verb was felt to need clarification; thus, at 38r2 (l. 71) *nec tibi uitetur* "let [it] not be avoided by you" has *tibi* glossed by *a te* "by you." This is a particularly common gloss with gerundives where

---

150. For discussion, see below, 64–67.

151. *uicta rogantis agat* RYL (corr.); *uicta rogantis aget* L, recc.

152. Occasional possible examples, using different prepositions, can be found elsewhere; for example, in the Southampton Psalter, 77:72, *intellectibus* is glossed by *in sensibus,* where the preposition may perhaps be intended to show that the lemma is ablative and not dative (*Psalterium Suthantonense* (ed. Ó Néill), 211).

153. For further discussion, see below, 76–78.

a dative pronominal agent is to be expected: thus at both 38v32 (l. 138) *tibi . . . accipienda . . .* and 38v36 (l. 142) *tibi tangenda*, the pronoun is glossed by *a te*.[154]

The use of *quid* to mean not only "what?" but also "for what reason? why?," which is more common in verse than prose, clearly required some explication; thus at 41r16 (l. 303) it was clearly felt to be important that the first *quid* "for what reason?" was glossed differently (with Old Welsh **padiu**) from *quid* "what?" two lines below (glossed with Old Welsh **pui**).[155] This example brings out an important aspect of the grammatical glossing: it often had the very local aim of explicating and distinguishing morphological features within the same couplet or larger sense unit. The choice to gloss or not to gloss was not gratuitous or random but rather had a very clear pedagogical aim—namely, to distinguish, for example, two adjacent words both ending in the same letter or two words identical in form but different in meaning.

Two examples are particularly illuminating in this respect as they show a glossator making mistakes, but ones which reveal his preoccupations and concerns. On a single line at 38r10 (l. 79) *et fora conueniunt quis credere possit amori* "even the fora are suitable for love (who would believe it?)," there are four glosses: *fora* is glossed by Old Welsh **datlocou** lit. "meeting places," *quis* by *in quibus*, *credere* by *permittere se*, and *possit* by *quis*. We may focus on the second and fourth of these glosses. The last gloss is simply showing that *quis* is the subject of *possit*, but by wrongly glossing *quis* as *in quibus*, the glossator is revealing that he is thinking of *quis*, the poetic dative plural of the interrogative pronoun, rather than the nominative singular. Although he might have been misled into thinking that it was dative following on from *conueniunt* ("fitting for those who . . ."), or perhaps after the *credere*, even so it reveals the kind of things he felt needed explanation and gloss—that is, grammatical features restricted to Latin verse and not found in prose. This pair of glosses also provides evidence for the accumulation and layering of glosses on this text; as they stand, the glosses are incompatible (*quis* cannot be both a dative plural and a nominative singular) and presumably arrived in the text at different stages.[156] The second case is at 37r29 (l. 29), where the first word of the line, *usus*, is glossed *genetiuus*, but in fact it is nominative singular (the second syllable scans short). The gloss should give us pause anyway in that it is the only occasion when a word is glossed in Latin as a genitive. Again it is revealing of his concerns: in terms of spelling *usus* is ambiguous and the glossator is

---

154. Cf. also the significant confusion caused by *cui defleta* 41v11 (l. 335); for which, see the Notes, 195.

155. The gloss, **padiu**, raises interesting issues for other reasons; for further discussion, see below, 117–18.

156. For further discussion of the accumulation of glosses, see 111–14.

keen to clear up the ambiguity. But he gets it wrong (and no doubt confused his students in doing so), which is helpful for us (if not for them).[157]

The grammatical glossing, therefore, in both Latin and Old Welsh reveals certain preoccupations of the part of the glossators. Primarily, they were interested in features of Ovid's verse not found in prose. As a consequence, much of the glossing focuses on nominal forms in the vocative, genitive, dative, and ablative singular.

Another strand of the glossing which stands out is what might be termed syntactic glossing. While most of the glossing relates to the analysis or explanation of a single word, and in this text mainly on nominal forms, some glosses have a broader syntactical function in aiding the reader or pupil to keep track of the overall structure. One type of marking is the glossing of verbs with *ut* to show that they are generally to be construed as part of a subordinate clause (and not just a clause requiring *ut* to be understood).[158] Construe marks also occur and are discussed in the following section, but we may also note glosses where verbs from the main text are repeated as glosses to show that the same syntactic structure is to be continued. For example, at 38r4 (l. 73) *nec uitentur* glosses *quaeque* but is in fact a reminder that the force of *nec tibi uitetur* (l. 71) is continued into the next couplet: "you should not avoid . . . and neither should you avoid." Likewise in the next line *nec te pretereat* is repeated as a gloss over *Cultaque* in the next line (l. 76): "And it should not pass you by . . . nor should [they] pass you by."[159] Rather than functioning as explanations, these glosses repeat crucial parts of the main text in order to provide structural guidance.

(b) Construe Marks

Other broader features are also marked, but not verbally with glosses. Construe marks also occur to mark agreement between adjectives and nouns, to indicate subjects of verbs, etc.[160] They are not found consistently but show a characteristic pattern: they are very dense in the first few pages but then become very patchy with the last set being found at fol. 41r22 (l. 311).[161] They typically mark agreement between nouns and adjectives when they

---

157. It also constitutes another instance where scansion should have come to the teacher's aid but does not; on the failure to exploit metrical features, see 84–85.

158. See the glosses on ll. 34, 35, 39, 93, 145, 205, 230, 263, 270, 274, 278.

159. Cf. also *inuenies* (l. 91) which is repeated as a gloss on *quodque* on l. 92.

160. These are marked here and in the edition below by * and, where necessary to distinguish a second set of marks, by †.

161. Construe marks occur in the following lines (at least a pair per line): 3–5, 8, 11, 12–22, 34, 120, 128, 197–99, and 309–10.

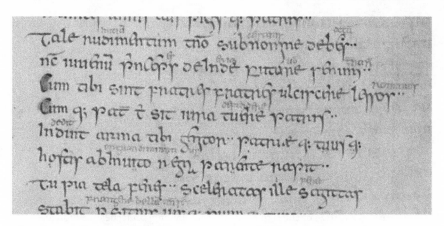

Plate 2.10. Oxford, Bodleian Library, Auct. F. 4. 32, fol. 39v13–19

are separated by other words in the line or indeed are in separate lines (see, for example, Plate 2.8): *citae . . . rates* (fol. 37r3 (l. 3)), *leuis currus . . . regendus* (fol. 37r4 (l. 4)), *animos . . . feros* (fol. 37r12 (l. 12)), *magnanimi . . . equi* (fol. 27r20 (l. 20)), *cupido . . . sinu* (fol. 38v22 (l. 128) where *cupido* might have been more than usually vulnerable to misinterpretation given the ubiquity of Cupid (*Cupido*) in this poem); or the subject of a verb and the verb itself, especially if the subject has more than one element or does not look as if it is the nom-inative: *automedon . . . erat* (fol. 37r5 (l. 5)), *tiphis . . . dicar . . . ego* (fol. 37r8 (l. 8)), *crimen erit* (fol. 37v1 (l. 34)). A particularly complex example is found at fol. 39v17–19 (ll. 197–99; see Plate 2.10) where the context is an imagined triumph for Gaius Caesar, grandson of Augustus, on his return from defeating the Parthians; Ovid is making a contrast between Gaius receiving his weapons from his father on the one hand and the Parthian king who had killed his father to gain power on the other:

> induit arma tibi *genitor *patriaeque *tuusque
> *hostis ab †inuito regna †parente rapit
> tu pia tela feres sceleratas *ille sagittas

> He presented you with arms, he who is both father of the country and of you;
> The enemy takes a kingdom from a father against his will.
> You will bear honourable weapons, he wicked arrows.

Three different pairs of signs are used. In the first line, *patriae* and *tuus* are linked to show that both go with *genitor,* "the father of the country and of you" rather than them being read with the next line. In the next line *inuito . . .*

parente are linked, but in addition *hostis* is linked to *ille* in the following line to show that they have the same referent.

These construe marks have been noted sporadically in the scholarship, but have received most attention in the context of Robinson's discussion of "syntactical" marks in manuscripts containing Old English.[162] He distinguished three types, the third of which is relevant for our purposes. While the other two types (using either letters of the alphabet or numbers of dots to indicate the order in which the words are to be taken) have to do with getting words in the right order for translation, the linking marks found here and elsewhere are doing something different:

> There is no vestige of the sequential principle which underlies the alphabetic and the dotting codes; it is made up entirely of linking symbols which call attention to grammatical relationships within the Latin text itself. In a way more sophisticated than the other codes, this system helps the Anglo-Saxon reader to understand the Latin syntax rather than showing him how to rearrange the Latin words mechanically into common Old English word order.[163]

The crucial advantage of this system is that it is not language-specific; because it treats Latin syntax on its own terms, it can be used as an aid to comprehension whether the target language for any putative translation is Old English, Old Welsh, Old Irish, or something else. While it might be tempting to think that, given the prevalence of construe marking in Anglo-Saxon England, these marks were added at Glastonbury, Robinson makes it clear that the technique was much more widespread, encompassing both early medieval Ireland and the continent, although it is as yet not clear where it might have originated.[164] A very similar pattern of construe marks, for example, occur in the manuscripts associated with Sulien and his family at Llanbadarn in the late eleventh century, which is described by Graham in ways which, mutatis mutandis, could be applied to the text of Ovid:

> The marks comprise, in a variety of combinations, dots, comma-shaped strokes, and horizontal lines which curve upwards at the right-hand end. The marks are attributable to Ieuan himself, as their ink appears to match that of his script and their forms resemble those of his characteristic marks for

---

162. Robinson, "Syntactical Glosses," 462 (n. 53), 467; Wieland, *Latin Glosses*, 98–207; Korhammer, "Mittelalterliche Konstruktionshilfen"; Blom, *Glossing the* Psalms; for earlier comments, see *New Palaeographical Society* (ed. Maunde Thompson et al.), pl. 82b.

163. Robinson, "Syntactical Glosses," 457, though we may note that Korhammer, "Mittelalterliche Konstruktionshilfen," argued that the alphabetic codes were not language-specific.

164. For discussion of early Irish examples, see Draak, "Construe Marks"; ead., "The Higher Teaching of Latin Grammar."

punctuation and abbreviation. . . . Ieuan's construe marks perform a variety of functions. They variously link a preposition with the noun which it governs; link an adjective with the noun which it qualifies; link a pronoun with the noun to which it refers; link the object of a verb with that verb; link a conjunction with the verb of the clause which that conjunction introduces; and link the various words which make up a single phrase or clause.[165]

For our purposes, the construe marks work alongside the other glossing and form part of a more complex matrix of grammatical and syntactic support for teachers and students. While tricky datives and ablatives need indicating, the bigger structural blocks have to be marked up in other ways. Ovid's word order is rarely less than complex and the student will have required some careful steering through the difficulties. Construe marks provide a simple and unobtrusive way of doing that. A consequence of this, too, is that it is very rare for nominatives and accusatives to be glossed in other ways, unless confusable with another case form.[166]

(c) The Order of Glossing

In the discussion above, it has been assumed without argument that the Old Welsh glossing reflects a later stage of glossing than the Latin. There are, of course, plausible a priori arguments for supposing that that might be the case. Arguments from the Latin perspective are presented below.[167] At this stage we might consider the physical arrangement of the glosses on the page. There are relatively few examples, but where a word is glossed both in Latin and Old Welsh, it is clear that the position of the Old Welsh gloss is secondary; that is, the Latin gloss was already in place. A relatively simple case is *cum* (fol. 38r33 (l. 102)), which is glossed by *donec uel* **cant** (Plate 2.11 overleaf):[168] the context is an explanation of why Romulus was the first to make games a source of sexual trouble (*sollicitos . . . ludos*), namely, that he masterminded the rape of the Sabine women. The *cum* introduces a clause, *cum iuuit uiduos*

---

165. Graham, "The Poetic, Scribal, and Artistic Work of Ieuan ap Sulien," 247–48.

166. Except perhaps in error; cf. the discussion of *usus* (37r29 (l. 29)) above, 63–64. There is one possible exception to this absence of glossing on accusatives which is the use of *per* discussed above, 62.

167. See below, 76–79.

168. This gloss has been omitted in most discussions of the Old Welsh glosses in this manuscript; it is not in either edition of Zeuss, *Grammatica Celtica* (where it should have appeared 1083 (1st ed.) and 1056 (2nd ed.)), nor in *VVB*, nor in *EGOW*. Bradshaw transcribed it in his manuscript notes, though it never made it into Stokes's edition. It was first published by Dumville, "A *Thesaurus Palaeoanglicus*?" 72 and 76, l. 33 (n. 56).

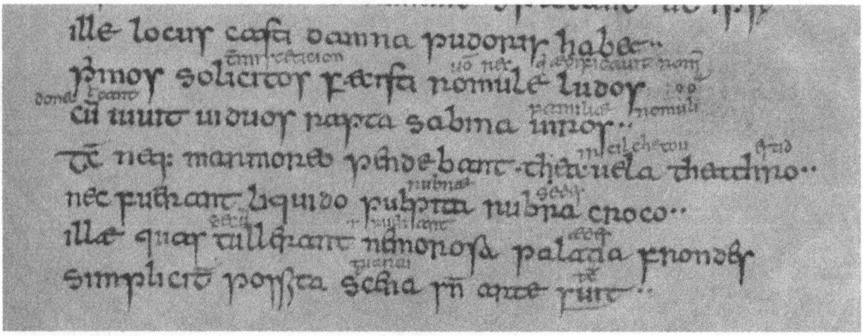

Plate 2.11. Oxford, Bodleian Library, Auct. F. 4. 32, fol. 38r31–37

rapta Sabina uiros "since the wifeless men were keen to snatch Sabine women." It looks as if *cum* was originally glossed in Latin by *donec* "until," but the Welsh glossator, perhaps recognizing that this was not the most obvious interpretation, offers an alternative (hence the *uel*), namely **cant**, the Old Welsh conjunction meaning "since, because." In this case the gloss is positioned more or less where it should be, though clearly secondary to the Latin gloss. But there are other cases where the Old Welsh gloss has to be displaced because of an existing Latin gloss. There are two clear examples: *occellos* (fol. 38v23 (l. 129)) is glossed both by Latin *oculos* and Old Welsh **grudou** in that order, with *oculos* placed centrally over the word and **grudou** trailing off into the right margin (Plate 2.9 above).[169] The phrase *miseris patruelibus* (fol. 38r4 (l. 73)) is glossed *fili aegypti* with the gloss positioned over *patruelibus*, though with a pointer to *miseris*, but, because of the space taken up by the Latin gloss, the Old Welsh gloss **dir arpeteticion ceintiru** is displaced after *patruelibus* over *ause* and runs on into the right margin (Plate 2.12, l. 4).

While there are only a handful of examples, it is clear that when the Old Welsh glosses were added to the text at least some Latin glosses were already in place and blocking the expected position for the Old Welsh gloss. There are only three double glosses and in all of them the Welsh gloss is offering something different from the Latin: a different interpretation of *cum*, **grudou** as "cheeks" rather than eyes, and in the last case an explanation of the meaning of *miseris patruelibus* as opposed to the Latin which identifies them as the sons of Aegyptus. In other words, they do not simply translate the Latin gloss but offer something different or at least supplementary, and in some cases possibly corrective. The fact that there is only a handful of examples, however, highlights the contrast with, for example, the Old Welsh glosses in

---

169. On the rewriting involved in this gloss and an image, see above 48.

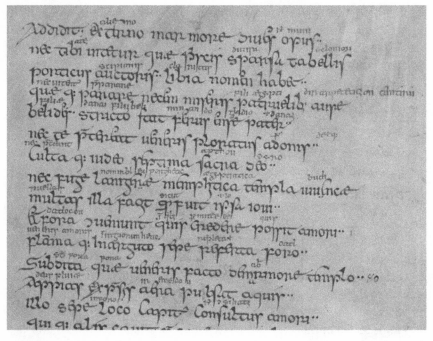

Plate 2.12. Oxford, Bodleian Library, Auct. F. 4. 32, fol. 38r1–14

the Juvencus manuscript where there are numerous examples of Latin / Old Welsh double glosses, often with the Latin gloss being translated by the Welsh gloss, e.g. Juvencus 5r22 *nomen genusque* glossed by *.i. tribus .i.* **be[m]hed**, where the Old Welsh gloss is glossing the Latin gloss *tribus*.[170] That raises the question, to which we shall return, as to what happened in our text when it was the Latin gloss which was felt to be in need of explanation. One possibility to be considered is that the Latin was simply replaced by an Old Welsh gloss.[171]

(d) Latin Glosses and Comment

There are just under five hundred Latin glosses spread over 421 lines of text (some 83 percent of all the glossing). The number is somewhat hazy in that it is sometimes unclear whether we are to treat a longer gloss as a single item

---

170. McKee, *The Cambridge Juvencus Manuscript*, 475; for further discussion, see Russell, "*An habes linguam Latinam?*," 210.

171. An interesting example is at 39v34 (l. 214) where **teg guis** (perhaps to be read as one word) partially overlays an erased *octauianus*; for discussion, see below, 116, 183–84. On the translation of glosses, see Lambert, "Old Irish *gláoṡnáthe*," etc.

or as several single-word glosses on separate words; furthermore, it is not always clear how one might classify the longer marginal comments. We may usefully distinguish the Latin interlinear glosses from the marginal comment and begin with the glosses, and among the glosses we may start with apparent cases of "collation glosses."[172]

The term "collation gloss" is used here to refer to glosses that have been created to record a different reading as the result of a scribe collating two different copies of the text. They are not always easy to detect as they can often look like a correction of an immediate scribal error unless we know that the reading is found in some other copy. In our manuscript one layer of such glosses is readily identified since they do not fit the distribution of the other glosses. While the glosses we are mainly concerned with occur in one main batch (ll. 1–389) and then in a small later batch (ll. 620–52), apparent "collation" glosses are found in other parts of the text and were presumably relatively late additions. This group offers a very useful control as to how they might be identified elsewhere. We may begin with glosses which appear in ll. 390–619 and 653 through the end. Some are clearly corrections of scribal errors (whether immediate or at a later stage is unclear): *da* (46v8 (l. 712) is added in the left margin having been accidentally omitted (or perhaps the scribe thought it was a gloss for *datiuus*); the *te* of *tedritiae* (46v18 (l. 721)) was originally omitted and then added above; likewise, the *se* of *misere* (47r22 (l. 768)) was omitted and added above perhaps as a result of misreading insular *r* and *s*.[173] That these are simple errors is suggested by the fact that no alternative was suggested and what was initially written simply does not make sense (and certainly does not correspond to readings elsewhere). More plausible instances of collation are where a case ending is adjusted, thus *innumeris* (47r14 (l. 760)) from *innumeras* (no other manuscript offers *innumeras*); confusions of agreement are a productive source of corruption in Latin verse and this may be one such case. Personal names, especially less familiar ones, might be spelt in different ways in different manuscripts; thus, at 47r15 (l. 761) *proteus* is changed to *protheus* perhaps by collation. Cast-iron cases of collation are where readings are not simply overwritten but an alternative reading is offered; thus at 46r19 (l. 684) *uel duas* (found in Y and P$_f$) is added at the end of the line after the punctuation as an alternative reading to *uenus* with which the line-ends, and at 47r20 (l. 766) *uel e* is added over *curua* offering the alternative reading *cerua* (found in R and Y).[174] In both cases they are

---

172. On some marginal comments, see 73–76.

173. Alternatively, the scribe had read it as *mere* (classical *maere* "weep!") before realizing his error.

174. Kenney, "Manuscript Tradition," 15.

readings attested in other manuscripts and are regarded by editors as the better reading.[175]

Within the more heavily glossed sections, this type is harder to identify. There are several cases where we have to assume straightforward correction of error: at 41r19 (l. 316) *tibi* is deleted as it was copied erroneously through eyeskip to the preceding line, *quid tibi.*[176] Another specific type is where error has arisen through misreading the various abbreviations involving *qu-*: thus, the addition of *-que* (40r3 (l. 218)), insertion of *quae* (40v14 (l. 265)), correction of *quod* to *quid* (38v36 (l. 142)).[177] Some may just be correction of a misunderstanding: 38r16 (l. 85) *diserto* is corrected from *deserto* (the latter perhaps being originally thought to agree with *loco* earlier in the line). Other types of change might be more likely to be the result of collation even though there is no evidence that the alternative reading is attested: for example, changes of tense or mood: 38r30 (l. 99) *specttentur* from *spectantur,* 40r1 (l. 216) *ne possint* glossed by *non possunt.* In the glossed sections of our manuscripts there are no instances of a *uel* offering an alternative reading. The closest to that is the gloss *peius tra* over *tractat* (39v2 (l. 182)) which seems to be suggesting a comparison with another reading; one possibility is that the scribe had seen a manuscript which had *tratat* or the like and was commenting on the inferiority of that reading.[178] Another instance is where *tollitur* (42r28 (l. 389)) is glossed by what looks like the imperative *tolle*; in fact this is probably a partial gloss intended to propose a change of tense from the present to a future (*tolletur*).

One particular example has occasioned more detailed discussion:[179] 38r7 (l. 76) reads *Cultaque iudeo septima sacra deo*; the line is heavily glossed: *cultaque* by *nec pretereant* (repeated from the preceding line to remind the reader that the syntax continued), *sacra* by Old Welsh **apthou** (for **aperthou**) "offerings," and *deo* by *syro.* The reading of *deo* as the last word was shared by one other later manuscript (P$_a$) but all the other older manuscripts and the majority of the *recentiores* read *uiro*. Most recent editors emend the text to *syro* here on the basis of the gloss in O, seemingly following Tafel's suggestion that *deo*

---

175. Interestingly, the only early manuscript which has both *duas* and *cerua* is Y (which also has *uenus* as a marginal gloss). On the admittedly thin basis of these two readings it is possible that the manuscript collated with O was either Y or a related manuscript. On the more general possibility that Carolingian manuscripts of Ovid travelled with alternative readings added in the margins, see Kenney, "Manuscript Tradition," 24–26; McKie, "Ovid's *Amores*," 237–38.

176. Cf. also 39v3 (l. 183) *natales* from *natalis*; 41r17 (l. 304) *nullus* from *nullas.*

177. Cf. Kenney, "Manuscript Tradition," 15, n. 1.

178. For further discussion, see below, 78–79, 180.

179. See Kenney, "Manuscript Tradition," 24 (cf. also Kenney, "Ovid, *Ars amatoria,* i.147," 10, n. 2); Charles-Edwards, "The Use of the Book in Wales," 402; id., *Wales and the Britons,* 646.

was a Christian interpolation.[180] However, at l. 416, a very similar line occurs: O has *culta palestino septima sacra deo,* but here *festa syro* is found in R and Y, and appears in the standard editions, *culta Palaestino septima festa Syro* (at this point there are no glosses in O, and S$_a$ is lacking). The reading *syro* is more firmly embedded in the tradition here than at l. 76 and likely to be correct at l. 416, but it is possible that the gloss in O was taken from here and that at l. 76 *deo* is correct.[181]

We may now turn to glosses which add content and context. A very common type of gloss is where personal pronouns are in need of clarification and are glossed with explanatory nouns or names;[182] this typically occurs with some frequency in scenes where there is, for example, more than one referent for a masculine or feminine singular pronoun. There are two good examples: first, at ll. 350–89 (where the glossing stops) Ovid argues that, if you seek to seduce the mistress (*domina* or *puella*), it is best first to get the maid (*ancilla,* often written *ancella*) on your side: *sed prius ancillam captatae nosse puellae | cura sit* (41v27–28 (ll. 351–52)).[183] A grammatical consequence of such a narrative is that there is more than one possible referent for a singular feminine pronoun, *hec* or *illa,* either the *domina* or the *ancella*; unexpressed subjects can be ambiguous and have to be supplied; and genitives need to be added as glosses to nouns to show who is being referred to. The glossing helps the reader to disentangle the referents: whereas *illa* (41v8 (l. 352) and 42r24 (l. 385)) and *hec* (42r16 (l. 377)) are glossed by *ancella, illa* (42r22 (l. 383)) and *hanc* (42r6 (l. 367)) are glossed by *domina* and *puellam* respectively; likewise, *ancella* is supplied in the gloss as the subject of *incitet* (42r7 (l. 368)), *dicat* (42r8 (l. 369)), and *narret* (42r10 (l. 371)), while *mens* (41v35 (l. 359)) is glossed by *dominae* to indicate whose *mens* is *apta capi* "suitable for capture."

The Pasiphaë episode (41r2–41v1 (ll. 289–325)) is even more complicated; we have two female referents, Pasiphaë herself and the cow which she imagines to be her rival for the affections of the bull, and two male referents, her husband, Minos, and the bull itself. The effect is that almost all the glossing in this passage is devoted to disentangling these referents (a consequence being that most of the glossing is in Latin). Pasiphaë herself (usually spelt *passiue* or *passiua*) figures as the gloss on *ipsa* (41r12 (l. 299)), *regina* (41r24 (l. 311)), as subject of *aspicit* (41r28 (l. 315)), and as subject of *dixit* (41r30 (l. 317)); but the following feminine singular forms are glossed by *uacca* (or the relevant

---

180. Kenney; Ramírez de Verger, et al. Kenney, "Ovid, *Ars amatoria,* i.147," 10, n. 2, notes: "Cf. Tafel, 16, who suggested that *deo* for *Syro* at i. 76, 416 might be a Christian interpolation" (cf. Kenney, "Manuscript Tradition," 15, n. 2; Tafel, *Die Überlieferungsgeschichte,* 16).

181. The *uiro* readings in some manuscripts in both places may be a scribal misreading of *siro.*

182. Hexter's type III.3; see Table 2.2 above (56).

183. The editions read *captandae* against the two oldest witnesses, both of which have *captatae.*

case form of it): *ista* (41r27 (l. 314)), as subject of *duci* (41r30 (l. 317)), *inmeritam* (41r31 (l. 318)), *altera* (41r37 (l. 324)), and *hanc* (41v1 (l. 325)).[184] Since Minos's name figures several times in the main text, there is less need for it to figure in the glossing, but it is used once to gloss *coniugis* (41r15 (l. 302)). On the other hand, the bull (*taurus*) is indicated in the following glosses: *illum* (41r6 (l. 293)), *iste* (41r17 (l. 304)), *ipsum* (41r28 (l. 315)), *meo* (41r35 (l. 322)), *dux* (41v2 (l. 326)).[185] Both of these extended examples demonstrate the importance of understanding the glossing within its close context.

Proper names, whether personal or topographical, receive considerable attention. In some instances, they are simply identified as proper names usually with the standard abbreviation for *pro* with a suspension mark above (representing *proprium* (sc. *nomen*)), thus *chiron* (37r17 (l. 17)), *adonis* (38r6 (l. 75)). Sometimes the gloss is expanded to specify that it is the proper name of some generic type; thus *automedon* (37r5 (l. 5)) is glossed by *proprium aurigae* "the proper name of a charioteer," *tiphis* (37r6 (l. 6)) by *proprium gubernatoris, clio cliusque sorores* (37r27 (l. 27)) by *propria nomina dearum*. Alternative interpretations can be introduced: for example, *thimia* (38r27 (l. 96)) where the full gloss is *flos uel proprium*; i.e. it is either a flower or a proper name.[186] This last example nicely points up the purpose of indicating that a word is a proper noun—namely, that it might not be. In the absence of the modern techniques for marking names, some words can be ambiguous; *thimia* is certainly felt to be one, and throughout the poem there are all kinds of playful ambiguity surrounding the use of *cupido* (whether the abstract noun or Cupid), most of which are introduced by the poet himself.[187] Proper names could also need explanation; thus, at 37v21 (l. 54), . . . *frigio graia puella uiro*, everything is explained: *frigio* and *graia* are glossed by *troiano* and *graeca* respectively, the former providing the more familiar name, the latter the non-poetical version, and *puella* and *uiro* by *helena* and *alaxandrio* respectively—details which Ovid could take for granted but the teachers of his texts could not. Striking too in this case is the importance of getting the details right in the particular context. Such contextualizing information was clearly thought to be crucial and so it is often the case that a generic noun is identified as a particular place: for example,

---

184. Cf. also the relentless (and often unhistorical) glossing of *puer* and *pater*, etc. with forms of *Octauianus* and *Cessar* in the section on the triumph (39r34–39v13 (ll. 177–228)); for further details, see the Notes on this section (below 179–85).

185. A particularly confusing set of glosses is on ll. 177–228 where Ovid is describing how to pick up a girl at a military triumph; for the historical context, see Hollis's edition, 65–73. The glossator seems to be seriously muddled, identifying various pronouns as *Cessar* or *Octauianus* more or less at random.

186. Cf. also the examples written by scribe E, discussed above, 41, where different abbreviations are used.

187. Cf. also 39v32 (l. 212) where *mars tuus* is glossed *bellum tuum* to indicate that in this instance Mars is a personification of war.

at 37v (l. 60), *urbe* is glossed *alba longa nomen ciuitatis quam aeneas aedificauit in otio* [*recte ostio*] *tiberis fluminis* to provide the contextualizing information which presumably a Roman audience could be assumed to know but which later audiences would get wrong, perhaps assuming it to refer to Rome. That the glossator's geography is not as accurate as it might be, Alba Longa not being on the estuary of the Tiber, is beside the point; the point is that they are showing us the kind of things medieval students needed to have explained.

Much of the glossing consists of single words or short phrases but, as the last example showed, longer comment was also possible and these can sometimes give us a better sense of what glossators were thinking about and what their sources were. At 40r8–9 (ll. 223–24), where the Tigris and Euphrates rivers are mentioned, marginal explanatory comments were added: *Eufratis fluuius mesopotamiae de paradisso oriens* "Euphrates, a river of Mesopotamia rising from Paradise" and *tigris de nomine bestiae uelocis quae dicitur tigris* "Tigres, deriving from the name of a swift beast which is called *tigris*." Both probably draw upon Isidore, *Etymologiae*, XIII.xxi.9–10: *Tigris fluvius Mesopotamiae de Paradiso exoriens. . . . Vocatus autem hoc nomine propter velocitatem, instar bestiae tigris nimia pernicitate currentis. Euphrates fluvius Mesopotamiae de Paradiso exoriens.* "The Tigris is a river in Mesopotamia, rising from Paradise. . . . It is called by this name on account of its speed, like that animal, the tiger (*tigris*), which runs exceedingly fast. The Euphrates is a river in Mesopotamia, rising from Paradise."[188] That these comments are derived directly from Isidore is confirmed by another explanatory gloss: at 37v24 (l. 57) *gargara* is glossed by *nomen regionis in india* "name of a region in India." It is easy to observe that the gloss is wrong; Gargara refers to the area of Mount Ida in the Troad. If, however, we assume that *gargara* was a misreading of *gangara*, the gloss can be seen to make sense by reference to Isidore, *Etymologiae*, XIII.xxi.8: *Ganges autem vocatus a rege Gangaro Indiae* "But Ganges is named after king Gangarus of India" (perhaps especially if *rege* was misread as an abbreviated form of *regione*). This comment comes from the sentence of Isidore which immediately precedes the sentences on the Tigris and Euphrates and indicates that sections of such texts could be profitably quarried for information. That such learned texts were familiar to the glossators is also indicated by the gloss on *cura* (40r23 (l. 238)), *eo quod urit cor* "because it burns the heart," where *cura* is explained as *cor* "heart" + *ur-* "burn," an etymology attested elsewhere in Isidore, *De differentiis*, and Servius's commentary on Virgil.[189]

The longer comments fall into three groups. We have already seen some examples of the first relatively straightforward type where the name of an

---

188. Translation from Barney et al., *Etymologies of Isidore of Seville*, 280–81.
189. For the details, see Maltby, *Lexicon*, 166.

individual is explained, e.g. *Automedon* glossed *proprium* (sc. *nomen*) *aurigae* (37r5 (l. 5)); a longer version of the same type explains that *tirinthius* (38v7 (l. 187)) refers to Hercules and explains why he is so called: *Hercolis quia in tirinthio oppido nutritus est* "of Hercules (sc. so called) because he was brought up in the town of Tiryns." In some instances the explanation is more specific to the context; thus, among a very confusing and error-strewn catalogue of those who have suffered for love, the fates of Dido and Phoenix are explained in close succession: *creuse* (41v11 (l. 335)), glossed *didonis quae se ipsam uiuam incendit*, and *phenix* (41v13 (l. 337)) glossed *.i. filius ageneroi qui prodidit consilia deorum et postea orbatus est* "i.e. the son of Agenor who betrayed the councils of the gods and was afterwards blinded."[190] Most of these comments are presumably intended to provide background information for a medieval audience who might need a little more help than the one originally intended by Ovid.

One particular type which became a staple of the later commentary tradition was the *mos (erat) . . .* comment: "(it was) a custom among the Romans to . . ."[191] In the section on the putative triumph of Gaius, Ovid remarks upon his youth and the glossator feels the need to comment on the precocity of the Caesars: *cessaribus uirtus contigit ante diem* (39v3 (l. 184)), glossed by *mos illis cessaribus a primordio iuuentutis suae fieri semper triumphales* "[it was] the custom among those Caesars always to celebrate triumphs from the very beginning of their youth." The tense is not indicated but the *illis* makes it clear that we are talking about the Caesars mentioned by Ovid. A similar observation made on the violent nature of men is found where Romulus is being taken to task for the rape of the Sabine women: *scisti dare commodus solus* (38v25 (l. 131)) is glossed *.i. quia placebat uiris uim facere* "i.e. because men used to like using force." The imperfect tense of *placebat* makes the point that we are to think of this as habitual behaviour of men in the past (and perhaps by implication not of men now in an enlightened Christian world). Such remarks with past reference can clearly be distinguished from those with a more moralistic tone which are clearly intended to apply to the glossator's own world.[192] The distinguishing mark is the tense of the verb which is always in the present in such moralistic remarks: for example, at 38v35 (l. 141), where Ovid is encouraging the young man to take advantage of the circus to sit close to the girl, the comment is intended to be of general application, "do it gently": *non bonum est per uim sed leniter*. Other comments have present reference and generalize from the point

---

190. For the details and an attempt to unpack the confusions, see the Notes on these lines, 195–96.

191. Cf. Hexter, *Ovid and Medieval Schooling*, 41.

192. See Hexter, *Ovid and Medieval Schooling*, 40–41, on the link between these and the comments in later commentaries.

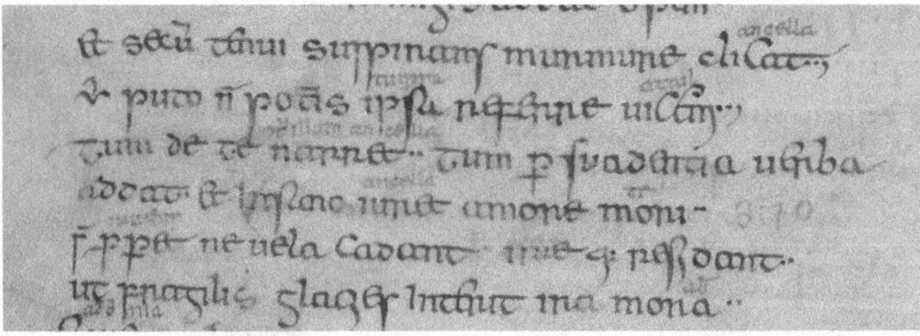

Plate 2.13a. Oxford, Bodleian Library, Auct. F. 4. 32, fol. 42r8–13

Ovid is making: *horaque formossam quamlibet illa facit* (40r35 (l. 250)) "and that hour makes anyone beautiful" is glossed *quando fuerint conuiuium et ignis unum colorem habent mulieres omnes* "when there is a banquet and a fire, all women have the same complexion." Another comment, which again is developing the Ovidian point, makes an explicit present-tense contrast between men and women: *parcior in nobis nec tam furiosa libido est* "in us lust is more restrained and not so raging" (40v31 (l. 281)) is glossed *libido uirorum habet finem libido mulierum non habet finem* "the lust of men has an end; the lust of women has no end." We even find a present-tense *mos est* assertion deriving from a comment of Ovid which is in the perfect tense and referring to a specific instance: *illic sepe animos iuuenum rapuere puellae* (40r28 (l. 243)) "then often have girls seized the minds of young men" is glossed *mos est mulieribus intellegere mentem iuuenum* "it is the custom of women to understand the minds of young men." Here the trope of *mos erat*, with its past reference, is subverted to refer to the behaviour of all women—*così fan tutte.*[193]

So far we have been discussing the Latin glossing as if it were all of a piece chronologically. But it will be argued below that the glossing was probably the outcome of a cumulative gathering of comment, and we have already suggested that some of the glossing with Latin prepositions may reflect a relatively late layer if they reflect the usage of Old Welsh.[194] At this point, however, we might usefully consider a layer of Latin glossing which almost certainly took place in a context where Celtic languages were being spoken. At 42r10 (l. 371), where Ovid is arguing that one way for a lover to pick up a

---

193. One Old Welsh gloss may well contain a moralistic interpretation, **cared** "sin, stain" glossing *nota*; but see above, 84, 174–75, and the Notes to l. 138. Another comment is less easily interpretable: at 39v1 (l. 181) in the right margin a comment is written in the format of a flat-topped triangle: *licet enumeratur octauianus uobiscum | nolite iracundiam | habere | cum | eo* "Although Octavian be counted with you, do not be angry with him"; see Notes, 180, for a possible interpretation.

194. See above, 62.

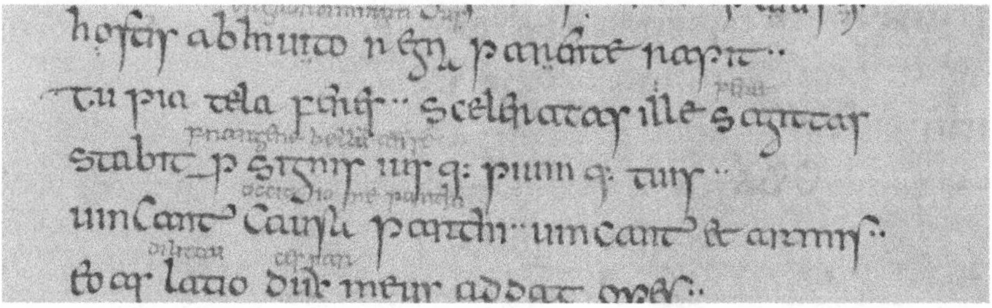

Plate 2.13b. Oxford, Bodleian Library, Auct. F. 4. 32, fol. 39v18–22

high-born lady (*domina*) is first to get her maidservant (*ancilla*) on his side so she will talk to her mistress about him: to a somewhat laconic phrase *de te narret* "let her (sc. the maidservant) talk about you" is added an expanding gloss *contra illam ancella* which is to be understood as supplying both the subject, *ancilla,* and to whom she is talking, her mistress (Plate 2.13a). The use of *contra* after a verb of saying is familiar in the Latin of Celtic-speaking countries, corresponding as it does to the use of Welsh *wrth* (Old Welsh **gwrth**), Irish *fri* "to" with verbs of saying and speaking.[195] A second instance of Celtic usage has already been recognized by David Dumville:[196] at 39v20 (l. 200), *stabit pro signis* "it (sc. *ius* "legitimate law") will stand before the standards" is glossed by *frangere bellum ante se* "war breaks before him," meaning "he wins" (Plate 13b). This idiom can be compared with the common Old Irish impersonal idiom *maidid (in cath) re* X *for* Y (lit.) "(the battle) breaks before X upon Y," meaning "X defeats Y"; we can also contrast the personal usage of *brissid* X *for* Y (lit.) "X breaks upon Y" again meaning "X defeats Y" which is paralleled in Welsh by *torri ar.*[197] Thus, *frangere bellum ante se* has to be understood as "he (*se*) wins." However, as Dumville has noted, there seems to be no Welsh parallel to the impersonal idiom of *maidid cath* and he concludes as follows:[198]

> The fact that the impersonal construction is attested in Latin in both Ireland and Wales gives pause for thought. We have no reason to argue that the Welsh example derives from an Irish exemplar or is the work of an Irishman in

---

195. See *Patrician Texts* (ed. Bieler), 225; Herren, "Latin and the Vernacular Languages," 128; Rittmueller, "Construe Marks," 539–40. While the tendency is to see this use of *contra* as reflecting Irish usage, it could just as well reflect Brittonic practice. For an example of this use of *contra* in another glossed manuscript of Ovid, see below, 107–11.

196. Dumville, "Notes on Celtic Latin," 286–88; and for other Latin examples, cf. also Dumville, "An Irish Idiom Latinised"; Löfstedt, "*Fregit bellum.*"

197. See Dumville, "Notes on Celtic Latin," 287, for Welsh examples.

198. Dumville, "Notes on Celtic Latin," 288.

Wales. In default of a parallel Brittonic vernacular construction, we must con-
sider the possibility that this Latin usage was common Celtic Latin dependent
ultimately on an Irish vernacular idiom.

In other words, it is claimed, the idiom which is perhaps of Irish origin had
been absorbed into the common currency of Celtic Latin. However, it will be
suggested below that there are other grounds for thinking that, just as with
the Juvencus manuscript, there were Irish influences on the glossing in this
manuscript, and these glosses may come under that heading.[199]

(e) Old Welsh Glosses

Aspects of the Old Welsh glossing which are shared with the Latin glossing
have been discussed above. What follows in this section relates to features
specific to the Old Welsh glosses. These glosses have the advantage that they
are all likely to have been added at much the same time and unlikely to have
been added anywhere but Wales.

There are about eighty-one Old Welsh glosses, mostly single words or
short phrases.[200] They broadly concern the same kind of thing as the Latin
glosses; although Tables 2.2 (based on Hexter's analysis) and 2.3 above (56 and
59) might suggest that the Old Welsh glosses are less interested in more gen-
eral comment, this really comes down to the fact that straightforward explan-
atory glosses, e.g. explaining a name or glossing one name with another, are
better, and more simply, done in Latin.

Generally, the Old Welsh glosses provide few problematic readings. Two
have already been discussed: the rewriting of **tru** as **grudou** (Plate 2.9 above),
and the gloss originally read as **penitra** (and thought to be Old Welsh) but
which is to be read as Latin *peius tra* (Plate 2.14a).[201] Two further difficult cases
remain to be discussed. At 38v16 (l. 122) *sine mente* is glossed by **hep amgnau-
bot** "without realizing" (Plate 2.14b). The preposition is unproblematic, but
the verbal noun, apparently a compound of **am-** and **gnaubot**, presents a
number of issues: first, above the **b** a small **p** is written, perhaps suggesting
that we should read **amgnaupot** which would be consistent with the Old
Welsh convention of using **p** for /b/.[202]

---

199. Another possible, but less persuasive, example is canvassed in the Notes to l.102 where
uiros is glossed *familiae romuli* where it might be argued that *familia* is used in the sense of "war-
band" (cf. MW *teilu* "warband." MnW *teulu* "family").

200. For discussion of their orthography, see the discussion at the beginning of the Notes,
153–56.

201. See above, 48 and below, 78–79, 180.

202. On the orthography of Old Welsh, see below 153–56.

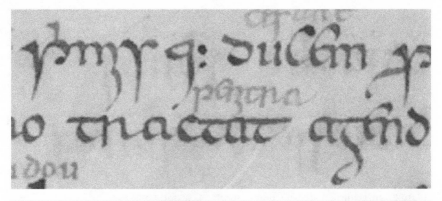

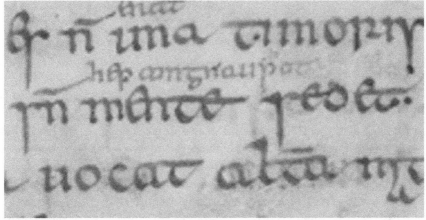

Plate 2.14a. Oxford, Bodleian Library, Auct. F. 4. 32, fol. 39v1–2
Plate 2.14b. Oxford, Bodleian Library, Auct. F. 4. 32, fol. 38v15–17

Although this compound is not attested in later Welsh, the basic verbal noun *gnabod* (itself a compound of *bod* "be") and other compounds (e.g. *adnabod*) are. According to the accepted patterns of Old Welsh orthography, we would expect the Old Welsh form to be something like **amgnapot**. It is not then just the **b** for **p** but the presence of an **au**-diphthong which is unexpected. However, it is worth noting that Breton versions of this verbal noun usually contain an internal -/v/- (e.g. Middle Breton *aznavout*).[203] One solution is we do not have an **au**-diphthong here at all and that our scribe was confusing a Breton form with internal -/v/- with a Welsh one: while in Old Breton the usual spelling of -/v/- would be *b*, it is possible to spell it with -*u*-, and so it is

---

203. Middle Cornish has a different form, *aswonvos*, which nevertheless follows Breton in having a lenited form of the verb 'to be' (-*vos*).

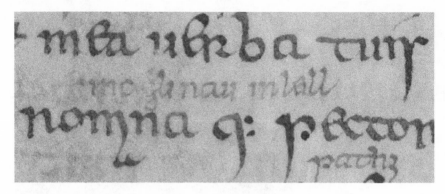

Plate 2.14c. Oxford, Bodleian Library, Auct. F. 4. 32, fol. 39v29

possible that a scribe started to spell the form as -**gnauot** but then corrected it to -**gnabot** part way through. It was subsequently corrected to represent the Welsh form -**gnapot**, which would be the preferred spelling for -/b/- in Old Welsh. It is difficult to build much on one gloss, but if we are to think this is more than just a simple error and that the variation of -**u/b/p**- is significant, then it is possible that a Breton or Cornish scribe was involved. That such a possibility is at least thinkable may be supported by noting that there may have been at least one Breton-trained scribe among the several scribes who added the vernacular glosses to the Juvencus manuscript.[204]

The second problematic reading is at 39v19 (l. 209), where *romana pectora* is glossed by **ingclinau ir leill** or however we are supposed to read this (Plate 2.14c). There is almost certainly a copying problem here somewhere; it is also possible that the first word begins with **h-**. Bradshaw read **hince$_d$linau**.[205] The reading remains uncertain and any analysis has to be tentative. The context is Ovid addressing Gaius and predicting his victory: *tergaque parthorum roman-aque pectora dicam* "I shall tell of Parthian backs and Roman chests" (i.e. the Parthians will be running away and the Romans in pursuit, though Parthians were notoriously more dangerous when they were retreating). In that context, the Old Welsh gloss may be tentatively understood as meaning something like "pursuing the others" (Welsh *y llaill* refers to "the others of two") and read as equivalent to later *yn glynu y lleill,* where **in** (later *yn*) is the particle which precedes a verbal noun to mark progressive aspect, and **gclinau** is some version of a verbal noun "follow"; in later Welsh compounds of *glynu*

---

204. McKee, *The Cambridge Juvencus Manuscript,* 20–23; on the layering of vernacular glossing, see, for example, Lambert, "Les gloses du manuscript BN Lat. 10290."

205. Note that in Stokes's copy of *VVB* (UCL Stokes's Collection 114.f.10), Loth's **cetlinau** is corrected to **cedlinau.**

(e.g. *dilyn*) mean "follow, pursue."[206] Another even less likely possibility is that this is a miscopying of something like **(h)in dilinu** or perhaps **(h)in cedlinu**, compound of *cyd-* "together, joint" and *glynu* "follow," although this compound is unattested in later Welsh.

The range of functions indicated by the Old Welsh glosses has been noted above; most are explanatory or grammatical.[207] Just as with the Latin glosses, a number of glosses have to do with explaining aspects of the Roman world which might have been unfamiliar to a medieval audience. Some of the knowledge displayed in the Old Welsh glosses is particularly impressive if we are to assume that most of these glosses originated in Wales and were not the product of translation from Latin.[208] They are impressive not just for the knowledge itself but the control of distinctive detail. For example, in the section on the theatre as a place to pick up girls (Plate 2.11), Ovid refers to different parts of the theatre; at 38r34 (l. 103) *uela,* used specifically of the awnings pulled over the seating to provide shade, is glossed by **ir cilchetou** "sheets, coverings," the point being that in Welsh *uela* would most naturally be translated by something like *hwylau* "sails" and so the choice of *cylchedau* displays specific knowledge. Similarly, the next word in the line, *theathro* is glossed **estid** "sitting," making it clear that the glossator knows which part of a theatre is being referred to. Three lines later, at 38r37 (l. 106), *scena* is glossed **guarai** "play(ing)," again indicating an awareness that the reference here is to the area where the performance took place.[209] In the same passage, it is also clear that the glossator understands the point of the rape of the Sabine women— that is, to increase the population of Rome; at 38v19 (l. 125) the adjective *genialis* in the difficult phrase *genialis preda* is glossed by **creaticaul plant**, best understood as "for creating children," which captures the precise sense of the Latin.[210] A slightly different case is where Ovid uses the same word in several different senses; in the case of *tabella* the glossator (in both Latin and Old Welsh) is fully alert to all the nuances: at 38r2 (l. 71) *tabellis* "panels of a marble frieze decorating a portico" is glossed **o cloriou** "panels"; at 39r18 (l. 161) *tabellam* "a programme used to fan the girl to keep her cool" is glossed *fabillam* "fan" (*recte flabillam*); at 42r22 (l. 383) *tabellas* "writing tablets" is precisely glossed *aepistolas.* Some of these senses might reasonably be gained from the context but the cumulative display of knowledge remains impressive.

---

206. Another less likely interpretation is that we have what in later Welsh would be spelt *ynglŷn â'r llaill* "in relation to the others."

207. See above, 59.

208. This possibility in some instances at least is discussed below, 114–18.

209. Cf. also the use of *guaroimaou* "(lit.) play places" to gloss *theathris* a little earlier at 38r20 (l. 89).

210. The form of **creaticaul** is striking as it should mean something like "created." It may well therefore be a calque on *genialis* with -**aul** corresponding to -*alis.*

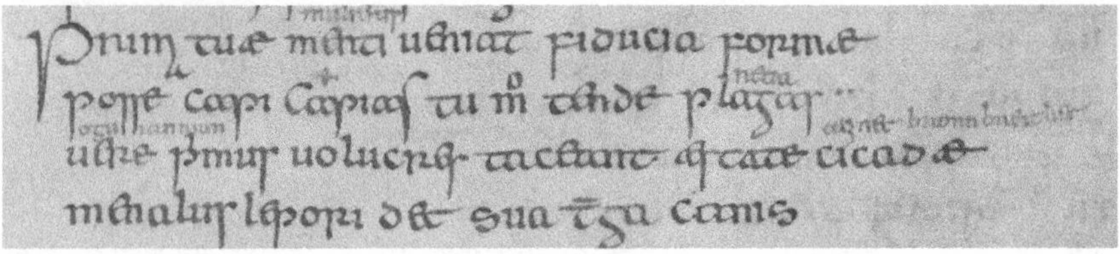

Plate 2.15. Oxford, Bodleian Library, Auct. F. 4. 32, fol. 40v18–21

That said, their grasp was not perfect. Three examples make the point. There can be simple lexical errors: at 42r9 (l. 370) *uicem* "in turn" is confusingly glossed by **atail** "building" (Plate 2.13a above); here it is likely that the scribe understood *uicem* as *uicum* "settlement" or the like and glossed accordingly. In another case, the error seems to be based on pardonable ignorance: at 40v21 (l. 271) *cicadae* "cicadas" is glossed by **cecinet bronnbreithet** "speckle-breasted woodpeckers" (Plate 2.15).[211] The line contrasts birds and cicadas: *uere primus* (*recte prius*) *uolucres taceant aestate cicadae* "in spring first let the birds fall silent, in summer the cicadas." Misled by the first part of the line, the Welsh glossator, presumably never having encountered a cicada, seems to have assumed that they were a type of bird and opted for a phonetically close form **cecin** "woodpecker, jay." He could have been encouraged in this belief that a cicada was a bird if he had read Isidore's *Etymologiae* (as we know at least some of the glossators had[212]) where *cicadae* are mentioned in the section on birds as the product of cuckoo spit.[213] The final example involves metrics. It has been noted sporadically above that metrical comment never features in the annotation and comment.[214] However, 38r13 (l. 83) provides compelling evidence that it should have done: *aera* is glossed **ir emedou** "the bronzes" (Plate 2.12 above) and at first sight appears to be an unproblematic lexical gloss, and indeed has been taken as such by all Celtic scholars.[215] However, the pentameter elegiac line scans as follows:

āppĭă|s ēxprēs|sī||s āĕră | pūlsăt ă|quīs
Appias (a fountain with a statue of Appias, the rain god) beats the air with squirted water

---

211. I take *bronnbreithet* as an adjective "speckle-breasted" with a repeated plural suffix taken over from the adjacent noun, though it has been taken as a separate noun "thrushes" (*EGOW*, 19).

212. See above at 74.

213. Isidore, *Etymologiae* (ed. Lindsay), XII.viii.10. For the tendency of glossators to explain something unfamiliar creature with reference to something more familiar, see *Glossae divinae historiae* (ed. Contreni and Ó Néill), 48.

214. See below, 84–85.

215. See *VVB* 117; *EGOW*, 53.

It emerges, then, that *aera* is not the disyllabic accusative plural of *aes* "bronze" but the trisyllabic Greek accusative singular of the loanword *āēr* "air." The glossator treated it as the former and glossed it accordingly. As such, it provides further evidence that metrical concerns were low on the list of priorities for explanation.[216]

(f) Glosses of Uncertain Origin

So far the discussion has generally made a clear-cut distinction between Latin and Old Welsh glosses. But it has been observed at various points in the preceding discussion that it is uncertain as to which language some glosses should be assigned. It may be useful here to bring the forms together.

The gloss usually read as **penitra**, glossing *tractat* (39v2 (l. 182)), was thought to be Old Welsh, though it had never been satisfactorily explained. It should, however, be read as Latin *peius tra* perhaps recommending that a reading in another manuscript was inferior.[217]

At 38v6 (l. 112) **ledit** glossing *pulsat* was only identified as Old Welsh in the 1930s, probably because it had previously been understood as Latin *l(a)edit* "he harms."[218] The Old Welsh interpretation provided a simpler reading, "he strikes," and a rare example of the absolute third singular verbal ending -**it** in Old Welsh.[219] Even so, it is worth noting that it remains an uncertain member of the Old Welsh dossier of forms.

Coorn, glossing *plausu* (38v7 (l. 113)), has never been certain; it has been understood purely on contextual grounds to mean "applause," but it is otherwise unattested in Welsh.[220] One possibility is that it is not Welsh at all but a miscopying of Latin *corona* in the sense of a crowd standing round in a circle.

Dur, glossing *dira* (41v10 (l. 334)), though formally acceptable as Welsh for "hard, harsh," may perhaps be a collation gloss on *dira* implying a reading *dura* in another manuscript.[221]

Finally, at (38v36 (l. 142)) Old Welsh **ir** was identified by Bradshaw and Bodden although, probably because it was read as Latin *in*, it never made its way into the standard collections of Old Welsh.[222] The context makes it much

---

216. For further discussion on the absence of metrical reflection, see below 84–85.

217. See above, 78.

218. Williams, "Glosau Rhydychen a Chaergrawnt," 213. Note also that *ledit* (for classical *laedit*) occurs in the main text at l. 443.

219. Rodway, *Dating Medieval Welsh Literature*, 91–95.

220. For a connection with W *orn* "blame, slander," cf. *VVB* 82.

221. On this form, see now Parina, "On the Semantics of Adjectives."

222. Although it was not noted in Stokes, "Cambrica," it was later added by Stokes in the lower margin of p. 165 of his copy of *VVB* (UCL Stokes's Collection 114.f.10).

more likely that it is the Old Welsh version of the conjunction found later as *yr* "on account of which."

(g) On Misunderstanding Ovid

At various points in this discussion, we have noted cases where the glossators have misunderstood the text: for example, understanding *uicem* as *uicum* and glossing it with Old Welsh **atail** "building," thinking that a cicada is a bird and that *quis* was a poetical dative/ablative plural rather than a nominative singular[223] In addition, we have also seen that they sometimes misunderstood the referent of a pronoun (l. 639), or how the syntax of a longer passage worked (e.g. l. 289) and what was to be understood from the preceding lines. All of these errors reveal something of the aims and preoccupations of the glossators; while it is easy to take some of the run-of-the-mill glosses for granted, their interests are brought into sharp relief when they get it wrong. The main aim was to explain terms and references unfamiliar to a medieval audience and Latin usage which was restricted to verse (or at least rare in the type of Latin they were used to). Hence the preoccupation with vocative, genitive, dative and ablative singulars, with specific poetical forms, such as second singular deponent verbs in -*re* (beside the prose ending -*ris*), and with the complexities of the word order of Ovidian verse.

A different type of error seems to have been perpetrated at l. 138 where an erroneous moralistic interpretation has been introduced. The main text does not contain any hint of judgement: *nec tibi per nutus accipienda nota est* "and (sc. in the Circus) a signal (*nota*) need not be communicated by nods." But *nota* is glossed by Old Welsh **cared** "stain, sin," which seems to be taking *nota* in that sense and thus by implication condemning the couple's behaviour as sinful.[224]

In all of this, one particular type of error deserves particular mention. As has been observed on several occasions, the glossators seem to have been particularly deaf to metre. The egregious case of a trisyllabic Greek accusative *aera* "air" being glossed with Old Welsh **emedou** "bronzes" as if the lemma had been disyllabic *aera* has been considered in detail.[225] Another striking example is 42r2 (l. 363), where *ilios* is glossed by *troianos* as if it were an accusative plural *iliōs* when in fact it is a feminine nominative singular *iliŏs* "Troy."[226] We have also encountered the incorrect case descriptions added to

---

223. For details, see 82.
224. For further discussion, see the Notes to l. 138.
225. See above, 82–83.
226. I am grateful to an anonymous reviewer for pointing out this particular instance.

usus (l. 29) as genitive when it is nominative, and to *remigis* as ablative plural when it is genitive singular.[227] Furthermore, there are several instances where the glosses are accurate but would have been unnecessary if the metrical pattern of the line had been taken into account, e.g. 37r11 (l. 10) *regi* glossed by *infinitiuus,* 37r12 (l. 11) *cythera* glossed by *.i. ablatiuus.* The evidence clearly points to the glossators not pronouncing the verse with classical quantities and in effect paying no attention to the metre as a diagnostic and explanatory tool. It follows then that they were probably pronouncing their Latin using the later pattern whereby stressed vowels were lengthened in open syllables and unaccented vowels reduced.[228] The vowel in a monosyllable could then only be pronounced long and the distinction in, for example, ll. 1–2 between an ablative singular *hōc* and a nominative/accusative singular *hŏc* would have been lost; the latter is glossed *.i. carmen* perhaps to make the distinction (though it would have scanned long before *legat* anyway). Likewise, at l. 10 *rĕgi* had to be glossed as an infinitive as it would have been indistinguishable from the dative singular *rēgi.* Metrically, *cythĕrā* (nom. sg.) would have been distinguishable from *cytherā* (abl. sg.), but in the later system both would have had a short final vowel; hence the need to gloss it as ablative. Mutatis mutandis, this corresponds exactly to the situation described by Wieland in relation to the pronunciation of the Latin verse of Aratus and Prudentius in Anglo-Saxon England where he describes the verse as being, as it were, prose and with the stress patterns of prose (rather than the ictus of verse).[229]

(h) Evidence for an Irish Element in the Glossing

It was noted above in relation to the Latin gloss *frangere bellum ante se* "war breaks before him" that it provides evidence of having been composed by speakers of Celtic Latin and that, if the point were pressed, it might show stronger evidence of Irish influence than Welsh.[230]

It has long been observed that the glossing in the Cambridge Juvencus manuscript (Cambridge University Library, MS Ff. 4. 42), though predominantly in Latin, contains a proportion of glosses in Old Welsh and Old Irish.[231] In what follows, I want to consider the possibility that there are hints of an

227. See above, 63–64.
228. On this change in late Latin, see Väänänen, *Introduction,* 29–35; Herman, *Vulgar Latin,* 28–38; Russell, "Recent Work," 24–26.
229. Wieland, *Latin Glosses,* 16–23.
230. See above, 77–78; on this matter, see also the discussion in Russell, "Beyond Juvencus."
231. For a facsimile of this manuscript, see *Juvencus codex Cantabrigiensis Ff.4.22* (ed. McKee); for a detailed edition of the text, see McKee, *The Cambridge Juvencus Manuscript*; and for discussion of the glossing and commentary, see Lapidge "The Study of Latin Texts," 111–13; Harvey, "The Cambridge

Irish context to the glossing in the Ovid manuscript which go beyond the two Latin glosses discussed above.

In addition to the Latin glosses noted above, at 39v22 (l. 202) *Latio* "Latium" (the area around Rome, now part of the modern region of Lazio) is glossed by Old Welsh **litau** "Brittany" (later *Llydaw*).[232] Again, if we turn to early Irish, Irish *Letha* is used to refer to both Brittany and Latium, and sometimes in a confused fashion;[233] for example, in Fiacc's Hymn, l. 10 (which is talking of Fiacc going to study with Germanus in Gaul), *conidfarcaib la German andes i ndeisciurt Letha* "so that he left him with German southwards in the southern part of Letha" (where *Letha* refers to a part of Gaul) is glossed *.i. Latium quae Italia dicitur eo quod latuit Saturnus fugens Iouem; sed tamen Germanus [erat] in Gallia, ut Beda dicit* "Latium which is what Italy is called because Saturn 'hid' there in flight from Jupiter; however, Germanus was in Gaul, as Bede says."[234] But as with the Latin glosses above, there is a more marginal Welsh example: in the genealogies the adjective *letewic* is used to refer to Aeneas, *Eneas letewic o Lydaw.*[235] The logic of the genealogy is that we have to do with Brittany as suggested by *o Lydaw*, but the adjective associated with Aeneas is suggestive of the same kind of confusion, or perhaps double use, found in Irish.[236]

This example, together with the two Latin cases, is tantalizing and, if they were encountered in the Juvencus manuscript, no one would hesitate to posit Irish influence, perhaps by way of translation of a gloss *letha* into Old Welsh **litau**. But, if we are to think along the same lines for the Ovid manuscript, the *frangere bellum* example indicates that the Irish contribution may run more deeply as this is found in a relatively late stratum of the Latin glossing—at least late enough for these glosses not to appear in any other Ovid manuscript. All of this is suggestive but nothing more. However, since we know that the Juvencus manuscript had a significant Irish input in its creation, a further step can be suggested.

The gloss **dir arpeteticion ceintiru** on *miseris patruelibus* (38r4 (l. 73)) was discussed above in the context of an Old Welsh gloss being relegated to the margins since a Latin gloss occupied the interlinear space above the lemma.[237] It was noted by Thomas Charles-Edwards some time ago that the form

Juvencus Glosses"; McKee, "Scribes and Glosses from Dark Age Wales"; Russell, "*An habes linguam Latinam?*," 206–14.

232. For discussion, see Koch, "New Thoughts," 17–19: ". . . the name which came, in Welsh and Irish, to designate 'Brittany,' and also, through confused pedantry, 'Latium'" (17); cf. also Koch, "*Ériu, Alba, and Letha,*" 20–21, Evans, "Royal Succession," 28, n. 99.

233. See *DIL,* s.v. *Letha.*

234. *Thesaurus Palaeohibernicus,* (ed. Stokes and Strachan), II.311–12 (my translation of the gloss); note that the gloss is referring to the etymology of Latium provided in Virgil, *Aeneid,* viii.322–23.

235. *Early Welsh Genealogical Tracts* (ed. Bartrum), 57 (*Bonedd y Saint* 19).

236. It is possible that *o Lydaw* was a later clarifying addition.

237. See above, 68–69.

ceintiru 'cousins' is southern Welsh in form (modern *ceindyrw*);[238] it is *cefn-dyrw* (plural of *cefnderw*) in northern Welsh. It may therefore provide a clue to the provenance of the manuscript (or the glossator). That the manuscript ended up in Glastonbury no more than a century later would make a southern Welsh provenance plausible simply on geographical grounds. There is, how-ever, a further hint to be gleaned from another gloss: at 39v8 (l. 188) *in cunis* (in the context of Hercules strangling the snakes in his cradle) is glossed by **mapbrethinnou** "swaddling clothes" which should be compared with the gloss in the Juvencus manuscript (5v3) where *conabula* (classical *cunab-ula*), here referring to the swaddling clothes of the infant Jesus, is glossed by **mapbrith .i. onnou.**[239] This gloss is spelt slightly differently and has clearly been miscopied perhaps by misreading a descender from the line above as *.i.* But the striking fact is that these are the only two attestations in Welsh of this compound and it would be tempting to think that there is a connection. Even if we think that both manuscripts might be southern Welsh productions, it may be premature to speculate as to whether they are products of the same scriptorium, not least because the scripts have little in common.[240] However one final point can be made: when one considers the productivity and use of the prefixed *map-* meaning "baby-, junior-, child-, etc." in Welsh there are relatively few medieval examples; the following are all the pre-1500 attesta-tions in *GPC*: *mabddysg* "early learning," *mabiaith* "chatter," *mablan* "grave," *mablygad* "pupil (of the eye)," *mabsant* "patron saint," and *mabwraig* "young girl."[241] For the purposes of this argument, we may leave aside *mablan* and *mabsant* where the semantics seem rather different. By contrast, Old Irish compounds in *mac-* are relatively frequent and many are early.[242] Jacobs has recently made a similar point about "loose compounds" containing Welsh *map*, in particular *mab llen* "student" (lit. "son of learning") in relation to Irish *mac léi(g)enn* of the same meaning:

> In general the idiom seems better developed and better exemplified in Irish than in Welsh, and while to suggest that the idiom itself is borrowed from Irish might be to carry speculation too far, it is likely, given the associated

---

238. Charles-Edwards, "Some Celtic Kinship Terms"; id., "*Nei, Keifn,* and *Kefynderw.*"

239. McKee, *The Cambridge Juvencus Manuscript,* 144–45, 528.

240. On the Juvencus manuscript, see McKee, *The Cambridge Juvencus Manuscript,* 27–39; McKee, "Scribes and Glosses from Dark Age Wales," 20–22.

241. See *GPC, s.vv.* Of these, *mablygad* (with its Breton cognate *mablagad*) is particularly striking as it is difficult to escape the thought that this is related to Old Irish *mac imblissen* "pupil (of the eye)," lit. "son of an iris (of the eye)." It is also worth adding that *macbrat,* a parallel formation to *mapbrethinnou,* is attested in Irish, but all the examples are late and so the parallel should not be pressed.

242. See *DIL,* s.v. 1 *macc* IV.

expressions containing *léi(g)enn* "(sacred) learning," that *mab llen* at least is a loose compound formed under Irish influence.[243]

The point that such forms are contextually much more embedded in Irish than in Welsh is well taken and applies to the prefixed forms as well. If so, it is arguable again that such a gloss (and indeed some of the other glossing practices in the Ovid manuscript) would be best understood as a product of a bilingual Irish-Welsh glossing context such as that posited for the Juvencus manuscript.

Moving from the lexical to the morphological, it is possible that the use of *priuatiuus* to indicate a subset of datives (the so-called dative of disadvantage) may, as Lambert has suggested, be attributed to an Irish milieu where subdivision of the basic case categories was more common.[244]

The proposal that there may be an Irish context to the glossing in the Welsh Ovid manuscript remains speculative. However, if a connection can be made between the Ovid and the Juvencus in terms perhaps of a shared scriptorium, then cumulatively the evidence is suggestive. If we accept that suggestion, we may be able to discern yet another strand, however faint, of the transmission of learning and scribes across the Irish Sea in the ninth century.

CONCLUSION

This chapter has focused solely on the glossing upon the text of Ovid in Bodley Auct. F. 4. 32. The aim has been to bring together all we can know about the glosses, both Latin and Old Welsh, and their relation to the main text and to each other. At various points, there have been references to the broader tradition of glossing on texts of Ovid which may well have been the forerunner of the later commentary tradition. This broader glossing tradition is the subject of the next chapter.

---

243. Jacobs, "Irish influence," 108–9; cf. also Charles-Edwards, *Wales and the Britons*, 603–4, 607. That *map lyen* is also attested in Cornish need not be a counter-argument as it is perfectly reasonable to assume that, if such a form could be taken over into Welsh, it could likewise be taken up in Cornish and Breton, or have been borrowed from one Brittonic language to another.

244. Lambert, "'Fraudatiuus.'"

3

THE LEARNED CONTEXT

Other Glossed Manuscripts of Ovid's Ars amatoria *I*

INTRODUCTION

So far the focus of the discussion has been on the text of Ovid's *Ars amatoria* I preserved in Oxford, Bodleian Library, Auct. F. 4. 32 (O). In this chapter we take a step back and assume a wider perspective. O is not the only glossed text of the *Ars amatoria,* and there are several others which are glossed in interesting and illuminating ways. In the discussion of the glossing in O we noted that, in addition to the main body of Latin glossing, at least two other layers could be distinguished, one in Latin (exhibiting features associated with Celtic Latin) and one in Old Welsh (probably the most recent layer apart from a few brief glosses on the first page added in Glastonbury).[1] But we have tended thus far to treat the rest of the glossing *en bloc.* Given the way that glossing is usually seen as a cumulative process, it is worth exploring what can be gleaned by examining the glossing in other manuscripts. One way of distinguishing layers in the glossing is to compare the glossing in other manuscripts so as to attempt to identify common glosses. If we can identify such a layer of glossing, it might tell us one of two things: (a) that such glosses were transmitted along with the main text and derive from an early stage of the transmission; or (b) that such glosses might be the result of the collation

---

1. See above, 76–78 and 78–83 respectively.

of manuscripts where scribes had more than one copy of the text in front of them and were copying across variant readings and glosses not recorded in their main copy. The two are in theory distinguishable in that the distribution of the former across manuscripts should correspond to the agreed relationship between the surviving manuscripts, while the latter would rather be the outcome of "horizontal" contact between manuscripts at a later point. This is of course easy to say but rather harder to put into practice. One particular issue which we shall have to grapple with is that our ability to distinguish between these two categories depends on an assumption that any given gloss is unique and that, if the same gloss occurs in two manuscripts, we have evidence of contact. But of course glossators were perfectly capable of creating the same gloss on the same word independently of one another, especially in an educational context where pupils would encounter the same difficulties whether they were construing and reading the text in Francia, Italy, Germany, England, or Wales. On that basis, it would be impossible to distinguish these two categories of glossing. But all is not lost as not all glosses are qualitatively the same; while, for example, the glosses over ll. 289–326 which identify Pasiphaë, Minos, the bull and the cow, or those over ll. 351–98 which clarify which pronouns refer to the mistress or the maidservant, are likely to have been generated independently in any copy used for educational purposes, there are some very distinctive glosses which may be diagnostic of contact. What follows then is a discussion of the range of the manuscript copies of *Ars amatoria* I which contain glosses. Not all such manuscripts are discussed in detail but only ones which show at least some interesting correlations with O. We begin with a brief overview of the relevant Ovid manuscripts and then focus on the ones which are of interest before ending with a comparative discussion of significant common features. For the most part we shall focus on the group of manuscripts described by Kenney as *antiquiores* but it is clear that some of the *recentiores* contain glossing derived from earlier manuscripts which may not otherwise have survived.[2]

As a starting point, Table 3.1 lists the manuscripts using their OCT sigla.[3] It also provides details of date and whether they contain glosses, etc. Included in the table are as many of the manuscripts of Ovid's *Ars amatoria* I as I have seen whether directly, on microfilm, or in photographs.[4] The Table contains both glossed and unglossed manuscripts, but the following discussion

---

2. See Kenney, "Manuscript Tradition" and above 22–23; for a stemma, see above 23 (Figure 2.1); cf. also McKie, "Ovid's *Amores*" which, even though it refers primarily to the *Amores,* has proved very useful.

3. The readings of Y were not used in the first edition (1961) as at that time it was thought be one of the *recentiores,* but they are reported in the second edition (1994) and in the Teubner edition of Ramírez de Verger (2003).

4. Most of the microfilms I have seen are housed at the IRHT in Paris; many of the photographs were kindly lent to me by Ted Kenney.

Table 3.1. List of manuscripts containing Ovid's *Ars amatoria* I

Siglum	Manuscript	Date	Notes on glossing
	Antiquiores		
O	Oxford, Bodleian Library, Auctarium F. 4. 32 (*S. C.* 2176)	s. ix	heavy glossing
R	Paris, BN, Latin 7311	s. ix	very occasional glosses
S$_a$	St Gall, Stiftsbibliothek, 821, pp. 94–96	s. xi	fragment (AA I, 1–230 only); glosses
Y	Berlin, Staatsbibliothek, Hamilton 471	s. xi	no significant glossing
	Recentiores		
A	London, British Library, Additional 14086, 3r–15v	ca. 1100	very heavy glossing
A$_a$	London, British Library, Additional 34749 (Phillips 1056), 85r–87v	s. xiii	fragment (*AA* I, 1–95 only); no glosses
A$_b$	London, British Library, Additional 21169, 46v37–53r1	s. xiii	some glosses
B	Bern, Burgerbibliothek 478, 156v–164v8	s. xii/xiii	glosses
B$_b$	Bern, Burgerbibliothek, 505, 1r–13r6	s. xiii	no glosses
D	Dijon, Bibl. mun. 497, 227va25–229rc8	s. xiii exc.	no glosses
E$_a$	Eton College 91 (Bk. 6. 18)	s. xiii	no glosses
H	London, British Library, Additional 49369 (*olim* Holkham 322), 81v8–88r37	s. xiii	some glosses
O$_a$	Oxford, Bodleian Library, D'Orville 170 (*S. C.* 17084)	ca. 1210	no glosses
O$_b$	Oxford, Bodleian Library, Canon. Class. 1 (*S. C.* 18582), 50r24–56v21	s. xiii	glosses
O$_g$	Oxford, Bodleian Library, Canon. Class. 18 (*S. C.* 18599), 1r1–13r3	s. xv inc.	glosses
P$_a$	Paris BN Latin 7993, 9ra1–10vb2	s. xiii	no glosses, but occasional collation
P$_b$	Paris BN Latin 7994, 63r1–69v2	s. xiii	no glosses
P$_c$	Paris, BN Latin 7997, 137r ff.	s. xv	no glosses
P$_f$	Paris BN Latin 8430, 25va1–31rb21	s. xiii	no glosses, but occasional collation
T	Tours 879, 26rb6–29va28	s. xiii inc.	no glosses

Table 3.1. List of manuscripts containing Ovid's *Ars amatoria* I (*continued*)

Siglum	Manuscript	Date	Notes on glossing
W	Perpignan, Médiathèque, 19 (*olim* Bibl. mun. 10), 2r–16v4	s. xiii	heavy glossing
	Fragmenta, excerpta, etc.		
b	Bamberg Msc. Class. 30 (M. V.18), fol. iii[1]	s. x	excerpts from *AA* I; no glosses
e	Escorial, Q. I. 14 (excerpts), 41r30ff.	s. xiv inc.	no glosses
l	Florence, Laur. 66.40 (excerpts)	s. xv	no glosses
o	Oxford, Bodleian Library, Rawlinson Q. d. 19 (*S. C.* 16044) (fragments found in the binding of Oxford, Bodleian Library, Liturg. E. 15 (*S. C.* 15823))	s. xiii	glosses
p_1	Paris BN Latin 7647 (excerpts), 67v–70r	s. xii exc.	no glosses
p_2	Paris BN Latin 15155 (excerpts), 67v26–71r11	s. xiii	some excerpts glossed
p_3	Paris BN Latin 17903	s. xiii	no glosses

1. Fragments of *AA* I are copied into the margin of a fragment of Eutyches, *De uerbo.*

concentrates on the former category, and especially on the glosses these manuscripts share with O.

THE GLOSSED MANUSCRIPTS OF OVID, *ARS AMATORIA* I

St Gall, Stiftsbibliothek, 821, pp. 94–96 (s. xi) (S_a)

The bulk of S_a is taken up with a complete copy of Boethius's Commentary on Aristotle's *Categoriae,* but copied in at the end is a three-page fragment of Ovid's *Ars amatoria* I which breaks off at l. 230 (Plate 3.1).[5] The text itself belongs to the *antiquiores.*[6] The glosses in the two oldest manuscripts, S_a and A (along with the relevant glosses in W), which correspond to glosses in O are tabulated in Table 3.2.

5. For online images, see http://www.e-codices.unifr.ch/en/list/one/csg/0821 (consulted 2 October 2014); for a description of the manuscript, see http://www.e-codices.unifr.ch/en/description/csg/0821.

6. Kenney, "Manuscript Tradition," 2, 13–16, 19–20.

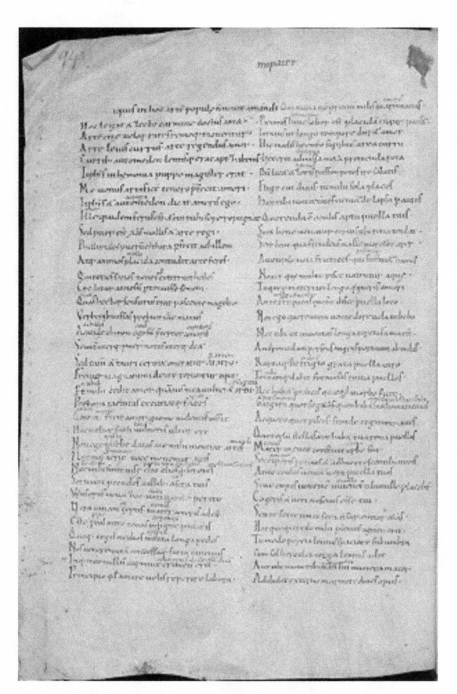

Plate 3.1. St Gall, Stiftsbibliothek 821 (S_a), p. 94

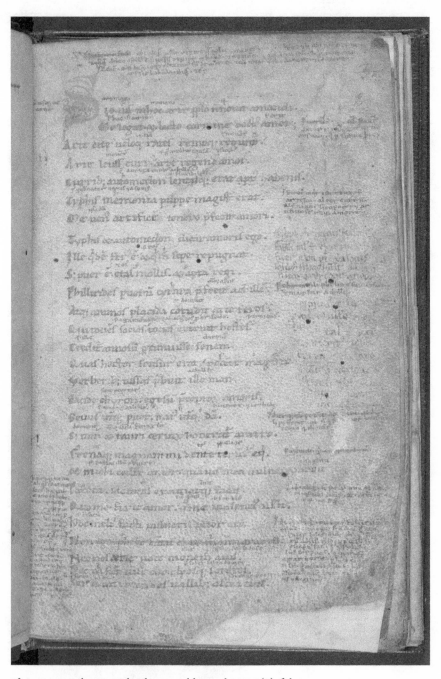

Plate 3.2. London, British Library, Additional 14086 (A), fol. 3r

There seem to be two layers of glossing: a first layer in dark-brown ink and a second in a light-brown ink which is collating the manuscript with a text close to one of the *recentiores,* e.g. l. 12 *placida* (gl. *molli*).[7] The overall density of the glossing is similar to that of O, but contains a few more collation-glosses, e.g. l. 13 *exterruit* (gl. *per* (indicating the reading *perterruit*)). Some, but not many, of the glosses are identical to those in O: e.g., l. 15 *quas* (gl. *manus*), l. 30 *mater* (gl. *uenus*), l. 41 *loris* (gl. *habenis*), ll. 71, 142 *tibi* (gl. *a te*), l. 110 *mouent* (gl. *cogitant*), l. 165 *puer* (gl. *cupido*), l. 213 *pulcherrime* (gl. *octauiane*). In addition, there are several glosses which are similar, but not identical, to glosses in O: e.g. l. 5 *automedon* (gl. *aurigae* (*proprium aurigae* O)), l. 57 *methymna* (gl. *oppidum in lesba insula* (*insola* O)), l. 80 *flammaque* (gl. *amoris* (*ueneris amoris* O)), l. 97 *cultissima* (gl. *ornatissima* (*ornata* O)), l. 140 *lateri* (gl. *mulieris* (*mulieri* O)), l. 193 *rudimentum* (gl. *documentum* (*initia* O)). There are also some Latin glosses in S$_a$ which correspond to Old Welsh glosses in O: l. 80 *arguto* (gl. *stridenti* (**guorunhetic** O)), l. 153 *dimissa* (gl. *prolixa* (**amlais** O)), l. 183 *natales* (gl. *dies festales* (**litolaidou** O)). As can be seen from Table 2, there are also a few glosses common to S$_a$ and A (though they are mainly similar, not identical, glosses).

Another aspect of this text, although more in passing than of direct significance, is that some glosses suggest that they may derive from a copy glossed in Francia. Two glosses are suggestive: at l. 168 *pignore* is glossed by *uuadio* "gage," a Latin term borrowed from Germanic, and at l. 180 *barbaricas* (which in the context refers to the Parthians) is glossed *britanicas,* which almost certainly refers to the Bretons. The latter probably arose in western Francia where the Bretons may have been regarded as the closest hostile barbarians.

London, British Library, Additional 14086, fol. 3r–15v (ca. 1100) (A)

The text of *Ars amatoria* preserved in A occupies an interesting intermediate position between the *antiquiores* and the later manuscripts.[8] Kenney has noted its importance for our understanding of the transmission of the *Ars amatoria.*[9] It is also heavily glossed and contains a large number of longer marginal comments (see Plate 3.2). Table 3.2 contains a complete list of the glosses common to A and O (as well as those in S$_a$ and W). Thirty-nine glosses are identical

---

7. See *AA* i.12 (and apparatus).

8. See Kenney, "Manuscript Tradition," 3; for a description, see Boutemy, "Un manuscrit inconnu" and "Une copie de l'*Ars amatoria*"; McKie, "Ovid's *Amores,*" 231–38; *Ovid, Ars amatoria, Book 3* (ed. Gibson), 44.

9. For a detailed discussion of the contribution of A, see Kenney, "Manuscript Tradition," 16–17.

Table 3.2. Matching glosses on *Ars amatoria* I

AA I, line no.	Lemma (from O)	Glosses in O	Old Welsh	Glosses in A	Glosses in S$_a$ (n.b. ll. 1–230 only)	Glosses in W
1	populo	romano		romano		romano
2	hoc	.i. carmen		hoc .i. carmen		carmen
3	citae	ueloces (Scribe E)				ueloces
5	automedon	proprium *above first letter*; aurigae *above word.*		auriga currus achillis		qui fuit auriga achilles
6	tiphis	proprium *above first letter*, gubernatoris *above word.*		gubernator nauis yasonis		qui fuit nauita iasonis
7	uenus	nomen deae		nomen proprium deae		
8	automedon	proprium nomen			auriga	
12	contudit	domuit		.i. domuit		
13	socios	graecos		.i. agamemnonem et alios grecos		grecos
13	hostes	.i. troianos		.i. troianos		troianos
15	quas	manus			manus	
15	magistro	pilliride				plydii
17	neacidae	.i. achillis			achillis	achillis
18	uterque	cupido et achillis ab tiphis et uenus				tam achilles quam cupido

Table 3.2. Matching glosses on *Ars amatoria* I (*continued*)

AA I, line no.	Lemma (from O)	Glosses in O	Old Welsh	Glosses in A	Glosses in S$_a$ (n.b. ll. 1–230 only)	Glosses in W
22	faces	titiones			ignes	
24	hoc	uulnere		.i. in . . . ?		
27	clio cliusque sorores	propria nomina dearum		[gloss]		
28	ascra	uocatiuus		[gloss]		
29	parete	o iuuenes		ó romani		
30	mater	uenus		.i. uenus	uenus	.i. uenus
31	este	este pro estote		estote		
31	insigne	signum		.i. signum		
32	instita longa	**a hir etem**	✓	ó .i. maritata		
36	miles	nouus		ó		
40	meta	uia		.i. ultra haec . . . praecepta non procedam		
41	loris	habenis			habenis	
47	noti	sunt		sunt		
47	frutices	**loinou**	✓	uirgulta		
53	andromedon	.i. nomen mulieris		[gloss]		
54	puella	helena		helena		helena
54	uiro	ablatiuus alaxandrio		paridi		

Table 3.2. Matching glosses on *Ars amatoria* I (*continued*)

AA I, line no.	Lemma (from O)	Glosses in O	Old Welsh	Glosses in A	Glosses in S_a (n.b. ll. 1–230 only)	Glosses in W
56	haec	roma		roma		roma
57	gargara	nomen regionis in india		terra uel ind. .tes		
57	metina	insola		regio	in lesba insula	
60	mater	uenus		uenus	uenus	uenus
60	urbe sui	alba longa nomen ciuitatis quae aeneas aedificauit in otio [*sic; recte* ostio] tiberis fluminis			roma	
63	iuuenem	iuuenculam		puellam		
63	iuuenes	iuuenculae			puelle	
69	aut	spatiare				spatiare illic
71	tibi	a te			a te	
74	pater	.i. danaus		.i. danaus		
77	memphitica	aegyptiaca				egyptiaca
80	flammaque	ueneris amoris		amoris	amoris	amor
80	arguto	**in ir guorunhetic**	✓		stridenti	
83	consultus	id est consiliatus			consilium	

Table 3.2. Matching glosses on *Ars amatoria* I (*continued*)

AA I, line no.	Lemma (from O)	Glosses in O	Old Welsh	Glosses in A	Glosses in S$_a$ (n.b. ll. 1–230 only)	Glosses in W
85	diserto	*corr. from* deserto; priuatiuus *above* dise; sapienti				sapienti
88	patronus	fuit				fuit
96	timia	flos uel proprium		flos dulcis apibus		
97	cultissima	ornata		ornata	ornatissima	ornatissima
110	mouent	cogitant			cogitant	cogitant
119	illae timuere	mulieres		puellae		puellae
121	una	erat				erat
130	pater	fuit				fuit
134	formosis	puellis		puellis		puellis
140	lateri	mulieri		puelle	muleris	
142	tibi	a te			te	a te
153	dimissa	**amlais**	✓		prolixa	
154	collige	erege			erige	
159	parua	officia			indicia	officia
159	animos	puellarum			puellarum	
161	tabellam	fabillam		.i. flabello		flabello
165	illa	in				in

Table 3.2. Matching glosses on *Ars amatoria* I (*continued*)

AA I, line no.	Lemma (from O)	Glosses in O	Old Welsh	Glosses in A	Glosses in S_a (n.b. ll. 1–230 only)	Glosses in W
165	puer	cupido filius ueneris		amoris	cupido	
166	qui	is		ille		
166	uulnera	amoris		amoris		amoris
168	pignore			uadimonio	uuadio	
172	cecropetas	athinenses		athinenses		athinenses
173	ab utroque mari	adriaticum et tuscium				.i. tuscano et adriatico
177	cessar	octauianus				augustus uel octauianus
179	dabis	sustinebis				sustinebis
180	signaque	uocatiuus crassi		ó romana		
180	barbaricas	parthorim [sic]		parthorum	britannicas	parthorum
181	ultor	.i. cessar		.i. cessar		
182	puer	octauianus		octauianus		
183	natales	litolaidou	✓	dies	dies festales	
191	auspicis	o coilou	✓		augurium	
191	patris	octauianus		iulii cesaris		
191	puer	octauianus		ó tu octauiane		
193	rudimentum	initium			documentum	

Table 3.2. Matching glosses on *Ars amatoria* I (*continued*)

AA I, line no.	Lemma (from O)	Glosses in O	Old Welsh	Glosses in A	Glosses in S_a (n.b. ll. 1–230 only)	Glosses in W
202	latio	**di litau**	✓	.i. italie		
202	dux	cessar		cesar	octauianus	cessar
203	cessarque	uocatiuus		ó		
204	eunti	cessari		octauiano		
205	alter es alter	cessar deus octauianus		.i. mars .i. cesar	cesar	
209	tergaque	in fugam				.i. fugam
211	quid	parthe		.i. cur o parthe		
213	pulcherrime	octauianus			octauianus	
214	aureus	**teg guis**	✓			aureis uestibus indutus
219	aliqua	puella			puella	
219	illis	puellis		puellis		puellis
221	si qua	puella				alia puella
223	hic	dic ita		ita dic		
225	hos facit	dic tu ita		et dic (*later in line over* haec)		
225	daneia	ciuitas (?) quae a danio fabricata		a dane matre praefer		

Table 3.2. Matching glosses on *Ars amatoria* I (*continued*)

AA I, line no.	Lemma (from O)	Glosses in O	Old Welsh	Glosses in A	Glosses in S$_a$ (n.b. ll. 1–230 only)	Glosses in W
231	possitis teneris	hominibus habitantibus		in comunibus hominbus		
247	luce	diem				in die
248	utramque	iuno et minerua		.i. iunonem et palladem		
255	baias	ciuitas in italia		nomen portus		
262	uulnera	amoris		amoris		
270	plagas	retia		.i. retia		retia
275	grata	est		est		est
279	femina	uacca		uacca		uacca
280	faemina	aequa		equa		
281	nobis	uiris		maribus		hominibus
281	libido	libido uirorum habet finem | libido mulierum non habet finem *in right margin*		quantum est in feminis		
283	biblia	proprium mulieris		proprium nomen		
292	cetera	membra		membra		

Table 3.2. Matching glosses on *Ars amatoria* I (*continued*)

AA I, line no.	Lemma (from O)	Glosses in O	Old Welsh	Glosses in A	Glosses in S$_a$ (n.b. ll. 1–230 only)	Glosses in W
293	gnosiades	cretenses		cretenses		
293	cidonaeque	nomen est cretae		cnosia et cidonia crete ciuitates fuerunt		
295	passiue	nomen mulieris		coniunx minois regis crete fuit		
299	ipsa	passiua		.i. pasiphae		pasiphae
302	coniugis	minois		.i. minois		minois
303	quid	**padiu**	✓	prodest	prodest	
304	iste	taurus		taurus (gl. adulter)		taurus
309	placet	tibi				tibi
311	regina	passiue				pasiphae
314	ista	uacca				uacca
315	istum	taurum				taurum
317	dixit	passiue		pasiphe		pasiphae contra minoim
317	duci	uaccam		illam uacam		uaccam
318	inmeritam	uaccam				uaccam
322	meo	tauro		amico		
324	altera	uacca		.i. io		

Table 3.2. Matching glosses on *Ars amatoria* I (*continued*)

AA I, line no.	Lemma (from O)	Glosses in O	Old Welsh	Glosses in A	Glosses in S_a (n.b. ll. 1–230 only)	Glosses in W
326	dux	taurus				taurus
330	auroram	ad				ad
331	filia	scilla filia nisi		scilla; nisi *added above* furata (*n.b. niso missing from text*)		
331	niso	priuatiuus				priuatiuus
336	parens	media pro amore iasonis		medeia		media
338	rabidi			ó		
342	acrior	ut mulierum cupiditas		feminea libido		
352	illa	ancella		ancilla		
364	laeta	troia		ylios		
372	mori	te		te		te
377	haec	ancella		ancilla		ancella
385	illa	ancella		ancilla		ancella
389	index	.i. ancella		proprium		.i. ancella
649	thraseus	proprium		proprium		
649	bussirin	nomen regis		regem egypti		

in the two manuscripts and another thirty-six are similar, but not identical. What clearly emerges is that there is a great deal of overlap between the two sets of glosses; many are relatively trivial, but some are more significant.[10]

Bern, Burgerbibliothek 478, 156v–164v8 (s. xii/xiii) (B)

The manuscript is now lost and the text can only be accessed through photographs and microfilm. The manuscript is heavily glossed but there are relatively few parallels with O and it seems generally to belong to a different tradition of glossing; for example, while O regularly marks vocatives with uō, in B they are marked with .o.[11] There are very few corresponding glosses: l. 12 *contudit* (gl. *domuit*), l. 63 *inuenem* [sic] (gl. *iuuenculam*), l. 159 *animos* (gl. *puellarum*), l. 235 *ille* (gl. *cupido*), etc.[12] Note also l. 193 *rudimentum* (gl. *documentum* (*documentum* A, *initium* O)) which is suggestive of some link with A.

B also contains a number of collation glosses which indicate collation with a manuscript similar to O: l. 32 *tenet* (gl. *tegis* (O text)), l. 147 *ephebis* (gl. *uel celestibus ibit eburnis* (*eburnis* ORYS$_a$ text)),[13] l. 249 *ignoratur* (gl. *ignoscitur* (O text; but *ignoratur* as gloss)),[14] l. 322 *meo* (gl. *deum* (*deo* O)). In most cases these readings are not unique to O but are at least suggestive of contact with one of the *antiquiores*.

Paris BN Latin 15155 (excerpts), 67v26–71r11 (s. xiii) (p$_2$)

This manuscript contains excerpts from *AA* I, mainly single lines or couplets, not all of which are glossed. Very few glosses are similar to those in O: l. 80 *arguto* (gl. *clamoso* (**guorunhetic** O)).

Oxford, Bodleian Library, Canon. Class. 1 (*S. C.* 18582), 50r24–56v21 (s. xiii) (O$_b$)

The text itself is more or less unglossed but the glosses together with a lemma from the text have been pulled out into the margins. The glossing tails off

10. For further discussion, see below, 111–14.
11. E.g. ll. 30, 65, 131, 145, 189, 191, and 267.
12. At l. 304 *adulter* is glossed by *taurus* in B, and while in O it is unglossed *iste* in the same line is glossed by *taurus*.
13. On the readings here, see Kenney, "Ovid, *Ars Amatoria* i. 147."
14. On this gloss, see the further discussion in the Notes, 188.

significantly after fol. 54v. The glosses are almost entirely explanatory and rarely grammatical; very few can be paralleled in O. It is also worth noting that the glossators were sensitive to variant readings; for example, at l. 77 O_b reads *niligenae* but was clearly aware of other readings, such as *lanigerae* (OA) and *linigerae* (RS_a) which are incorporated in the notes.

One noteworthy gloss which seems deeply embedded in the tradition is l. 12 *contudit* (gl. *domuit*), which is also found in A and B as well as O.[15] The significance of this gloss is that it is by no means obvious and therefore unlikely to have been invented more than once; indeed, it is sufficiently striking for the O_b glossator to offer an explanation of ll. 11–12: *sicut phillirides chiron filius philliridis domuit achillem . . . contudit .i. domuit.*

Another interesting gloss should also be noted: at l. 303 (52v33) *quid tibi Pasiphae* is glossed by *quid tibi pasiphae prodest* where the verb *prodest* is provided to explain the syntax of *quid tibi* and to distinguish it from the syntax of *quid tibi* two lines further down at l. 305. The importance of this will be discussed in greater detail below, but the same gloss occurs in W and A and may be the starting point for Old Welsh **padiu** in O.[16]

Oxford, Bodleian Library, Rawlinson
Q. d. 19 (*S. C.* 16044) (s. xiii) (o)

This manuscript contains fragments from *Ars amatoria* I which were found in the binding of Oxford, Bodleian Library, Rawlinson Liturg. E. 15 (*S. C.* 15823). The fragments only contain *Ars amatoria* I ll. 64–437 and they are bound in the wrong order.[17] The layout is similar to that of O_b with the text in the centre of the page with commentary pushed out into the wide margins. While there is little grammatical glossing, there are some glosses shared with O: l. 134 *formosis* (gl. *puellis*), l. 165 *puer* (gl. *filius .i. cupido (cupido filius ueneris* O)), l. 166 *uulnus* (gl. *amoris*),[18] l. 179 *dabis* (gl. *sustinebis*), l. 181 *ultor* (gl. *.i. aug romanorum* (cf. *.i. cessar* O)), l. 320 *pelicis* (gl. *uacce illius* (*meretrix* O, *uacce* W), l. 326 *dux gregis* (gl. *taurus*). Of these, *dabis* (gl. *sustinebis*) is striking in that it is one of the group of unexpected glosses which occurs in a number of manuscripts (O but also W). At l. 161 the text reads *flabello* beside O *tabellam* (gl. *fabillam*) and W *tabellam* (gl. *flabello*), and it looks as if a gloss might have been incorporated in the text in o. One further point to note is that at l. 129 *corrumpis* is glossed

---

15. See below, 111–14, for further discussion.
16. See below, 117–18.
17. For the order of the lines, see Kenney, "Manuscript Tradition," 6, n. 2.
18. The gloss in o is on *uulnus,* but in O it is on the preceding word, *uulnera.*

o pu, an abbreviation for *o puella*; this provides corroboration for reading the gloss *pu* on O l. 120 *in nulla* as *puella.*

London, British Library, Additional 49369 (*olim* Holkham 322), 81v8–88r37 (s. xiii) (H)

This version has some glosses, but fol. 81r is the beginning of a quire and the lower part is very worn, as are the lower parts of fols. 82v–83r. Generally, it only has a few glosses in common with O, notably at l. 12 *domuit* glossing *contudit*,[19] and lacks the consistent grammatical glosses found in O. In some instances, the same words are glossed but not in the same way, e.g. l. 281 *furiosa* glossed by *in mulieribus* (*feminis* O). However, we can note that, like a number of other manuscripts (WAOO_b), at l. 303 *quid* is glossed *prodest* while at l. 305 *quid* is glossed *est.*

Perpignan, Mediathèque, 19 (*olim* Bibliothèque municipale 10), 2r–16v4 (s. xiii/xiv) (W)

As one of the *recentiores,* W does not figure significantly in most discussions of the text.[20] However, it is very heavily glossed and in some places the glosses are so tightly packed that they are almost illegible; they are also in several different hands and inks and are clearly the product of several layers of glossing and comment (Plate 3.3). In addition to the interlinear glossing, there is a long and detailed marginal commentary which goes far beyond the occasional notes in O.

W deserves closer inspection than can be given here. But it is worth noting that, according to the nineteenth-century description in the *Catalogue général,* the manuscript itself is of Italian origin:

> Nombreuses gloses et notes marginales et interlinéaires du XIVe siècle. Écriture italienne. Parchemin. 161 feuillets. 217 sur 132 millim. Initiales ornées. Quelques figures peints en tête des divers livres. Les "Epistolae ex Ponto" sont écrites avec une encre différente et semblent d'une écriture un peu plus ancienne que le reste du manuscrit. On lit, au fol. 161v: "hic liber est Angeli Decembris, poete Mediolanensis." Les épigrammes de ce poète, au fol. 107, ont été écrites au XVIe siècle. Demi-rel. modern.[21]

---

19. For further discussion of this gloss, see below 111–114.
20. Cf. Kenney, "Manuscript Tradition," 5; McKie, "Ovid's *Amores,*" 231–38.
21. *Catalogue général* XIII, 86–87 (cf. http://ccfr.bnf.fr/portailccfr/jsp/ccfr/sitemap /ead_sitemap_view.jsp?record=eadcgm%3AEADC%3AD19050074 (consulted 11 April 2014)). A more recent discussion is that of Scarcia Piacentini, "Angelo Decembrio," 267–68.

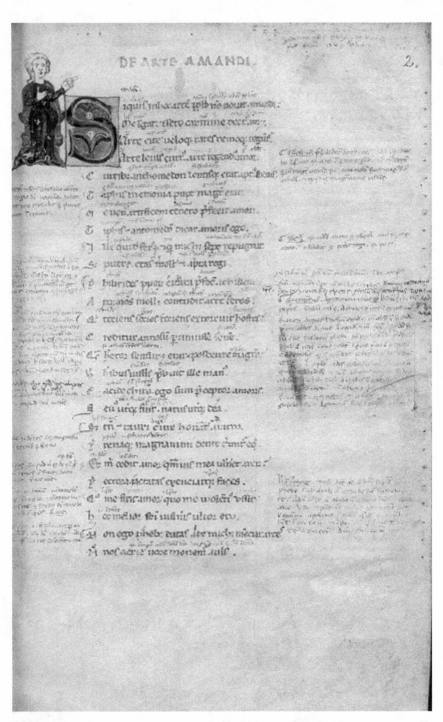

Plate 3.3. Perpignan, Médiathèque, 19 (olim Bibliothèque municpale, 10), fol. 2r

However, Michael Reeve has suggested that the manuscript had a more excit-
ing career than this note suggests.[22] Angelo Decembrio appears to have visited
Spain briefly in 1450 and then lived there from 1458 to 1465.[23] On his return
to Italy in 1465 retainers of Jean d'Armagnac stole his consignment of books
at Rodez near Toulouse. When he finally reached Italy, Decembrio produced a
list of the stolen items for Borso d'Este who he hoped might help him recover
the books; the list is preserved in Milan.[24] Importantly for our purposes it
has been suggested by Reeve that the first item on the list, *Omnia opera Ouidii
minora in duobus voluminibus vetustissime et pulcherrime scripta ac circumscripta,*
might be Perpignan 19.[25]

The glosses (listed in Table 3.2, along with the glosses from S_a and A) are
also in part of a different character to those in O; they are far less interested in
grammar but are mainly explanatory;[26] sixty-two glosses, almost all explana-
tory, are shared with O, but strikingly twenty-six of them are shared uniquely
with O. In other words, it may be that comparison with W reveals a different
layer of glossing which reached an ancestor of O from a different source. That
said, the glosses are not markedly different in character to glosses also found
in A and S_a, but they are simply glossing different words. However, as we shall
see, the glosses show some interesting, indirect connections with O.

It is also clear that at some point W, or an earlier version, was collated
with one of the *antiquiores,* as there are number of collation glosses which link
it to O or one of the others of the earlier group; the following are examples
where the alternative reading proposed in the gloss corresponds to the read-
ing of O:[27] l. 57 *dodona* (gl. *uel methina*), l. 63 *petis* (gl. *uel cupis*), l. 69 *numinibus*
(gl. *uel muneribus*), l. 176 *lesit* (gl. *uel tor* (*torsit* O)),[28] l. 177 *urbi* (gl. *uel orbi*), l. 230
inter (gl. *uel preter*), l. 236 *colet* (gl. *uel noc* (*nocet* O)), l. 256 *manat* (gl. *uel fumat*),
l. 287 *amara* (gl. *uel odora*), l. 328 *continuisse* (gl. *uel posse placere* (*posse carere* O,
posse placere RYAω), l. 338 *pauidi* (gl. *uel rapidi* (*rabidi* O)).[29]

---

22. Reeve, "Rediscovery of Classical Texts," 234–38 (and especially n. 25); cf. also Scapaticcio,
"Il 'PHerc,'" 85, n. 4. On Angelo Decembrio more generally, see Scarcia Piacentini, "Angelo Decem-
brio," and Cappelli, "Angelo Decembrio."

23. Scarcia Piacentini, "Angelo Decembrio," 250–51, 258, 271.

24. Milan, Archivio del Stato, cl. Autografi, sez. Letterati, Supplica a Borso d'Este; for an image,
see Scarcia Piacentini, "Angelo Decembrio," Plate II.

25. Reeve, "Rediscovery of Classical Texts," 238, n. 25.

26. W also shares with B the marking of vocatives with .o. rather than uō.

27. Note that the lemma presented here is that found in W and by definition will not be found
in the text of the standard editions.

28. Note that in O *torsit* is glossed by *laesit.*

29. On the penultimate of these examples, see the discussion by Kenney, "Notes on Ovid: II,"
247–48 and "First Thoughts," 268. On the last, see the discussion by Kenney, "Notes on Ovid: II,"
248; Goold, "*Amatoria critica,*" 62–63; and Kenney's response, "First Thoughts," 268, 270–71.

Three points are worth noting. First, the last two more complex examples suggest that at least some of the collation was with a manuscript closer to A than to O. Secondly, there are a few examples here of a partial alternative reading being suggested, that is, the verbal stem is changed but not the ending, e.g. *uel tor, uel noc*. While such practice is not common in O, there is one possible example at 1. 389 where *tollitur* is glossed by *tolle*; at first sight the gloss looks like the imperative but it is probable that the gloss is intended to suggest a change of tense from *tollitur* (present) to *tolletur* (future). Furthermore, this does give us license to think that at O, l. 182, the gloss *peius tra* is criticizing a particular reading; the text has *tractat,* and it is possible that the glossator knew of but rejected a reading *tratat* or the like.[30]

Two particular features of the glossing in W call for further comment. First, in the glossing on O we have noted one example of the Celtic-Latin usage of *contra* after a verb of saying or speaking to denote the addressee: l. 371 *de te narret* (gl. *contra illam ancella*) which together means "let her, the maidservant, speak about you to her (i.e. the mistress)."[31] In W 8r3 (l. 317) *dixit* is glossed by *pasiphae* to indicate who is speaking, but the gloss continues with a dense row of abbreviations which can be disentangled to read *contra minoim* "to Minos," thus expanding the *dixit* of the text to mean "Pasiphaë said to Minos." If this is right, we have another gloss composed by a glossator writing in a Celtic-Latin idiom. The gloss has almost certainly been copied into W from elsewhere (and it cannot be from O, which does not have this gloss), but it does indicate that at least one item of the glossing in a manuscript other than O had at some point been composed in a Celtic-Latin environment.

Second, while it has been noted that much of the glossing in W is explanatory and very little is grammatical (apart from the ubiquitous marking of vocatives), it shares with O one striking grammatical gloss. On two occasions in O (ll. 85 and 331) we have noted the use of the gloss *priuatiuus* to gloss a dative "of disadvantage," where the dative has to be read as "from" rather than "to."[32] One of these is at l. 331 where *niso* was thus glossed; in W 8r17 the same word is also glossed with *priuatiuus*. Furthermore, O and W also share a gloss at l. 85 where O also has *priuatiuus*; in this case the shared gloss is *sapienti* which glosses *diserto* in both texts. If it is correct, as was suggested above, that this type of grammatical glossing which subdivides the broad case terminology into smaller units is confined to Celtic glossing, this is another

---

30. This would be consistent with the teachings of the *Appendix Probi* (ed. Powell), items 154–55, where *-t-* for *-ct-* is stigmatized. For further discussion of this gloss, which had originally been read as *penitra* and claimed to be Old Welsh, see above, 78–79, and the Notes, 180. A third possible example is discussed in the Notes to l. 138, but eventually rejected.

31. See above, 76–78.

32. See above, 61, and the Notes, 167 and 195.

link with O, though probably indirectly through the collation of glosses from different manuscripts.

Oxford, Bodleian Library, Canon. Class. 18
(*S. C.* 18599), 1r1–13r3 (s. xv) (O$_g$)

This manuscript contains a heavy gloss and commentary in a number of different hands especially in the early folios, though it begins to tail off after the first two or three folios. Overall, although a similar range of words are glossed, the glosses tend to be different from those in O; some are similar to glosses in W, e.g. l. 6 *Tiphis.* Again the glossing does not tend to be about grammar, while displaying the same preoccupation with vocatives as B and W. The following glosses are shared with O: l. 11 *perfecit* (*prefaecit* O) (gl. *docuit*), l. 12 *contudit* (gl. *domuit*), l. 13 *qui tociens* (gl. *achilles*), *socios* (gl. *grecos*), l. 30 *mater* (gl. *uenus*), l. 54 *graia puella* (gl. *elena*), *uiro* (gl. *paridi* (*alexandrio* O)), l. 60 *mater* (gl. *uenus*), l. 74 *bellides* (gl. *filii beli*), l. 264 *thalia* (gl. *musa* (*diana* O)), l. 314 *ista* (gl. *vacha*), l. 336 *sanguinolenta parens* (gl. *.i. medea*), l. 378 *illa* (gl. *.i. ancilla*), l. 623 *preconia forme* (gl. *laudes* (*laudationis* O)). The one common grammatical gloss, l. 154 *immunda* (gl. *ablatiuus*), is striking as it is intended to show that it agrees with *humo* later in the line and that *humo* is feminine.[33]

SIGNIFICANT PARALLEL GLOSSES

In his discussion of the manuscript tradition of Ovid's love poetry, Kenney proposed that the archetype of the tradition, his α, was

> a French minuscule manuscript fairly close in date to the oldest members of the group. . . . A date *circa* 800 would seem probable. Insular influence played some part in the tradition: witness O and the insular characteristics of b.[34]

The significance of b (Bamberg, Msc. Class. 30 (M. V. 18) (s. x)), which consists of excerpts on the margins of fol. 110b–112b, has not really played any role in our discussion as it is not glossed, but the fact that it too has insular features is suggestive of an early line of transmission in Britain or, if not in Britain, at least involving insular scribes on the Continent.[35] Kenney goes on

---

33. See the Notes, 177.

34. Kenney, "Manuscript Tradition," 24; cf. also McKie, "Ovid's *Amores,*" 228–30.

35. For b, see Leitschuh and Fischer, *Katalog,* s.n.; Kenney, "Manuscript Tradition," 6; McKie, "Ovid's *Amores,*" 231–38.

to observe that the *recentiores* do not derive from the α-group but form a distinct group, which he tentatively calls β; his reservations are based on the fact that the readings of this group may be "the product of more than one stream of tradition."[36] He concludes that "In the Carolingian period it is certain that there existed at least two manuscripts (α, β), independent of each other, though possibly equipped with variant readings to an extent which already blurred the distinction between the texts which they presented."[37] He goes to make the point that these manuscripts "stand at the end of a long tradition of 'horizontal transmission.'"[38] It is in this context that we have to consider the glossing on O.

What has emerged from the above survey of glossed manuscripts of *Ars amatoria* I is that we first have to make a distinction between glosses which (a) are so predictable that they might have been invented at any point in the tradition and probably several times over—glosses explaining pronouns, identifying who is who, etc.—which will be ignored in what follows, and those which (b) may have been created only once at different stages in the tradition and disseminated from there. However, we do not observe these glosses following the lines of transmission of the base text but rather they are a product of the "horizontal transmission" noted by Kenney; just as collation glosses travelled horizontally so did some glosses intended to clarify the grammar or sense of the text. Crucially for our purposes, there are glosses in category (b) which are sufficiently distinctive that it is unlikely that they were created more than once, and it is upon these that we shall focus the discussion.

The following list of eight glosses seems to fulfill the criteria for a type (b) gloss in that they are distinctive and in different ways unexpected; that is, they are not a straightforwardly predictable translation or explanation of the lemma:[39]

l. 12   *contudit* (gl. *domuit* $OABHO_bO_g$)

l. 80   *arguto* (gl. **guorunhetic** O, *stridenti* S_aB, *clamoso* p_2)

l. 85   *diserto* (gl. *sapienti* OW)

l. 110   *mouent* (gl. *cogitant* OS_aW)

l. 153   *dimissa* (gl. **amlais** O, *prolixa* S_a)

l. 161   *tabellam* (gl. *fabillam* O, *flabello* W (glossing *tabellam*), *flabello* (o main text))

l. 179   *dabis* (gl. *sustinebis* OWo)

l. 303   *quid* (gl. **padiu** O, *prodest* AWO_bH)

---

36. Kenney, "Manuscript Tradition," 25; see the stemma above, 23 (Figure 2.1).

37. Kenney, "Manuscript Tradition," 26; cf. also McKie, "Ovid's *Amores*," 236–38. On the Carolingian context, see, inter alia, Bischoff, "Benedictine Monasteries"; id., "Libraries and Schools."

38. Kenney, "Manuscript Tradition," 26.

39. For details, see the discussions in the Notes on each item.

What is striking here is that the distribution of each of these glosses across the surviving glossed manuscripts of Ovid's *Ars amatoria* is different. We know that, when manuscripts were copied, glosses could have been copied at the same time; after all, the simple fact that scribe A of O was copying both text and glosses is indicative of glosses travelling through the manuscript tradition. Each copy could then be subject to further glossing which would then be incorporated into the tradition when the next copy was made; for example, the three glosses were added on the first page of O (37r) in a later hand and a darker ink and would have been absorbed into the tradition if a copy had been made. Moreover, it is clear too from O that the Old Welsh glossing simply represents the final stage of the accumulation of glosses in this manuscript. In two instances in particular we have seen that, probably in the archetype of our manuscript, the Latin gloss must have already been in place when the Old Welsh gloss was added and that the latter has been displaced; for example, at 38r4 (l. 73) *miseris patruelibus* is glossed above in Latin by the explanatory gloss *fili aegypti* "the sons of Aegyptus" with the Old Welsh gloss, **dir arpeteticion ceintiru** "the wretched cousins" in the right margin.[40] While the Latin gloss is providing explanation, the Old Welsh gloss is simply translating the main text but could not have been added interlinearly as the space was already occupied by the Latin gloss. The point is that the Latin gloss had to be in place for the Welsh glossator to react against it. We have also noted contradictory glosses, both of which cannot be true at the same time, and which must be the product of accumulated glossing: for example, at l. 79 (38r10) *quis* is glossed by *in quibus* and *possit* by *quis*.[41]

Returning to the list of distinctive glosses above, the pattern of distribution seems haphazard but is indicative of a process of collation of manuscripts and the horizontal transmission of glosses from one unrelated copy of a text to another. In some cases, the texts may not even share the same readings in the base text, and so a collation gloss might be added.[42] In others, it is possible that a scribe declined to copy a gloss as the manuscript already contained a similar but different gloss which was doing the same job; in other words, the absence of a gloss is probably not diagnostic. Furthermore, as evidenced by the unglossed parts of O and the survival of late unglossed manuscripts of Ovid's love poetry, it was possible for the main texts to be copied without glosses; if Kenney is right that the earlier manuscripts often travelled with at

---

40. For further discussion , see above, 68–69; on the preposition **di** "to" (combined with the definite article) being used to mark the case of the Latin as dative, see above, 60–61. Cf. also 38r33 (l. 102) where *cum* is glossed *donec uel* **cant**; on the accident-prone nature of this gloss, see above 67–68 and n168.

41. See above, 63.

42. See, for example, l. 259 *satirbane* (recte *suburbane*), gl. *ciuitatis,* where the gloss looks as if it might have been copied from a manuscript with the correct reading.

least collation glosses (and I have argued that they probably had other glosses as well), the later clean copies may well be the result of "deglossing."

In the list above, apart from O, only S$_a$ of the *antiquiores* is glossed but it only shares three of these glosses with O. A shares two. But the most interesting cluster is the five shared with W. We have noted above that W also shares with O some glosses which look as if they have been created in a Celtic linguistic context, the use of *contra* to mean "to" with a verb of speaking, and the use of *priuatiuus* to indicate a dative of disadvantage. Together these at least point to a closer connection between O and W than is obvious from an initial consideration of the two manuscripts.

The evidence then is clear not only in O itself but through an examination of the other surviving glossed manuscripts containing Ovid's *Ars amatoria* I that the glossing is a product of a long and slow process of accumulation from at least the Carolingian period onwards, though there is no reason to suppose it started then. There is nothing startling in this. As has been demonstrated by Lambert in a more narrowly Celtic context, comparison of different glossed copies of the same text can be illuminating; he has shown that there are glosses shared between different manuscripts of Priscian's *Institutiones* and of the works of Bede and Orosius, and of the *Collectio canonum Hibernensis*.[43] Furthermore, McKee has argued that the distribution of glosses (Latin, Old Welsh, and Old Irish) in the Cambridge Juvencus (CUL Ff. 4.42) was probably the outcome of a process of cumulative glossing built up from different sources.[44]

GLOSSES WHICH CAN HELP IN UNDERSTANDING O

We may now return to O. We have noted above several instances where the glossing on another manuscript can help to explain something in O: for example, W's reading at l. 138 *uenus* rather than O's *nota* may perhaps help with the Old Welsh gloss **cared**;[45] the abbreviation *pu* at o (l. 129) again gives us a way of explaining the same gloss in O (l. 120).[46] However, there is one particular aspect of the glossing which may be illuminated by consideration of the glosses in other manuscripts, and that relates to the Old Welsh glosses in O.

---

43. Lambert, "Les gloses du manuscript BN Lat. 10290" ; id., "Les gloses en vieux-breton"; id., "Gloses en vieux-breton: 6–9," 342–59.

44. McKee, *The Cambridge Juvencus Manuscript,* 43–75; ead., "Scribes and Glosses from Dark Age Wales," 12–20.

45. See above, 84, and the Notes on 174–75.

46. See below, 172.

While most of the Old Welsh glosses do not correspond to glosses in the other manuscripts of Ovid, the following nine correspond to Latin glosses in the other manuscripts:

37r32 (l. 32) *instita longa* (gl. **a hir etem** "long material (voc.)" O, *ó .i. maritata* A)

38v14 (l. 47) *frutices* (gl. **loinou** "bushes" O, *uirgulta* A)

38r11 (l. 80) *arguto* (gl. **in ir guorunhetic** "noisy" O, *stridenti* S$_a$, *clamoso* p$_2$)

39r10 (l. 153) *dimissa* (gl. **amlais** "loose" O, *prolixa* S$_a$)

39v3 (l. 183) *natales* (gl. **litolaidou** "festal" O, *dies* A, *dies festales* S$_a$)

39v11 (l. 191) *auspicis* (gl. **o coilou** "auspices (abl.)" O, *augurium* S$_a$)

39v23 (l. 202) *latio* (gl. **di litau** "Latium/Brittany (dat.)" O, *.i. italie* A)

39v34 (l. 214) *aureus* (gl. **teg guis** "leader(ship)" (?) O, *aureis uestibus indutus* W)

41r16 (l. 303) *quid* (gl. **padiu** "for what is?" O, *prodest* AWO$_b$H)

Why these might be worth considering in greater detail has to do with the broader context of glossing in Celtic languages. It has been argued over the last few decades that one factor in the generating of vernacular glossing was a process of translating glosses either from one vernacular into another or from Latin into a vernacular. Lambert has discussed this phenomenon in a number of Continental manuscripts, mainly those containing Old Breton glosses which can be shown to be closely related to, and in part dependent on, glossing in other vernaculars.[47] It has already been suggested above that there may have been an Irish element in the glossing in O. That suggestion is in part influenced by the long-recognized association between the Old Welsh and Old Irish glosses in the Cambridge Juvencus manuscript. Some of the slightly odd Old Welsh glosses have in the past been thought to be errors perhaps perpetrated by Irish speakers writing Welsh. However, some may represent a less-than-perfect translation of Old Irish glosses into Old Welsh.[48] For those who seek to understand the nature of vernacular glossing in Latin manuscripts, the Juvencus manuscript is crucial: in addition to the arguable evidence for translation, the fact that the manuscript was copied, glossed, and more generally commented upon by six different scribes highlights the cumulative nature of the glossing process; had only a fair copy of this manuscript survived, we would have no clue to the complex layers of glossing which have gone into the making of the manuscript text. In some respects, though, the Juvencus manuscript has no more or less complex a transmission than many

---

47. See, for example, Lambert, "Les gloses du manuscrit BN Lat. 10290"; id., "Les gloses grammaticales brittoniques"; id., "Gloses en vieux-breton: 1–5"; id., "Gloses en vieux-breton: 6–9"; id., "Old Irish *gláosnáthe*"; id., "La typologie des gloses en vieux-breton"; id., "Les gloses en vieux-breton."

48. Harvey, "The Cambridge Juvencus Glosses"; Russell, "*An habes linguam Latinam?*," 212.

others; the complexity is simply visible. It is this type of complex transmission we have proposed for O, even though we only have a fair-copy version to deal with.

The nine glosses listed above correspond to glosses in the other manuscripts and, in the light of what we have seen in other manuscripts it might be worth considering whether any of them looks like a translation of a Latin gloss. We might immediately rule out **hir etem** since the gloss in A does not correspond verbally; it first marks the phrase as a vocative and then comments on the married status of the woman who would wear such a dress. A problematic instance is **litau**, which has been discussed above as a reflex of the ambiguity of Irish *Letha,* and perhaps Old Welsh **litau** (MW *Llydaw*), meaning both "Brittany" and "Latium," the latter perhaps being a secondary reading based on the similarity of form.[49] We should also bear in mind the potential for a misreading of a gloss like that in A, *.i. italia,* as **litau.** On the other hand, **teg guis** is difficult for other reasons, not least because there is some debate about its meaning. In this case, however, it might be possible to make some progress. If we accept with Williams that it is an abbreviated form of **tegirn guisc** "princely clothing," then it could be claimed to be a translation of the form of the gloss in W, *aureis vestibus indutus.*[50] However, another possibility is that **teg guis** is interpreted as corresponding to Middle Welsh *tywys* "leadership," in which case there is no correspondence to the gloss in W. In this case, matters are complicated by the fact that there seems to be a deleted gloss just after, or partially under, **teg**; if the deleted gloss is read correctly as an erased *octā* (as elsewhere in this text), then **teg guis** might be a way of interpreting (but not necessarily translating) *octauianus.* A clearer connection might be argued if **teg guis** was treated as an abbreviation of **tegguisauc,** corresponding to Middle Welsh *tywysauc* "leader." But the fact that the Old Welsh gloss overlays an erased Latin gloss is significant; as pointed out above, it is relatively rare in this manuscript to see double glosses (consisting of a Latin element and a Welsh element), a feature which contrasts sharply with the many double glosses in the Juvencus manuscript. Could it be that the Old Welsh glosses were replacing Latin ones?

Those three examples aside, most of the others, **loinou, guorunhetic, amlais, litolaidou,** and **coilou** could be claimed to be translations of the kind of Latin gloss attested in the other manuscripts. In particular, a plausible case could be made for **amlais** being a translation of *prolixa* since neither is a direct or easy rendering of *dimissa* in the context. Even so, on the basis of these five

---

49. See above, 86.
50. For further discussion, see the Notes 183–84.

forms it is impossible to make a strong case for the Old Welsh being a translation of a Latin gloss.

There is one case, however, where a stronger case can be made. At 41r16–19 (ll. 303, 305, and 306) three lines begin with *quid tibi* (though *tibi* in l. 306 is deleted). We may note at the outset that these are not the readings of the standard edition by Kenney which reads *quo tibi . . . quid tibi . . . quid totiens . . .* If that is a correct understanding of the archetype, it is likely that our text has been created through several eye-skips, and it might be argued that such a text might be in greater need of glossing so as to recover some sense from it. At first sight it would appear reasonable to understand all three instances of *quid* in O as "why?": "Why do you dress up? . . . Why do you look in the mirror? . . . Why do you keep fiddling with your hair?" But the glossator seems to have had other ideas and attempted to distinguish the senses of *quid,* the first being glossed with Old Welsh **padiu**, the second with Old Welsh **pui**, and the third left unglossed. Now while **pui** can unproblematically mean "what?," **padiu** needs further discussion. As we have observed, it is a feature of the glossing in this manuscript that much of it is designed to focus on features which are unique to Latin verse and especially to make distinctions between homonyms which only arise in Latin verse, and it may be that the glossator had a sense that *quid* was being used in different ways here. This is supported by some of the glossing in the other manuscripts: at the corresponding place in several of the other manuscripts (AWO$_b$H) the first *quid* is glossed by *prodest* to indicate that *quid tibi* means in this case "what does it benefit you . . . ?"[51] In the manuscripts where this gloss occurs, it is written with the conventional abbreviations for *pro* and *est* and this may be significant for our understanding of the Old Welsh gloss. A noteworthy aspect of the use of Old Welsh **padiu** here is, as Caerwyn Williams had pointed out, that it does not conform to the usage of this form elsewhere in Welsh.[52] He concluded that the core sense of the word is "to whom is" (used in both an interrogative and a relative sense) but that our example, which is the only Old Welsh instance, is an outlier which does not fit the usage of the other attestations; interestingly he suggests that the Ovid example might be understood as "beth a dycia?" [what does it avail?], but that is in effect a reading back from the sense of the Latin.[53] If the editors of the standard editions are right to emend the text to *quo,* it may be that in l. 303 the original had *quo tibi* glossed *quid prodest* and that

---

51. H also shares the gloss *prodest* with A (see above, 107), but has added *est* above the *quid* on l. 305, as if to make the distinction crystal clear.

52. Williams, "*Difod, Diw, Pyddiw,*" 221–23, and especially 229; cf. also *GMW,* 77–78.

53. Williams, "*Difod, Diw, Pyddiw,*" 229.

the *quid* was incorporated into the main text in place of *quo*.[54] With regard to **padiu**, I propose that it is a reading of the abbreviation for *pro* as **pa** and *est* translated into Welsh as **iu** (later *yw*). The reading of *pro* as **pa** may have been aided by the tendency of scribes writing in Welsh minuscule to use subscript vowels, e.g. *magistro* (l. 15) together with their general tendency to confuse the abbreviations for *pro, pre,* and *per*. While it might be possible to see the -**d**- of **padiu** as continuing the -*d*- of *prodest*, it is possible that it reflects the Old Welsh preverbal particle **id**, thus ***pa id iu** > **padiu**.[55] In short, the Welsh glossator on these lines was clear that the first two instances of *quid* in these lines were to be read neither as "what . . . what . . . ?" nor as "why . . . why . . . ?" but as "why . . . what . . . ?" For the moment, however, the important point for our purposes is that we may have here a case of a scribe attempting to translate a Latin gloss into Welsh; put another way, it is difficult to see how the Old Welsh gloss would have this form, if it were not dependent on Latin *prodest*. As such, then, it leaves the door open for the possibility that some of the other Old Welsh glosses (where there are corresponding Latin glosses in another manuscript) were also created by reference to, or by the replacement of, a Latin gloss.

CONCLUSIONS

This chapter has taken a broader view of the manuscripts of Ovid's *Ars amatoria* I, and we have observed that a strong case can be made for the steady accumulation of glossing and comment from at least the Carolingian period onwards. While glosses can be infinitely reinvented in the schoolroom, there are a few which are more specific and look like one-off inventions in that they are by no means predictable from the text itself; such glosses would then have been just absorbed into the tradition. The complex interrelationship of the glosses suggests a messy and unpredictable process of horizontal transmission of glosses along with collation-readings—and we should also not forget that part of that process may well have been the removal of glosses and the cleansing of texts—but it is clear that some of the glosses are sufficiently widespread across the tradition to belong to early strata of the glossing. Combined with our understanding of the later insular strata of glossing, these findings cast light on the complex history of these texts which goes far beyond the classicists' preoccupation with the base text. Another feature discussed is the relationship between the Old Welsh and Latin glosses. In the

---

54. As Kenney notes ("First Thoughts," 267–68), *quo* was a conjecture by Nicolaus Heinsius which was subsequently supported by a glossing hand in Y; cf. Munari, *Il codice Hamilton 471*, 21.

55. For **id**, see *GMW*, 171.

context of Brittonic glossing there are hints, but no more than that, that a few of the glosses might have been based on Latin glosses, though one might hesitate to call it translation. The example of **padiu** : *prodest* is particularly telling in this respect. If nothing else, through an examination of the broader context of glossing in these other manuscripts, we have learnt much more about the development of the glossing in O.

4

OVID, *ARS AMATORIA* I

Edition

he text is transcribed from Oxford Bodley Auct. F. 4. 32; all glosses in the apparatus are above the word in question unless otherwise indicated; if the gloss relates to a phrase, the phrase is given; Old Welsh glosses are in **bold**. The line numbering follows Kenney's OCT edition. The symbol * is used to indicate words marked by construe marks (in the manuscript the marks are usually underneath the word in question); where several words in a line are so marked they are to be understood as being linked by the construe marks. Where there are different construe marks in a line, the second one is marked by †. In the glosses, expansions of Latin abbreviations are indicated by italics, as are editorial comments in English. Where a suspension mark at the end of a gloss has been expanded, it has been assumed that the case ending is the same as that of the lemma unless there is a good reason for thinking otherwise.

ouidii nassonis artis amatoriae liber primus incipit··,[1]   [37r]   *Hand A*

SI quis in hoc artem populo[2] non nouit amandi
   hoc[3] legat et lecto carmine doctus amet··
arte *citae[4] ueloque *rates remo que mouentur·
   arte *leuis *currus arte *regendus amor··
Curribus *automedon[5] lentis que *erat aptus abenis··   5
   tiphis[6] in hermonia[7] pupe[8] magister erat··
me uenus[9] artificem tenero prefecit[10] amori··
   *tiphis et automedon[11] *dicar amoris *ego··
ille quidem ferus erat et oui[12] mihi sepe repugnet
   sed puer[13] est aetas mollis et apta regi··[14]   10
*pillirides[15] puerum cythara[16] *prefaecit[17] achillem··
   atque *animos molli contudit[18] arte *feros··
*qui[19] toties *socios[20] toties *perterruit hostis[21]
   creditur *annossum pertenuisse[22] senem··
*quas[23] *hector *sensurus[24] erat poscente magistro[25]   15
   uerberibus iusas *prebuit *ille[26] manus··

---

1. *Title added in the same hand as the main text in the top margin; above the beginning is written* Christe; *in the top margin and into the right margin the following has been added:* Ovidii de arte amandi lib. prim. cum Britt. notis. | Anno Domini 1161| vid. Archaeologia | Britt. Lhuyd | page 226
   2. romano "Roman"
   3. .i. carmen "i.e. poem"
   4. .i. ueloces "i.e. swift"; *scribe E in a darker ink*
   5. *proprium* "proper (sc. name)" *above first letter;* aurigae "of a charioteer" *above word*
   6. *proprium* "proper (sc. name)" *above first letter;* gubernatoris "of a helmsman" *above word*
   7. insola "island" (*Hexter* insvla)
   8. naue "ship"
   9. nomen deae "name of a goddess"; *scribe E in a darker ink*
   10. .i. ornauit "i.e. (she) adorned"
   11. *proprium nomen* "proper (sc. name)"; *scribe E in a darker ink.*
   12. *error for* qui
   13. cupid "Cupid"
   14. *infinitiuum* "infinitive"
   15. *proprium* "proper (sc. name)" *above first letter;* citharistae "of a cithara player" *above word*
   16. *ablatiuus* "ablative"
   17. docuit "he taught"
   18. domuit "he tamed"
   19. achilis "Achilles"
   20. graecos "Greeks"
   21. .i. troianos "i.e. Trojans"
   22. achiles "Achilles"
   23. manus "hands"
   24. passurus "would suffer"
   25. pilliride "Phyllirides"
   26. achilis "Achilles"

neacide²⁷ *chiron²⁸ ego sum *preceptor amoris··

    Seuus²⁹ uterque puer natus uterque³⁰ dea··

Sed tamen et tauri ceruix oneratur aratro··

    frenaque *magnanimi dente teruntur *equi   20

et mihi cedet amor·· *quamuis mea uulneret arcu

    pectora iactatas *excutiatque faces··³¹

quo me fixit amor quo me uiolentius ussit

    hoc³² melior facti uulneris ultor ero··

non ego phae phe³³ datas a te mihi mentiar artes··   25

    nec nos aeriae uoce monemur auis··

nec mihi uisae sunt clio³⁴ cliusque sorores

    seruanti pecodes uallibus ascra³⁵ tuis··

usus³⁶ opus mouet hoc uati parete³⁷ perito

    uera canam ceptis mater³⁸ amoris ades··   30

este³⁹ procul uittae⁴⁰ tenues insigne⁴¹ pudoris

    queque⁴² tegis medio⁴³ instita⁴⁴ longa pedes··

nos uenerem⁴⁵ tutam concessaque furta canemus⁴⁶

    inque meo nullum carmine *crimen *erit··,   [37v]

Principio⁴⁷ quod amare uellis reperire⁴⁸ labora⁴⁹   35

    qui noua nunc primum miles⁵⁰ in arma uenis··

---

27. .i. achilis "i.e. Achilles"

28. *proprium* "proper (sc. name)"

29. *est* "is"

30. uterque dea] cupido et achilis ab tiphis et uenus "Cupid and Achilles from Typhis and Venus" *running into right margin*

31. titiones "torches"

32. uulnere "wound"

33. *uocatiuus* "vocative"

34. clio cliusque sorores] propria nomina dearum "proper names of goddesses"

35. *uocatiuus* "vocative"

36. *genetiuus* "genitive"

37. o iuuenes "o young men"

38. uen*us* "Venus"

39. este pro estote "*este* for *estote*"

40. uittae tenues] **a mein funiou** "slender bands (voc.)"

41. signum "sign"

42. .i. estote "i.e. *estote*"

43. **or garr** "the lower leg (abl.)"

44. **a hir etem** "long border (sc. of a dress) (voc.)"

45. uoluntatem *under* uenerem "desire"

46. ut "that"

47. primo "first" *above*; prologus huc usque "thus far the prologue" *in left margin*

48. ut "that"

49. *imperatiuus* "imperative"

50. nouus "new"

proximus[51] huic labor est placitam exorare[52] puellam
 tertius[53] ut longuo tempore duret amor··
hic modus[54] haec nostro signabitur[55] aerea[56] curru··
 haec erit admissa[57] meta[58] terenda rota··[59]   40
dum licet et loris[60] passim[61] potes ire solutis··
 elege cui dicas tu mihi sola places··
Haec[62] tibi non tenues[63] ueniet delapsa per auras··
 querenda est oculis apta puella tuis
scit bene uenator ceruis ubi retia tendat··   45
 scit bene qun[64] frendens ualle moretur aper··-
Aucupibus noti[65] frutices··[66] qui continet hamos
 nouit[67] quae multo pisce natentur aquae··
Tu quoque materiam longuo qui queris amori[68]
 ante frequens quo sit disce puella loco··   50
non ego querentem uento[69] dare uela iubebo··
 nec tibi[70] ut inuenias longua terenda uia est··,
Andromedon[71] perseus nigris portauit[72] ab indis··
 raptaque[73] sic frigio[74] graia[75] puella[76] uiro··[77]
Tot tibi tamque dabit formosas roma puellas   55

---

51. se*cundu*s "second"
52. exorare puellam] rogare usque dum inuenies "to ask until you find"
53. *est* "is"
54. liber "book"
55. ut "that"
56. **ir digatma** "the circus"
57. adsumpta "taken up"
58. uia "road"
59. **o olin** "wheel (abl.)"
60. habenis "reins"
61. ubique "everywhere"
62. puella "girl"
63. nisi quaeras "unless you ask"
64. *error for* qua
65. sunt "are"
66. **loinou** "bushes"
67. .i. is "i.e. he"
68. da*tiuus* "dative"
69. .i. cum "i.e. with"
70. .i. a te "i.e. by you"
71. .i. no*men* mulieris "i.e. name of a woman"
72. duxit "(he) led"
73. est "is"
74. troiano "Trojan"
75. graecia "Greece"
76. helena "Helen"
77. ab*latiuus* alaxandrio "ablative, Alexandrian (of Alexandrus (Paris))"

haec⁷⁸ habet ut dicas quidquid in orbe fuit··
gargara⁷⁹ quot⁸⁰ segites quot habet metina⁸¹ racemos
    aequore quot pisces fronde teguntur aues
quot caelum stellas· tot habet tua roma puellas··
    mater⁸² in aeneae constitit⁸³ urbe⁸⁴ sui··   60
Seu⁸⁵ caperis primis et adhuc crescentibus annis
    ante oculos ueniet uera puella tuos
SIue cupis iuuenem·⁸⁶ iuuenes⁸⁷ tibi mille placebunt··
    cogeres et uoti conscius esse tui··
seu te forte iuuat sera⁸⁸ et sapientior⁸⁹ aetas   65
    hoc quoque crede mihi plenius agmen erit··
tu modo popeia lentus⁹⁰ spatiare⁹¹ sub umbra
    cum sol herculei terga leonis adit··
Aut⁹² ubi muneribus⁹³ nati sui munera mater⁹⁴
    Addidit externo⁹⁵ marmore diues opus··⁹⁶   70 [38r]
nec tibi⁹⁷ uitetur quae priscis sparsa⁹⁸ tabellis⁹⁹
    porticus auctoris··¹⁰⁰ libia¹⁰¹ nomen habet··
quaeque¹⁰² parare¹⁰³ necem miseris patruelibus¹⁰⁴ ause¹⁰⁵

---

78. roma "Rome"
79. no*men* regionis in india "the name of a region in India"
80. *habent* "they have"
81. insola "island"
82. uen*us* "Venus"
83. stat "stands"
84. urbe sui] alba longa no*men* ciuitatis q*uam* aeneas aedificauit in o[s]tio tib*er*is flu*minis* "Alba Longa, the name of the city which Aeneas built at the mouth of the river Tiber"
85. si "if"
86. iuuenculam "young girl"
87. iuuenculae "young girls"
88. tarda "slow"
89. **guobriach** "more dignified"
90. sec*urus* "free from care"
91. specta "gaze at"
92. aut ubi] spatiare "sc. *spatiare* (from line 67)"
93. **di aperthou** "offerings (dat.)"
94. uen*us* "Venus"
95. alieno "from another country"
96. i *est* munus "i.e. gift"
97. a te "by you"
98. diuisa "divided"
99. **o cloriou** "panels (abl.)"
100. scipionis "of Scipio"
101. claritas "fame"
102. nec uitent*ur* "and they are not to be missed" (picking up the verb from l. 71)
103. p*re*parare "to prepare"
104. fili aegypti "the sons of Aegyptus"
105. **dir arpeteticion ceintiru** "the wretched cousins (dat.)" *referring to* miseris patruelibus

belides[106] · stricto stat ferus[107] ense pater··[108]

nec te pretereat ueneris ploratus adonis··[109]   75

    Cultaque[110] iudeo septima sacra[111] deo··[112]

nec fuge lanigerae[113] memphitica[114] templa iuuencae[115]

    multas[116] illa facit quod[117] fuit ipsa[118] ioui··

et fora[119] conueniunt quis[120] credere[121] possit[122] amori··

    flammaque[123] in arguto[124] sepe referta[125] foro··[126]   80

Subdita[127] quae[128] ueneris facto de marmore[129] templo··

    appias[130] expressis aera[131] pulsat aquis··

illo sepe loco[132] capitur consultus[133] amori··

    quique alis cauit non cauet ipse sibi··

illo sepe loco[134] desunt sua uerba deserto··[135]   85

    resque nouae ueniunt causaque agenda sua est··

nunc[136] uenus e templis quae sunt confinia ridet··

---

106. belides et stricto] filiae danai filius beli "the daughters of Danaus, the son of Belus"

107. ferus ense] minando gladio "by threatening with a sword"

108. .i. danaus "i.e. Danaus"

109. *proprium* "proper (sc. name)" *above first letter*; deestque "and she is missing (sc. him)" *in right margin*

110. nec pretereant "and let them not pass by" (picking up the verb from l. 75)

111. **apthou** "offerings"; *for* aperthou (cf. l. 69) *but lacking the suspension mark*

112. Syro "Syrian"

113. **nom ir bleuporthetic** "the wool-wearing one (gen.)"

114. aegyptiaca "Egyptian"

115. **buch** "cow"

116. puellas "girls"

117. sicut "just as"

118. .i. io "i.e. Io"

119. **datlocou** "meeting places"

120. in quibus "in which"

121. *permittere* se "to allow oneself"

122. quis "who?"

123. ueneris amoris "of Venus, of love"

124. **in ir guorunhetic** "in the noisy . . ."

125. repleta est "was filled"

126. **datl** "meeting"

127. *sunt* fora "are," "forums"

128. fora "forums"

129. ab*latiuus* "ablative"

130. deus pluiae "the god of rain"

131. **ir emedou** "the bronzes"

132. in foro "in the forum"

133. id est *consiliatus* "i.e. advising"

134. ab*latiuus* "ablative"

135. *corrected to* diserto "eloquent"; priuatiuus "privative" *above* dise; sapienti "wise" *over end of word and running into right margin*

136. tunc "at that time"

qui[137] modo patronus[138] nunc cupit esse cliens··[139]
sed tu precipue[140] ceruis uenare[141] theathris··[142]
   hec loco sunt uoto[143] fertiliora tuo··   90
illic inuenies quod ames quod ludere possis··
   quodque[144] semel tangas quod tenere uelis··
ut redit itque[145] frequens longum formica per agmen
   granifero solidum cum uechit ore cibum
Aut ut apes saltusque suos et olentia nanctae   95
   pascua per flores et thimia[146] summa uolant
sic ruit ad celebres cultissima[147] femina ludos··
   copia iudicium[148] sepe morata meum est··
spectatum[149] ueniunt ueniunt specttentur[150] ut ipse
   ille locus casti damna pudoris habet··   100
primos solicitos[151] faecisti romule[152] ludos
   cum[153] iuuit uiduos rapta sabina uiros··[154]
tunc neque marmoreo pendebant .thea.[155] uela[156] theathro··[157]
   nec fuerant liquido pulpita rubra[158] croco··
illae quas tullerant[159] nemorosa[160] palatia[161] frondes   105
   simpliciter possita scena[162] sine arte fuit··[163]

---

137. fuit "was"
138. index "indicator" (*but perhaps for* iudex "judge")
139. **dauu** "member of a retinue"
140. ad*uerbum* "adverb"
141. **helghati** "hunt (2sg. imperative)"
142. **guaroimaou** "plays, play places"
143. dat*iuus* "dative"
144. inuenies "you will find"
145. ut "that"
146. flos uel proprium "flower or a proper (sc. name)"
147. cultissima] ma *added above; glossed* ornata "decorated"
148. copia iudicium] deficile est elegere ab eis "it is difficult to choose from them"
149. ad sspectandos [*sic*] alios "in order to watch others"
150. [*sic*]; *altered from* spectantur; ab alis "by others"
151. **termisceticion** "confused"
152. uocatiuus rex qui aedificauit romam "vocative, the king who built Rome"
153. donec uel **cant** "until or since"
154. familiae romuli "the families of Romulus"
155. thea] *preceded and followed by* puncta delentia; *the scribe anticipated* theathro
156. **ir cilchetou** "the sheets"
157. **estid** "the seating area"
158. rubrae sedes "red seats"
159. se*cum* "with them"
160. .i. fuerant "i.e. they had been"
161. aedes "houses"
162. **guarai** "play, stage"
163. *tunc* "at that time"

in gradibus[164] sedit populus de cispite[165] factis   [38v]
    qualibet hirsutas fronte tegente comas
respiciunt oculisque notat[166] sibi quisque puellam
    quam uelit et tacito pectore mutta[167] mouent··[168]   110
dumque rudem prebente modum tubicine[169] tusco
    lidius aequatam ter pede pulsat[170] humum··,
in medio plausu[171] plausus[172] tunc arte carebant··
    rex populo predae signa petenda dedit··
protinus exiliunt animum clamore fatentes··[173]   115
    uirginibus cupidas iniciunt que manus··
ut fugiunt aquilas[174] timidissima turba columbae
    ut fugit uissos agna nouella[175] lupos
SIc illae[176] timuere uiros sine lege furentes··[177]
    *constitit in *nulla[178] qui fuit ante *color··   120
nam timor unus erat facies non una[179] timoris:·
    pars laniat crines pars sine[180] mente sedet··
altera[181] mesta[182] silet frustra uocat altera matrem··
    hec[183] queritur stupet hec manet illa fugit··
ducuntur raptae genialis[184] preda puellae··   125
    et potuit multas[185] ipse decere pudor··
SI qua[186] repugnarat nimium comittemque[187] repugnat

---

164. .i. **cemmein** "i.e. steps"
165. *tellure* "earth"
166. *elegit* "he picked out"
167. *consilia* "plans"
168. *cogitant* "they consider"
169. tubicine tusco] **pippaur tuscois** "Tuscan piper"
170. **ledit** "he strikes"
171. **coorn** "applause" (*but cf. Notes*)
172. *clamoris* "shouting"
173. *fatigantes* "tiring"
174. *ante* "in front of"
175. *iuuenis* "young"
176. illae timuere] .i. mulieres "i.e. women"
177. *furio* "I rage"
178. **pu** "girl" (*abbreviation for* puella; *see Notes*)
179. *erat* "was"
180. sine mente] **heb amgnaupot** (*small* b *above* p) "without realising"
181. *puella* "girl"
182. *tristis* "sad"
183. *una* "single (sc. girl)"
184. genialis] **creaticaul plant** "for producing children" *in right margin linked by a signe de renvoi*
185. *puellas* "girls"
186. **nepun** puella "someone, a girl"
187. comitemque repugnat] si ire *over* -que re-

sublatam[188] *cupido uir tulit ipse *sinu··
Atque ita quid teneros lacrimis corrumpis occellos[189]
    Quod matri pater[190] est hoc tibi dixit ero··   130
romulae[191] militibus scisti[192] dare commoda solus··
    hec mihi si dederis commoda miles ero··
scilicet ex illo solemnia more teathra[193]
    nunc quoque formosis[194] insidiosa manent··
nec te nobilium fugiat[195] certamen[196] equorum··   135
    multa capax populi commoda circus[197] habet··
nil[198] opus est digitis[199] per quos arcana[200] loquaris··
    nec tibi[201] per[202] nutus accipienda nota[203] est··
proximus a domina[204] nulla prohibente sedeto··[205]
    iunge tuum lateri[206] qua potes usque latus··   140
nec bene[207] quod[208] cogit si nolit linia iungi··
    quid[209] tibi[210] tangenda est lege puella loci
hic[211] queratur socii sermonis origo··
    et moueant primos puplica uerba sonos··   [39r]
Cuius equi ueniant facito studiosse requires··[212]   145

---

188. puella*m* "girl"
189. oculos **grudou** "eyes, cheeks"; *the Old Welsh seems to have been rewritten (see Notes)*
190. fuit "was"
191. u*ocatiuus* "vocative"
192. scisti dare commoda solus] .i. quia placebat uiris ui*m* facere "i.e. because men used to like causing violence"
193. **guaroiou** "plays"
194. puellis "girls"
195. *preteriat* "let it go past"
196. currus "of a chariot"
197. **digatma** "circus"
198. nil opus] *non* necesse *est* "it is not necessary"
199. ut nutas "as you nod"
200. **ringuedaulion** "secrets"
201. a te "by you"
202. per nutus] **troi enmeituou** "by means of nods"; *line over* ou *showing that it is part of the same word*
203. **cared** "sin"
204. quasi dominae "as if *dominae* (dat.)"
205. sede "sit" (imperative)
206. mulieri "woman"
207. *est* "is"
208. quod cogit si nolit] *non* bonum est *per* uim *sed* leniter "it is not good by force but gently"
209. quid *changed to* quod; **ir** "on account of"
210. a te "by you"
211. ibi "there"
212. ut "that"

nec²¹³ mora quisquis²¹⁴ erit cui fauet illa faue˙˙
At cum pompa²¹⁵ frequens celestibus ibit eburnis²¹⁶
   tu ueneri dominae plaude²¹⁷ fauente²¹⁸ manu
utque fit in gremium puluis si forte puellae
   deciderit digitis excusiendus erit²¹⁹   150
et si nullus erit puluis tamen excute nullum˙˙²²⁰
   quelibet²²¹ officio causa sit apta tuo˙˙
pallia si terra nimium dimissa²²² iacebunt
   collige²²³ et inmunda²²⁴ sedulus effer²²⁵ humo˙˙
protinus officio²²⁶ pretium patiente puella   155
   contingent oculis crura uidenda tuis˙˙
respice preterea post uos quicunque sedebit˙˙²²⁷
   ne premat²²⁸ oppossito mollia terga genu˙
parua²²⁹ leuis capiunt animos²³⁰ fuit utile multis˙
   puluinum facili conpossuisse manu˙˙   160
profuit²³¹ et tenui uento mouisse tabellam˙˙²³²
   et caua sub tenerum scamna dedisse pedem˙˙
hos aditus circusque²³³ nouo prebebit amori˙˙
   sparsaque solicito²³⁴ tristis²³⁵ harena foro˙˙,
illa²³⁶ sepe puer²³⁷ ueneris pugnauit harena˙˙   165

---

213. nec mora] .i. cito "i.e. quickly"
214. *uel bonus uel malus* "either good or bad"
215. *pompea MS, with e erased*
216. r *written above the n of eburnis, then* dentes eliphantis "elephant's tusks" *written either side of it*
217. roga "ask (imperative) on behalf of"
218. *pro* fauenti "for *fauenti*"
219. **hac boi** "and it will be"
220. **ir ansceth** "the nonexistent thing"
221. excute "brush off" *over* que; erit "it will be" *over end of word*
222. **amlais** "loose"
223. erege "gather up"
224. ab*latiuus* "ablative"
225. erege "gather up"
226. tuo "your"
227. *post tergum* "behind"
228. quis "anyone"
229. officia "duties"
230. puella*rum* "of girls"
231. multis "many"
232. fabillam [*sic for* flabillam "fan"] (*see Notes*)
233. **ir digatmaou** "the circuses"
234. ab*latiuus* "ablative"
235. sordida "dirty"
236. in "in"
237. cupido filius ueneris "Cupid, the son of Venus"

et qui[238] spectauit uulnera[239] uulnus habet··
dum loquitur tangitque manum poscntque[240] libellum[241]
    et querit possito pignore uincat uter
Saucius ingemuit telumque uolatile sensit··
    et pars spectati[242] muneris ipse[243] fuit··   170
Quid modo cum belli naualis imagine cessar
    persidas induxit cecropetasque[244] rates
nimphe[245] ab utroque mari[246] iuuenes ab utroque puellae
    uenere atque ingens orbis in urbe fuit
uir non inuenit[247] turba quod[248] amaret in illa··   175
    heu[249] quam[250] multos aduena torsit[251] amor··
ecce parat cessar[252] domito[253] quod defuit orbi
    addere nunc[254] oriens[255] ultime noster eris··
pathe[256] dabis[257] penas grassi[258] gaudete sepulti··[259]
    signaque[260] barbaricas[261] non bene[262] passa manus··   180
ultor[263] adest primisque ducem[264] profitetur in annis·[265]   [39v]

---

238. is "he"
239. amoris "of love"
240. poscntque] sic
241. **ir caiauc** "the little book"
242. *promisi* "promised"
243. *qui* poscit "who demands"
244. *athinenses* "Athenians"
245. quia "because"
246. adriaticum et tuscium "Adriatic and Tuscan"
247. *inter* "among"
248. .i. id "i.e. that"; *different ink and perhaps different hand*
249. **mortru** "so sad"
250. quam multos] **mor liaus** "so many"
251. laesit "it harmed."
252. octouianus "Octavian"
253. **or dometic** "the tamed . . ."
254. *tunc* "at that time"
255. uocatiuus "vocative"
256. uocatiuus "vocative"
257. sustinebis "you will endure"
258. proprium "proper (sc. name)"
259. uocatiuus "vocative" *over word;* **ha arcibrenou** "buried ones (voc.)" *running into right margin*
260. uocatiuus crassi "vocative, of Crassus"
261. Parthorim (*recte* Parthorum) "of the Parthians"
262. non bene passa] **ni cein guodemisauch** "you did not suffer well"
263. .i. cessar "i.e. Caesar"
264. cesarem "Caesar"
265. licet enumeratur octauianus uobiscum | nolite iracundiam | habere | cum | eo "although Octavian may be counted among you, do not be angry with him" *in right margin in a triangular shape*

bellaque non puero²⁶⁶ tractat²⁶⁷ agenda puer⁓²⁶⁸
parcite natales²⁶⁹ timidi numerare deorum⁓
    cessaribus uirtus contigit ante diem⁓²⁷⁰
ingenium celeste tuis uelocius annis   185
    Surgit et ignauae²⁷¹ fert male damna morae
paruus erat manibusque duos tirinthius²⁷² anguis
    presit²⁷³ et in²⁷⁴ cunis iam ioue²⁷⁵ dignus erat⁓
nunc quoque qui puer es quantus²⁷⁶ tum bache²⁷⁷ fuisti⁓
    cum timuit thyrros²⁷⁸ india uicta tuos⁓   190
Auspicis²⁷⁹ annisque patris²⁸⁰ puer²⁸¹ arma mouebis
    et uinces annis auspicisque patris⁓²⁸²
Tale rudimentum²⁸³ tanto sub nomine²⁸⁴ debes⁓²⁸⁵
    nunc iuuenum princeps²⁸⁶ de inde²⁸⁷ future²⁸⁸ senum⁓²⁸⁹
Cum tibi sint fratres fratres ulciscere lessos⁓²⁹⁰   195
    Cumque pater tibi sit iura tuere²⁹¹ patris⁓
induit²⁹² arma tibi *genitor *patriaeque *tuusque

---

266. dat*iuus* "dative"
267. peius tra "*tra* is worse" (*see Notes*)
268. octau*ianus* "Octavian"
269. natales] *corrected from* natalis; *glossed* **litolaidou** "feast-days"
270. mos illis cessarib*us* a primordio iuentutis suae fieri sem*per* triumphales "it is a custom for those Caesars always to be celebrating triumphs from their earliest youth" *in right margin*
271. stultae *uel* tardae "stupid or slow"
272. Hercolis quia in tirinthio oppido nutritus est "of Hercules, (sc. so called) because he was brought up in the town of Tiryns"
273. com (*addition of prefix to indicate compound verb*)
274. in cunis] **mapbrethinnou** "swaddling-clothes"
275. ioue dignus] **hin map di iob** "that one is a son of Jupiter"
276. *interrogatiuus* "interrogative"
277. liber pater "Liber his father"
278. uettes "bands"
279. **o coilou** "auspices (abl.)"
280. octau*ianus* "Octavian"
281. octau*ianus* "Octavian"
282. octau*ianus* "Octavian"
283. initiu*m* "beginning"
284. cessaris "of Caesar"
285. octau*ianus* "Octavian"
286. es "you are"
287. *error* ia "error for *ia*"
288. *uocatiuus* "vocative"
289. *terrarum* "of lands"
290. romanos "Romans"
291. defendere "to defend"
292. dedit "gave"

†hostis ab²⁹³ *inuito regna *parente rapit··
Tu pia tela feres·· sceleratas †ille²⁹⁴ sagittas
    stabit pro²⁹⁵ signis iusque piumque tuis··   200
uincantur causa²⁹⁶ parthi·· uincantur et armis··
    eoas latio²⁹⁷ dux²⁹⁸ meus addat opes··
marsque²⁹⁹ pater cessarque³⁰⁰ pater date numen³⁰¹ eunti··³⁰²
    nam deus e nobis alter³⁰³ es alter eris··
auguror³⁰⁴ euinces³⁰⁵ uotiuaque carmina reddam··³⁰⁶   205
    et magno³⁰⁷ nobis³⁰⁸ ore³⁰⁹ sonandus eris··
consistes³¹⁰ aciemque meis ortabere³¹¹ uerbis··
    o³¹² desint animis ne mea uerba tuis··
Tergaque³¹³ parthorum romanaque³¹⁴ pectora dicam··
    telaque ab aduerso quae iacit hostis³¹⁵ aequo   210
quid³¹⁶ fugis ut uincas quid uicto³¹⁷ parthe relinques··
    parthe³¹⁸ malum iam nunc mars³¹⁹ tuus habet··
ergo erit illa dies qua tu pulcherrime³²⁰ rerum³²¹
    quatuor in niueis aureus³²² ibis aequis·

---

293. ab inuito] **or guordiminntius** "the unwilling one (abl.)"; us *separated from* i *by descender*
294. feret "will bear"
295. pro signis] frangere bellum ante se "wins the war"
296. occitione parthi "by killing a Parthian"
297. **di litau** "Latium/Brittany (dat.)"
298. cessar "Caesar"
299. uocatiuus deus belli "vocative, the god of war"
300. uocatiuus "vocative"
301. auxilium "help"
302. cessari "Caesar"
303. alter es alter] cessar deus octauianus "Caesar, Octavian a god"
304. presagio "I prophesy"
305. ut "that"
306. dicam "I shall speak"
307. per "by means of"
308. ablatiuus "ablative"
309. carmine "poem"
310. **gurt paup** "against all"
311. **nerthiti** "you will strengthen"
312. optatiuus "optative"
313. in fugam "in flight"
314. romanaque pectora] **(h)incglinau ir leill** "following the others"
315. pathus [*sic*] "Parthian"
316. parthe "o Parthian"
317. **budicaul** "defeated" (*see Notes*)
318. uocatiuus "vocative"
319. bellum tuum "your war"
320. octauiane "Octavian"
321. hominum "of men"
322. octauianus "Octavian" *deleted and partially overwritten by* **teg guis** "prince" (*see Notes*)

ibunt ante³²³ duces³²⁴ onerati colla catenis··³²⁵   215
     ne³²⁶ possint tuti qua prius esse fuga··   [40r]
spectabunt laeti iuuenes mixtaeque puellae
     Defundetque³²⁷ animos omnibus ista dies··
Atque aliqua³²⁸ ex illis³²⁹ cum³³⁰ regum nomina queret
     que loca qui montes queue feruntur aquae   220
omnia responde nec³³¹ tantum siqua³³² rogabit··
     et que nescieris ut bene³³³ nota refer··
hic³³⁴ est eufrates³³⁵ precinctus³³⁶ harundine³³⁷ frontem³³⁸
     cui coma dependet cerula tigris³³⁹ erit··
hos³⁴⁰ facit armenios³⁴¹ hec est daneia³⁴² persis··   225
     urbs in achemenis³⁴³ uallibus ista fuit··
ille uel ille duces³⁴⁴ et erunt quae nomina dicas
     si poteris uere si minus apta³⁴⁵ tamen··
Dant etiam possitis³⁴⁶ aditum conuiuiuia mensis
     est aliquid preter uina quod³⁴⁷ inde petas··   230
Sepe illic possitis³⁴⁸ teneris adducta lacertis³⁴⁹
     purpureus bachi cornua presit amor··

---

323. ant*ea* "in front"
324. captiuos "prisoners"
325. ab*latiuus* "ablative"
326. ne possint] *non* possunt "they cannot"
327. que *added later*
328. puella "girl"
329. puellis "girls"
330. si "if" *under* cum
331. referes "you will reply"
332. puella "girl"
333. *conscius* "knowledgable"
334. dic ita "speak as follows"
335. Eufratis fluu*ius* mesopotamiae de paradisso oriens "The Euphrates is a river in Mesopotamia arising from Paradise" *in left margin*
336. ornatus "decorated"
337. **o corsenn** "reed (abl.)"
338. *per* "along"
339. forma bestiae "the shape of a beast"; tigris de no*mine* bestiae uelocis qu*ae dicitur* tigris "the Tigris from the name of a swift beast which is called a tiger" *in right margin*
340. hos facit] dic tu ita "you then speak as follows"
341. habitator armeniae "inhabitant of Armenia"
342. ciuitas quae a danio fabricata "a city which was built by Danius"
343. caldaicis "Chaldaean"
344. dicas "you should say"
345. confirma "be firm"
346. de (*addition of prefix to indicate compound verb*)
347. ut "that"
348. possitis teneris] hominibus habitantibus "for living people"
349. ab*latiuus* "ablative"

uinaque cum[350] bibulas sparsere cupidinis[351] alas··
    permanet et cepto stat grauis[352] illa[353] loco··[354]
ille[355] quidem pennas uelociter excutit[356] udas··[357]   235
    sed tamen et spargi pectus amore nocet··
uina parant animos faciuntque caloribus[358] aptos··
    Cura[359] fugit multo diluiturque mero··[360]
Tunc ueniunt risus tum pauper[361] cornua sumit··
    Tum color[362] et curae[363] rugaque[364] frontis abit··   240
Tunc aperit mentes[365] aeuo rassissima[366] nostro
    simplicitas artes excutiente deo··
illic sepe animos iuuenum rapuere puellae··[367]
    et[368] uenus in ueneri ignis[369] in igne fuit··
nec tu fallaci nimium ne crede lucernae··   245
    iudicio[370] formae noxque merumque[371] nocent··
luce[372] deas caeloque pares[373] spectauit aperto··
    cum dixit ueneri[374] uincis utranque[375] uenus
Nocte[376] latent mendae[377] uitioque ignoscitur[378] omni··

---

350. *tunc* "at that time"

351. cupid "Cupid"

352. **guobri** "serious"

353. puella "girl"

354. initiu*m* *conuiuii* "the beginning of the feast"

355. cupido "Cupid"

356. tinguit "he dipped"

357. alas "wings"

358. *ab*lat*iuus* "ablative"

359. eo quod urit cor "because it burns the heart"

360. habundante uino "plentiful wine"

361. *sine* muliere "without a woman"

362. qui an*tea* fuit "which it was previously"

363. abiunt "they leave"

364. **criched** "wrinkledness"

365. mentes aeuo rassissima nostro] quia sagaciores sunt quam *quomodo* fuer*unt* "because they (i.e. *mentes*) are wiser than how they were"

366. rassissima] sic *for* rarissima

367. mos est mulieribus intellegere mentem iuuenum "the custom is for women to understand the minds of young men" *in right margin*

368. uol*uptas* "desire"

369. amor "love"

370. dat*iuus* dative"

371. et nouu*m* uinu*m* "and new wine"

372. di*em* "day"

373. alaxanter "Alexander"

374. datiuus "dative"

375. iuno et minerua "Iuno and Minerva"

376. quando fuerint "when they were"

377. **ir anamou** "the blemishes"

378. ignora*tur* "it is not known"

horaque formossam quamlibet illa facit·^{·379}   250

consule³⁸⁰ de gemmis detincta³⁸¹ murice³⁸² lana·,³⁸³

   consule³⁸⁴ de facie corporibusque die·   [40v]

quid tibi femineos caetos uenatibus aptos

   enumerem numero cedet harena meo·

quid referam baias³⁸⁵ praetextaque³⁸⁶ litora bais·   255

   et que de calido solphore fumat aquam·

hinc aliquis uulnus referens in pectore dixit·

   non haec³⁸⁷ ut fama est unda salubris erat·

ecce³⁸⁸ satirbane³⁸⁹ templum memorale deanae·

   partaque³⁹⁰ per gladios regna nocente manu·^{·391}   260

illa quod est uirgo quod tela cupidinis odit

   multa dedit populo uulnera³⁹² multa dabit·

hac tenus unde³⁹³ legas quod ames ubi retia pones

   precipit inparibus uecta thalea³⁹⁴ rotis·

nunc tibi que³⁹⁵ placuit³⁹⁶ quas sit capienda per artes   265

   dicere precipue molior³⁹⁷ artis opus

quisquis³⁹⁸ ubique³⁹⁹ uiri⁴⁰⁰ dociles auertite mentes·

   pollicitisque fauens uulgus adesse meis·

Prima tuae menti⁴⁰¹ ueniat fiducia formae

   posse capi capias⁴⁰² tu modo tende plagas·^{·403}   270

---

379. quando fuerint *conuiuium* et ignis *unum* colorem *habent* mulieres omnes "when there is a feast and a fire, all women have the same complexion" *above whole line*

380. prouide "beware"

381. **ir tinetic** "the extracted . . ."

382. **o ceenn** "(from) a shell"

383. **gulan** "wool"

384. prouide "beware"

385. ciuitas in italia "a city in Italy"

386. *concaua* "curved"

387. aqua "water"

388. *est* "is"

389. ciuitas "city"

390. parata "prepared"

391. multitudine "crowd"

392. amoris "of love"

393. ut "that"

394. diana "Diana"

395. *inserted*

396. mulier tibi "woman," "to you"

397. memoro "I recall"

398. aduerte "turn (imperative)"

399. es "you are"

400. uocatiuus "vocative"

401. mulieris "of a woman"

402. ut "that"

403. retia "nets"

uere[404] primus uolucres taceant aestate cicadae[405]
    menalus lepori det sua terga canis
faemina quam iuueni blanda temptata repugnet··
    hec quoque quam[406] poteris credere nolle uolet··
atque uiro furtiua uenus[407] sic grata[408] puellae··   275
    uir male disimulat[409] texius[410] illa cupit··
conuenient[411] maribus[412] ne quam[413] nos ante rogemus··
    faemina iam partes[414] blanda rogansque cogat··[415]
Mollibus in pratis admugit femina[416] tauro··
    faemina[417] cornipedi semper adhinnit aequo··   280
parcior in nobis[418] nec tam furiosa[419] libido[420] est··
    legitimum finem flamma uirilis habet··
biblia[421] quid referam· uetito quae fratris amore
    arsit et est laqueo fortiter ulta nefas··
murra[422] patrem sed non qua filia debet amabit:.   285
    et nunc obducto cotice pressa latet··
illius e lacrimis quas arbore fundit odora
    ungimur et dominae nomina gutta tenet··   [41r]
forte sub umbrosis nemorose uallibus idae
    candidus armenti gloria taurus erat··   290
SIgnatus tenui media inter cornua nigro··
    una fuit[423] labes·· caetera[424] lactis erant··

---

404. o guiannuin "spring (abl.)"
405. cecinet bronnbreithet "speckle-breasted woodpeckers"
406. ut "that"
407. uoluntas "will" (but cf. Notes)
408. est "is"
409. celat "he hides"
410. secretius "more secretly"
411. interogatiuus "interrogative"
412. nobis unus "for us, one"
413. utř perhaps for utrum (cf. Notes)
414. per "through"
415. ut "that"
416. uacca "cow"
417. aequa "mare"
418. uiris "for men"
419. feminis "for women"
420. libido uirorum habet finem | libido mulierum non habet finem "the lust of men has an end; the lust of women has no end" in right margin
421. proprium mulieris "proper (sc. name) of a woman"
422. proprium mulieris "proper (sc. name) of a woman"
423. sordida "dirty"
424. membra "limbs"

illum⁴²⁵ gnosiades⁴²⁶ cidonaeque⁴²⁷ iuuencae

    optarunt tergo sustenuisse suo··

passiue⁴²⁸ fieri gaudebat adultera tauri··   295

    inuida formosas oderat illa boes··

Nota⁴²⁹ cano non hoc centum quae⁴³⁰ sustinet urbes

    quamuis sit mentax creta negare potest··

ipsa⁴³¹ nouas frondes et prata tenerima tauro⁴³²

    fertur inadsueta subsecuisse manu··   300

et comes armentis nec itura cura moratur⁴³³

    coniugis⁴³⁴ et minos a boe uictus⁴³⁵ erat··

quid⁴³⁶ tibi passiue formossas sumere uestes

    iste⁴³⁷ tuus nullas⁴³⁸ sentit adulter opes··

quid⁴³⁹ tibi cum speculo montana armenta petenti··   305

    Quid tibi⁴⁴⁰ toties positas⁴⁴¹ fingis inepta comas··

credita mens speculo quod te negat esse iuuencam··⁴⁴²

    quam cuperis fronti cornua nata tuae

SIue⁴⁴³ placet⁴⁴⁴ *minos nullus queratur adulter··⁴⁴⁵

    SIue *uirum mauis fallere falle uiro··⁴⁴⁶   310

in nemus⁴⁴⁷ et saltus⁴⁴⁸ thalamo regina⁴⁴⁹ relicto

---

425. tauru*m* "bull"
426. cretenses "Cretans"
427. *nomen est* cretae "it is a name for Crete"
428. *nomen* mulieris "name of a woman"
429. iura "laws"
430. creta "Crete"
431. passiua "Pasiphaë"
432. dat*iuus* "dative"
433. sentit "feels"
434. minois "Minos"
435. **guoguith** "defeated"
436. **padiu** "for what is?"
437. taurus "bull"
438. *corrected from* nullus
439. **pui** "what?"
440. *crossed out in the MS.*
441. positas *corrected from* possitas
442. aspiciebant *autem* forma*m* sua*m* in speculo "but they used to gaze at their own beauty in a mirror" *in right margin*
443. si "if"
444. tibi "to you"
445. **guas marchauc** "adulterer"; melior erat etecum si cornua fuissent nata de fronte tuo "you too would be better off if horns had grown from your brow" *in right margin, but relates to preceding line (l. 309)*
446. ablatiuus "ablative"
447. ire "to go"
448. in "into"
449. passiue "Pasiphaë"

fertur ut aonio concita bacha⁴⁵⁰ deo··
a⁴⁵¹ quoties uaccam uultu spectauit⁴⁵² iniquo··
    et dixit domino cur placet ista⁴⁵³ meo··
aspicit⁴⁵⁴ ante ipsum⁴⁵⁵ tenerisque exultet in herbis··   315
    nec dubito quin est ulta decere⁴⁵⁶ putet··
dixit⁴⁵⁷ et ingenti iamdudum⁴⁵⁸ de grege duci⁴⁵⁹
    iusit et inmeritam⁴⁶⁰ sub iuga curua trachi··
aut cadere ante aras commentaque⁴⁶¹ frena coegit··
    et tenuit laeta pelicis⁴⁶² exta⁴⁶³ manu··   320
pelicibus⁴⁶⁴ quoties placauit numina cessis··
    Atque ait exta tenens ite placete meo··⁴⁶⁵
et modo se europen fieri modo⁴⁶⁶ postulat io··,
    altera⁴⁶⁷ quod bos est altera uicta boe··,⁴⁶⁸
Hanc⁴⁶⁹ tamen impleuit uacca deceptus⁴⁷⁰ acerna   325   [41v]
    dux⁴⁷¹ gregis et partu⁴⁷² proditus⁴⁷³ auctor⁴⁷⁴ erat··
cressa⁴⁷⁵ thiesteo si se obstenuisset amore
    et⁴⁷⁶ quantum⁴⁷⁷ est uno posse carere uiro
non medium rupisset iter curruque⁴⁷⁸ retorto

---

450. dea "goddess"
451. *interiectio doloris* "exclamation of grief" *in left margin*
452. aspecit "she gazes at"
453. uacca "cow"
454. passiue "Pasiphaë"
455. tauru*m* "bull"
456. debere "ought"
457. passiue "Pasiphae"
458. dicto citius "more quickly than said"
459. uacca*m* "cow"
460. uacca*m* "cow"
461. machinata "devised"
462. meretrix "whore"
463. **ir onguedou** "the entrails"
464. obidius dicit "Ovid says" *in left margin*
465. tauro "bull"
466. aliqu*ando* "sometimes"
467. uacca "cow"
468. ab ioue "by Jupiter"
469. uacca*m* "cow"
470. **malgueretic** "deceived"
471. taurus "bull"
472. minotauri "of the Minotaur"
473. **diguolouichetic** "revealed (dat.)"
474. dedalus "Daedalus"
475. **ir cretuis** "the Cretan (sc. woman)"
476. si "if"
477. qm *changed to* qnm *MS*
478. *non* "not"

auroram[479] uersis phephus abiisset aequis   330
filia[480] purpureos niso[481] furata[482] capillos··
    pube[483] premit rabidos inguinibus[484] que canes··
qui martem[485] terra[486] neptunum effugit in undis
    coniugis atrides uictima[487] dira[488] fuit··
cui non defleta[489] est ephireae flamma creuse··[490]   335
    et nece[491] natorum[492] sanguinolenta parens··[493]
fleuit aginorides per inania lumina phenix··[494]
    hipolitum rabidi diripuistis aequi[495]
quid fodis inmeritis phinetus[496] sua lumina natis··
    paena reuersura est in caput ista tuum··   340
omnia faeminea sunt ista[497] cupidine plena
    acrior[498] est nostra[499] plusque furoris habet:.[500]
ergo age ne dubita cunctas sperare puellas·
    uix erit e multis que neget una tibi··
quae dant[501] queque negant gaudent tamen esse rogate   345
    ut iam[502] fallaris[503] tuta repulsa tua est··
Sed cur fallaris cum sit noua grata uoluntas··
    et capiant animis plus aliena suis··

---

479. ad "to"

480. scilla filia nisi "Scylla daughter of Nisus"

481. priuat*iuus* "privative (sc. dative)"

482. est "is"

483. **o caitoir** "pubic hair (abl.)"

484. **hac or achmonou** "and the groins (abl.)"

485. *deus* belli "god of war"

486. troiae "of Troy"

487. **aperth** "offering"

488. **dur** "harsh" (*but cf. Notes*)

489. .i. deflenda *est* "i.e. it is to be wept over"

490. didonis quae se ipsa*m* uiua*m* incendit "of Dido who burnt herself alive" *running into right margin*

491. ablat*iuus* "ablative"

492. filioru*m* "of sons"

493. media *pro* amore iasonis "Medea for love of Jason"

494. .i. filius agenero*i* q*ui* prodidit *con*silia deoru*m* et postea orbatus *est* "i.e. the son of Agenor who betrayed the advice of the gods and afterwards was blinded" *in right margin*

495. uo*catiuus* "vocative"

496. ide*m* et phenix "the same person as Phoenix"

497. miracula "miracles"

498. ut mulieru*m* cupiditas "as is the desire of women"

499. qua*m* "than"

500. femina "woman"

501. responsa "replies"

502. *etiam* "also"

503. licet "although"

fertilior seges est alienis semper in agris·
    uicinum[504] pecus grandius uber habet··   350
sed prius ancellam captatae nosse puellae
    cura sit accessus molliat[505] illa[506] tuos··
proxima consilis dominae sit an illa uideto··
    ne ue[507] parum[508] tacitis conscia fida locis[509]
hanc tu pollicitis hanc tu corrumpe rogando··   355
    quod petis ex facili[510] si uolet illa feres··[511]
illa leget tempus medici quod[512] tempora seruant··
    quo faciles dominae mens sit et apta capi·
mens[513] erit apta capi tum·· cum laetissima rerum[514]
    ut seges in pingui luxoriauit humo··   360
pectora dum gaudet non sunt astricta dolore··,
    ipsa patent blanda tum subit arte uenus   [42r]
Tum cum tristis erat defensa est ilios[515] armis
    militibus grauidum laeta[516] recipit aequm:.
Tum quoque temtanda est cum pelice[517] lessa[518] dolebit··   365
    tu facies opera ne sit inulta tua··
Hanc[519] matutina pectentem[520] ancella capillos
    incitet[521] et uelo[522] remigis[523] addat opem··
et secum tenui suspirans murmure dicat··,[524]
    ut puto non poteris ipsa[525] referre uicem··,[526]   370

---

504. proximum "closest"
505. ut agnoscat "that she is aware"
506. ancella "maidservant"
507. ne ue] *in gloss-sized text*; sit "may it be"
508. *non* "not"
509. *read as* locis "places" *by Kenney, but it could be a "tall" i and read as* iocis "pastimes"
510. opere "labour"
511. inuenies *uel* adepiscaris "you will find or obtain"
512. sicut "just as"
513. dominae "mistress"
514. hominum "of men"
515. troianos "Trojans"
516. troia "Troy"
517. meretrice "whore"
518. concubina "concubine"
519. puellam "girl"
520. **ha crip** "with a comb"
521. ancella "maidservant"
522. ablatiuus "ablative"
523. datiuus "dative"
524. ancella "maidservant"
525. tu ipsa "you yourself"
526. **atail** "building" (*cf. Notes*)

tum de te narret·.[527] tum persuadentia uerba
    addat et insano iuret[528] amore mori·.[529]
sed properet[530] ne uela cadant iraeque residant·.
    ut fragilis glacies interit ira mora·.[531]
Queris[532] hanc ipsam prosit uiolare ministram·.   375
    talibus admissis alea[533] grandis inest·
hec[534] a concubitu fit. sedula[535] tardior illa·.
    hec dominae munus te parat illa[536] sibi·.
cassus[537] in euentu est· licet hic indulgeat ausis
    consilium tamen est abstenuisse meum·.   380   *Hand B*
non ego per preceps[538] et acuta cacumina cadam·.
    nec iuuenum quisquam me duce captus erit
si tamen illa[539] tibi dum dat recipitque tabellas[540]
    corpore non tantum sedulitate placet·.-
fac domina podiare prius[541] comes illa[542] sequatur·.   385
    non tibi ab ancella est incipienda uenus·.
hoc unum[543] moneo· si quod modo creditur arti
    nec[544] mea dicta rapax per mare uentus agit·.
aut non temptasses aut perfice[545] tollitur[546] index·.[547]
    cum semel in partem creminis ipsa uenit·.   390
non auis utiliter uiscatis effugit alis·.
    non bene de laxis cassibus exit aper·.
saucius abrepto piscis teneatur ab amo·.

---

527. *contra illam* ancella "to her, the maidservant"
528. ancella "maidservant"
529. te "you"
530. iuuenis "young man"
531. ab*latiuus* "ablative"
532. a domina "from a mistress"
533. alea grandis] si inuenies ambas "if you find both women"
534. ancella "maidservant"
535. promta "ready to hand"
536. ancella "maidservant"
537. cassus in euentu est] promissum dominae et de ancella sua "a promise of a mistress and about a maidservant"
538. iter "a journey"
539. domina "mistress"
540. aepistolas "letters"
541. prius comes] post dominam "after the mistress"
542. ancella "maidservant"
543. ius "rule"
544. si "if"
545. non "not"
546. tolle *changing* tollitur *to* tolletur "will be removed" (*see Notes*)
547. .i. ancella "i.e. maidservant"

perprime temptatam nec nisi uictor abii‥ 394
    two lines omitted
sed bene celetur bene si celabitur index‥ 397
    notitiae suberit semper amice tuae‥
Tempora qui solis operossa collentibus arua
    fallitur et nautis aspicienda putat‥ 400
nec semper credenda ceres fallacibus aruis‥
    nec semper uiridi concaua pupis aquae‥ [42v]
nec itera semper tutum captare puellas
    sepe dato melius tempore fiet idem‥
siue dies suberit natalis siue kalendae 405
    quas uenerem marti continuisse luna
siue erit ornatus non ut fugit ante figillis
    sed regum possitas circus habebit oues
differ opus tunc tristis hiems tunc pyludes instant‥
    nunc tener equorea mergitur hedus aqua‥ 410
Tunc bene desinitur‥ tunc siqui creditur alto
    uix tenuit lacere naufraga membra ratis‥
tu licet incipias qua flebilis allia lucae
    nostris uulneribus sanginolensa[548] fuit‥
quaque die rediunt. reuus minus apta regendis 415
    culta palestino septima sacra deo‥
magna superstitio tibi sit natalis amice‥
    quaque aliquid dandum illa sit atra dies‥
cum bene uitalis tamen auferet inuenit artem
    femina qua cupidi carpat amantis opes‥ 420
institor ad dominam ueniat discinctus emacem‥
    expedeat merces tece sedente suas‥
quas illa inspiciens rapere ut uideare rogauit
    oscula deinde dabit deinde rogauit emas‥
hoc fore contendam multos iurauit in annos‥ 425
    nunc opus esse sibi nunc bene dicet emi
si non esse domi quos des caisabere[549] nummos
    littera poscetur. ne didicisse iubet‥
quid quasi natali cum poscit munera libo‥
    et quoties opus est nascitur illa sibi‥ 430
Quid cum mendaci damno mestissima plorat
    elapsusque caua fingitur aure lapis

---

548. *second* s *overwritten by* t
549. sic *for* causabere

multa rogant utenda dari data reddere nolunt‥
    perdis et in damno gratia nulla tuo
quid mihi scrilegas[550] meritricum ut persequar artes‥   435
    cum totidem linguis sint satis ora decim‥
coera uadum temptet raris infusa tabellis‥
    coera tuae primum nuntia mentis erit‥
blanditias ferat illa tuas imitataque amoitum
    uerba nec exiguas quisquis es adde preceps‥   440   [43r]
hectora donauit priamo prece motus achiles‥
    flectitur iratus[551] uoce rogante deus‥
promittas facito quid enim promittere ledit‥
    pollicitis diues quilibet esse potest‥
spes teneret in tempus semel est si credita longum‥   445
    illa quidem fallax sicut tamen apta dea est‥
si dederis aliquid poteris ratione relinqui‥
    pretium tulerit perdideritque nihil‥
At quod non dederis semper uideare daturus‥
    sic dominum sterilis sepe fefellit ager‥   450
sic ne perdiderit non cessat perdere lusor‥
    et reuocat cupidas alea sepe manus‥
hoc opus hic labor est primo sine munere iungi‥
    ne dederit gratis que dedit usque dabit‥
ergo eat et blandis perhornetur littera uerbis‥   455
    exploretque animos primaque temptet iter‥
littera cidippen primo perlata fefellit‥
    insciaque est uerbis apta puella tuis‥-
Disce bonas artes‥ moeneo romana iuuentus
    non tantum trepidos ut tueare reos‥   460
quam populus iudexque grauis letusque senatus
    tam dabit eloquio uicta puella manus‥
sed lateant uires ne sis in fronte desertus‥
    effugiant uoces uerba molesta tuae
quis nisi mentis inops tenere declamat amice‥   465
      six lines omitted
    tempore lenta pati frena docentur equi‥   472
ferreus assiduo consumitur anulus usu‥
    iterit assidua uomer aduncus humo‥
quid magis est saxo durum quid mollius unda‥   475

---

550. sic *for* sacrilegas
551. tus *added above*

dura tamen molli saxa cauantur aqua
penelopen ipsam persta modo tempore uinces··
    capta uides sero pergama capta tamen··
legerit et noli rescribere cogere noli··   [43v]
    Tu modo blanditias fac legat usque tuas··   480
que uoluit legisse·· uolet rescribere lectis··
    per numeros uenient ista gradusque suas··
forsitan et primo ueniet tibi littera tristis··
    queque roget ne se sollicitare uelis··
quod rogat illa timet quod non rogat optat ut instes··   485
    insequere et uoti postmodo compos eris··
INterea sibi bellatore sopina feretur··
    lecticam dominice dissimulanter adi··
neue aliquis uerbis odiossas oferat aures··
    quam potes ambiguis callidus abde notis··   490
seu pedibus uacuans illis spatiosa teretur
    porticus· hic socias tu quoque iunge moras··
et modo precedas facito modo terga sequaris··
    et modo festinaes et modo lentus eas··
nec tibi de medis aliquot transirae columnas   495
    sit pudor· aut lateri continuisse latus
nec sine te curuo sedeat speciosa theathro··
    quod spectes humeris afferet illa suis··
illam respicies illam mirare licebit··
    multa supercilio multa locare notis··   500
et plaudas aliqua mittem saltante puellam··
    ut faueas illi·· quisquis agatur amans
consurgit surges donec sedet illa sedebis··
    arbitrio domine tempora perde tuae··
sed tibi nec ferro placent torqueare capillos··   505
    nec tua mordaci punice cura terras
ista iube faciant quorum cibeilea mater
    concinitur frigus exululata modis··
forma uiros neglecta decet menoida theseus
    abstulit a nulla timpora comptus acu··   510
hipolitum pedra nec erat bene cultus amauit··
    cura dee sirulis aptus adonis erat··   [44r]
munditie placeant fuscentur corpora campo··
    sit bene conueniens et sine labe toga··
linguam ne rigeat careant rubigine dentes··   515
    nec uagus in laxa pes tibi pelle natet··

Nec male deformet rigidos tonsura capillos˗
    sit coma sit tuta barba refecta manu˗
ut nihil eminat et sint sine sordibus unges˗
    inque caua nullus stet tibi nare pilus˗   520
nec male odorantis sit tristis hanelitus oris˗
    nec ledant nares uirque paterque gregis˗
caetera lasciue faciant concede puellae
    et si quis male uir querit habere uirum˗
ecce suum uatem liber uocat hic quoque amantes   525
    adiuuat et flamme qua calet ipse fauet˗
gnosis in ignotis amens errabat harenis˗
    qua breuis equores india fertur aquis˗
utque erat e somno tonica uelata recinta
    nuda pedem croceas inrelegata comas   530
thesea crudelem surdas clamabat ad undas
    indigno teneras imbre rigante genas˗
clamabat flebatque simul sed utrumque decebat˗
    non facta est lacrimis turpior illa suis
iamque iterum tundens mollissima pectora palmis   535
    perfidus ille abit quid mihi fiet ait
quid mihi fiet ait˗ sonuerunt cymbala toto
    litore˗ et attonita timphana pulsa manu˗
excidit illa metu rupitque nouissima uerba˗
    nullus in exanimi corpore sanguis erat˗   540
ecce mimallonides sparsis in terga capillis˗
    ecce leues satiri preuia turba dei˗
ebrius atque senex pando silenus assello˗
    uix sedet˗ et preses continet arte iubar˗
dum sequitur bachas bachae fugiuntque petuntque   545
    quadripedem ferula dum calce urget eques
in caput aurito cecidit delapsus asello˗
    clamarunt satiri surge age surge senex˗
iam deus in curru quem summum texaret uuis˗   [44v]
    tigribus adiunctis aurea lora dabat˗   550
et color et theseus et uox abire puellae˗
    terque fugam petiit terque retenta metu est
horruit ut steriles agitat quas uentus aristus˗
    ut leuis in madida fanna palude tremit˗
cui deus en adsum tibi cura fidelior inquit˗   555
    pone metum bachum gnosias exoreris˗
munus habe caelum caeli spectabere sidus˗

sepe rege dubiam cressa corona ratem··
dixit et e curru desilit ne tigris illa timeret··
    desilit inposito cessit harena pede··   560
inplicitamque sinu neque enim pugnare ualebit··
    abstulit·· en facili est omnia posse deo··
pars hymenea canunt·· pars clamant euhio euhoe··
    sic coeunt sacro nupta deusque thoro··
ergo ubi contigerint positi tibi munera bachi   565
    atque erit in soci femina parte tori
nucteliumque patrem nocturnaque sacra precare··
    ne iubeant capiti uina nocere tuo··
hic tibi multa licet sermone latentia tecto··
    Dicere que dici sentiat illa sibi·   570
blanditiasque leues tenui perscribere uino··
    ut dominam in mensa se legat illa tuam··
Atque oculus oculis spectare fatentibus ignem··
    sepe tacens uocem uerbaque uultus habet··
fac primus rapias illius tacta labellis   575
    pocula quaque bibet parte puella bibas
et quemcumque cibum degitis libraberit illa
    tu pete dumque petes sit tibi tacta manus··
sint etiam tua uota uiro placuisse puelle··
    utiliter uotis factus amicus erit··   580
huic si forte tibi sortem concede priorem
    huic detur capiti missa corona tuo
si uellit inferior seu par prior omnia sumat··
    nec dubites illi uerba secunda loqui··
Tuta frequensque uia est per amici fallere nomen··   585
    tuta frequensque licet sit uia crimen habet··
inde procurator nimium quoque multa procurat··
    et sibi mandari plura uidenda putat··   [45r]
certa tibi a nobis dabitur mensura bibendo
    officium prestent mensque pedesque suum   590
iurgia precipue uino stimulata caueto··
    et minimum faciles ad fera bella manus··
occidit urytion stulte data uina bibendo··
    aptior est dulci mensa merumque ioco··
si uox est canta si mollia brachia salta··   595
    et quacumque potes tote placere place··
ebrietas ut uera nocet ·sic ficta iuuabit··
    fac titubet blesso subdola lingua solo··

ut quicquid facias dicasue proteruius aequo
    credatur nimium causa fuisse merum   600
et bene dic domine bene cum quo dormiat illa··
    sed male sit tacita mente precare uiro··
at cum discedet mensa conuiua remota
    ipsa tibi accessus turba locumque dabit··
insere te turbe leuiterque admotus eunti   605
    uelle latus degitis et pede tange pedem··
conloqui iam tempus adest fuge rustice longuae··
    hinc pudor audentem forsue uenusque iuuat··
non tua sub nostras ueniat facundia leges··
    fac tantum cupias sponse disertus eris   610
est tibi agendus amans·· imitandaque uulnera uerbis··
    hec tibi queratur qualibet arte fides··
nec crede labor est sibi queque uidetur amanda··
    pessima sit nulli non sua forma placet··
sepe tamen uere cepit simulator amare··   615
    sepe quod incipiens finxerat esse fuit··
quo magis o faciles imitantibus esse puelle··
    fiet amor uerus qui modo falsus erat··
blanditis animum furtim ut deprehendere non sit··
    ut pendes liquida⁵⁵² ripa subetur aqua··   620
nec faciem nec te pigeat laudare capillos··
    et teritis digitos exiguumque pedem··
Dilectant etiam castas⁵⁵³ preconia forme··⁵⁵⁴
    uirginibus curae⁵⁵⁵ grataque forma sua est··
nam cur in frigis⁵⁵⁶ iunonem et pallada siluis··   625
    nunc quoque iudicium non tenuisse pudet··
laudatas ostendit auis iunonia pennas·   [45v]
    si tacitus spectis·· illa recondit⁵⁵⁷ opus··⁵⁵⁸
quadrupedem⁵⁵⁹ inter rapidi certamina cursus·
    depexeque iuuae plausaque colla iubant··   630
Nec timide promitte trachunt promissa puellas··

---

552. in "in"
553. puellas "girls"
554. laudationis "of praise"
555. *datiuus* "dative"
556. frigea "Phrygian"
557. renouat "renews"
558. **hi ataned** "its wings" *under* pennas
559. quadrupedem *corrected from* quadripedem

pollicito[560] testis quoslibet adde deos··
iupiter ex alto periura[561] ridet amandum··[562]
    et iubet eolios inrita ferre nothos··
per stiga[563] iunoni falsum[564] iurare solebat··[565]   635
    iupiter exemplo nunc[566] fauet ipse suo··
expedit esse deus et ut expedit esse putemus··
    dentur in antiquos dura merumque focos··
nec secura est quies illis[567] similisque sopori
    detinet innocue uiuite numen adest··   640
reddite adpossitum·· pietas sua fidera seruet··[568]
    fraus absit uacuas cedes habete manus··
ludite[569] si sapitis solas inpune[570] puellas··
    hac magis est una fraude pudenda fides··
fallite fallentes·· ex magna parte profana   645
    sunt genus in laqueos quos possuere cadant··
dicitur egiptus caruisse iuuantibus arua[571]
    imbribus atque annos[572] sicca fuisse nouem··
Cum[573] thraseus[574] bussiren[575] adit monstratque piare
    ospitis effusso sanguine posse iouem··   650
ille busseris fies[576] iouis hostia primus··
    incedit egipto tu dabis ospis[577] aquam··
et phallaris tauro uiolendi membra pericli
    torruit infelix imbuit auctor[578] opus·
iustusque uterque fuit neque enim lex equor ulla est   655
    quam necis artifices arte perire sua

---

560. *datiuus* "dative"
561. **anutonou** "oaths"
562. *iurauit iupiter multum iunoni per stiga infer*[. . . *in right margin* "Jupiter swore much to Juno by the Stygian underworld"
563. *per stidgia* "by the Stygian . . ."
564. *aduerbum* "adverb"
565. *iupiter* "Jupiter"
566. *tunc* "at that time"
567. puellis "girls"
568. *.i. est* deus "i.e. he is a god"
569. fallite "you make a mistake"
570. *sine* pena "without punishment"
571. *per* "through"
572. *per* "through"
573. *tunc* "at that time"
574. *proprium* "proper (sc. name)"
575. *nomen* regis "name of a king"
576. eris "you will be"
577. *uocatiuus* "vocative"
578. *c has been added above*

ergo ut periuras merito periuria fallent
    exemplo doleat femina lessa suo
et lacrime prosunt lacrimis adamanda mouebis
    fac madidas uideat si potes illa genas   660
si lacrime neque enim ueniunt in tempore semper
    difficient cuncta lumina tange manu
quis sapiens blandis non misceat oscula uerbis
    illa licet non det non data sume tamen
pugnauit primo fortassis et improbe dicet   665
    pugnando uinci se tamen ipsa uolet   [46r]
tantum ne noceant teneris male rapta labellis
    neue queri possit dura fuisse caue
oscula qui sumpsit si non et cetera sumpsit
    hec quoque que data sunt pendere designis erit   670
quantum defuerat pleno post oscula uoto
    ei mihi rusticitas non pudor ille fuit
uim licet appelles·· grata est tuis ista puellis
    quod iubat inuitae sepe dedisse nolunt
quaecumque est ueneris subita uiolata rapina   675
    gaudet et inprobitas muneris instar habet
at quae cum posset cogi non tacta recessit
    ut simulet uult gaudia tristis erit
uim passa est phebei uis est allata sapori
    et gratus raptae raptor uterque fuit   680
fabula nota quidem sed non indigna referri:
    scyrias hemonio iuncta puella uiro
laudea⁵⁷⁹ laudate dederat mala premia formae
    colle sub ideo uincere digna uenus·· uel duas··⁵⁸⁰
iam nurus ad priamum diuerso uenerat orbe··   685
    grataque in iliacis moenibus uxor erat··
iurabant omnes in lessi uerba mariti··
    nam dolor unius puplica causa fuit··
turpe nisi hoc matris precibus tribuisset achiles
    ueste uirum longua desimilatus erat··   690
quid facis eaeacide non sunt tua munera lane··
    tu titulos alia palladis arte petis··
quid tibi cum calathis clepeo manus apta terenda est
    pensa quid in dextra qua cadet hector habes··

---

579. *miscopied by eye-skip; recte* dea
580. uel duas *added after the punctuation in same hand and ink*

rence succinctos operosa stanne fusos··   695
 quas scanda est ista pelias hasta manu··
forte erat in thalamo uirgo regalis eodem··
 hec illum stupro comperit esse uirum··
uiribus illa quidem uicta est ita credere oportet
 sed uoluit uinci uiribus ipsa tamen   700
sepe mane dixit·· cum iam properaret achiles··
 fortia nam possito sumpserat arma colo··
uis ubi nunc illa est quid blanda uoce morasus
 autorem stupri deidamia tui··
scilicet ut pudor est quandam coepisse priorem 705 [46v] *Hand C*
 sic alio gratum est incipiente pati··
a nimia est iuueni propriae fiduciae formae
 expectet sicis dum prior illa roget··
vir prius accidat·· vir uerba precantia dicat··
 excipiat blandas comiter illa preces·   710
ut posiare roga tantum cupit illa rogari··
 da⁵⁸¹ causam uoti principiumque tui··
iupiter ad ueteres supex heroidas ibat··
 corripit magnum nulla puella iouem··
si tamen a precibus tumidos abscedere flatus   715
 senseris incepto parce referce pedem··
quod refuit multae cupiunt odere quod instat··
 lenius instando tedia tolle tui··
nec semper ueneris pes est profidenda rogandi··
 intret amicitiae nomine tectus amor··   720
hoc auditu uidi tedritie⁵⁸² data uerba puaellae
 qui fuerat cultor factus amator erat··
candidus in nauta turpis est color equoris undo
 debet et a radis sideris esse niger··
turpis et agriculae quam uomere semper adunco· 725
 et grauibus rastris sub ioue uersat humum··
et tua pallaide petitor cui fama coronae
 candida si fuerint corpora turpis eris··
palleat omnis amans hic est color aptus amandi
 hoc decet hoc multi non ualuisse putant··   730
  one line omitted

---

581. *added in left margin*
582. te *added above*

pallidus in lenta mude daphnis erat··   732
arguat et macies animum nec turpe putamus
    palliolum nitidis inpossuisse comes··
At tenuant iuuenum uigilate corpora noctes··   735
    curaque et in magno qui fit amore dolor··
ut uoto potiare tuo miserabilis esto·
    ut qui te uideat dicere possit amans··
conquerar admoneam mixtum fas omne nefasque
    nomen amicitia est nomen inane fides··   740
ei mihi non tutum est quod ames laudare sodali
    cum tibi laudanti credidit ipse subit··
at non autoridis lectum temerabit achilles··
    quantum ad pirithoum phedra pudica fuit··
hermonen pilades quod palda phoebus amauat··   745
    quodque tibi geminus tindare castor erat·
Siquis item superat iacturas poma miricas·   [47r]   Hand D
    Supet et e medio flumine mella petat·
Nihil tibi turpe iuuat cure sua cuique uoluptas·
    Haec quoque ab alterius grata dolore uenit·   750
Heu facimus non est hostis metuendus amandi·
    Quos credis fidos effuge tutus eris·
Cognatum fratremque caue carumque sodalem·
    Prebebit ueros haec tibi turba metus·
Finiturus eram sed sunt diuersa puellis·   755
    Pectora mille animos excipe mille modis·
Nec tellus eadem parit omnia uitibus illis·
    Conuenit hec oleis hic bene farra uirent·
Pectoribus mores tot sunt quot in orbe figure·
    Qui sapit innumeras[583] moribus aptus erat·   760
Utque leues proteus[584] modo se tenuabat in undas·
    Nunc leo nunc arbor nunc erit hirtus aper·
Hic iaculo piscis illic capiuntur ab hamis·
    Haec caua contenta retia fune trahunt·
Nec tibi conueniat cunctos modus unus ad annos·   765
    Longius insidias curua[585] uidebit anus·
Si doctus uideare rudi petulansue pudenti·

---

583. as *corrected to* is
584. h *added above*
585. uel e *added above, suggesting the reading* cerua *for* curua

Diffidet mire[586] protinus illa sibi·
Inde fit ut que se timuit committere honesto·
   Uilis in amplexus inferioris eat·   770
Pars superat cepti pars est exhausta laboris·
   Hic teneat nostras anchora iacta rates·   FINIT

---

586. se *added above.*

5

NOTES TO THE EDITION

he first word cited is the lemma and the gloss is printed after the colon; suspension marks are not indicated. Old Welsh glosses are printed in **bold**. References to Bradshaw are to his partial transcription in Celtic Papers (CUL, Add. 6425, fols. 558–67) unless otherwise indicated. References to previous discussion of the Old Welsh glosses are generally confined to *EGOW*, from which earlier references can be derived (note that page references to *EGOW* come in the order of the elements in the gloss). Other references are provided if relevant to the discussion. For background contextual information on Ovid's text, the commentary in Hollis, *Ovid: Ars Amatoria I* has been used. To aid understanding of the Old Welsh glosses, a brief overview of the spelling of the glosses follows.

OLD WELSH ORTHOGRAPHY

The adoption of a Latin-based script to write Welsh presented a number of interrelated difficulties (for discussion of these issues, see Lewis, "Disgrifiad"; Russell, *Introduction,* 207–29; Charles-Edwards and Russell, "Hendregadredd Manuscript," 421–25; Sims-Williams, "Emergence"; on specific Old Welsh texts, see Jenkins and Owen, "Welsh Marginalia," 117–20 (Chad Memoranda); Watkins, "Englynion y Juvencus"; McKee, *Juvencus,* 71–73). First, a Latin script did not provide enough vowel signs: while the lower vowels of Welsh, /e a o/, provided no real problem, the high vowels did with only **i** and **u** available to spell /i ɨ ə/ and /u ʉ/ respectively together with the semivowels /j w/. In later Old Welsh documents **y** was imported to help spread the load (see Kitson, "Old English Literacy"), but at all stages up to around 1300 there was a tendency to use **e** for the high front vowels along-side **i** and **u** (and later **y**); this use of *e* later became fixed in the spellings of diphthongs such as *ae* and *oe*. Within Old Welsh *u* was used for /u/ and /ʉ/, but internal -/w/- was usually spelt *gu*; because initial mutations were not marked, both initial /gw/- and its mutated form /w/- were spelt (-)*gu*- and, on the model of this, internal -/w/- was also spelt -*gu*-, thus *petguar* 'four' (Modern Welsh *pedwar*). Furthermore, and related to this problem was the fact that Welsh had developed a series of fricatives, mainly in the first instance in medial and final positions, /f v μ ð θ γ χ/ which Latin did not have. Additional issues were posed by the system of initial mutations and more generally the differing orthographical demands of initial, medial and final consonants.

Essentially, in Old Welsh the general state of affairs is that **p t c** repre-sented /p t k/ in initial position but /b d g/ medially and finally, while **b d g** represented /b d g/ initially but /v ð γ/ medially and finally, and initial muta-tions were not marked. That said, in unstressed elements like the preposition **di** "to" it is almost certainly the case that the initial consonant was /ð/ at this point (and similarly perhaps the **g** of **gurt** should be understood as /γ/). Unvoiced fricatives were often spelt with a digraph involving **h**, thus **th** /θ/ and **ch** /χ/ though in both cases there was considerable experimentation, e.g. for /θ/ h th ht tth t d dh tt (and even s sh ssh) (Jenkins and Owen, "The Welsh Marginalia," 117–20). We may note that in these glosses there is one case, **litolaidou**, where **d** is used for /θ/, if we think that the word corre-sponds to the later plural *llidolaethau*.

The orthography of the Old Welsh glosses on Ovid broadly follows this scheme. The spellings are set out below; the examples are not exhaustive but should be sufficient to illustrate the distribution (if there is any doubt as to the relevant letter in an example, it has been underlined); further discussion can be found in the Notes.

Vowels

a   /a/: **aperthou, arpeteticion, digatma**

e   /e/: **etem, aperthou**; /ɨ/: **etem**; /ə/: **emedou**; /ei/: **estid**

i   /i/: **hir, bleuporthetic, guobriach**; /ɨ/: **olin, estid**; /ə/: **ir, arcibrenou, brethin-nou, guordiminntius, termisceticion**; /j/ **funiou, cloriou, arpeteticion**

o   /o/: **o, olin, guobriach, cloriou**

u   /ʉ/: funiou, nepun, grudou, budicaul; /u/: tuscois (?); /w/: ceintiru; /v/:
     dau̱u̱

ai   /ai̵/: amlais, caiauc, litolaidou

ei   /ei̵/: cemmein, cein, mein, ceintiru

oi   /ui̵/: loinou, tuscois, troi, boi; /oi̵/: guaroimaou, coilou

ui   /ui̵/: guiannuin, pui, cretuis

au   /au/: da̱u̱u̱, pippaur, caiauc, paup, liaus

eu   /ew/: bleuporthetic

iu   /i̵u/: padiu

ou   /oʉ/: -ou (plural marker)

Consonants

p   /p/-: padiu, pippaur, plant; -/b/-: nepun, bleuporthetic, aperthou; -/b/:
     hep, map, paup, crip

pp   -/b/-: pippaur

b   /b/-: bleuporthetic, buch; -/v/-: guobri, arcibrenou, bronnbreithet; -/v/:
     iob

f   /f/-: funiou

t   /t/-: tuscois, termisceticion; -/d/-: etem, digatma, arpeteticion, caitoir;
     -/d/: ledit, cecinet; -/θ/: gurt (in mutation position /d/-: mor tru)

d   /d/-: digatma, datlocou; /ð/-: di; -/ð/-: emedou, ledit, grudou; -/θ/-: lito-
     laidou; -/ð/: estid, cared, criched

th   -/θ/-: brethinnou, bleuporthetic; -/θ/: aperth, ansceth

c   /k/-: ceintiru, cared, cloriou; -/g/-: datlocou, arcibrenou, cec̱inet; -/g/:
     caiauc, marchauc, bleuporthetic (in mutation position /χ/-: ha crip)

ch   -/χ/-: cilchetou, criched, marchauc; -/χ/: guobriach, buch, guodemisauch

g   /g/-: grudou, garr; -/γ/-: digatma

gh   -/γ/-: helghati

gu   /gw/-: gulan; guodemisauch, guarai; -/w/-: ringuedaulion

r   /rʰ/-: ringuedaulion; -/r/-: cloriou, guobri, arpeteticion; -/r/: ir, hir

l   /ɫ/-: loinou, ledit; -/l/-: olin, datlocou, cloriou; -/l/: datl, budicaul (in muta-
     tion position /l/-: liaus)

m   /m/-: marchauc, mein; -/v/-: dometic, digatma, emedou, guaroimaou;
     -/v/: etem, nom

mm   -/m/-: cemmein

n   /n/-: nepun, nom, nerthiti; -/n/-: loinou; -/n/: nepun, mein, olin,
     arpeteticion

s   -/s/-: estid; -/s/ guas

h   /h/-: hir, helghati; -/h/-: guorunhetic

Among the vowels we may note the use of **e** for /e/ but also /i/, /ə/ and /ei/. Similarly, **i** and **u** are overworked. None of this is inconsistent with other Old Welsh texts. One interesting feature is the spelling of the diphthong /uɨ/; in the early part of the text it is spelt with **oi** (examples in ll. 47–150) but later in the text (examples in ll. 271–327) as **ui**. The change does not correspond to the change between scribe A and scribe B but does look significant; might it reflect a change of scribe in the exemplar from which the text and glosses were copied?

The spelling of consonants again is largely consistent with what is found in other texts, in particular the different values accorded to **p t c b d g** whether initial or medial and final. Two points are worth noting, however. Both **b** and **m** are used medially and finally for /v/ reflecting the historical fact that -/b/(-) lenited to -/β/(-) and -/m/(-) to -/μ/(-); both fricatives fell together as -/v/(-) in late Old Welsh. Generally the **b** and **m** spellings in these glosses accurately reflect their historical origins except for **arcibrenou** (< **are-kom-reg-* (*EGOW* 10)) which we would expect to be spelt **arcimrenou. The **b**-spelling suggests that by the date of these glosses (late ninth or early tenth century), /β/ and /μ/ had already fallen together at least in this environment before /r/ which may have been where the merger took place earliest (Russell, "*Rowynniauc, Rhufoniog*," 39–41). A second related point can be made about **dauu** where the final -**u** seems to reflect the final fricative of an original */daːm/-. The question here is why **u** for /v/ or /μ/ was used and not **m**. Although the most common spelling of labial fricatives in Old Welsh was **b** or **m**, I have argued that **u** and **v** were also in use (Russell, "*Rowynniauc, Rhufoniog*," 32–36), and this may be a possible example parallel to the spelling **frauu** "River Frome" in Asser. That said, in both cases, it is possible that there was minim confusion and a single stroke was lost from ***daum** and ***fraum**.

The spelling of the Latin, both in the main text and the glossing, is relatively unproblematic. One point to note is that there are occasional spellings which suggest that internal *b* and *u* were both pronounced -/v/- (the classical form is in brackets): l. 72 *Libia* (*Livia*), l. 321 *obidius* (in a gloss), 415 *reuus* (*rebus*), l. 745 *amauat* (*amabat*). In addition, l. 144 *puplica* seems to be using -*p*- for -/b/-; it is tempting to think that this is an example of an Old Welsh spelling. Note also l. 37 *placita* for *placida*, l. 144 *puplica* for *publica*, and l. 385 *podiare* for *potiare*.

NOTES

1–34 Prologue: Ovid presents his credentials for teaching about love. The main challenge here for the glossator is to explain the mythological references, many of which are to Greeks whose names do not have conventional Latin case endings; thus, in l. 5 a nom. sg. in -on has to be glossed.

1 populo: romano. The gloss is presumably a reminder to a medieval audience of which *populus* is being referred to.

2 hoc: .i. carmen. The gloss picks up *carmine* from later in the line, but may also be intended to distinguish this *hoc* (acc. sg.) from the *hoc* (abl. sg.) in the previous line. This is not a case where the metre could be used to distinguish the two as here *hoc,* though acc. sg. with a short vowel, could be scanned long before *legat;* for discussion, see 84–85 above.

3 citae . . . rates. These words are joined by construe marks presumably to show that *citae* agrees with *rates.*

citae: .i. ueloces. The gloss is by scribe E, the later hand, which only adds a few glosses to first eight lines of the text; note that the gloss is also found in W (see above 107–11). It is tempting to wonder whether the choice of gloss was influenced by the next word in the main text, *ueloque* and, if so, whether the gloss was originally intended as a correction.

4 leuis currus . . . regendus. These words are linked by construe marks to indicate that they are to be taken together; in fact, *leuis currus* is nom. pl. and cannot be directly understood with *regendus,* but presumably *regendi* is implied, and the construe marks indicate that this is the verb which has to be construed with *leuis currus.*

5 automedon . . . erat. These words are joined by construe marks presumably to show that *automedon* is the subject and because it looks an unlikely nom. sg.

automedon: proprium aurigae. The gloss (sc. *nomen*) is the standard mode of marking a proper name. Scribe E has a different mode; see below, l. 11. Hexter, *Ovid and Medieval Schooling,* 37, reads *auriagae.*

6 hermonia: insula. Names for things are often identified simply by the common noun.

pupe: naue. A poetical term for a ship is glossed with the standard prose word.

8 tiphis . . . dicar . . . ego. These words are joined by construe marks to show that they are to be taken together: "Let me be called the Typhis and Automedon of love."

automedon: proprium nomen. The gloss is by scribe E who has a distinctive way of marking proper names different from the other scribes (cf. l. 5 above), and also a distinctive way of abbreviating *nomen* (cf. l. 7 for another example).

10 puer: cupid. There is no suspension mark for -*o*; the gloss simply reads *cupid* but is to be understood as referring to Cupid (cf. also l. 233 where the same form occurs). It is the kind of error which might easily be made when a gloss is being copied.

regi: infinitiuum. The lemma needed to be marked as an infinitive so
that it was not taken as the dat. sg. of *rex*; although the two forms would
have differed metrically (*rĕgi : rēgi*), metrical considerations seem not to
have figured (for discussion, see 84–85 above).

11 pillirides . . . prefecit. These words are joined by construe marks to show
that *pillirides* is the subject of the verb even though it looks plural.

cythara: *ablatiuus*. In *New Palaeographical Society* (ed. Maunde Thompson
et al.), pl. 82b, the gloss was mistakenly read as *tibia*. The gloss is presum-
ably intended to ensure that the student does not think that *cythara* is the
subject of *prefaecit*. Again note that the gloss would not have been neces-
sary had metrical considerations been taken into account by which the abl.
sg. and nom. sg. might be distinguished (for discussion, see above 84–85).

prefaecit: docuit. The gloss clarifies the sense of *prefaecit*. The abbre-
viation for *pre-* is slightly ambiguous; it has the macron shape over the
p- for *pre-*, but the tail at the right-hand end suggests it might have been
intended for *per-* (the reading of the editions). However, here it is taken as
pre- as the suspension mark is identical to that in *prebuit* (l. 16) and *precep-
tor* (l. 17).

12 animos . . . feros. The construe marks make the elementary point that
these two words are meant to be taken together but, in the context of
learning how to read Latin verse where nouns and agreeing adjectives
may be some distance apart, it is a useful gloss.

contudit: domuit. The gloss again explains the metaphor embodied in
animos . . . contudit "knocked their wild spirits into shape." This somewhat
unexpected gloss is found in several other manuscripts and seems well
embedded in the tradition; see 112–14 for discussion.

13 qui . . . socios . . . perterruit. The construe marks link both the subject and
object to the verb.

socios . . . hostis: graecos. . . . i. troianos. The glosses on this line seem
to be intended to remind a medieval audience of who was who at Troy.

14 annossum. It is not clear whether the mark under *annossum* is a construe
mark as it is not picked up elsewhere; perhaps a mark under *senem* was
omitted.

15 quas hector sensurus. These words are linked by construe marks perhaps
to indicate that *hector* and *sensurus* are to be taken together and that *quas*
is to be taken as the accusative following the participle.

16–18 The glosses again add names to a common noun, a pronoun, and a patr-
onymic in an attempt to keep the student in control of who is who.

16 prebuit ille. The construe marks show that *ille* is the subject of the verb.

17 chiron . . . preceptor. The construe marks link these words, no doubt
because *chiron*, like *automedon* above (ll. 5 and 8), looks an unlikely nom. sg.

18 Seuus: est. The gloss provides the relevant part of the verb "to be" which is so often omitted in Latin verse; cf. also ll. 38, 47, 54, 88, 121, 130, 141, 194, 259, 267, 275, 331, and 354.

puer. This is marked by a construe mark, but it is unclear what it is being linked with.

uterque dea: cupido et achilis ab tiphis et uenus. The gloss provides the names of the two boys and the two goddesses who are their mothers though apparently in chiastic order. I take it that *tiphis* is an error for *thetis* (perhaps via a spelling *tethis*). The preposition *ab* seems to have been added between them although the names of the goddesses are not in the ablative. Perhaps in an earlier version of the gloss there were just four names in the nominative to which a glossator added *ab* "from" to clarify the relationship.

20 magnanimi . . . equi. Construe marks link these words, perhaps for the same reason that *animos . . . feros* (l. 12) are joined, simply that they are a long way apart in the line.

21–22 quamuis . . . excutiatque. The words are joined by construe marks probably to indicate that *excutiat* as well as *uulneret* are to be construed with the conjunction.

22 faces: titiones. An interesting example where in providing the rarer word for "torches" the gloss seems to be doing the opposite of the normal practice. However, in medieval Latin *fax* in the sense of "firebrand" is rarer than *titio* (*DMLBS*, s.vv.), and so by medieval standards the glossing may be working in the right direction.

25 *phae phe* (= *Phoebe*): uocatiuus. The gloss notes the vocative case which is consistent with practice elsewhere in this text which is to mark many of the forms in final -*e*, and also to mark any vocative which might be confused with another case (especially in the context of a second person pronoun or verb, as in l. 28 below). In *New Palaeographical Society* (ed. Maunde Thompson et al.), pl. 82b, it is mistakenly assumed that it is an error for *nomen* "name" even though elsewhere names are glossed by *proprium* (cf. ll. 5, 6, 7, 8, 11, 27, etc.).

28 ascra: uocatiuus. The gloss is clearly designed to indicate the referent of the following *tuis*. Again *New Palaeographical Society* (ed. Maunde Thompson et al.), pl. 82b, it is mistakenly assumed that it is an error for *nōmen* "name."

29 usus: genetiuus. In *New Palaeographical Society* (ed. Maunde Thompson et al.), pl. 82b, it is mistakenly expanded as *generaliter*. Genitives are rarely glossed in this text (cf. l. 77 where Old Welsh **nom** marks a genitive). A fifth-declension genitive would particularly need to be distinguished from a nominative when metrical criteria were not taken into account.

However, in this case the gloss is incorrect; *usus* is in fact nominative: in *usus opus mouet* "experience drives the work" the second syllable of *usus* scans short. This is another example of the glossators' unwillingness, or inability, to bring an understanding of scansion to bear on their analysis; for discussion, see above, 84–85.

parete: o iuuenes. The text shifts to the second pl. and the gloss carefully changes the referent.

31 este: este pro estote. The gloss suggests that the future imperative might be expected here (with perhaps the implication that *este* is a metrical expedient) which might be influenced by the future *canam* in the preceding line; thus, "I shall sing the truth . . . ; and you, young women and matrons, keep away (sc. and stay away in the future)." Hollis, 38, notes that *este* is the usual ceremonial form.

uittae tenues: **a mein funiou** "slender bands (voc.)" (cf. Middle Welsh *mein* and *ffuniau*). EGOW 1, 59, and 111. For the use of the vocative particle to mark the case of the Latin lemma, see above 60–61. The regular plural ending in most Old Welsh glosses is **-ou** (MW *-eu*, MnW *-au*).

insigne: signum. The gloss indicates that the adjective is being used substantivally.

32 queque: .i. estote. The practice of repeating a word or phrase from a preceding line is used to counter the naturally elliptic form of Ovid's verse; cf. also l. 73. Here the gloss seems to be reminding the student to repeat the verb from the preceding line, though in fact the verb provided in the gloss is the earlier gloss and not the lemma; this may be suggesting that the future sense is to be maintained too.

medio: **or garr** "lower leg" (abl.). EGOW 60, s.v. *garn*. For the use of a preposition to mark the case of the Latin lemma, see above 60–61. The previous scholarship is based on reading the gloss as *garn*, but the final letter should be read as *r*, rather than *n*, thus *garr* "lower leg." VVB has **garn** but this was corrected by Stokes in his copy (UCL Stokes's Collection 114.f.10) to **garr**. In the context, the gloss supplies (with the ablative of the lemma marked by **o**) the noun which we have to understand with *medio*. The text in O is faulty; *medio* does not scan as it would elide with *instita*, and the editions correctly read *medios* agreeing with *pedes*. The Ovidian text is to be understood to mean that the dress of a Roman matron (*maritata*) comes down to the ground, thus *medios . . . pedes* "because the long *stola* cuts the feet in half, leaving only the front part exposed" (Hollis, 38–39). The reading *medio* may therefore have caused difficulty for the glossator who seems to have provided a noun **garr** to explain *medio*. Taken literally, the glossator seems to have imagined a shorter dress.

instita: **a hir etem** "o long border (sc. of a dress)" (MW *hir edeu*). *EGOW* 1, 56, 85. Note that **hir** seems to have been corrected by the scribe from **nir** with the lengthening of the first stroke. For the use of the vocative particle to mark the case of the Latin lemma, see above 60–61. The Middle Welsh form is probably to be understood as /edev/ (*GPC*, s.v. *edau*). *EGOW* quotes Gaelic *aitheamh* "fathom, arm span" as a cognate, which is possible if the sense developed from a length of yarn or string.

33 uenerem: uoluntatem. Unusually, the gloss is written under the lemma probably because the space above *uenerem* is clogged with descenders from the line above, and, as this is the last line on the page, there is plenty of space underneath.

canemus: ut. A number of verbs in this text are glossed by *ut* which seems to be indicating that they are to be taken to be in some sense subordinate; cf. also ll. 35, 39, 145, 205, 230, 263, 270, and 278.

34 crimen erit. These words are linked by construe marks perhaps to indicate that *crimen* is the subject even though it does not look like a nom. sg. For this type of syntactic glossing, see 64–67.

35–36. Introduction to the main theme of the first part of the book which contains most of the glossing on where and how to find girls.

35 reperire: ut. Cf. l. 33. Here the infinitive is marked as subordinate to the following imperative, *labora*: "work hard to find . . ."

35 miles: nouus. The text expresses the same sentiment with a transferred epithet: *qui noua nunc primum miles in arma uenis* "you who now first come as a soldier to new weapons." The gloss simply moves the epithet back to the subject.

37 proximus: secundus. By glossing *Principio* in l. 35 as *primo*, and taking up the *tertius* of the next line, it is natural to gloss *proximus* in this way.

exorare puellam: rogare usque dum inuenies. The gloss seems to miss the point; the third stage is to keep the pleasing girl and *exorare* "to prevail over her."

38 tertius: est. On supplying of parts of the verb "to be," cf. l. 18 above.

39 modus: liber. On this gloss, see Hexter, *Ovid and Medieval Schooling*, 40, n. 78, who discusses it as a possible example of a literary gloss.

signabitur: ut. Cf. l. 33. Here the gloss *ut* may be indicating that the tense of the verb should not be taken as a straight future; given the programmatic nature of the assertion, it may easily be taken as meaning something closer to "let the area be marked out."

aerea: **ir digatma** "the circus" (later Welsh *dyadfa*); cf. l. 136 where *circus* is glossed with the same Old Welsh word, and l. 163 where the plural, **ir digatmaou**, glosses *circus*. *EGOW* 45, 94–96. The form is a derivative of the verb *di-gad- with the suffix -ma (later -fa) signifying a place where something happens (on -fa, see Russell, "Verdunkelte Komposita," 116). On the sense here, see Isaac, *The Verb*, 329.

40 meta: uia. The gloss seems intended to remove the metaphor of the turning post and to replace it with the simpler sense of "road," but in doing so rather obscures the sense of the rest of the line; on this line, see Hollis, 40–41.

rota: **o olin** "wheel (abl.)" (cf. MW *olwyn*). EGOW 122–23, 125. The spelling of the diphthong in the second syllable may be an error, perhaps for *oloin or *oluin; cf. the plural *holoinou* glossing *rotis* (Angers 12b), *crunnolunou* "round wheels" glossing *orbiculata* (Mart. Cap. 4ba).

41 loris passim: habenis ubique. Both glosses provide the more common word.

43 tenues: nisi quaeras "unless you ask." As Hexter, *Ovid and Medieval Schooling*, 38, n. 74, points out, the gloss is actually on the whole line: "A girl will not fall out of thin air (sc. unless you ask)."

47 noti: sunt. On supplying parts of the verb "to be," cf. l. 18 above.

frutices: **loinou** "bushes" (cf. MW *llwyn*). EGOW 106. The regular plural ending in most Old Welsh glosses is **-ou** (MW -eu, MnW -au).

48 nouit: .i. is. The gloss provides a pronominal subject which refers to a generic hunter/fisherman.

51 uento: .i. cum. The gloss implies that the lemma is to be taken as an ablative; we might wonder whether the use of the preposition is a Latin version of the Old Welsh practice of marking case with prepositions (in Old Welsh an ablative would be marked by **o** "from"); cf. also 60–61 for general discussion. If so, this might be a relatively late gloss. However, the gloss may be incorrect; the idiom of *uela dare* suggests that *uento* is dative.

52 tibi: .i. a te. It is common in this text for the dative of the agent *tibi* to be glossed by *a te*; for discussion, see above 62–63, and cf. ll. 71, 138, 142, etc.

53 andromedon: .i. nomen mulieris. The standard reading here is *andromedan* but our form seems to be modelled on the *automedon* in ll. 5 and 8, and therefore perhaps in need of being identified as the name of a woman.

54 raptaque: est. On supplying of parts of the verb "to be," cf. l. 18 above.

frigio graia puella uiro: troiano graecia helena ablatiuus alaxandrio. The densely packed glosses provide all the necessary information to disentangle the allusive poetical terms: *troiano* on *frigio*, *graecia* on *graia*. The last word of the line has a double gloss marking it as ablative but also identifying the man concerned as Alexander (Paris), but glossed with an adjective rather than the noun.

56 haec: roma. The gloss connects the demonstrative with *roma* in the preceding line; given the subject matter, clarifying the referent of a feminine singular demonstrative would have been important since the default assumption would be that it referred to a woman.

57 gargara: nomen regionis in india. For discussion of this gloss, see above 74. Gargara was in the Troad (see Hollis, 43), not in India, but it is suggested above that the gloss arises from a misunderstanding of a passage in Isidore which is exploited elsewhere in the glossing.

quot: habent. The text requires the verb to be supplied from later in the line, but the gloss provides the plural *habent* perhaps on the correct assumption that *gargara* is neuter plural; cf. Virgil, *Georgics,* i.103, *ipsa suas mirantur Gargara messes* "Gargara itself marvels at its own harvests," where the verb is also plural (Hollis, 43).

metina: insola. An unfamiliar name is explained as the name of an island.

60 constitit: stat. The change in tense from the perfect of the lemma to the present of the gloss seems to indicate that the sense of *constitit* is that of a present state resulting from a past action, i.e. "she has settled in her son's city and continues to stand in her son's city."

urbe: alba longa nomen ciuitatis quam aeneas aedificauit in otio [*recte* ostio] tiberis fluminis. The long explanatory (but misleading) gloss is presumably aimed at a medieval audience who would have been confused by the city being identified as Alba Longa instead of Rome; see above, 73–74.

61 Seu: si. The poetical form is glossed with the more common conjunction.

63 iuuenem iuuenes: iuuenculam iuuenculae. The glosses are intended to show them to be female (Hexter, *Ovid and Medieval Schooling,* 36, n. 64).

65 sera: tarda. The lemma *sera* "late" is glossed by a more specific reference to old age, *tarda* "slow."

sapientior: **guobriach** "more dignified" (MW *gofriach*). EGOW 71. This is a comparative form, marked with the -*ach* suffix (GMW 38), of the adjective **guobri**, which is attested at l. 234 glossing *gravis.*

67 lentus spatiare: securus specta. The glosses emphasize the leisurely nature of the activity; "stroll slowly" is glossed as "look about you in a carefree manner."

67–88. The colonnades and forums of Rome: this is one of the most heavily glossed sections in the whole text (for the statistics, see 50–51) with much of the glossing focusing on the Roman features which would need explanation for a medieval readership and in the schoolroom. For discussion of the cumulative effect of all the glossing on this passage, see Russell, "Teaching between the lines," 140–45.

69 Aut ubi: spatiare. The gloss repeats the verb from l. 66 which is to be understood in this clause as well.

muneribus: **di aperthou** "offerings (dat.)" (cf. MW *aberth*). EGOW 9. The preposition marks the dative case. The regular plural ending in most Old Welsh glosses is -**ou** (MW -*eu*, MnW -*au*). The gloss is written with a suspension mark for **er**, rare in vernacular glosses; cf. also l. 334 where the singular **aperth** is written in full and l. 76 where the suspension mark has been omitted on **apthou**.

70–104. For a sample edition of this page (38r) of the manuscript, see Dumville, "A *Thesaurus Palaeoanglicus*?," 75–76 (with a brief discussion on 71–73).

70 externo: alieno. The gloss clarifies the ambiguity of the lemma which could mean both "marble facing" (i.e. marble on the outside; thus Green, *Ovid. The Erotic Poems,* 168) or "foreign marble" (i.e. marble from elsewhere; thus Hollis, 46); rightly or wrongly, the gloss opts for the latter.

opus: i est munus. Bradshaw reads *hoc est munus,* but the gloss is *i* followed by the abbreviation for *est,* perhaps attempting to expand the *.i.* abbreviation for *id est.*

71 tibi: a te. On *tibi* glossed by *a te,* see above l. 52.

tabellis: **o cloriou** "panels (abl.)" (MW *clawr*). EGOW 122–23, 33 (and also 32, s.v. *claur*). The regular plural ending in most Old Welsh glosses is -**ou** (MW -*eu,* MnW -*au*). On how the glossators (both Latin and Welsh) understand the different senses of *tabella,* as marble panels on an arcade, a programme, and writing tablets, see 81 above.

72 libia: claritas. Note the spelling of *b* for -/v/- in the lemma; cf. also the converse in l. 415 *reuus* (for *rebus*), l. 745 *amauat* (for *amabat*). The point of the gloss is unclear, though it is possible that an abstract noun is being used to define her by her most notable characteristic.

73 quaeque: nec uitentur. The gloss repeats the negative verb from l. 71.

miseris patruelibus: **dir arpeteticion ceintiru** "the wretched cousins (dat.)" (cf. MW *cefnderw*). EGOW 12, 24, 42–43. On the displacement of this gloss out towards the right margin because an explanatory Latin gloss, *fili aegipti,* was already occupying the space above the lemma, see above 68. On the significance of **ceintiru** as a southern form, see Charles-Edwards, "Some Celtic Kinship Terms," and "*Nei, Keifn,* and *Kefynderw,*" and 86–87 above. The adjective **arpeteticion** is otherwise unattested in Welsh but is formed with the suffix -*etic* (pl. -*eticion*) which is often used to gloss Latin adjectives and often past participles; for its form, see Russell, *Celtic Word-Formation,* 76–80, 103–8. The myth (Hollis, 46) seems to have needed explanation for a medieval audience, and its cast list is gradually presented through the glosses in this line and the next: . . . *miseris patruelibus* (gl. *fili aegypti*) . . . *ause* (gl. **dir arpeteticion ceintiru**) . . . *belides* (gl. *filiae danai filius beli*) . . . *pater* (gl. *.i. danaus*).

74 belides . . . pater: filiae danai filius beli. . . . i. danaus. For discussion of these explanatory glosses, see the previous note.

ferus ense: minando gladio. Taken by Bradshaw as two separate glosses (that is, *ferus* glossed by *minando* and *ense* by *gladio*), but they make more sense as one; he is (lit.) "wild with a (drawn) sword" glossed by "by threatening with a sword."

75 adonis: proprium; deestque (in left margin). The gloss *proprium* (sc. *nomen*) is the standard mode of marking a proper name; cf. ll. 5, 6, 8, 11, 17, 96, 179, 283, 285, 649. It is useful here to remind us that we are talking about individuals, since *uenus* is often used by Ovid to mean "love." The latter gloss is odd: the logic of the syntax suggests that Adonis is the subject and so literally "is lacking to her" (i.e. she is missing him) which may have been intended to explain why he is being wept over by her. However, the force of the *-que* remains unclear and something one might expect in a quotation or collation gloss. While the older manuscripts have *ueneris,* the *recentiores* have *ueneri* (printed in fact by Ramírez de Verger); one possibility is that the *deestque* gloss originated in a text containing the dative *ueneri.*

76 Cultaque: nec pretereant. This gloss again repeats a verb from a previous line (here from l. 71); cf. l. 73.

sacra: **apthou** "offerings." For **aperthou,** see l. 69, though here it lacks the suspension mark, but note also l. 334 *uictima* glossed by **aperth** written out in full. Bradshaw nevertheless transcribed it here as *aperthou.* The regular plural ending in most Old Welsh glosses is **-ou** (MW *-eu,* MnW *-au*).

deo: Syro. A collation reading. For discussion, see 71–72 above, and Kenney, "Manuscript Tradition," 24 (cf. also Kenney, "Ovid, *Ars Amatoria,* i. 147," 10, n. 2); Charles-Edwards, "The Use of the Book in Wales," 402; id., *Wales and the Britons, 350–1064,* 646.

77 lanigerae: **nom ir bleuporthetic** "the wool-wearing one (gen.)" (cf. W *blew* "hair, fur" and *porthi* "bear, carry" borrowed from Latin *portāre*). *EGOW* 120–21, 94–96, 16; on *-etic* as an adjectival and participial marker, see the note above on l. 73. This is a hapax legomenon in Welsh and has probably been calqued on *lanigerae.* Note that the reading *lani-* "wool" is restricted to a small group of manuscripts; most of the others have *lini-* "linen"; see above 60n143. The particle **nom** (also *nou* and *inno*) seems to be used in Old Welsh to mark the genitive case in the Latin lemma (just as prepositions are used for other oblique cases). Its origin is debated (*EGOW* 121); see in particular Lambert, "Vieux gallois *nou, nom, inno.*"

memphitica: aegyptiaca. The gloss provides a more general geographical location.

iuuencae: **buch** "cow" (cf. MW *buwch, buch*). *EGOW* 19. This seems a rather obvious gloss, but it is presumably intended to clarify that here *iuuenca* really does mean "cow" and is not a metaphor for a girl as in the glosses on l. 63, and it is also probably to be taken with the gloss in the next line where *multas* is glossed by *puellas* as a way of distinguishing the two female groups being discussed here.

78 multas: puellas. See the discussion above on l. 77.

ipsa: .i. io. For discussion, see Hexter, *Ovid and Medieval Schooling*, 39, n. 75; Bodden, 'Study,' 200–201, Lambert, "Les gloses grammaticales," 292 (cf. *EGOW* 106); the gloss is almost certainly Latin *Io* and not Old Welsh *Io* "calf," as Bradshaw and Stokes thought (cf. 28n45 above).

79 fora: **datlocou** "meeting places" (cf. Middle Welsh *dadl* "meeting" (later "argument") and *lloc* "place" < Latin *locus*). Note also **datl** at l. 80 below. *EGOW* 41; see also Charles-Edwards, "*Gorsedd, Dadl*, and *Llys*," 101–3. The regular plural ending in most Old Welsh glosses is -**ou** (MW -*eu*, MnW -*au*). Here, by using a compound containing *lloc* "place," the glossator is clear that he is talking about the place where debate takes place, though in the next line it is less clear whether he has the place in mind rather than the process of debating.

quis . . . possit: in quibus . . . quis. For the confusion of these two contradictory glosses (*in quibus* seems to be taking *quis* as a poetical dative plural), which must be the product of two distinct layers of glossing, see the discussion above, 63, where it is suggested that, even though *in quibus* is wrong, it shows what the glossators were looking for—poetical forms not found in prose.

80 in arguto . . . foro: **in ir guorunhetic . . . datl** "in the noisy . . . meeting" (cf. MW *dadl* "meeting"). *EGOW* 91–92, 94–95, 74, 40. It is possible that **datl** is intended as an abbreviation for **datloc** following on from **datlocou** (l. 79 above). The gloss had originally been read as *guorimhetic,* but Lewis, "Nodiadau Cymysg," 84, was the first in print to realize that it was a derivative of *gorun* "noise," and the minims should be read as -*un*- and not -*im*-, though Stokes, in his copy of VVB (UCL Stokes's Collection 114.f.10) corrected Loth's reading to **guorunhetic**. However, if the stem has been correctly identified, we would expect it to be spelt *gorun*-, not *guorun*-, as it does not etymologically contain **guo*- from **wo*- (cf. *EGOW* 71–75 for forms in *guo*-). It would appear then that it has been reanalysed as containing the *guo*-/*go*- prefix. For -*etic* as an adjectival and participial marker, see the note above on l. 73.

referta: repleta est "was filled." The gloss provides *est* to complete the sense (for which see l.18), but seems to be trying to explain the sense of *referta,* though *repleta* does not really convey anything useful.

81 Subdita: sunt fora "are," "forums." The glosses are probably intended to be taken separately and not as "there are forums." Thus *sunt* provides the verb with *subdita* to show that this is a plural finite verb and not simply a participle; and *fora* indicates the plural subject as there would have been room for confusion since *flamma* in the preceding line might otherwise have been assumed to be the subject.

quae: fora "forums." The fact that both *subdita* and *quae* are glossed by *fora* looks like overload, but it is possible that they were added at different times.

82 appias: deus pluiae. In the context of a fountain, the gloss provides a relevant explanation of the lemma; on Appias, see Hollis, 49.

aera: **ir emedou** "the bronzes" (cf. MW *efyd*). *EGOW* 94–95, 53–54 (s.vv. *emedou* and *emid*). The regular plural ending in most Old Welsh glosses is -**ou** (MW -*eu*, MnW -*au*). What has not been noticed by previous commentators (who seem as unwilling to scan the text as the glossators) is that *aera* is trisyllabic and the Greek acc. sg. of *aer* "air" and therefore it has been glossed in error as if it were the disyllabic acc. pl. of *aes* "bronze"; for discussion, see above 82–83.

83 loco: in foro. The gloss helpfully reminds us both that *loco* is ablative (cf. l. 85 below), and that we are still in the Forum, though our attention has momentarily moved away from the lawyers.

consultus: id est consiliatus "i.e. advising." The gloss seems to be making the point that *consultus* seems to mean "one who is consulted" when in fact the sense is the converse; the point of Ovid's text is that here is a person who is happy to give advice on legal matters but, when love strikes, he is the one in need of advice.

83–86 Hollis (49) notes that "every line contains a double meaning based on legal terminology—a notable tour de force." This does not trouble the glossators who are having a hard enough job simply construing the Latin.

85 loco: ablatiuus. Here, too (cf. l. 83), we need to be reminded in the absence of a preposition that *illo . . . loco* is ablative, and especially next to *desunt*, which is usually construed with the dative.

deserto: priuatiuus. The lemma was corrected by the scribe to *diserto*; evidently he thought it agreed with *illo . . . loco* earlier in the line, when in fact it is a dative after *desunt*: "In that place words are often lacking even for an eloquent man." The gloss, which relates to the (*dativus*) *privativus*, the dative of disadvantage, is correct; for this gloss, cf. also l. 331. On "privative" datives, see above, 61.

87 nunc: tunc "at that time." The gloss *tunc* is used on several occasions as a distancing adverb, reminding the reader that events are in the past. Here, specifically, it changes the temporal focus from Ovid's present to the Roman past of the reader's perspective. But cf. ll. 106, 634, and 649 where the gloss is used to distance a Roman present from an earlier past, and l. 178, where it is used to remind the reader that Ovid's present is in the past for a medieval readership. Cf. also the shift in tense in the *mos . . .* glosses discussed above, 75–76.

88 qui: fuit. On supplying of parts of the verb "to be," cf. l. 18 above.

patronus: index. The gloss is clearly *index* but may be a misreading of *iudex.*

cliens: **dauu** "member of a retinue" (cf. MW *daw*). *EGOW* 41. This is an interestingly specific gloss which shows a precise understanding of the nature of a *cliens.*

89–134 The best place to find girls is the theatre, and it has been so since the time of Romulus.

89–91 A construe mark joins *theathris* to *illic* in l. 91 to show that *illic* is referring to the theatre.

89 precipue: aduerbum. An unremarkable gloss but perhaps necessary to distinguish the words in the same line ending in *-e.*

ceruis. The correct reading is *curuis* but *ceruis* "stags" might have been encouraged by the following word, *uenare.* Cf. also the collation gloss at l. 766 suggesting *cerua* for the main text *curua.*

uenare: **helghati** "you (sg.) hunt (imperative)" (cf. MW *hely/hela*). *EGOW* 82. The verb is **helgha** with a second sg. affixed pronoun **ti**. This is one of only two verbs glossed in this text (cf. l. 207 *ortabere* gl. **nerthiti**) and it is suggested above (60) that the poetical second sg. deponent ending *-e* rather than the standard *-is* was confusable with nominal case forms and adverbs; cf. earlier in the line *precipue*, also ending in *-e*, glossed with *aduerbum.*

theathris: **guaroimaou** "plays, play places" (cf. MW *gwarwyua*). *EGOW* 64–65. The regular plural ending in most Old Welsh glosses is -**ou** (MW *-eu*, MnW *-au*). Cf. also l. 106 **guarai** glossing *scena* and l. 133 **guaroiou** glossing *teathra.* It is not clear whether any distinction is intended between a **guarai** and a **guaroima**; if there were, it may be between the place where generally plays take place (**guaroima**), i.e. a theatre, and a play or part of the theatre where the play itself takes place (**guarai** (l. 106) which is glossing *scena* "stage"). Note also that l. 103 where *theathro* is used to refer to the seating area over which the awning can be drawn is glossed with **estid** "seating." On the suffix *-ma*, see the note to l. 39n above, s.v. **digatma**.

90 uoto: datiuus. The line in O is even more confusing because the reading *loco* (perhaps introduced from l. 85) for the correct *loca* of the editions introduces yet another dative/ablative singular. The lemma is specifically marked as dative as there would have been room for misunderstanding next to a comparative adjective where it could have been interpreted as an ablative. If we follow the glossator in taking *tuo . . . uoto* as dative, a reading "these (places) are more fertile for (sc. the fulfilment of) your prayer" imposes itself. In fact, modern scholars have treated *tuo . . . uoto* as ablative: "These (places) are even more productive than you could wish" (Hollis, 50).

92 quodque: inuenies. The gloss indicates that the verb is to be repeated from the previous line; for such repetition, compare also ll. 211, 151, 328, and 388.

93 itque: ut. The gloss repeats *ut* from the beginning of the line to show that it goes with both verbs: "just as an ant comes and (just as) it goes."

96 thimia: flos uel proprium. The gloss offers alternative interpretations: either the flower, thyme, or a proper name. The latter (sc. *nomen*) is the standard mode of marking a proper name.

98 copia iudicium: deficile est elegere ab eis. The gloss is really a comment on the whole line: "Their large number (i.e. of women) has often slowed my decision."

99 spectatum: ad sspectandos [*sic*] alios. In the gloss the two *s*'s are different in form, the first *s*, the second the insular form. The glossator assumes that the women come to watch men (*alios*), not women, and to be watched themselves.

spetttentur [*sic*]. The scribe originally wrote the indicative *spectantur*. To be absolutely clear, the gloss explains they have come to be watched by others (*ab alis*).

101 solicitos: **termisceticion** "confused" (cf. MW *teruysg*). EGOW 146–47. For -*etic* as an adjectival and participial marker, see the note above on l. 73.

romule: uocatiuus rex qui aedificauit romam. The gloss provides both grammatical information and an explanation of who Romulus was.

102 cum: donec uel **cant** "since" (cf. MW *gan*). The Old Welsh element of this gloss was not recognized until it was published by Dumville in 1992, "A *Thesaurus Palaeoanglicus?*," 72 and 76 (l. 33 (n. 56)). It was not noted in VVB or EGOW; in Stokes's copy of VVB (UCL Stokes's Collection 114.f.10) the gloss was added by him in the left margin of p. 64, though wrongly attributed to the text of Eutyches. For discussion, see 67–68, and n. 168 above. While *cant* is attested elsewhere in Old Welsh as a preposition, in this case it is functioning as a conjunction as it does regularly in Middle and later Welsh in the form *gan* (GMW 234).

uiros: familiae romuli. Romulus's men are identified as his *familiae* "families" or perhaps "household," which could be intended to anticipate their familial status having taken the Sabine women. However, it is possible that this is intended more in the sense of "retinue, warband, household" and be more redolent of the Latin terminology of north-west Europe; cf., for example, MW *teulu* which originally meant "warband" but came to mean "household, family."

103 uela: **ir cilchetou** "the sheets" (cf. MW *cylched*). EGOW 28, 94–95, and also 81 above where it is noted that interpreting *uela* as "sheets" rather than "sails" displays a very specific understanding of the way awnings worked

on a Roman theatre. The regular plural ending in most Old Welsh glosses is -**ou** (MW -*eu*, MnW -*au*).

    theathro: **estid** "the seating area" (cf. MW *iested*). *EGOW* 56, and, for the specificity of the knowledge of Roman theatres in being able to distinguish the seating areas from the stage, see the discussion above at 81, and the notes to l. 89.

104 pulpita rubra: rubrae sedes. At first sight these appear like two independent glosses, but in fact it is a two-word gloss on a two-word lemma; this is the only way to explain the form of *rubrae* as agreeing with *sedes*.

105-6. Ovid here is playing with the present and past state of the Palatine Hill—now (i.e. in Ovid's period) covered in palaces and then (i.e. in Romulus's time) in woods. But it is also perhaps suggesting that those woods were the *palatia* of their time where the Romans-to-be dwelt. The readings of our text have caused the glossator(s) some difficulty. Our text reads *illae* (*illic* Kenney) *quas tullerant nemorosa palatia frondes* | *simpliciter possita* (*positae* Kenney) and is very difficult to translate coherently, but seems to suggest that "they (the women?) brought boughs," and "the woody Palatine Hill was placed," while the edited text should probably be read as "boughs, which the woody Palatine Hill bore there, were placed simply." This is perhaps why *tullerant* was glossed *secum* as the glossator seems to think that the women are bringing boughs with them, which is in fact mentioned in l. 108 (or at least is in the standard editions which read *fronde tegente,* while our text reads *fronte tegente*). As an anonymous reader points out, the gloss *aedes* (plural) on *palatia* may signal the glossator's unease with the poetic plural *palatia* who has glossed a plural word with singular meaning with another word with similar semantics.

105 tullerant: secum. See the preceding discussion.

    nemorosa: .i. fuerant. The gloss reminds the medieval audience that this is what the Palatine hill with its *palatia* had been like—that is, covered in woods.

106 scena: **guarai** "play, stage" (cf. MW *gwarae, chwarae*). *EGOW* 64, and above in the notes to l. 89.

    fuit: tunc. On the use of adverbial *tunc* as a gloss, see l. 87 above for discussion.

107 gradibus: .i. **cemmein** "steps" (MW *cam* (pl. *cemmein*)). *EGOW* 25. Note that here *gradibus* refers to physical steps, not the action of stepping which is the usual sense of *cam* (pl. *cemmein*).

    cispite: tellure. The gloss slightly misses the point in explaining "turf, sod" as "earth."

109 oculisque notat: elegit. Lhuyd, *Archaeologia Britannica,* 226, quotes this gloss as an example of a Welsh gloss (though he was not followed in

this by subsequent scholars); he seems to have assumed that *elegit* was intended to gloss *oculis* even though it is above *notat*. I think that he read it as *e legit* (Modern Welsh *ei lygaid* "his eyes"); however, in Old Welsh that would almost certainly have been spelt *liceit* or the like (cf. the singular *licat* "spring" frequently in the boundary clauses in the *Book of Llandaff* (see *GPC*, s.v. *llygad* (2)), which is a semantic adaptation of the same word). In the context of the rape of the Sabine women, the gloss can readily be understood as "he picked out" and glossing the whole phrase.

110 mutta: consilia. The standard edition has *multa* and the gloss *consilia* would fit that too. The reading *mutta* "silent," if not simply an error, may have been triggered by the preceding *tacito pectore*.

111 tubicine tusco: **pippaur tuscois** "a Tuscan piper." I follow Bradshaw in reading *pippaur* rather than *pispaur* (*VVB*, s.v., but Stokes has corrected this to *piipaur* in his copy (UCL Stokes's Collection 114.f.10)) or *piipaur* (Williams, "Glosau Rhydychen a Chaergrawnt," 113; *EGOW* 131, s.v. *pii-paur*, 152). **Pippaur** is a derivative created with the agent-noun suffix *-awr* (Latin *-ārius*) based on *pib* "pipe." I have taken *-pp-* to represent *-/b/-* but it may be an attempt to spell an intervocalic *-/p/-*. The adjectival suffix in **tuscois**, *-wys* in later Welsh (< Latin *-ēnsis*), is used with names of places to refer to people or things deriving from that place. The stem is spelt with *-u-* which I take to be Latin influence (from *Tusc-*) as we would have expected an Old Welsh spelling in *i* or *e* for /təsk/-.

112 pulsat: **ledit** "strikes" (cf. MW *llad*, stem *lled-*). This gloss was a late arrival in the scholarship; it was first added to the Old Welsh dossier by Williams, "Glosau Rhydychen a Chaergrawnt," 113; see also *EGOW* 101 and above, 83–84. One might wonder whether it was missed by earlier scholars (Zeuss, Stokes, Ebel, et al.) because they thought it was for classical Latin *laedit* "harms, hurts," which would not be an untenable gloss on *pulsat*. But, if it is Old Welsh, it contains the original "absolute" ending of the verb (cf. Old Irish *slaidid* "strikes") which became obsolete in later Welsh, though still exploited by poets; for discussion, see *GMW* 118–19, and Rodway, *Dating Medieval Welsh Literature*, 91–95. Note also that here the verb still has its original sense of "strike" as opposed to the later sense of "kill."

113 plausu: **coorn** "applause" (unattested in later Welsh). For discussion of this problematic form, see *EGOW* 34–35; because it is only attested once, it is not clear how it is to be analysed even though the sense is tolerably clear. For the digraph spelling of the vowel, we might compare *ceenn* (l. 251). However, the form remains uncertain, and it is possible that it is a miscopying of Latin *corona* "crowd" (or perhaps of the gen. sg. *corone*); on such uncertain forms, see above, 83–84. It could be a miscopying of an Old Welsh **corun** borrowed from Latin *corona* in this sense, though

there is no evidence that Welsh *corun*, which was borrowed in the sense of "crown," ever meant "crowd." *VVB* 82 suggests a connection with W *orn* "blame, slander."

plausus: clamoris. The gloss could perhaps be interpreted as explaining the type of applause, but I think it more likely that the glossator mistakenly thought that *plausus* was genitive.

115 fatentes: fatigantes. The gloss seems to indicate a different understanding of the main text; the participle in *animum clamore fatentes* "revealing their intention with a shout" seems to have been understood as something like "tiring, wearing out."

117 aquilas: ante. The gloss provides the extra semantic detail of the doves fleeing with the eagles on their tail.

118 furentes: furio. This is one of the few verbs glossed in the whole text and it is glossed with a first sg. verb. The reading *furentes* is only found in O and O_g; elsewhere, the reading is *ruentes*. The lemma is part of *furo, -ere*, but I take it that the gloss is trying to suggest that the participle is of a different verb. One possibility is that the glossator thought it was part of the transitive verb *furio, -are*; did the glossator interpret the line as "the women who were making the men rage out of control grew afraid"? The notion that the women were the cause of the men's rage would fit with some of the comments added later about the women's lust (see the discussion and references on 75–76). We might observe that such a gloss would be more suited to a text like Eutyches's *De uerbo* (a fragment of which now forms part of the same manuscript but which was originally separate (see above, 12–14)) earlier in the manuscript, where the first sg. of a verb form is used as a citation form.

119–28. Note the number of glosses in these lines where feminine singular or plural pronouns are glossed with a case form of *puella* (ll. 119, 120, 123, 126, 127, 128).

119 illae: .i. mulieres. The gloss clarifies the referent of the pronoun in a context where several feminine nouns intervene, *aquilae, columbae, agnae*.

120 constitit . . . in nulla . . . color. These words are linked by construe marks probably to mark out the basic structure of subject (*color*), verb (*constitit*), and prepositional phrase (*in nulla*).

in nulla: pu. I take *pu* here as an abbreviation for *puella*; as a parallel, cf. *tolle* (l. 389, glossing *tollitur*), which is intended to change the tense to the future. Cf. another Ovid fragment, o, where at l. 129 *corrumpis* is glossed *o pu*, clearly an abbreviation of *o puella*, providing a vocative to explain the second sg. verb; on o, see above, 106–7.

121 una: erat. The gloss repeats the verb from earlier in the line; on supplying of parts of the verb "to be" (cf. l. 18 above).

122 sine mente: **hep amgnaupot** (with **b** written above the **p**) "without real-
izing" (cf. MW *adnabot*). EGOW 83, 5; and for the Middle Welsh forms, GMW
148; it is considered in greater detail above, 78–80. The usual form in
Middle Welsh is *adnabot* (with *b* for /b/) and it is possible that the form
here has a different preverb. But the main issue is the central consonant
which in Middle and Modern Welsh is pronounced -/b/-, though in Breton
aznavout it is -/v/-. Arguably, the spellings here hesitate between the two.

124 hec: una. Given the number of women involved in this episode, it is impor-
tant that the gloss marks *hec* as feminine singular.

125 genialis: **creaticaul plant** "for producing children" (cf. MW *creadigawl* and
plant). EGOW 36 and 132, and also above, 81. Although the gloss extends
over the top of *preda*, it seems to be an expansion of *genialis* in the sense
of "producing children" rather than anything to do with plunder; it looks
as if the adjectival form of **creaticaul** is calqued on *genialis*, but then the
sense has been developed by adding **plant** "children."

127 qua: **nepun** puella "any girl" (cf. MW *nebun*). It looks as if the glosses
were added piecemeal; the scribe copied *puella* as a gloss on *qua* (above
and slightly to the right), and then the Old Welsh gloss was added imme-
diately above *qua*. On **nepun**, see EGOW 118; GMW 106.

128 cupido . . . sinu. The words are linked by construe marks to show that
cupido does not for once refer to Cupid but is the adjective agreeing with
sinu.

129 occellos: **grudou**. VVB has **trudou**; in Stokes's copy (UCL Stokes's Collec-
tion 114.f.10) it was corrected to **grudou**. The Welsh gloss has been over-
written and the **d** inserted above. Bradshaw suggested that the gloss had
originally been *cruou*, but the first letter is **t**- overwritten to make a **g**-, and
the plural ending -**ou** (the regular plural ending in most Old Welsh glosses
(MW -*eu*, MnW -*au*)) seems to be added later and then the **d** added above.
The order of reworking may have been as follows: the original gloss, there-
fore, was **tru** "pitiful" perhaps intended as an exclamation (as in **mor tru**
below (l. 176) glossing *eheu*); it then may have had the plural ending added
suggesting that a glossator thought it was intended as a gloss on *occellos*
and so making it agree in number; finally, since it was over *occellos* it was
rewritten as **grudou** by adjusting the **t**- to **g**- and inserting the **d**. For fur-
ther discussion, see above, 48 and 68.

130 pater: fuit. On supplying of parts of the verb "to be," cf. l. 18 above; here it
is important to make the past tense explicit in contrast to the future tense
in the latter part of the line: *"quod matri patri* (sc. *erat), est hoc tibi," dixit, "ero"*
"'What your father was to your mother, this is what I shall be to you.'"

131 romulae: note here the overextension of the *ae* spelling for *e* (here a short
e which would never have been *ae*).

scisti: .i. quia placebat uiris uim facere. For discussion of moralistic comments among the commentary on this text, see 75–76 above. The glossator is perhaps reading too much into the text and seems to understand the *commoda* (rendered "fringe benefits" by Hollis (57)) to be the act of rape, when in fact Ovid may been intending them to be simply the women themselves.

133 teathra: **guaroiou** "plays" (cf. MW *guarwy*). *EGOW* 65; see also the discussion above, l. 89. The regular plural ending in most Old Welsh glosses is **-ou** (MW *-eu*, MnW *-au*).

135–62 Finding a girl at the chariot races.

135 fugiat: preteriat. Bradshaw read it as *praetereat.* The gloss is written *ptiat* with a long line over the *pt* which I take to be for *preter*; thus, "may it (not) pass (you) by." The gloss may have been intended to reshape the idiom into that found in ll. 71ff and 75–76.

136 circus: **digatma** "circus." *EGOW* 45, 94–96, and also above at l. 39.

137 digitis: ut nutas "just as you nod." The glossator anticipates the next line.

arcana: **ringuedaulion** "secrets" (cf. MW *rinwedawl*). *EGOW* 138.

138 tibi: a te. On *tibi* glossed by *a te*, see above l. 52.

per nutus: **troi enmeituou** "by means of nods" (cf. MW *trwy* and *amnaid, emneid*). *EGOW* 151, 55. The regular plural ending in most Old Welsh glosses is **-ou** (MW *-eu*, MnW *-au*).The phrase is split up between the descenders of the letters of the line above thus: *troien | meit | uou*. In the light of the later forms, we might have expected the Old Welsh form to have been something like *emneituou* and it is possible that in the process of copying the gloss between the descenders resulted in a minim error, mis-segmenting the minims as *-nm-* rather than as *-mn-*. The ending is not as clear as it might be: the plural would normally be in *-ou* but we seem to have an extra *-u-*; is it possible that the original form had a plural in *-uo*, rather than in *-ou*, as is sometimes found in Old Breton?

nota: **cared** "sin, stain" (cf. MW *cared*). *EGOW* 22. The main text does not contain any hint of judgement: "and (sc. in the circus) a signal (*nota*) need not be communicated by nods." However, the same word is used to gloss *nequitiae* in the Juvencus manuscript (46v36); McKee's note on the Juvencus gloss renders Ovid's *nota* as "mark (of ignominy)" (*Juvencus*, 479). It may be that this is a case of a glossator introducing a moralistic interpretation to what in the Ovid is depicted as a relatively innocent activity. It is worth pointing out that Welsh *caredd* later acquires the sense of "love" (perhaps via "lust"?) presumably by interpreting the stem *car-* as "love" (cf. *caru*, etc.); cf. *GPC* s.v. In the light of this later development it is probably worth noting that, where O has *nota est* at the end of the line, W has *uenus est*, which has been deleted and *uel nota .i. notita est* added over the top and *nota est* added after it. The text of W therefore has been corrected by reference to a manuscript with the *nota* reading. It could be argued that the later sense of **cared** might be related to the *uenus est* reading. But this is unlikely given the otherwise late attestation of the Welsh meaning of "love." Another outside possibility is worth bearing in mind: that it is to be read as *caret* "there is a gap" and it is being used to indicate that something is missing; that said, it is not at all clear that anything is missing at this point.

139 a domina: quasi dominae. The gloss points out that the phrase is to be construed with *proximus* and a dative ("next to") would be expected.

    sedeto: sede. The archaic imperative (for which see Hollis, 59) is glossed by the regular form; cf. l. 31, where a slightly different but related issue arises with imperatives.

140 lateri: mulieri. The gloss is clearly dative (though a genitive could have been expected here); if so, it is to be understood to be in apposition to the lemma: "join your side to her side (i.e. to the woman)." It is possible however that it is a copying error for *mulieris.*

141 bene: est. On supplying of parts of the verb "to be," cf. l. 18 above.

142 quid (*corrected to* quod): **ir.** Bradshaw and Bodden both rightly read Old Welsh **ir** rather than Latin *in*; VVB has no entry but in Stokes's copy (UCL Stokes's Collection 114.f.10) **ir** (gl. *quod*) has been added in the lower margin of p. 165, though wrongly attributed to the text of Eutyches. Note also that the main text has *quid* which was changed to *quod* which is the standard reading. No good sense can be extracted from Latin *in* as a gloss here, but it is possible that a Welsh glossator understood *quod* as relative (*et bene . . . quod* "and what a good thing it is that") and then added **ir** as the preposition, taking it as "for which, on account of which" (for which see *GMW* 219–20 (MW *yr*, MnW *er*)); thus "and what a good thing it is . . . on account of which the girl may be touched by you."

    tibi: a te. On *tibi* glossed by *a te,* see above l. 52.

143 hic: ibi. The lemma does not seem to have been intended spatially (Hollis, 59–60), thus "at this point" rather than "here, in this place," but is taken as such by the gloss.

144 puplica. Note the Brittonic-style spelling of internal -/b/- as *p*; for other examples, see above, 156.

145 requires: ut. The gloss makes explicit the colloquial syntax of *facito* (sc. *ut*) *requires* "make sure you ask."

146 quisquis: uel bonus uel malus. The gloss, picking up on the *studiosse* of the preceding line ("as if you were a fan" (Hollis, 60)), provides the extra explanatory detail: "ask her which horse she favours and back that one (sc. no matter whether it is good or bad)."

147 eburnis: dentes r elephantis. There seem to be two glosses here which have been merged; they can be distinguished by ink colour. Originally, the adjective *eburnis* had *r* written over the *n,* perhaps suggesting a reading *eburris* (or at least the potential of confusion between *r* and *n* in the exemplar) or perhaps that a gen. sg. *eburis* was intended (which would not have scanned). Subsequently *dentes eliphantis* "elephant teeth" (referring to ivory) was written either side of the *r.* This example provides clear evidence for two phases of copying at some point in the glossing process, possibly in this version.

148 plaude fauente: roga pro fauenti. I take it that there are two glosses here: *roga* and *pro fauenti*; there is no space between *pro* and *fauenti,* which is perhaps more evidence for copied glosses). The context is showing favour to one's preferred goddess as their statues pass by in parade (Hollis, 60). The imperative *plaude* is glossed *roga* "ask" indicating that the glossator has rightly understood the point of *plaude* as a request to one's favoured goddess. The glossator seems to be understanding *fauente* as a dative agreeing with *ueneri* (even though it seems necessary to take *fauente* with *manu*) and has indicated this with the gloss *pro fauenti* (i.e. "*fauente* is for *fauenti*"); a further possibility is that *fauenti* is a collation gloss.

150 erit: **hac boi** "and it will be" (cf. MW *bo, bwy*). For the analysis, see *EGOW* 159; cf. also *GMW* 137. Note that we should probably understand this as a regular spelling (regular, that is, for this manuscript) as /buɨ/; some, but not all, examples of the spelling *oi* are for /uɨ/, e.g. **loinou, troi, tuscois,** etc. (see above 156) We have here a present subjunctive form being used in a future sense.

151 nullum: **ir ansceth** "the non-existent thing" (cf. MW *ysgeth* "appearance"). *EGOW* 94–95, 8 (following Williams's correct explanation, "Glosau Rhydychen a Chaergrawnt," 113–14). The point of the main text is that, if there is a speck of dust in the girl's lap on her dress, he should brush it off, and if there is no speck of dust, he should brush off a non-existent speck (*nullum*) just to be able to touch her. The Old Welsh form, a negative form of a word meaning "appearance," literally "non-appearance," has been created to express this precise sense of something which has no existence.

152 quelibet: excute (over *que*) erit (over the end of *libet*). The first gloss repeats the verb from the preceding line, while *erit* seems intended to be taken with *quelibet* "whatever it will be." The glossator seems unwilling to take *quelibet* with the rest of the line: "whatever may be the reason suitable for your cause."

153 dimissa: **amlais** "loose, hanging down" (cf. MW *amlaes*). *EGOW* 6. Here the point is that if her dress is hanging too loose (*dimissa*) and dragging on the

ground, then he should gather it up on the off chance that he might get to see her legs.

154 collige ... effer: erege ... erege "gather up ... gather up." Both imperatives in this line are glossed in the same way; the glossator seems to be getting overexcited.

inmunda: ablatiuus. The gloss indicates that the adjective agrees with *humo* and will remind the student that *humus* is feminine.

158 premat: quis. The gloss provides the indefinite subject implied from the previous line.

159 parua: officia. The glossator assumes that the adjective is referring back to *officio* in l. 155, or more generally to the tasks that the lover carries out for his lady in the intervening lines, but here *parua* could simply mean "little things."

161 profuit: multis. Hexter reads *multas* (*Ovid and Medieval Schooling*, 38). The gloss seems to be supplementing the generic sense of *profuit* "it has been of use."

tabellam: fabillam; almost certainly this is an error for *flabillam* "fan" (classical *flabellam*) rather than being a late spelling for *fauillam* (with *b* for /v/). This is supported by the fact that one of the little *officia* which can be performed to keep her comfortable is to fan her with the programme, and this is what the gloss is elucidating. Some of the later manuscripts have the main text reading *flabello,* and it is not impossible that this is a collation gloss (see above 70–72) based on such a reading. The error may have arisen because the scribe had the *puluis* of l. 151 still in mind, even though the narrative has moved on, and thought that *fabilla* for *favilla* 'ash' had been intended.

163–77. Finding a girl at a gladiatorial display. Much of the glossing is devoted to explaining the mythological references.

163 circusque: **ir dirgatmaou** "the circuses." *EGOW* 45, 94–96; for other forms of this same noun, see l. 39 above. The regular plural ending in most Old Welsh glosses is **-ou** (MW *-eu,* MnW *-au*).

164 solicito: ablatiuus. The gloss may have been intended to indicate that the lemma is an adjective agreeing with *foro* and should not be interpreted as a verb.

165 illa: in. The preposition was added to show that *illa ... harena* is ablative, "in that sand/arena." This may be another example of a preposition being used in a Latin gloss to mark case; cf. l. 51 *uento* gl. *cum* and the note there; cf. also 61–62 for general discussion.

166 qui: is. The gloss may be intended to show that the antecedent of *qui* is someone other than Cupid (mentioned in the previous line) which might be the assumption otherwise.

uulnera: amoris. The conceit here is that the spectator is as wounded as the fighters in the arena (Hollis, 62–63, who suggests that Ovid has in mind the brutalizing of the spectators at the arena), but the glossator seems to be anticipating what happens in the next few lines and assuming that the spectator is wounded by love or Cupid; this is not unreasonable in the light of how Ovid elsewhere in this book depicts love striking in unlikely places, such as in a forum full of lawyers. If so, it would have made more sense had *uulnus* (and not *uulnera*) been glossed, and it may be that in copying the gloss the scribe's eye skipped back a word.

167 libellum: **ir caiauc** "the little book (lit. the bound thing)." *EGOW* 20, 94–96. I take it that this is the gladiatorial equivalent of the *tabellam* which may be being used as a fan in l. 161.

170 spectati . . . ipse: promisi . . . qui poscit. The point of the line is that the spectator, pierced by Cupid's arrow, has now become part of the show which is being watched. The gloss, *promisi,* on *spectati* relates partly to the notion of a *munus* as the entertainment promised by the sponsor(s). The gloss, *qui poscit,* on *ipse* is less clear; I take it that, unlike most of the participants in the show, he has been asking for it and got what he asked for.

172 cecropetasque: athinenses. Here we are back into explanatory glossing of poetical terms not familiar to a medieval audience.

173 nimphe: quia. The gloss attempts to provide the simple explanation of the lemma (for *nempe*), but in this instance *nempe* is used adverbially, "of course, certainly."

ab utroque mari: adriaticum et tuscium. Ovid seems to be suggesting something wider than just both sides of Italy, though it is a serviceable gloss for a medieval audience (see Hollis, 64).

175 Our text has lost some of the rhetorical force by beginning the line with *uir* rather than the *quis* of the standard editions; "a man has not found" rather than "who has not found."

inuenit: inter. Has the glossator read *inuenit turba* as going together and assumed a preposition was needed?

quod: id. The gloss, which is in a different ink and maybe a different hand (perhaps scribe E), provides the antecedent pronoun for the relative; on this scribe, see 41 above.

176 heu: **mortru** "so sad!" (cf. MW *mor* "so, how!" and *tru* "sad"). *EGOW* 114–15, 151; for another possible form, see l. 129 above, where **tru** seems to have been overwritten to create **grudou.**

quam multos: **mor liaus** "so many!" (cf. MW *mor* "so, how!" and *lliaws* "numerous"). *EGOW* 114–15, 103.

torsit: laesit. The gloss extracts the sense from the metaphor.

177–228. Finding a girl at a military triumph. This is another very highly glossed section (see 50–51 for statistics). Throughout this next section, the glossator is at pains to distinguish which pronouns refer to Caesar, using either *ces(s)ar* or *octauianus*, and which to the Parthian(s), and to mark out clearly the vocative phrases (especially in ll. 178–79, 203). That said, the glossator displays at the same time a less than perfect control of the history; on Ovid's treatment of this episode in Roman history, and the imagined triumph after the return of Gaius Caesar from victory in Parthia, see Hollis, 65–73.

177 domito: **or dometic** "the tamed (sc. world) (abl.)." *EGOW* 49, 94–96.

178 nunc: tunc. On this use of adverbial *tunc* as a gloss, see l. 87 above for discussion.

179 dabis: sustinebis. The gloss seems to be strengthening the point of *pathe dabis penas* "you, Parthian, will be punished," thus "you will endure"; but for the student this may be a way of understanding the idiom of *poenas dare.* Note that this somewhat unexpected gloss also occurs in O and W, and may belong to a relatively early stratum of glossing (see above, 107–11).

grassi: proprium (sc. nomen). For a medieval readership, perhaps unfamiliar with the details of Crassus and the Parthian disaster, such glosses would have been very helpful.

sepulti: **ha arcibrenou** "O buried ones" (cf. MW *argyvrein*). On the vocative plural, *grassi . . . sepulti,* see Hollis, 73–74; *EGOW* 79 (s.v. *ha⁵*), 10. The regular plural ending in most Old Welsh glosses is **-ou** (MW *-eu*, MnW *-au*). The **ha** is the vocative particle indicating that *sepulti* has been correctly construed as a vocative. The morphology of the noun is curious and looks like a one-off calque: the stem, to which the plural marker **-ou** has been added, seems to be the verbal noun which has been pluralized in order to gloss a plural past participle passive in the Latin; we might more typically have expected a form in *-eticion,* something like **arcibreticion* or **cladeticion.* On the spelling with *-b-* instead of *-m-*, see above, 156.

180 signaque: uocatiuus crassi. The glosses are to be separated. The former marks *signa* (and indeed the whole line) as vocative, while the latter indicates that the standards in question belonged originally to Crassus (Hollis, 74).

non bene passa: **ni cein guodemisauch** "you did not suffer well" (cf. MW *cein* "fine" and *godef* "suffer, endure"). *EGOW* 119–20, 24, 71. Again the vocative is indicated but this time by a finite verb in the second pl. *s*-preterite. The word order seems to be following that of the Latin; however, it is possible that an adverbial *cein* could be used in this position in Old Welsh, between the negative and the finite verb, as can be done in Old Irish, e.g. *caín·rognatha* "well have they been done" (Thurneysen, *Grammar*, 241).

181 A long gloss has been written in a triangular shape in the right margin, the point of which is unclear. It addresses a plural *uobis* and tells them not to be angry with Octavian. Within the main text, the preceding lines provide the two buried *Crassi* and the standards as possible referents, but it is far from clear why these words would be addressed to them. It is possible that it is to be linked to the next long comment on l. 184 which refers to the propensity for Caesars to win triumphs. Could this be making the point that Octavian was only a Caesar by adoption? Another possibility is that the *uobis* who are addressed are the gods who are addressed in l. 183, and this is a reference to Augustus's deification.

182 puero: datiuus. The gloss indicates that this is the dative of the agent with the gerundive *agenda.*

tractat: peius tra "*tra* is worse." For discussion, see 78–79 above, and on the possibility of a spelling *tratat,* see the note below to l. 654. The gloss was read by Bradshaw as *penitra* and thought to be Old Welsh. It was omitted from *EGOW.* Even if it is read as Latin, it seems to be suggesting that the reading is inferior, but no other variants are suggested in the apparatus to the editions.

puer: octauianus. The glossator has misunderstood the point of the references to a boy; this is referring to the young Gaius Caesar.

183 natales: **litolaidou** "feast days." *EGOW* 105. The regular plural ending in most Old Welsh glosses is -**ou** (MW -*eu,* MnW -*au*). Zeuss (followed by Stokes) read *cenitolaidou* imagining that the first stroke was for ɔ (the insular abbreviation for *con-,* but also *cen-* and *cin-* in Old Welsh). Bradshaw read it as *utolaidou,* but, as Williams saw, the first stroke is clearly taller and not the first minim of a *u,* and so it should be read as *litolaidou.* The equivalent gloss in A and S_a is *festales,* and the Old Welsh gloss might be a translation of a Latin gloss such as this.

184 Another long comment has been added in the right margin generalizing the theme developed in these lines of how the Caesars were accustomed to victory from an early age; on the *mos est / erat* theme in commentaries, see above 75–76.

187 tirinthius: Hercolis quia in tirinthio oppido nutritus est. *Quia* is abbreviated and may be an error for *qui.* The gloss provides for a medieval readership the necessary explanation of the connection between Tiryns and Hercules.

188 presit: com. The gloss provides the preverb and may thereby have made the verb more familiar; one characteristic of Latin verse was a tendency to revert to simple verbs when the compound was more common in prose. Cf. also l. 229 (*de*)*possitis.*

in cunis: **mapbrethinnou** "swaddling clothes" (cf. MW *map* "son, baby-," *brethyn* "covering, cloth"). It is not clear whether the space between the **p** and the **b** (slightly wider than is usual between letters within a word but narrower than other spaces between words) is intended to indicate word break or not; I have taken it as a single word since it has to be treated as a compound. *EGOW* 109–10, where a suggestive parallel form in the Juvencus MS is noted; for further discussion of this form, see above 87–88. The regular plural ending in most Old Welsh glosses is -**ou** (MW -*eu,* MnW -*au*).

Ioue dignus: **hin map di iob** "that one is a son of Jupiter" (cf. MW *hyn* "that one," *map* "son"). *EGOW* 85, 109, 43 (s.v. *di⁴*). This is an explanatory gloss: he is worthy of Jupiter (*Ioue dignus*) because he is his son.

189 quantus: interrogatiuus. The glossator thinks that *quantus* is interrogative, as does Green, *Ovid. The Erotic Poems,* 171 (l. 189): "What age were you when . . . ?" But it would be possible to read it as exclamatory. The same gloss is used at l. 277.

191–93 The glossator is having difficulty with *pater* and *puer* in these lines, and thinks that both are Octavian.

191 Auspicis: **o coilou** "auspices (abl.)" (cf. MW *coel*). *EGOW* 122–23, 32. The regular plural ending in most Old Welsh glosses is -**ou** (MW -*eu,* MnW -*au*).

193 sub nomine debes: cessaris octauianus. The glossator is still thinking that the addressee is Octavian and that the *tantum nomen* is that of his adopted father, Julius Caesar.

194 princeps: es. The gloss provides the missing verb; on supplying of parts of the verb "to be," cf. l. 18 above.

de inde: error ia. The gloss is unclear but it is possible that under the influence of the mention of India in l. 190, the glossator, who actually wrote *er ia,* has misunderstood the temporal adverb *deinde* as *de India* "from India" (aided by the use of a tall *i,* thus *de Inde*) and corrected accordingly. If so, this provides evidence that the glossator was thinking as he copied and was accustomed to correcting the text he was copying.

senum: terrarum. Ovid is contrasting Gaius's present leadership of the young with a potential future leadership of the old, though Hollis (77) suggests that *senum* is an oblique reference to the Senate. It is not at all clear then what the glossator is thinking by glossing *senum* with *terrarum;* does he think *senum* is a place name?

195 lessos: romanos. Ovid's intended sense is, "Since you, Gaius, have brothers, avenge these other brothers who have been harmed (the four Parthian hostages who had been supplanted by their half-brother Phraataces—the supposed reason for the planned expedition; on this, see Hollis, 77–78)." The glossator seems to be assuming that *fratres lessos* are the Romans defeated and captured at Carrhae.

197–99 The syntax of these lines is carefully marked out with construe marks and the glosses should be read in conjunction with them; for discussion, see above, 64–67. Note that different marks are used to link *patriaeque* with *tuusque* (l. 197), *inuito* with *parente* (l. 198), and *hostis* (l. 198) with *ille* (l. 199).

198 ab inuito: **or guordiminntius** "the unwilling one (abl.)" (cf. MW *gordy-fynt*). *EGOW* 122–23, 73, and also 47–48 above, where it is suggested that originally there were two glosses, **or guordiminnt** over *ab inuito* and *ius* over *regna,* and a later copyist merged them into one word, influenced perhaps by misreading **diminnt***ius* as the grammatical term *diminutiuus.*

199 ille: feret. The gloss supplies the verb in the correct person from earlier in the line: "You will bear righteous weapons, he (sc. will bear) treacherous arrows."

200 pro signis: frangere bellum ante se. On the Celtic nature of the Latinity of this gloss, see above, 77–78.

201 uincantur . . . uincantur. The manuscript readings vary here as to whether these verbs (or one of them) are subjunctive, future, or present; the standard editions read *uincuntur . . . uincantur.*

causa: occitione parthi. Ovid's text is probably to be understood (allowing for variation in the mood and tense of the verbs) that the Parthians have already been overcome by a just cause and now they are to be defeated in war. While it would appear that *causa* has correctly been understood by the glossator as an ablative, the sense has been misunderstood.

202 latio: **di litau** "Latium/Brittany (dat.)" (cf. MW *Llydaw* "Brittany"). *EGOW* 42–43 (s.v. *di¹*), 104, and also 86 above where the issue of Irish *Letha* is discussed. Another less likely possibility is that the gloss has been misread from *Italia,* though it is clear that a glossator thought it was Welsh as it is prefixed with the preposition marking it as a dative.

204 alter es alter: cessar deus octauianus. It is not immediately clear how the glosses are to be segmented. Taking the line as a whole, *nam deus e nobis alter es alter eris* "for the one of you, descended from us, is a god, the other of you will be," I take it that *cessar* refers to the first *alter* and *deus* can be understood from earlier in the line; if so, then *deus* in the gloss can be understood as going with *octauianus.* Thus, *deus . . . alter* (sc. *cessar*) *es, alter* (sc. *deus octauianus*) *eris.*

205 euinces: ut. The gloss makes explicit the colloquial syntax of *auguror euinces.*

206 magno . . . ore: per . . . carmine. There are two distinct glosses here. The gloss, *per* "by means of," explains the force of the ablative *magno . . . ore,* and *carmine* clarifies the sense of *ore* in this context.

nobis: ablatiuus. The gloss indicates that *nobis* is marking the agent but grammatically it is dative (marking the agent after the gerundive), not ablative. Dative marking of agents with gerunds and gerundives seems to be an issue which the glossators feel obliged to deal with; cf. *tibi* glossed by *a te* (see the note on l. 52).

207 consistes: **gurt paup** "against all" (cf. MW *wrth paub*). *EGOW* 76, 128. The prepositional phrase in the gloss provides an extra development of the sense of *consistes* "you will stand," though it is not clear that *consistes* has the sense of "standing against" as opposed to "standing upright."

ortabere: **nerthiti** "you will strengthen" (cf. MW *nerthu*). The verb is **nerthi** with a second sg. affixed subject pronoun **ti**. *EGOW* 119, where it is suggested that the gloss is to be understood as a second sg. imperative, but the lemma is second sg. future, and there is no reason to think that the gloss is to be interpreted otherwise; in Welsh synthetic present forms can be used to refer to the future as well. Cf. also l. 89 *uenare* gl. **helghati**, the only other verbal form glossed in this text.

208 o: optatiuus. The lemma usually indicates a vocative and so it was necessary to gloss it here as expressing a wish before the subjunctive verb.

209 Tergaque ... romanaque pectora: in fugam ... **(h)incglinau ir leill**. The reading of the Old Welsh is difficult, and what is printed here is tentative. *VVB* has **cetlinau**, which was corrected to **cetdlinau** in Stokes's copy (UCL Stokes's Collection 114.f.10) and Loth's translation corrected to "pursuing the others." Bradshaw reads **hincedlinau irlleill**, with the *d* written subscript (*EGOW* 156 and above 80–81 for a fuller discussion of the difficulties of this gloss); there I take the phrase as the equivalent of a later *yn glynaw yr llaill* "following the others" (i.e. the Romans pursuing the Parthians). The glosses on this line contrast the backs of the Parthians turned in flight with the chests of the Romans in pursuit of the Parthians.

211 quid: parthe. The gloss brings forward from later in the line the vocative which is repeated relentlessly over the next few lines.

uicto: **budicaul** "victorious" (cf. MW *budugaul*). *EGOW* 20. The gloss, which must mean "victorious," seems to misconstrue the lemma; the context—*quid uicto, Parthe, relinques?* "What is left for you in defeat?" (Green, *Ovid. The Erotic Poems*, 172)—clearly suggests that *uicto* must be interpreted as "defeated," not "victorious." Cf. also l. 302 *uictus* gl. **guoguith**.

213 pulcherrime: octauiane. The gloss ensures that the student is clear that this vocative does not refer to the Parthians, unlike most of the vocatives in preceding lines.

rerum: hominum. The gloss seems to be a correction of the sense: "most beautiful of men" rather than "most beautiful of things."

214 aureus: octa*uianus*; this seems to have been deleted and partially overwritten by **teg guis** "leadership." Traces of what looks like the standard *octauianus* gloss are still visible but partially concealed by the **teg** of **teg guis**. The Old Welsh gloss has been difficult to interpret (*EGOW* 145). The lemma *aureus* here means something like "dressed in gold," and *VVB*, 219, interpreted it as *teg* "fine" and *guis*, the Welsh equivalent of Irish *fís* "vision,

sight," thus a comment on the lemma, "a fine sight"; however, Welsh *gwys* has a different sense (*GPC*, s.v.). Zeuss (*Grammatica Celtica*, 1088 (1st ed.), 1058 (2nd ed.)) followed by Williams "Glosau Rhydychen," 8; and "Glosau Rhydychen a Chaergrawnt," 114) took *guis* as an error for *guisc* "clothing," thus "finely dressed"; Williams went on to suggest that *teg* was also an error or an abbreviation for *tegirn*, thus "royally dressed." There is still a problem that we would expect *tec* in Old Welsh, unless the final -**g** was anticipating the initial **g**- of the next word. Support for this interpretation may come from a source unknown to Williams; in W the parallel gloss is *aureis vestibus indutus* "dressed in golden clothes" (the discussion above, 116). Another possibility takes into account that *octauianus* was deleted and that the Old Welsh gloss might be a replacement: **teg guis** has always been printed as two words, but in fact there is a descender between the two words, and so we could take it as one word: **tegguis** "leadership," corresponding to Middle Welsh *tywys*, which would be an appropriate gloss in the context. In fact, it may even be, following Williams's train of thought, an abbreviation for **tegguisauc** "leader." The **gg** can be explained by assuming that the scribe wrote the first **g** and then realized that he could not fit in the whole word and so recopied the **g** after the descender. One possible objection is that **e** for /ə/ is not the default spelling in Old Welsh, though it is not uncommon: e.g. *remedaut* (Juv. 9 (5.1); cf. Middle Welsh *ryfeddaut*); *cellell* (*De raris fabulis* 42b; cf. MW *cyllell*); *cemecid* (*De raris fabulis* 42b; MW *cyfegyd*), etc.

215 ante: antea. The sense of *ante* in the text is adverbial and the gloss may be intended to indicate that, not least to prevent a reading of *ante duces* "in front of the leaders."

    catenis: ablatiuus. The gloss is presumably intended to clarify the ambiguous case form (cf. l. 231 below).

216 ne possint: non possunt. The gloss reduces the subordinate clause to a simple main-clause assertion.

219 aliqua ex illis: puella . . . puellis. Attention shifts finally back from the triumph to the spectators, and so we are reminded that, as frequently but not always in this text, feminine pronouns refer to girls.

221 nec: referes. The gloss supplies the verb for the second part of the line since *responde* is not quite to the point: "Answer everything and (sc. you will not keep talking) just to answer her questions."

222 ut bene nota: conscius. The gloss clarifies the sense of the phrase: "Reply as if you know everything (sc. even if you don't)."

223 hic: dic ita. I take the gloss as "speak as follows." Hexter, *Ovid and Medieval Schooling*, 36, n. 64, takes it as the imperative *dicita* (to *dicitare*) "keep on

saying"; the *dic* and *ita* are separated by the descender of *quae,* and so they could be considered to be joined. However, at l. 225 below in a similar context *hos* is glossed *dic tu ita,* thus justifying *dic ita* here.

eufrates: Eufratis fluuius mesopotamiae . . . (in left margin). On the source of this gloss in Isidore, see above, 74.

harundine: o **corsenn** "reed (abl.)" (MW *cors, corsen*). *EGOW* 122–23, 35. The gloss is the singulative form (referring to a single item of something which normally occurs in groups or masses) of *cors* "reeds."

frontem: per "along." On the use of *per* to mark non-object accusatives, see the discussion above, 62; cf. also ll. 647–48.

224 tigris: forma bestiae ; tigris de nomine . . . The second long gloss is in the right margin. On the source of this gloss in Isidore, see above, 74. Note that Lindsay, *Early Welsh Script,* 56, mistakenly took the last clause *quae dicitur tigris* as a continuation of the long gloss on *daneia* (l. 225). To judge by its position, slightly set out into the right margin, its addition may postdate the gloss on *daneia.*

225 hos: dic tu ita. See the note on l. 223.

daneia: ciuitas quae a danio fabricate. The gloss provides the necessary information for a medieval reader. Lindsay, *Early Welsh Script,* 56, reads *damo* (for *danio*), but it is probably to be understood as *danio* to make the etymology work.

226 achemenis: caldaicis. Again the gloss provides the necessary kind of information for a medieval reader.

227 duces: dicas. At first sight the gloss looks like it may be a collation gloss or a correction, but in fact it brings forwards the verb which is to be understood from later in the line.

228 apta: confirma. The final syllable of *apta* is short and it is therefore the adjective; the sense is "if you know their names, say so; if you don't, then say something suitable (*apta*)." But the glossator clearly thought it was the imperative, thus reading it as "if you don't know their names, adapt, make it up"; *confirma* clarifies that, and gives some added sense "and sound as if you know what you are talking about."

229–52 Finding a girl at a party and in other crowded places: at this point Ovid shifts scene, and so the nature of the glossing changes; now we are back to marking feminine pronouns as *puella(e),* and indicating when the subject of a third sg. verb is a girl or Cupid.

229 possitis: de. The gloss provides the preverb to produce the more familiar compound verb. Cf. also l. 188 (*com*)*presit.*

conuiuiuia. Note that the scribe has generated an extra syllable in our manuscript by overdoing the minims.

230 quod: ut. The gloss seems to indicate more than that a subordinate clause follows, perhaps that the following verb is subjunctive: "there is something more than wine which you may seek there."

231–36. On these lines, which both glossator and commentators have found difficult, see Hollis, 83–84.

231 possitis teneris: hominibus habitantibus. The context is unclear but it has been interpreted as Cupid and Bacchus involved in a wrestling match, but it remains completely unclear as to how that might generate a gloss about men living somewhere unless one of the words has been misread as a place name.

 lacertis: ablatiuus. The gloss is presumably intended to clarify the ambiguous case form (cf. l. 215 above).

233 cum: tunc. Here *tunc* seems not to be reminding us of a different time period (cf. above l. 87), but simply the precise time when Cupid is grounded—that is, when his feathers are soaked in wine.

 cupidinis: cupid "Cupid." The gloss seems to be lacking a suspension mark on the end; cf. l. 10.

234 grauis: **guobri** "serious" (MW *gofri*). For the comparative of this adjective, see l. 65 above where **guobriach** glosses *sapientior*. In the context the sense of *grauis* is "heavy" rather than "serious."

 illa: puella. The reading *illa* is an error in this text for the correct reading *ille*, but the gloss clearly refers to *illa*, and so must have been added to this text or its exemplar; in other words, it is a recent gloss to a text with this reading.

 cepto . . . loco: initium conuiuii. Although the gloss is over *loco*, it seems to refer to the phrase with *initium* reflecting *cepto* (for *coepto*).

235 excutit: tinguit. The gloss seems to have misunderstood where we are in the narrative; literally, "Cupid shakes off his damp feathers," the feathers having been soaked in wine. This has been taken to mean not just that Cupid shook his damp feathers like a bird but that he flew away (Hollis, 85). The gloss "dipped" seems either to have misunderstood or it is possible that the gloss has been misplaced, perhaps from *sparsere* (l. 232).

 udas: alas. The gloss supplies a noun for *udas* even though *pennas* occurs earlier in the line.

237 caloribus: ablatiuus. The gloss is presumably intended to clarify the ambiguous case form, but here it is mistaken as *aptus* is construed with the dative.

238 Cura: eo quod urit cor "because it burns the heart," an etymological gloss on *cura*; see 74.

 mero: habundante uino. Although the gloss is over *mero*, it may have been intended to gloss *multo . . . mero*. It also seems to take *mero* as a general word for wine and not for undiluted wine which is the point of the oxymoron in the last words of the line, *diluitur mero* (Hollis, 86).

239 pauper: sine muliere. In the context, *pauper* literally means "poor, impoverished," and the point is that the poor man will not allow himself to be pushed around (Hollis, 86), but the gloss takes *pauper* to mean "poor" in the sense of not having a girl.

240 color: qui antea fuit. The gloss reads *an* with a macron over the *n* which in the context is probably to be expanded as *antea*. The line refers to the previous concerns and expressions which are removed by the consumption of wine. The gloss simply explains this.

curae: abiunt. The gloss repeats the verb from the end of the line in the correct number to agree with the multiple subjects.

rugaque: **criched** "wrinkledness" (not otherwise attested in Welsh until the eighteenth century). *EGOW* 36, where it is suggested that **criched** is an adjective, but it is the abstract noun "wrinkledness" glossing a noun; in fact the sense is such that it makes better sense for it to be a gloss on *ruga ... frontis.*

241 mentes aeuo rassissima nostro: quia sagaciores sunt quam quomodo fuerunt "because they are wiser than how they were." The gloss is rather difficult to decipher as it is broken up by the descenders from the line above. It is best understood in the context of the whole couplet: *tunc aperit mentes aeuo rassissima [recte rarissima] nostros simplicitas artes excutiente deo* "then (i.e. after the consumption of wine) a simplicity, very rare in our age, opens out minds as the god dissipates guile," which, the gloss adds, makes our minds wiser as they used to be in simpler times.

rassissima. The scribe looks as if he has confused his *r*'s and *s*'s, easily done in any version of insular script, and skipped to the *ss* of the superlative suffix and failed to write the second *r* of the stem.

243 puellae: mos est mulieribus ... Here we see Ovid depicting the girls as for once taking advantage of the situation. The gloss frames this as a habitual activity; for discussion of the *mos est / erat ...* trope, see above, 75–76.

244 et uenus ... ignis: uoluptas ... amor. The glosses seem to be intended to clarify the abstract and metaphorical language of the text.

246 iudicio: datiuus. The gloss indicates the case which follows from *nocent.*

merumque: et nouum uinum. The explanatory gloss explains the lemma, including *et* for *que.* For the glossator's understanding of *merum,* cf. l. 238.

247 luce: diem. Lindsay, *Early Welsh Script,* 56, reads *die* which matches the case of *luce,* but does not account for the suspension mark.

248 ueneri: datiuus. The gloss presumably indicates the case in order to distinguish it from other possible forms in *-eri, -ere,* etc.

utranque: iuno et minerua. A medieval audience may well have needed some help with the narrative of the beauty contest on the slopes of Mount Ida.

249 Nocte: quando fuerint. The gloss was initially copied in the wrong place and was repeated in its full form on the next line (see below). This kind of error suggests that the scribe may have been copying a section of main text and then going back and adding glosses; it would be difficult to make this kind of error if glosses were being copied *pari passu* (see 40–41 above for discussion).

mendae: **ir anamou** "blemishes" (cf. MW *anafau*). *EGOW* 7. The regular plural ending in most Old Welsh glosses is -**ou** (MW -*eu*, MnW -*au*).

ignoscitur: ignoratur. The gloss is either an attempt to explain *ignoscitur* as a negative of *gnoscitur* or a suggested alternative reading; *ignoratur* is not noted as a variant in the standard editions, but it is found in B glossed by *ignoscitur*.

250 horaque formossam quamlibet illa facit: above the whole line *quando fuerint conuiuium et ignis unum colorem habent mulieres omnes* "when there is a feast and a fire, all women have the same complexion." Hexter (*Ovid and Medieval Schooling*, 41, n. 83) reads *fuerunt*. Although the gloss does not have the *mos est* of other glosses, it has the air of a generalization as it summarizes the point of these lines.

251 consule: prouide. The same gloss is repeated in the next line. I take it that the gloss was intended in part to ensure that *consule* was not read as an ablative.

gemmis. Lindsay, *Early Welsh Script*, 56, reads *geminis*, but, while the final *i* is written as *í*, there is no accent on the middle minim, and so it should probably be read as *gemmis*.

detincta murice lana: **ir tinetic o ceenn gulan** "the wool dyed (?) with *murex*" (cf. MW *ken(n)*, *gwlan*). The gloss is discussed here as a phrase (for ease of treatment), although the order of the Old Welsh glosses was clearly intended to match the Latin. For discussion of the individual glosses, see *EGOW* 94–96, 148, 122–23, and 23–24 (where the lemma is wrongly printed as *mirice*), 70; on -*etic* as an adjectival and participial marker, see the note above on l. 73. The lemma is printed as in the manuscript with *detincta* rather than the correct *de tincta* of the editions (the text runs (ll. 251–52) *consule de . . . de tincta . . . consule de . . .* "think about . . ."); *detincta . . . lana* is ablative singular, but is not glossed with **o** in the Old Welsh, and it may be that the Welsh glossator read it as *detincta . . . lana* "dyed wool" using the article to show simply that it was definite. Note again that there is no evidence that the glossator was using the metre to help decide on the case; for discussion, see 84–85 above. On the other hand, *murice* is glossed with the preposition **o** as ablative (but see below); here, though, the interesting issue is why **ceenn** (lit.) "skin, rind" was used to gloss *murice*. We have seen elsewhere that there is evidence for the glossators' familiarity with Isidore, and this may be another example: Isidore, *Etymologiae* (ed. Lindsay), XII.vi.50 talks of *haec tinctura ex testae humore elicitur* "this dye is drawn out from the liquid of the shell" (trans. Barney et al., *Etymologies*, 262). While **gulan** is a straightforward gloss on *lana*, **tinetic** is less obvious. *EGOW* 148 offers no explanation except for a cryptic "Cf. Lat. tingo 'dye, colour'" which suggests that the stem was thought to be based on Latin *tingo* (in fact the Isidorean quotation above uses the noun from this verb). One possibility is that **tinetic** is a participle based on *tynnu* "pull, extract" (thus later Welsh *tynnedig*), and that it is to be understood as "extracted (from)"; this might make better sense if we understand the Latin as the glossator did, namely as *detincta* "dyed from" which might be easily interpreted as "extracted from" with the following *murice*. If so, we need not take the **o** as marking the ablative but as the literal sense of the preposition; thus, "the wool (sc. the colour of which is) extracted from the shell."

252 consule: prouide. Cf. l. 251 above.

255 baias: ciuitas in italia. The gloss provides just enough information for a medieval audience to keep track of what is going on.

pretexta: concaua. The relationship between lemma and gloss is unclear. The lemma means something like "decorated" but has been glossed by an adjective "curved" which makes sense as a description of *litora* but is not a perfect rendering of *pretexta*; could the gloss originally have been on *litora* but in error was copied over *pretexta*? The reading of our text is not very easy with the repetition of case forms of Baiae; for discussion of alternatives, see Hollis, 88.

258 haec: aqua. The gloss picks up the referent from l. 256 and may have been intended to mark *haec* as not agreeing with either *fama* or a putative *puella*, which seems to be the default reading of any fem. sg. pronoun.

259 ecce: est. On supplying of parts of the verb "to be," cf. l. 18 above.

satirbane: ciuitas. For discussion of this gloss, see above, 46, 113n42. This reading of the lemma is unique to this manuscript; elsewhere, the text is *suburbanae* for which the gloss would be appropriate.

memorale. Note that the standard reading is *nemorale*.

260 partaque: parata. It is not clear whether this is a collation reading or an explanation (Hexter, *Ovid and Medieval Schooling*, 39, n. 76).

manu: multitudine. The gloss provides the less familiar sense of *manus* as "band, group," but one which reveals no understanding of the details of the priesthood in the grove of Diana, which involves a single priest, not a crowd (cf. Hollis, 88–89).

262 uulnera: amoris. Although many of the wounds in this poem are inflicted by love, this is not one of them; the virgin Diana notoriously loathed love and desire and so had inflicted, and will inflict, wounds on the visitors.

263–88. How to catch the girl once she has been found.

263 unde: ut. The gloss probably marks *unde* out as a subordinating conjunction; cf. l. 33 above.

264 thalea: diana. The glossator has assumed that Thalea is another name for Diana, but the name Thalea is rather confusingly associated with one of the Muses, one of the Graces, a Nereid, and a nymph.

265 que placuit: mulier tibi "woman," "to you." The *que* (for classical *quae*) is an insertion and was probably omitted in error. The glosses should be read separately; *mulier* provides a gloss on *quae,* thus providing an explicit antecedent for *placuit,* and then *tibi* is repeated from earlier in the line.

266 molior: memoro. The gloss does not really fit the lemma, but it may perhaps have been intended to gloss *dicere . . . molior* "I shall endeavour to say."

267 quisquis: aduerte. The gloss, which has been overwritten, repeats the imperative from later in the line but makes it singular to agree with *quisquis.*

ubique: es. On supplying of parts of the verb "to be," cf. l. 18 above. The first part of this line is glossed by second sg. verbs: "whoever you (sg.) are, wherever you (sg.) are." The latter part turns to the plural.

269 menti: mulieris. The gloss is confusing; the sense of the line is "first let confidence come to your mind." Thus it is the man's mind, not the woman's.

270 capias: ut. The gloss marks *capias* as a verb in a subordinate clause. For *ut* in this usage, cf. l. 33.

plagas: retia. The gloss provides the more familiar word for "nets, snares."

271 uere: **o guiannuin** "spring (abl.)" (MW *gwaeanwyn,* MnW *gwanwyn*). *EGOW* 67–68.

cicadae: **cecinet bronnbreithet** "speckle-breasted woodpeckers" or "woodpeckers (and) thrushes" (cf. MW *cegin, bronnureith*). *EGOW* 23, 19. For **cecinet,** Bradshaw read *aetinet.* For consideration of how *cicadae* comes to be glossed with the name(s) of birds, see above, 82. It is likely that the choice of **cecinet** to gloss *cicadae* was triggered by the parallel of *cic-*: **cec-**. What remains unclear is whether we are dealing with a single bird name with an adjective, or the names of two birds. *Cegin* (pl. *cegined*) can mean "woodpecker" (or "jay") and *bronfraith* "(mistle) thrush." However, the latter is morphologically an adjective "speckle breasted" (*bronn* "breast" + *breith* "speckled," substantivized as the noun for "thrush," and it seems more likely that the gloss is referring to one species, thus matching the lemma; we might otherwise have expected an *and* or *or* between the two words. The issue, then, is whether to take the -**et** ending on the latter as a spelling of the suffix *-eit* (MnW *-aid*), e.g. *eureit* "golden, gilded," or as a copying of the plural ending of the preceding noun. Given that the preceding word has -/ei/- spelt as such, it would be strange for the spelling to change in the final syllable of the next word. It is therefore more likely that it is a copy of the plural ending of the noun.

274 quam: ut. Here the gloss in unclear but may be pointing out that the relative clause, *quam poteris credere nolle,* is a subordinate clause.

275 uenus: uolu*ntas.* The gloss is clearly *uoluntas* "will," but it is tempting to think that this is an error earlier in the transmission for *uoluptas* "desire," perhaps through a misreading of a suspension mark.

grata: est. On supplying of parts of the verb "to be," cf. l. 18 above.

276 disimulat texius: celat secretius. Both glosses use more familiar and simpler vocabulary.

277 conuenient: interogatiuus. For the use of this gloss to mark a question, see l. 189 above.

maribus: nobis unus. The first word of the gloss is clear and identifies "husbands" with "us," but the point of *unus* in the nominative is less clear, unless it was added as an afterthought, "every single one of us," but one would have expected it to be in the dative.

ne quam: utr̄. The expansion of the gloss is uncertain; there is clearly a horizontal stroke over the *r.* One possible explanation is that the gloss is partial and intended to convert *nequam* into something like *neutrum*(*que*) or *ne utrumque.* The text is difficult at this point. The conventional understanding is that *ne quam nos ante rogemus* means something like "(were it agreed among men) that we (i.e. men) do not ask any (sc. girl) first" (i.e. "should we males agree never to take the initiative" (Hollis, 91)). But it is possible that the glossator understood it to mean that "we (i.e. men and women) do not ask each other first" and glossed accordingly.

278 cogat: ut. The gloss may be intended to indicate that *cogat* is subjunctive. For discussion of this line and its glossing, see above, 62. Relative to the standard editions (. . . *uicta rogantis aget* (Kenney)), the second half of this line is very corrupt.

279 femina: uacca. The gloss is to be read together with the gloss on *faemina* in the next line. In this line it is glossed *uacca* "cow" but *aequa* (for classical *equa*) "mare" in the next.

280 faemina: aequa. See the previous line for discussion.

281 nobis: uiris. The gloss clarifies the extent of the first-plural reference; it is restricted to men as opposed to women.

furiosa: feminis. The gloss should be taken in contrast to *nobis* (see previous gloss).

libido: libido uirorum habet finem libido mulierum non habet finem. This long gloss in the right margin can be taken as summarizing the whole line. For discussion of these longer moralistic comments, see above, 75–76.

283 biblia: proprium mulieris. The gloss identifies the proper name; as does the same gloss at l. 285.

285 murra: proprium mulieris. The gloss identifies the proper name; cf. l. 283.

289–326. Pasiphaë and the bull (and other mythological examples): the glossator's preoccupation in this passage is to gloss the pronouns to distinguish her (sometimes glossed with a case form of *passiua*) from the rival cow (often glossed with a case form of *uacca*) on the one hand and Minos from the bull (usually glossed with a case form of *taurus*) on the other; for discussion, see above, 72–73. Most of these simple identificatory glosses are not discussed individually below.

292 fuit: sordida. The gloss is presumably intended to modify *labes*. The bull is completely milk-white except for one *labes* "spot" between his horns which looks like a speck of dirt, hence *sordida*.

caetera: membra. The gloss clarifies the rather vague *caetera* "the rest of him."

293 gnosiades cidonaeque: cretenses nomen est cretae. There are probably two separate glosses here: *cretenses* on *gnosiades,* and *nomen est cretae* on *cidonaeque.* The poetical terminology referring to Crete and Cretans would have required clarification for a medieval reader.

295 passiue: nomen mulieris. Pasiphaë's name is spelt variously in this text and would have needed marking.

297 nota: iura. The lemma seems naturally to be neuter plural, "familiar things," but the gloss suggests a more precise sense perhaps not so much what is "known" about Crete but what the law is in Crete.

quae: creta. The gloss provides the antecedent from the next line.

299 tauro: datiuus. The gloss indicates that she picked the leaves and grass *for* the bull.

301 moratur: sentit. The gloss clarifies the sense of *nec itura* (*ituram* codd.) *cura moratur | coniugis* "and, as she sets off, concern for her husband does not slow her down." The gloss only seems to make sense if *cura* is being read as *curam* which would be easy with the following *moratur,* i.e. "as she sets off, she feels concern for her husband."

302 uictus: **guoguith** "defeated" (not otherwise attested in Welsh; the translation is derived from its context). See *EGOW* 71 where it is interpreted as connected to the stem of the Welsh verbal noun *amwyn* (cf. *EGOW* 5, s.v. *amgucant*).

303 quid: **padiu** "for what reason is?" *EGOW* 127. Hexter reads *padui*; the fact that he is quoting it at all suggests he thinks it is Latin. It is Old Welsh; see the discussion above, 117–18, where it is argued that it seems to represent an attempt to render *prodest* in Welsh and, as such, it constitutes key evidence for the translation of Latin glosses into Old Welsh. The gloss has to be understood in the context of l. 305 *quid . . .* (see below).

305 quid: **pui** "what" (cf. MW *pwy*). *EGOW* 134. Were it not for the fact that the *quid* in l. 303 needed to be glossed in order to distinguish its meaning from this *quid,* it is unlikely that there would be a gloss on this word. It provides an excellent example of why it is important to read glosses in their context.

307 iuuencam: aspiciebant autem formam suam in speculo. The comment in the right margin is probably to be understood as a general statement relating to the whole line. Note that the first half of the line is corrupt in our text; the standard editions read *crede tamen speculo* rather than *credita mens speculo* (for discussion, see above 44–45).

309 SIue: si. The gloss provides the simple version of the conjunction.

adulter: **guas marchauc** "adulterer" (lit. "servant of a horseman, squire") (MW *gwas marchauc*). *EGOW* 65.

The long gloss in the right margin, *melior erat etecum . . .* , is positioned to refer to this line but in fact relates to the previous line (l. 308). I take *etecum* to be a scribal compression of *et tecum*: "it would be better for you too that . . ."

placet: tibi. The gloss reminds the reader that this line is being addressed to Pasiphae.

310 uiro: ablatiuus. The gloss attempts to clarify the sense of Ovid's line: "if you prefer to deceive your husband (*uirum*), at least deceive him with a man (*uiro* (abl.))!"

311 nemus: ire. The gloss suggests that the glossator may have read *fertur* not as "she takes herself off" but rather as "it is said," and so thinks an infinitive is required, hence *ire.*

saltus: in. The gloss repeats the preposition for the preceding phrase perhaps to show that *saltus* is accusative.

312 bacha: dea. The glossator seems to think that *bacha* is a goddess, but instead it refers to a follower of Bacchus, a maenad.

313 a: interiectio doloris. The gloss is presumably intended to distinguish this *a* from the preposition.

spectauit: aspicit. The verb seems to be picked up from l. 315 below.

315 aspicit . . . ipsum: passiue . . . taurum. This line provides a good example of the clarification of the referents which is ubiquitous in this passage.

316 decere: debere. The gloss looks like it may be suggesting an alternative reading, but it is not attested elsewhere. Note that the reading of our text

is corrupt: for *se stulta decere putet* of the editions it reads *est ulta decere putet,* perhaps influenced by the vengeance depicted in the following lines.

317 iamdudum: dicto citius "more quickly than said." The gloss clarifies the sense of the lemma which can also mean "long ago."

318 commentaque: machinata. The gloss provides an explanation of the rarer word in the lemma.

320 pelicis: meretrix. An explanatory gloss as in l. 318. Note however, as can sometimes be the case with explanatory glosses, they do not match in case.

exta: **ir onguedou** "the entrails" (not otherwise attested in Welsh; the meaning is derived from the context). *EGOW* 94–96, 125. The regular plural ending in most Old Welsh glosses is **-ou** (MW *-eu,* MnW *-au*).

321 pelicibus: obidius dicit (left margin). Note the use of *-b-* to spell intervocalic *-/v/-,* for which see above, 156.

323 modo: aliquando. The gloss may well be intended to gloss the double . . . *modo . . . modo . . . " . . .* sometimes . . . sometimes. . . ."

324 boe: ab ioue. The phrase *altera uicta boe* "the other overcome by an ox" refers to Europa in the preceding line, and the gloss explains *boe* (note that the reading in the editions is *altera uecta boue*) However, it may have triggered an idea in a glossator's mind that the text might be read as *ab ioue.*

325 deceptus: **malgueretic** "deceived" (not otherwise attested in Welsh; the meaning is derived from the lemma). *EGOW* 109; on *-etic* as an adjectival and participial marker, see the note above on l. 73.

326 partu . . . auctor: minotauri . . . dedalus. The glossator here shows impressive control of the myth—Daedalus made a model cow for Pasiphae with which to fool the bull and the outcome was the Minotaur.

proditus: **diguolouichetic** "revealed" (cf. MW *llewychu*). *EGOW* 46; on *-etic* as an adjectival and participial marker, see the note above on l. 73. Falileyev's translation, "bright, shining," cannot be right. Lambert, "Gloses en vieux-breton: 6–9." 348, proposes that the form represents a confusion between *diguolo-* "uncover" and *louich-* "shine"; however, while confusion is possible, it could be between the latter and an Old Welsh *guolou* "light." It is likely therefore that it is a compound **di-guo-louich-etic** "brought out into the light," i.e. "revealed."

327 cressa: **ir cretuis** "the Cretan (sc. woman)." The form is omitted from *EGOW* but see 94–96 for the article *ir.* It is a derivative in *-uis* based on a Welsh form of the word for "Crete"; for the formation, cf. l. 111 **tuscois.**

328 et: si. The gloss suggests that *si* in the preceding line needs to be repeated here.

329 curruque: non. The gloss repeats the negative from the beginning of the line to show that the second clause is also negative.

330 auroram: ad. The gloss provides the preposition to clarify the poetical use of a simple accusative of motion towards.

331 filia: scilla filia nisi. The gloss provides the detail which may have been necessary for a medieval audience. Hollis, 97, notes that Ovid has conflated two Scyllas here: the daughter of Nisus and the Scylla who became a sea monster. The gloss is trying to offer clarification.

niso: priuatiuus. The gloss relates to the (*dativus*) *privativus*, the dative of disadvantage. For this gloss, cf. also l. 85. On "privative" datives, see above 61.

furata: est. On supplying of parts of the verb "to be," cf. l. 18 above.

332 pube: **o caitoir** "pubic hair (abl.)" (MW *cedor*). *EGOW* 122–23, 20. While **o** could be marking the form as ablative (which the lemma is), the sense of the Latin is actually "from her groin" and so the preposition could be taken literally.

ingunibus: **hac or achmonou** "and the groins (abl.)" (MW *achfen*). *EGOW* 122–23, 3. Bradshaw mistakenly transcribed the lemma as *inguinibus*. The **o** could be treated literally as "from"; cf. the note on the previous line. The regular plural ending in most Old Welsh glosses is -**ou** (MW -*eu*, MnW -*au*).

333 terra: troiae. The gloss would remind a medieval reader that we are talking about Agamemnon fighting at Troy here.

334 uictima: **aperth** "offering" (MW *aberth*). Cf. ll. 69 and 74 where the plural **aperthou** occurs, the former with a suspension mark for *er* and the latter, **apthou**, where it has been omitted.

dira: **dur** "harsh" (MW *dur*). *EGOW* 51, and Parina, "On the Semantics of Adjectives." It has always been assumed that this is an Old Welsh gloss, but it is possible that it is a partial collation gloss carried over from a manuscript which read *dura* rather than *dira*.

335 defleta: .i. deflenda est. The purpose of the gloss is not clear; the text means "by whom has the burning of Creusa not been wept over?" Since the gloss scans it may be a collation gloss. Alternatively, it may be a gloss for an audience contemporary with the glossator; i.e. this is what you should weep over.

creuse: didonis quae se ipsam uiuam incendit. The glossator has confused Creusa, wife of Jason who was burnt to death by Medea, with Dido, possibly through confusing this Creusa with Aeneas's first wife who, according to the *Aeneid*, died at Troy.

336 nece: ablatiuus. Another example of case forms ending in -*i* or -*e* being explained.

natorum: filiorum. The poetical use of *natus* "son" is explained by the basic term.

sanguinolenta: media pro amore iasonis. The gloss fills in the detail of why Medea killed her sons.

337 phenix: .i. filius ageneroi . . . In theory, the gloss provides the mythological background necessary for a medieval audience, but the text and narrative is so muddled that only confusion would have resulted. First, the text of O is corrupt in reading *aginorides* earlier in the line (against *amyntorides* in the editions). The error probably arose from confusing two different Phoenixes, namely the son of Agenor, the founder of Phoenicia, with Phoenix, son of Amyntor (the one who should be mentioned here) who was blinded by his father. The glossator therefore has been set off on the wrong track from the start. There may also be a miscopying of *ageneroi* for an abbreviated *agenorides* as in the text, but that then produces a confused narrative of why he was blinded. It involves him upsetting the *consilia deorum,* when the whole point of these *exempla* is that they involve men being destroyed by the rage of women. Matters are not helped in l. 339 where *phinetus* [*recte phineus*] is glossed *idem et phenix,* thus introducing yet another Phoenix into the plot line. The Phineus in question seems to have been another son of Agenor, thus compounding the confusion. In fact, the gloss on l. 337 may be better applied to the Phineus of l. 339 except that in our text he is Phinetus. Hollis, 98–99, provides a helpful discussion of the main text.

338 aequi: uocatiuus. The gloss marks the lemma out as vocative and as the addressees of the verb *diripuistis*; presumably this was to guard against it being interpreted as a gen. sg. or a nom. pl.

339 phinetus: idem et phenix. The lemma is corrupt; other manuscripts have the vocative *Phineu.* But the glossator has confused this story with the one mentioned above in l. 337; see the discussion above.

341 ista: miracula. The gloss refers to the preceding myths, and the sense is closer to "amazing things" than to "miracles" (*DMLBS,* s.v. *miraculum*).

342 acrior: ut mulierum cupiditas. For this sentiment, cf. also the glosses on ll. 243 and 281, and for the moralistic tone, also 75–76.

nostra: quam "than." The gloss has a double purpose: it both supplies the *quam* "than" which follows from *acrior* and also indicates by implication that *nostra* is ablative.

345 dant: responsa. The gloss supplies an object for the lemma, though the glossator's interpretation is unclear: it is possible that *dant responsa* is thought to mean "they say yes" in contrast to the following *negant.*

346 fallaris: licet. The gloss provides the clearer conjunction than the *ut* of the text.

350 uicinum: proximum. The gloss seems slightly to miss the point that it is the herd of one's neighbour (*uicinus*) which has fuller udders (i.e. "the grass is always greener . . ." (Hollis, 99)).

351–98 This section discusses the ways in which a lover can make use of the mistress's maid to get closer to her. The glossing is preoccupied with distinguishing the referents of the feminine singular pronouns, either the *ancella* or the *domina,* or in other instances concerned with showing that a fem. sg. pronoun or adjective does not refer to either but to something or someone else.

352 molliat: ut agnoscat. I take the gloss to refer to the maid being aware of the lover's intentions.

354 ne ue: sit. The lemma is written in gloss-sized text and looks like the correction of an error. The gloss provides the verb; on supplying of parts of the verb "to be," cf. l. 18 above.

356 ex facili: opere. The lemma is adverbial in sense "easily" but the glossator assumes that it is a prepositional phrase.

  feres: inuenies uel adepiscaris. The gloss provides more semantic precision for the verb.

357 quod: sicut. The gloss seems to be suggesting that the explanatory force of the *quod* be adjusted towards a comparative "just like."

359 rerum: hominum. The gloss seems to be assuming that the mistress is not unreasonably "very happy with men," but the sense is probably more general (see Hollis, 101).

363 ilios: troianos. The poetical term relating to Troy is glossed by the more familiar term; cf. l. 54 where *frigio* is glossed by *troiano.* The gloss seems to be taking *ilios* as accusative plural when it is in fact nominative singular with a short *o*. This is another case where the glossator is deaf to the metrical patterns; for discussion, see above 84–85. An anonymous reviewer wonders whether the gloss *troia* on l. 364 was originally glossing *ilios.*

364 laeta: troia. The gloss is important in ensuring that the reader does not think that the lemma refers to the mistress or maidservant, but cf. the preceding note for the possibility that *troia* is a misplaced gloss.

365 pelice: meretrice. The same gloss is used at l. 320 above.

  lessa: concubina. The gloss here seems confused; *lessa* refers to the mistress.

367 pectentem: **ha crip** "with a comb" (MW *crib*). EGOW 79, where it is interpreted as a verb in a relative clause "who combs"; cf. also Rodway, *Dating Medieval Welsh Literature,* 94, n. 299. Falileyev's observation that "most interpretations of this entry consider it as a gloss over *cum pectine*" is confused: there is no *cum pectine* in the text; this is Zeuss's Latin rendering of the Old Welsh gloss (*Grammatica Celtica,* 1089 (1st ed.), 1059 (2nd ed.)). Almost certainly the gloss means "with a comb" (as Zeuss had noted) but is a supplementary gloss on *pectentem . . . capillos* "combing her hair (sc. "with a comb")."

368 uelo remigis: ablatiuus datiuus. The glosses propose that *uelo* is ablative and *remigis* dative. In fact, they are probably to be construed as a dative and genitive respectively: *addat opem uelo remigis*: "let him add to the sail the help of rowing" (cf. Hollis, 101). The final syllable of *remigis* is short and so it must be genitive. This is another example both of the general preoccupation of the glossator with oblique case forms and of the inability of the glossator to take metrics into account in the analysis.

369 ipsa: tu ipsa. The gloss indicates that *ipsa* is vocative.

370 uicem: **atail** "building" (cf. MW *adeil*). EGOW 12, where the gloss is taken at face value; but it is clear that the gloss has confused *uicem* "in turn" with *uicum* "settlement" (see 82 above).

371 de te narret: contra illam ancella. On this gloss as an indicator of Celtic Latin, see the discussion at 76–77.

372 mori: te. The gloss provides the accusative pronoun: "let her (i.e the maid-servant) swear that *you* are dying of insane love."

373 properet: iuuenis. The gloss marks the change of subject in the row of the third sg. verbs from the maidservant to the young man.

374 mora: ablatiuus. The gloss is intended to show that *mora* is ablative beside the nominative *ira*.

375 Queris: a domina. Given the complex interchanges between the young man, the maidservant and the mistress, the gloss clarifies whom the glossator thinks the young man is addressing. However, it is more likely that this is a general enquiry not necessarily addressed to anyone in particular.

376 alea grandis: si inuenies ambas. The gloss is probably a comment on the whole line, but the sense of the line seems to have been misunderstood: in the previous line Ovid is contemplating seduction of the maidservant, but acknowledges that this involves great risk, *alea grandis*. The gloss seems to imagine that he is planning to seduce both maidservant and mistress.

377–78 hec . . . illa: ancella . . . ancella. The glossing here is, I think, confused. The sense of the lines is that "the one (*hec*) becomes painstaking , the other (*illa*) more slow; the one (*hec*) prepares you as a gift for her mistress, the other (*illa*) for herself." The *illa* in l. 378 therefore refers to the mistress, while in both lines *hec* refers to the maidservant. The glossing arises from the general necessity in this section to clarify which fem. sg. pronouns refer to the mistress and which to the maidservant.

377 sedula: promta. The gloss provides a simpler equivalent to the lemma, but has the effect perhaps of narrowing the sense slightly. The lemma has the sense of "painstaking, precise, attentive," while the gloss suggests something closer to "quick to act."

379 cassus in euentu est: promissum dominae et de ancella sua. The lemma "the uncertain fate lies in the outcome" (cf. Hollis, 102) is glossed by the reminder that the *euentus* involves both the mistress and the maidservant.

380 The scribe of the main text changes here to scribe B; however, the remaining glosses in this section (as far as l. 389) were copied by scribe A. For discussion , see 36–41 above.

381 per preceps: iter. The gloss, *it̄,* might give pause. I expand it here as *iter* "journey" and understand it as providing a noun by which to interpret *preceps* "steep." But it could be a miscopied abbreviation for *inter* of which one form could be *it̄.* If so, then the gloss is explaining *per preceps et acuta cacumina* "through steep places and sharp peaks" as "among. . . ."

384 tabellas: aepistolas. For discussion of the clear comprehension of the different senses of *tabella,* etc. in this text, see above 81.

385 podiare. Note the spelling for *potiare* "(sc. make sure that) you take control of (+ abl.)" which may reflect a Welsh pronunciation of the intervocalic -/t/-; cf. also the spellings *Libius,* and in a gloss *Obidius,* and the discussion above, 156 (with other examples).

prius comes . . . illa: post dominam . . . ancella. Although the gloss is written over both words, and might suggest that the glossator thought that *prius* was to be construed with the second half of the line (when it is an adverb modifying *podiare*), the gloss refers to the maidservant following on behind the mistress.

387 unum: ius. The text can be read simply as "I advise this one thing," but the gloss suggests a more precise "I advise this one principle."

388 nec: si. As with several other glosses (cf. ll. 92, 211, 151, 328), here the *si* is repeated from the preceding line to remind the reader that the *nec* clause is still part of the conditional clause.

389 perfice: non. The glossator wrongly thought that the negative should be continued from the beginning of the line into the second half, but the sense is "either don't start or finish it properly" (on the textual crux here, see Hollis, 103).

tollitur: tolle. The gloss looks like an imperative, but it is more likely that it was intended to change the tense of the verb to a future; thus, *tolletur* rather than *tollitur,* and so instead of "the informer (i.e. the maidservant) is removed (sc. as a problem) once she is implicated in the *crimen*"), the gloss suggests it is to be understood as "the informer will be removed. . . ."

The first batch of glosses ends here.

439 amoitum. An error for *amantem?*

446 sicut. For the abbreviation *sī* occasionally used for *sicut,* see Lindsay, *Notae Latinae,* 287.

503 consurgit. The insular abbreviation for *con-* is used here.

508 concinitur. The insular abbreviation for *con-* is used here.

620 The second batch of glosses runs from here to l. 652, and was copied by scribe B, the scribe of the main text at this point. The main text is largely concerned with one's proper obligations to the gods and how lovers' promises carry no penalty.

    liquida: in. The *in* may be intended to mark *liquida* (and indeed *aqua*) as ablative but, since the line is corrupt, the ablative may simply have been construed as needing a preposition. The editions follow Axelson in emending the verb to *subestur* "is eaten away" which explains the ablative "by the flowing water."

623 forme: laudationis. The gloss, although genitive, seems to refer to the whole phrase *preconia forme* "the proclaiming of beauty." The gloss is slightly unexpected, but we may compare the gloss on the same phrase on O_g (see 111 for discussion).

624 curae: datiuus. The gloss indicates the predicative dative, a notoriously difficult construction for students to grasp.

625 frigis: frigea. The gloss seems to be indicating that the adjective (printed *Phrygiis* in the editions) is related to Phrygia.

628 recondit: renouat "renews." The gloss is a misunderstanding; see below for discussion.

    pennas: **hi ataned** "his/its wings" (cf. MW *adein*). Omitted from *VVB* and *EGOW* (though see 84 for **hi** "her, its"). The words somewhat confusingly gloss *opus,* but the fact that they are immediately beneath *pennas* might encourage us to think that they have been misplaced. But it is *opus* which is in need of explanation: the peacock will show off its feathers when praised, but if you gaze at it in silence, it will hide (*recondit*; the gloss, *renouat,* is mistaken) its *opus* (i.e. its masterpiece—its wings). Note here that in the Latin and the Welsh the peacock is being treated as feminine in gender as it is the *auis Iunonia,* even though it is the male which displays.

632 pollicito: datiuus. The gloss points out that *pollicito* should not be construed as an ablative, but as a dative after *adde:* "add to what is promised."

633 periura: **anutonou** "perjuries" (MW *anudon*). *EGOW* 8; the regular plural ending in most Old Welsh glosses is -**ou** (MW *-eu,* MnW *-au*).

    The marginal note, *iurauit iupiter multum iunone per stiga infer*[. . . , was not recorded by Bradshaw even though he transcribed the couplet; he presumably thought that, as it referred to the whole line and the more general context, it was not relevant. It is in fact misplaced; it related to l. 635.

635 per stiga: per stidgia. See the discussion on l. 633 above.

falsum: aduerbum. The gloss indicates that *falsum* is to be treated adverbially "falsely."

solebat: iupiter. The subject of the verb is in need of clarification here.

636 nunc: tunc. The gloss *tunc* is relatively common; see l. 87 for discussion; it indicates that *nunc* refers to Ovid's presence which is the glossator's and reader's past.

639 illis: puellis. Dative and ablative plural pronouns are potentially confusing as they are not marked for gender, hence the gloss. However, the gloss is wrong; in the context it refers to the gods. The glossator can, however, be forgiven, since so many of the pronouns in this text do refer to girls.

641 seruet: .i. est deus. The gloss reminds the reader that Jupiter is overseeing all of these activities, which therefore should be carried out properly.

643 ludite: fallite. The gloss repeats the verb from l. 645 below, and may be suggesting that *ludite* is an error.

impune: sine pena. The gloss provides the simple prose explanation.

647–48 arua . . . annos: per . . . per. On the glossing of these lemmata by *per*, see the discussion above, 62. On Busiris and Phalaris, see Hollis, 135–36.

649 Cum: tunc. The gloss *tunc* is relatively common; see l. 87 for discussion.

thraseus bussiren: proprium . . . nomen regis. The glosses provide the necessary information so that the student need spend no further time trying to understand their meaning.

651 fies: eris. The gloss provides both tense and sense for this poetical usage of *fio* in place of the verb "to be."

652 ospis: uocatiuus. Since third-declension nouns do not have a distinct vocative, the gloss provides useful support for the student.

The second batch of glosses ends here.

654 auctor. The *c* is a later addition in what may be a pronunciation error; cf. *Appendix probi* (ed. Powell), 155, *auctoritas non autoritas*: the preceding entry (154) is partly illegible but the final *autor* would allow us to infer *auctor non autor*. The gloss *peius tra* on l. 182 *tractat* may be similar in its import to the strictures of the *Appendix probi*; although no such reading as *tratat* is attested, it is possible that the glossator has seen it and felt obliged to deter anyone wishing to adopt it (for discussion, see 78–79, 180).

684 uel duas. This is added after the punctuation and looks like a collation gloss, and indeed is the reading printed in the editions in place of *uenus*. On this type of gloss, see the discussion above at 70–72.

760 innumeras. The final syllable is corrected to *is,* which is the correct reading according to the editions. On this type of correction, see the discussion above at 70–72.

766 curua: uel e. The gloss offers the alternative *cerua* accepted as correct by the editions; cf. also l. 89 where the text reads *ceruis* against the correct *curuis.* On this type of gloss, see the discussion above at 70–72.

6

POSTSCRIPT

The Later Life of Ovid in Medieval Wales

Naso legendus erat tum cum didicistis amare;
idem nunc uobis Naso legendus erit.[1]

You had to read Ovid at that time when you learnt to love;
now you'll have to read the same Ovid.

Os da gennyt dyscu garu ne orderchu, keis lyvyr ovit yr hwnn a elwit naset . . . (Middle Welsh translation of *Disticha Catonis)*[2]

If you want to learn how to love or be a lover, seek out the book of Ovid, who was called Naso.

INTRODUCTION

It is impossible to discuss the fragment of *Ars amatoria* examined in the rest of this volume without being drawn into thinking about the presence of Ovid in later medieval Welsh literature. For, if in no other respect, his name (in Welsh *Ofydd* in various medieval spellings[3]) figures so regularly in the work of medieval Welsh poets, and especially in the work of Dafydd ap Gwilym and other *cywyddwyr*—poets writing mainly in the *cywydd* metre from the early fourteenth century onwards (also known as *Beirdd yr Uchelwyr* "poets of the nobles"). Previous discussions have tended to focus on the work of Dafydd ap Gwilym, but the greater bulk of evidence which can be extracted from the recent editions of the work of

---

1. *Remedia amoris* (ed. Kenney), ll. 71–72. I am grateful to Barry Lewis and Maredudd ap Huw for reading and commenting on a draft of this chapter.

2. Williams, "Testunau," 22 (text from NLW Llanstephan 27ii (ca. 1400)), translated from *Disticha Catonis* (ed. Boas), 90; for discussion of this text, see below, 218–20; for a survey of early scholarship on *Disticha Catonis*, see Bieler, "Nachaugustische nichtchristliche Dichter," 226–39; Alcamesi, "Remigius' Commentary," 145–47.

3. The convention among the editors of the poetry under discussion is to print the text in modern orthography, and that convention is followed here; examples from earlier sources will be printed in the orthography of the manuscript. The modern form is *Ofydd* representing /ovið/, but in Middle Welsh it was spelt as either *Ouyd* or *Ouyt*, both spelling /ovið/.

the *cywyddwyr* has turned the question into a more complex one with a much wider application: "Did they (or any or some of them) know their Ovid?" But the broader the range of poets we are considering, the less we should expect there to be a simple answer. But if there is any indication that they were familiar with the works of Ovid, then the obvious question is how they might have known them, and that brings us back to how scholars have handled the specific evidence. The discussion then moves on to what we might know or surmise about the knowledge of classical authors, and in particular of Ovid, in the period between ca. 900 and ca. 1400. Most discussions have focused on a particular aspect of the issue (e.g. the survival of books), but the intention here is to approach the question from several different angles and involves a certain amount of lateral thinking and extrapolation. As Sims-Williams has reminded us, it is all too easy for a discussion about the absence of evidence for books to slide into asking why there are so few books, and for that reason we need to maximize what we can do with what we have.[4] Another way of putting it is that what follows attempts to join up a range of scattered dots without necessarily knowing what the picture might be. It explores what we can glean from manuscript survival, from evidence in writers of this period for knowledge of classical authors, and from what we understand about the educational practices of the period. At the end of the chapter we attempt to think laterally about how a term like *ofydd*/*Ofydd* was used; we take two other terms which are based on personal names of figures from antiquity, *Fferyll* (< *Virgilius*) and *Dwned* (< Middle English *Donet* < *Donātus*), and compare their use in the same and similar sources as a way of seeing whether an argument by analogy might be developed to help us move forward.

OFYDD: POET, LOVE POET, AND LOVE POETRY

In what follows, a full list of the references to *Ofydd* is presented in the Appendix to this chapter and only representative examples are provided within the body of the discussion. Translations are my own unless otherwise indicated and aim to be as literal as possible. It is assumed at this stage, following the general practice of most editors, that references to *Ofydd* refer to Ovid, although it will be argued below that some, if not all, the examples refer more generally to love poetry, or indeed to the pangs of love itself. The following examples are illustrative: *dan gyrs Ofydd* "under the branches of Ovid,"[5] *prydydd cerdd Ofydd ddifai* "poet of Ovid's faultless song,"[6] *digrifaf dyn deigr Ofydd*

---

4. Sims-Williams, "The Uses of Writing," 18–24.

5. *GDG* 22.3 (= *CDG* 60.3).

6. *GDG* 28.21 (= *CDG* 159.21).

"most pleasant man of Ovid's tears,"[7] *Iefainc wyf ar fainc Ofydd* "I am a youth on the bench of Ovid,"[8] *Dyn wyf ym mhurdan Ofydd* "I am a person in the purgatory of Ovid,"[9] *sathr Ofydd serch* "trampling the love of Ovid,"[10] *dull Ofydd* "Ovid's method."[11] There is one instance where there are hints of something more specific; the poet Gutun Owain looks as if he is aware of the person and some of his biographical details: *Mae gennyd—tau yspryd da—oes, iaith y gwr o Sithia* "Tu as—car tu possèdes un esprit bien formé—oui, le langage de celui de Scythie."[12] At least there is some indication here of familiarity with at least one biographical fact about the poet—namely, his exile to the Black Sea coast, though that might easily have entered the tradition via the *accessus* "introductions" to the works of Ovid which commonly prefaced his works from the eleventh and twelfth centuries onwards.[13]

We may begin by making two points. The first relates to the form of the name. Generally the form of the name is clear although Lloyd-Jones noted that there was potential confusion with the lenited form of *gofydd* "oppressor" in at least one instance and with *dofydd* "lord" in compounds where the first element ended in -*dd*.[14] More importantly, it is clear that the form of the name must have been acquired relatively late in learned and literary contexts (and perhaps in a written form); if it has been inherited as part of the general stock of words borrowed from Latin, we would expect it to have undergone internal *i*-affection so as to produce **Efydd* or the like (cf. *efydd* "bronze" < *omiio*- (cf. Old Irish *umae*)). It is also worth adding that there are two cases in the works of early to mid-sixteenth-century poets where the name seems to reflect even later learned influence: Sir Dafydd Trefor has one instance of the form *Ofyd* with final -/d/ rhyming with *byd* "world," and Lewys Morgannwg went one stage further in producing *Ofid* with -/i/- for the expected /i/ and final -/d/.[15] Both changes probably reflect later learned pronunciations of Latin *Ovidius*, in part perhaps influenced by English. Secondly, and this is something to which we shall return, it is worth observing that the term *Ofydd* always occurs in the context of love poetry and never in relation to a wider

---

7. *GDG* 31.60 (= *CDG* 19.58).

8. *GLl* 7.63.

9. *GLM* At.ii.1 = *GTA* CXXII.1.

10. *GLlGMH* 12.53.

11. *GDG* 116.34 (= *CDG* 46.30). A striking example of the alternative reading is *GDG* 148.8 (= *CDG* 24.8) *cywydd gwiw Ofydd*, which is translated at http://www.dafyddapgwilym.net/ (consulted 2 July 2014) as "it is a worthy love poem" (though the note at *CDG*, 617, suggests that the editors still have the specific poet in mind).

12. *GO* I.3–4.

13. See above, 3, and also *Accessus* (ed. Huygens).

14. See Lloyd-Jones, "Nodiadau," 199.

15. *CYSDT* 11.57–8 and *GLM* II, 54.21, respectively.

range of contexts which might be imagined if the poets were familiar with the full range of Ovid's work.

The fashion of referring to *Ofydd* is older than the work of the *cywyddwyr* which dates from the early fourteenth century; three examples are found in the work of the Gogynfeirdd, the court poets of the Welsh princes, whose work dates from the early twelfth century to the last decades of the thirteenth. Two of the references are datable to the mid-twelfth century, and the third is found in one of only three poems surviving from the work of Iorwerth Fychan from the end of the thirteenth century: *boen Ouyt gennad* "messenger of Ovid's pain";[16] *Ked bwyf i cariadavg certed Ouyt* "though I be a lover in the manner of Ovid";[17] *Ys mawr vy angof na bvm Ouyd* "Great is my oblivion (sc. that I have fallen into) that I was not Ovid."[18] In the two earlier examples we find a similar use of the name as we have seen in the later verse, but Iorwerth Fychan seems to be referring much more specifically to the poet himself and comparing himself unfavourably with him. The relative infrequency of references to Ovid in the work of the Gogynfeirdd is difficult to assess: it might indicate the beginning of the fashion to refer to Ovid in relation to love poetry, but since love poetry forms a relatively small proportion of the output of these poets the small number of references may not be surprising.

When we turn to the *cywyddwyr*, one striking group within the references are to *llyfr Ofydd* "Ovid's book": *Nid gwas . . . llwfr ar waith llyfr Ofydd* "I'm no coward at the work of Ovid's book";[19] *Nid oes dwyn a dwys dyno . . . nas medrwyf . . . heb y llyfr hoywbwyll Ofydd* "There is no hillock or thickset meadow which I do not make for . . . without the book of a lively-minded Ovid";[20] *Salm i'm cof o lyfr Ofydd* "I have a psalm from the book of Ovid in my memory";[21] *Gwyddost, Cadi, . . . Lyfr Ofydd* "You knew, Cadi, . . . the book of Ovid";[22] *lifreifardd ar lyfr Ofydd* "a liveried poet of the book of Ovid";[23] *Llafur Ieuan, llyfr Ofydd* "the work of John, the book of Ovid";[24] *Dugum gof o lyfr Ovydd* "I took my recollection from the book of Ovid."[25] On the face of it, they seem to refer to

---

16. *CBT* II (Owein Cyfeiliog) 15.17.

17. *CBT* II (Hywel ab Owain Gwynedd) 6.40; on the difficulty of this line, see also Lloyd-Jones, "Nodiadau," 199.

18. *CBT* VII (Iorwerth Fychan) 30.63.

19. *GDG* 58.20 (= *CDG* 72.20); translation at http://www.dafyddapgwilym.net/eng/3win.htm (consulted 2 July 2014).

20. *GDG* 83.39–42 (= *CDG* 96.39–42); my translation is based mainly on Loomis, *Dafydd ap Gwilym*, 177.

21. *GDG* 50.1 (= *CDG* 95.1; cf. *GSRh* 11.55); translation at http://www.dafyddapgwilym.net (consulted 2 July 2014).

22. *GSH* At. ii.4.

23. *GLl* 5.6.

24. *GILlF* 5.8.

25. *GST* I 200.27.

specific books of Ovid's love poetry; comments by editors in the editions of the poetry explore the full range of possibilities, some suggesting that they do indeed refer to a very precise book of Ovid, be it *Ars amatoria* or the *Amores*, while others are more cautious and reserve judgement as to the precise referents.[26] But it is at least worth considering that, if *Ofydd* could be used in a more general sense to refer to "love" or "love poetry," then these references need not be understood so precisely. It might be objected that, if the basic sense is possible in the context and period, then there is no point in arguing for a more general sense. But it is suggested below that it is not clear that a precise sense would have necessarily been possible throughout this period.

There is a particularly striking, though relatively late, example of the use of *Llyfr Ofydd* which has not been brought into the discussion previously. Four manuscripts, all locatable in Glamorgan and dating from 1400 to the end of the sixteenth century, survive of a Welsh translation of Richart de Fornival's *Bestiaire d'amour*.[27] The earlier two are in Middle Welsh and the latter two in early modern Welsh, but they seem to be the reflexes of a single Welsh translation made perhaps in the fourteenth century. Of these versions, the latter two, preserved in NLW 13075 (Thomas's "Text C"), copied by Llywelyn ap Siôn, and BL Additional 15038 (Thomas's "Text D") are, according to the editor, sister manuscripts.[28] The text is "in the form of a letter from a lover to his beloved in which he analyses his love for her and his relationship with her, and makes observations on the relationship between men and women with reference to the nature of animals."[29] The striking aspect for our purposes is the title in each manuscript: while the two earlier versions lack titles, Text C is entitled *Llyma lyfr a elwir Llyfr Ovydd* "Here is the book which is called the Book of Ovid," and Text D has a more complicated version, *Llyma llythyr o ueith Ouydd yn anfon at i gariad* "Here is the letter from the work of Ovid which he is sending to his beloved."[30] The precise wording of the title in the exemplar from which these two versions were copied is unclear, but it is almost certain that *Ofydd* figured somewhere in it and that his name had been associated with this text by about the late fifteenth century, if not earlier. The text is demonstrably not a rendering of an Ovidian text, but it is a book about love, and this is probably why it has been designated *Llyfr Ofydd*. It therefore provides clear evidence that the term *Ofydd* could be used in this more general

---

26. Typical is *GGM* 3.65n; *CYSDT* 11.57n; a more subtle exploration is that in *CDG* 95.1n. On the idea of *llyfr Ofydd* as "anything pertaining to love," see Edwards, *Dafydd ap Gwilym: Influences and Analogues*, 21.

27. For an edition and discussion of these texts, see *A Welsh Bestiary of Love* (ed. Thomas).

28. *A Welsh Bestiary of Love* (ed. Thomas), xix–xxii and xxv; Text C with variants from Text D is printed at 11–24.

29. *A Welsh Bestiary of Love* (ed. Thomas), xiii.

30. Ibid., 11.

sense in the later medieval period in Wales. On the other hand, the Text D version refers to it as a *llythyr*, which in the context must mean "letter," and that still leaves the question of whether there is some implicit reference here to Ovidian works, such as the *Heroides, Tristia, Epistulae ex ponto,* all of which took an epistolary form.

Hints of a more generic reading are also provided by instances of the abstract term, *Ofyddiaeth* (lit. "Ovid-ship," or perhaps "love poetry"): *gwir ofyddiaeth* "true lovemaking,"[31] *Gwawd graffaf . . . gwaethwaeth heb ofyddiaeth Ofydd* "The most assured verse . . . will decline without Ovid's art."[32] But balanced against that is the single reference to Ovid in prose which is quoted at the head of this chapter: *Os da gennyt dyscu garu ne orderchu, keis lyvyr ovit yr hwnn a elwit naset* "If you want to learn how to love or be a lover, seek out the book of Ovid, who was called Naso." This is the Middle Welsh translation of the *Disticha Catonis,* a set of moral precepts dating from the third or fourth century AD, which was a popular teaching text in the medieval period; it is not then a reliable guide to literary choice the better part of a thousand years later.[33] Even so, the original Latin text reads *Si quid amare libet, vel discere amare legendo, Nasonem petito,* which strikingly recalls the beginning of *Ars amatoria* I, *Si quis in hoc artem populo non nouit amandi, hoc legat,* and it might be tempting to think that the Welsh poets were aware of the connection. Furthermore, it is noteworthy that the translator felt the need to state that he was also known as *Naset* "Naso"; this may be related to the fact that in medieval French and English sources he is known only by his cognomen and never as "Ovid."

The *Cywyddwyr* and *Ofydd*

These specific references to *Ofydd* unsurprisingly figure in the broad discussion of the relationship between the *cywyddwyr* and other medieval literatures from outside Wales. As can be seen from the selection of references above, and the others in the Appendix, *Ofydd* and related terms are common across the whole tradition and, as more of the works of the *cywyddwyr* become available in modern editions, the clearer that becomes. Earlier discussions were very much constructed in relation to Dafydd ap Gwilym, as more of his work was accessible to earlier generations of scholars, and often framed as

---

31. *GDG* 14.22 (= *CDG* 7.22).

32. *GDG* 20.60 (= *CDG* 22.60).

33. The Middle Welsh version is edited in Williams, "Testunau"; for further discussion of this text, see below, 218–20; for the original Latin, see *Disticha Catonis* (ed. Boas), 90; cf. the discussion in Lapidge, "The Study of Latin Texts," 201–5, where it is discussed in an Anglo-Saxon context.

questions such as "Did he or didn't he know any text of Ovid?" and "Had he ever encountered a manuscript of Ovid?" From the work of Chotzen onwards, there has been an increasingly sophisticated appreciation of the influence of medieval English and French literatures on Dafydd's work.[34] Scholars, however, have differed markedly as to the nature and range of that influence. Bromwich regarded the references to Ovid as "suggestive" and saw it as significant that Ovid is "the only poet which Dafydd gives evidence of so much as having ever heard the name," but at the same time she recognized that many of the apparently Ovidian and other themes can be traced to *Roman de la rose*.[35] Others have tackled related but different aspects: Fulton, while acknowledging that some of the apparent links may reflect parallel but similar developments, is still inclined to see Latin sources lying behind some of the Ovidian allusions.[36] Edwards, however, is more concerned with the manner of these connections and argues that some of the lines of transmission are at the subliterary level.[37] More recently, Heather Williams has suggested that these identifiable Ovidian themes may have been mediated through medieval English and French sources;[38] for example, she argues that medieval French treatments of the Ovidian theme of the theatre as a good place to pick up girls replace the theatre with the church and that this might be the model on which Dafydd's poem on the girls of Llanbadarn is based.[39]

The question for our purposes is whether these references indicate access to texts of Ovid in later medieval Wales or whether they are to be interpreted more generically as references to love and poetry about love. It has always been the case that some of the references have been regarded as generic; the editors of *Geiriadur Prifysgol Cymru* acknowledge this in their inclusion of *ofydd* as a common noun in the sense of "(a) love poet, litterateur; lover, sweetheart, darling; (b) master, champion."[40] What is not clear in the published entry is whether the editors' analysis reflects a decision that these particular entries must be generic and that others are not, and so must refer to the Latin poet or whether they are just making a selection. The latter seems more likely given the way the dictionary has been compiled, but in view of the ambiguity

---

34. Chotzen, *Recherches sur la poésie de Dafydd ap Gwilym*, 141–44. In addition to the work cited below, cf. also Mari Jones, "Byd y Beirdd" (an excellent discussion of these issues); cf. also Parry, "Dafydd ap Gwilym," Williams, "Cerddi'r Gogynfeirdd i Wragedd a Merched," esp. 100–101; Johnston, *Llên yr Uchelwyr*, 115–16.

35. Bromwich, *Aspects of the Poetry of Dafydd ap Gwilym*, 70–73.

36. Fulton, *Dafydd ap Gwilym and His European Context*, 28–30.

37. Edwards, *Dafydd ap Gwilym: Influences and Analogues*, e.g. 82–83, 98.

38. Heather Williams, "Dafydd ap Gwilym and the Debt to Europe."

39. Ibid., 188–89 (esp. n. 23).

40. *GPC*, s.v. *ofydd*.

of many of the examples, clear-cut decisions are always going to be difficult.[41] There is always going to be a tendency for the scholarly discussion to polarize and fall into a binary mode: either these are references to the Latin poet and to specific passages, and therefore Dafydd ap Gwilym (on whom most of the discussion has focused), or the poet in question, knew his Ovid, or they refer generically to love poetry, or in a slightly more precise version whereby *Ofydd* does not refer to Ovid himself but to *Roman de la rose* or the like.

Even instances which seem very precise, and seem to present a clear case, may not be as solid as they appear. We may take Dafydd's poem on crossing the River Dyfi where he addresses and scolds the river for preventing him from getting across and reaching his love, Morfudd, awaiting him in Llanbadarn. A link between this poem and *Amores* III.6, in which Ovid curses a river which is blocking his path to his lover, has long been suggested.[42] In what is a model discussion of the issues surrounding literary influences of this kind, Barry Lewis has set a penetrating discussion of the possible relationship between these two poems into a broader consideration of first how such influences can be gauged, and secondly of the play between Dafydd ap Gwilym, a poet of nature and the country, and the urban and indeed urbane Ovid.[43] His conclusion is agnostic: the situation might easily have arisen in Dafydd's own experience and provided the stimulus for the poem, or he got the idea from some other source (whether or not influenced by Ovid himself), or he had read Ovid, *Amores* III.6—it is impossible to tell. He concludes:

> I believe that we have to recognize this hard fact, draw a line under an argument that is unlikely, in the absence of new evidence, to go anywhere, and move on to do something worthwhile with the literary works themselves.[44]

It is clear that direct evidence, with which this question might be settled, is lacking and likely always will be. There are, however, ways to approach these issues obliquely, and this is what the rest of this chapter attempts to do, first by exploring what classical texts might have been known in medieval Wales and second by thinking laterally about the use of terms parallel to *Ofydd*.

---

41. The practice of the editors of *GPC* is to follow the view of the most recent editors of the poetry; the effect of this is that, if editors are being conservative and playing it safe, then so does the dictionary. I am grateful to Gareth Bevan for discussing this with me.

42. See Bromwich, *Aspects*, 72.

43. Lewis, "Bardd Natur yn Darllen Bardd y Ddinas?"

44. My translation of the original Welsh: "Credaf fod yn rhaid inni gydnabod y ffaith galed hon, tynnu llinell dan ddadl nad yw'n debygol, yn absenoldeb tystiolaeth newydd, o fynd i'r unlle, a symud ymlaen i wneud rhywbeth gwerth chwil gyda'r gweithiau llenyddol eu hunain" (Lewis, "Bardd Natur yn Darllen Bardd y Ddinas?," 18–19).

KNOWLEDGE OF CLASSICAL TEXTS
IN MEDIEVAL WALES, 900–1400

Surviving Books and Monastic Catalogues

When Llywelyn Bren was executed in Cardiff in 1317, after a rebellion in 1315–16, among his possessions (*des bies Lewelyn Bren*) were listed: *j romanz de la rose, iij liures Galeys, iiij autres lyures* "one *Roman de la rose*, three Welsh books, and four other books."[45] What these Welsh and "other" books were cannot be known, though the latter may have been books of personal devotion in Latin. The reason for beginning this section with such a laconic list is that it is one of very few lists of books from medieval Wales, and it serves to highlight the severe paucity of evidence and the real difficulty of saying anything useful about books in medieval Wales.

The prime concern here is with classical texts, and in particular those of Ovid, but we need to cast the net more widely. Our view of knowledge of Ovid in medieval Wales would be rather different if, for example, there were numerous manuscripts of Virgil, Juvenal, and Persius surviving but none of Ovid, than if there were no classical manuscripts surviving at all. If the latter were the case, then it would be reasonable to assume a general loss or dearth of texts but, if the former, then it would look as if some deliberate process of selection was going on. If, on the other hand, there was a good survival rate for devotional texts but a poor one for all kinds of classical texts, then the questions we might ask would be different.

Our interest here mainly has to do with non-vernacular books from medieval Wales, but we might begin by noting that Daniel Huws's lists of surviving manuscripts in Welsh (1250—ca. 1400) lists approximately 69 manuscripts.[46] By contrast, it is very difficult even to begin listing manuscripts in other languages from Wales, and the task would not take long. Much of the basic work in terms of identifying and listing books has been carried out by Ceridwen Lloyd-Morgan, and what emerges is a very short list strikingly short of evidence for the classical authors generally. In a study of the medieval manuscripts from Wales in the National Library of Wales in Aberystwyth she notes the thirteenth-century Tintern Bible (NLW 22631C), the late fourteenth-century Penpont Antiphonal, the late thirteenth-century copy of Giraldus Cambrensis

---

45. *Cardiff Records* (ed. Matthews), 58; another record which refers to the possessions of a Lewelin ap Griffith lists *Treys liveres escritz de Galeys et un liure de Romaunces* "three books in Welsh and one book of *Roman de la rose*" (57); the lists are so similar that they look like two lists of the same person's belongings.

46. Huws, *Medieval Manuscripts*, 1–4, 58–60 (lists); cf. also Huws, "Vernacular Literature." No manuscript written predominantly in Welsh survives from before 1250. Some manuscripts counted here are bound together with other manuscripts.

from St Davids (NLW 3024C) which contains the autograph of the poet Dafydd Nanmor (fl. 1450–59), and a few others, but the list is depressingly small.[47] The reasons are not hard to find: the natural wastage rate and loss of manuscripts was exacerbated by factors such as the destruction wrought by the Glyndŵr rebellion, the lack of any university in Wales at the Dissolution which might have stepped in and taken manuscripts into their care, and the lack of cathedrals of the wealth and power of Hereford or Worcester.[48] There are very few clear examples of surviving books which can be traced to a monastic library in Wales: Lloyd-Morgan notes that several books can be tracked back to Llanthony Prima (in the Black Mountains), mainly because they ended up at Llanthony Secunda in Gloucestershire.[49] But they do at least allow us to get a faint glimpse of what might have been in Welsh monastic libraries: none of those, which ended up in Llanthony Secunda, is liturgical and some are secular, including, Gregory, Jerome, Isidore, Cicero, and Higden's *Polychronicon*.[50] Recent work on monastic library catalogues has only served to highlight the fact that so few catalogues survive from Wales:[51] there is a partial list from Margam and a list from Llanthony Secunda mentioned above.[52] Apart from the Margam list, and in contrast to the situation in England, a striking absence is a catalogue from any of the Cistercian monasteries in Wales.

If we broaden the search to include England, the early part of our date range is still not densely populated with manuscripts.[53] For the Anglo-Saxon

---

47. Lloyd-Morgan, "Medieval Manuscripts"; cf. also ead., "Manuscripts and the Monasteries," and "The Book in Fifteenth-Century Wales"; and Marx, "Middle English Texts." On the date of NLW 3024C, see Rooney, "Manuscripts," vi, 81–82, 93–94.

48. Lloyd-Morgan, "Manuscripts and the Monasteries," 212

49. Lloyd-Morgan, "Manuscripts and the Monasteries," 211–12; the difficulty here is identifying books at Llanthony Secunda which came from the earlier monastery. Ker notes eight items which came from Llanthony Prima (Ker, *Medieval Libraries of Great Britain*, 108–12; 119–20). Lloyd-Morgan also argues (loc. cit.) that books ended up in Llanthony Secunda from Carmarthen after 1421, but it is unclear that the evidence need be interpreted in this way; my hesitation arises out of discussion with Georgia Henley who is working on this material. For the Llanthony Secunda catalogue, see *The Libraries of the Augustinian Canons* (ed. Webber and Watson), A16 (36–94).

50. It has also been suggested that part of a *florilegium* containing extracts of the works of Ovid, and preserved in Lambeth Cathedral Library 421, fols. 136–41 (s. xii–xiii), came from Llanthony but whether Prima or Secunda is unclear; see James, *Descriptive Catalogue*, 581–83.

51. See the Corpus of British Medieval Library Catalogues (CBMLC), edited by Richard Sharpe and others: for example, *The Libraries of the Augustinian Canons* (ed. Webber and Watson); *St. Augustine's Abbey, Canterbury* (ed. Barker-Benfield); *Libraries of the Cistercians, Gilbertines and Premonstratensians* (ed. Bell); *English Benedictine Libraries* (ed. Richard Sharpe et al.), etc. For the Cistercians, cf. also Lawrence, "English Cistercian Manuscripts." Note that the *Registrum Anglie* (ed. Rouse and Rouse), a catalogue of books in English, Welsh, and Scottish monastic libraries compiled in the early fourteenth century by perambulating Franciscans from Oxford, was highly selective and did not include literary texts, focusing rather on *patristica et spiritualia* (*Registrum Anglie* (ed. Rouse and Rouse), lxxiii–lxxiv).

52. For Margam, see Patterson, *The Scriptorium*, 64 (and n. 114), 66.

53. For an overview, see Gameson, "From Vindolanda to Domesday"; cf. also Ó Néill, "Celtic Britain"; Ogilvy, *Books Known to the English*.

period, Lapidge's work has identified two copies of Ovid's *Ars amatoria* in Oxford, Bodleian Library, Rawlinson G 57 and 111 (s. xi), and Paris, Sainte Geneviève, 2410 (s. x/xi Canterbury), and a copy of the *Metamorphoses* in Vatican BAV, Reg. Lat. 1671 (s. x/xi Worcester).[54] For a slightly later period, Ziolkowski has noted a text of Ovid's *Remedia* and *Epistulae ex ponto* in Bodleian Rawlinson G 109 (s. xii²–xiii¹), copied from a French exemplar.[55] But consideration of the monastic library catalogues from England can at least give us a baseline from which to work. They can also be set alongside McKinley's work on the manuscripts of Ovid in medieval England from 1100 to 1500, though most are listed from the later part of the period.[56] In addition to our Ovid manuscript, there seems to have been an *Ovidius magnus* at Glastonbury according to the 1247 catalogue (Cambridge, Trinity College R 5. 33 (7241), fol. 104r).[57] Similarly, if we focus on libraries close to the march of Wales, Hereford provides evidence for an *Ovidius moralizatus* which tantalizingly was owned by a Welshman in the fifteenth century: Hereford, Cathedral Library, O. I. 9, contains an inscription "ex dono M. Oweyni Lloyd," who has been identified as a canon of Exeter from 1468 and then at Hereford until his death in 1478.[58] Although he has a Welsh name, it is unclear whether the book was ever in Wales, but at least it can be minimally described as a book of Ovid owned by a Welshman. Two other manuscripts at Hereford, O. I. 2 and P. I. 15, also suggest knowledge of Ovid in the twelfth and thirteenth centuries as both quote couplets from the *Tristia*.[59] According to its table of contents, Worcester Cathedral Library Q. 55 ended with a text of *Remedia amoris* which was lost at some point before 1733–34.[60] In addition to the copies of Ovid listed at Glastonbury, the wealth of the English Benedictine libraries is represented by the significant presence of texts of Ovid in library catalogues: *Ovidii magni* are listed at Ramsey, Rochester, and the *Fasti* at Rochester and St Albans.[61]

---

54. Lapidge, *Anglo-Saxon Library*, 323.

55. Ziolkowski, "University and Monastic Texts," 236–37.

56. McKinley, "Manuscripts of Ovid in England"; cf. also Munk Olsen, "Ovide au Moyen-Age"; id., *L'étude des auteurs classiques latins*, II.111–81. There are no works of Ovid listed in Gameson, *The Manuscripts of Early Norman England*.

57. *English Benedictine Libraries* (ed. Sharpe et al.), 206 (B39.312). An *Ovidius magnus* was usually an omnibus volume containing all of Ovid's elegiac verse and sometimes also the *Metamorphoses*; such books were popular in the twelfth century.

58. McKinley, "Manuscripts of Ovid in England," 15; Mynors and Thomson, *Catalogue of the Manuscripts of Hereford Cathedral Library*, 9.

59. Mynors and Thomson, *Catalogue of the Manuscripts of Hereford Cathedral Library*, 4 and 72, respectively.

60. Thomson, *Descriptive Catalogue*, 154.

61. *English Benedictine Libraries* (ed. Sharpe et al.): respectively, B39.401, B.68.314, B79.213, B.79.191, B.86.4; cf. also the Ovidian works listed in *The Libraries of Collegiate Colleges* (ed. Willoughby), 1047; *The Friars' Libraries* (ed. Humphries), 119, 125; *Henry of Kirkstede* (ed. Rouse and Rouse), 376–78; *Peterborough Abbey* (ed. Friis-Jensen and Willoughby), 213.

It has been observed by Sims-Williams that the absence of Benedicti-nism in Wales may have been a significant factor in the lack of books from Wales.[62] The presence of the Cistercians may have had a similar effect. While no library catalogues survive from the Cistercian monasteries of Wales, it is unlikely that they would reveal any great wealth of secular books. It has been noted that "barely a dozen books can now be identified with certainty as belonging to a Welsh Cistercian house," and all of those are either devotional or historical books.[63] Books there certainly were, but it is not clear what they had; in the early thirteenth century the monasteries of Basingwerk and Aber-conwy had a dispute over "five books";[64] and in 1284 a fire at Strata Florida burnt the choir books.[65] Views of the Cistercians have also been coloured by Gerald's poor opinion of them; notably, in 1199–1202 he lent his library to Strata Florida for safekeeping and then they refused to give them back.[66] The lists from English Cistercian libraries provide no evidence for texts of Ovid apart from a reference to an *Ibis* in a list from Meaux, and indeed very little evidence for classical texts at all.[67] Extrapolation from this suggests that, had lists survived, there would have been a dearth of secular texts including Ovid. Even though the catalogues may not be a perfect guide, the obvious inference is that the libraries probably did not contain such texts.

Intertextual Knowledge of Classical Texts in Medieval Wales

While there is no direct evidence for texts of Ovid in Wales after the ninth century, another approach is to consider what books extant authors appear to have been reading. Much useful work has recently been carried out for both Wales and England, and an overview of what we know for the latter might provide us with at least some context to think about the former.

Anglo-Saxon England seems to have been relatively well stocked.[68] Gwara has noted that the surviving schoolbooks show contact with Virgil, Jerome, Ovid's *Ars amatoria*, Statius, Juvenal, Persius, and Macrobius;[69] Aldhelm's library seems to have contained Virgil, Ovid's *Metamorphoses*, Statius, and Juvenal, while

---

62. Sims-Williams, "The uses of writing," 20.

63. Lewis and Williams, *The White Monks in Wales,* 14.

64. Williams, *The Welsh Cistercians,* 25.

65. Ibid., 49.

66. Ibid., 30; cf. also Cowley, *The Monastic Order in South Wales,* 122.

67. *Libraries of the Cistercians, Gilbertines and Premonstratensians* (ed. Bell), 73 (Z 14.286c).

68. In addition to works cited below, a useful point of reference is Gneuss and Lapidge, *Anglo-Saxon Manuscripts.*

69. Gwara, "Anglo-Saxon Schoolbooks," 519–20.

Bede seems to have had access to Ovid's *Ars amatoria*.[70] Ganz has noted that there are no surviving copies of Horace or Lucan from Anglo-Saxon England.[71]

For Wales the evidence is necessarily thinner but work by Lapidge and others on the output of Sulien and his sons at Llanbadarn in the decade either side of 1100 suggests that they studied Virgil, Ovid (*Ars amatoria, Metamorphoses, Epistulae ex ponto, Fasti*—perhaps in the form of an *Ovidius magnus*), Lucan, Juvencus, and perhaps Statius, Horace, and Juvenal.[72] Outside Wales but relating to Wales, we may also note the range of reference available to Geoffrey of Monmouth and Gerald of Wales.[73] Even if the libraries they were accessing lay outside Wales—Oxford, Hereford, and Lincoln—they were in part writing for Welsh audiences and it is reasonable to suppose that the range of reference in these works would not have been totally lost on them. Likewise, Walter Map, writing in the first quarter of the twelfth century at least in part to explain the Welsh to the court of Henry II has a similar range of reference, and perhaps for the same reasons.[74] The author of the Latin *Vita Griffini filii Conani*, on the other hand, composed in perhaps St Davids or Gwynedd in the second quarter of the twelfth century, seems to have been a cleric who had a detailed (though imperfect) control of biblical quotation and a clear awareness of the conventions of classical biography, but did not reach into classical literature for quotation or allusion (though he is clearly aware of the narrative of the assassination of Julius Caesar).[75]

The death of the Lord Rhys in 1197 unleashed a torrent of grief and lamentation.[76] Three features are striking for our purposes. First, the long and difficult Latin death notice in the *Cronica de Wallia* is notable for an enormous number of classical references, some of which, such as the list of heroes with whom he is compared, could have been extracted from authors such as Statius or Dares Phrygius, but the complex reference to the Boethian wheel of fortune and the fates (which confused, if not defeated, most of the medieval Welsh translators) requires a more sophisticated grasp of classical texts.[77] Secondly,

---

70. Orchard, "Aldhelm's Library"; Love, "The Library of the Venerable Bede," 630.

71. Ganz, "Anglo-Saxon England," 96.

72. Lapidge, "Welsh-Latin Poetry," 69–70; Howlett, "Rhigyfarch ap Sulien"; Zeiser, "Latinity, Manuscripts and the Rhetoric of Conquest."

73. Wright, "Geoffrey of Monmouth and Bede"; id., "Geoffrey of Monmouth and Gildas"; id., "Geoffrey of Monmouth and Gildas Revisited"; Henley, "Quotation, Revision and Narrative Structure"; ead. "Through the Ethnographer's Eye."

74. Walter Map, *De Nugis Curialium* (ed. James), 524–25.

75. *Vita Griffini* (ed. Russell), §14/15 (64–65); 43–45 (for possible places of composition). The later Welsh translation (perhaps early thirteenth century) tends to add a layer of New Testament quotation and paraphrase.

76. For a more detailed discussion of the Latin literature occasioned by his death, see Russell, "'Go and look in the Latin books,'" 215–30.

77. For the text, see Jones, "'Cronica de Wallia,'" 30–31; and for discussion, Henley, "Rhetoric, Translation and Historiography" and Russell, "'Go and look in the Latin books,'" 215–19; for the

embedded in an early fourteenth-century Welsh version of this text, preserved in NLW Peniarth 20, is a Latin lament in elegiac couplets.[78] Although the phrasing of the lament is strikingly Welsh in tone, the language of the poem would have required a very sophisticated grasp of Latin metrics; it looks back to Rhigyfarch's lament of a century earlier, reworks a line of Boethius, and foreshadows the *marwnad* "death poem" for Llywelyn ap Gruffudd by Gruffudd ab yr Ynad Coch some eighty or so years later.[79] Thirdly, and most remarkably for our purposes, preserved in the PRO E 164/1 version of *Annales Cambriae* under the year 1197 we have a ten-line obituary of the Lord Rhys in elegiac couplets.[80] Lines 7–8 s*ed piger ad poenas princeps, ad praemia uelox, / quicquid do quo [sic] cogitur, esse ferox* "But as a prince he was slow to punish but swift to reward, / ... he is forced to be fierce" are taken from Ovid, *Epistulae ex ponto*, I.ii.120–22.[81] The context of these lines in the *Epistulae* is significant; Ovid, in exile in Tomis, is petitioning Fabius Maximus to plead his case with Augustus, and the lines in question refer to Augustus and here have been transferred to the Lord Rhys. In other words, the Lord Rhys is being portrayed as a second Augustus.

In the middle of the thirteenth century, a Latin version of the Welsh laws was copied in Gwynedd. The text, preserved in BL Cotton Vespasian E. xi (s.xiii^med.) and conventionally known as Latin Redaction B, begins with a version of a relatively standard preface presenting and validating the supposed origins of the text.[82] These prefaces vary in detail, but this preface uniquely contains two quotations from Horace, one from the *Epistles* (I.i.17) and the other from the *Satires* (I.i.106–7). Emanuel has noted that the quoting from classical authors as a way of validating law texts was widespread and that the practice may have been taken over from English law texts such as Bracton; he concludes that "it seems probable that Bracton and the Redaction B compiler were following the contemporary legal fashion in introducing into their writings quotations from Classical Latin poets."[83] However, these lines of Horace, appropriate though they are to a law text with their references to "right" and "courage," are not, as far as I am aware, attested elsewhere

---

title, which may be *Cronicon*, see Crick, "The Power and the Glory," 38.

78. ByT (Pen. 20), 140–41; and Henley, "Rhetoric, Translation and Historiography" and Russell, "'Go and look in the Latin books,'" 220–25.

79. For Rhigyfarch's lament, see Lapidge, "Welsh-Latin Poetry," 88–93; for the poem by Gruffudd ab yr Ynad Coch, see *CBT* VII.36 (414–33), and for discussion, see Matonis, "Rhetorical Patterns."

80. The text was printed in *Annales Cambriae* (ed. ab Ithel), 60–61, and has been more recently edited and translated into modern Welsh by Pryce, "Y Canu Lladin," 222–23; neither noted the Ovidian borrowing. See Russell, "'Go and look in the Latin books,'" 226–29.

81. The first half of the second line is corrupt, but easily understood as a scribal miscopying of Ovid's *Quique dolet quotiens . . .*

82. *Latin Texts of the Welsh Laws* (ed. Emanuel), 193; cf. also *Prologues* (ed. Russell), 23–25.

83. *Latin Texts of the Welsh Laws* (ed. Emanuel), 30–31 (quotation on 31).

within the legal tradition. It is possible therefore that, in following current fashion, the redactor was drawing on other sources for his quotations. Even so, we cannot rule out the possibility that they were extracted from a *florilegium,* and so such quotations do not constitute prima facie evidence for a text of Horace in medieval Gwynedd. Nowhere else in the Welsh legal tradition do we encounter a similar use of classical quotation, but Latin Redaction B is the closest thing we have to an antiquarian collection of law, and if we were to expect to find such quotation anywhere it would be in this kind of text. Such usage may point to classical texts (or *florilegia*) surviving in antiquarian contexts but not perhaps in general use.

The scattered fragments of evidence suggest that in the centuries after the Oxford Ovid left Wales for Glastonbury, there was some kind of access to classical literature reflected in the references by Sulien and his family and at a later stage in writings both in Wales and about Wales. There is then a disjunction between this and the lack of surviving manuscripts, and it may indicate that texts of the classical authors were known in some form even though the manuscripts are now lost.

Education in Medieval Wales

Another approach is to consider educational practice. For it is possible that some of the classical texts might have been encountered at a younger age as part of the more elementary stages of education. Such texts may have been available in certain places, but it is not clear, from what we know of the contents of their libraries, that the Cistercian monasteries would have been useful storehouses. On the other hand, there are hints that the Cistercians were involved in the provision of local education, as Thomson has shown for the Cistercian monasteries of Basingwerk and Valle Crucis in the late fifteenth century.[84] Similarly, in addition to the evidence from north-east Wales, Orme's work on medieval schooling provides evidence for schools in Wales from Brecon (1165), Caernarfon (mid-fifteenth century), Haverfordwest (1325, 1488), Montgomery (ca. 1518 and 1548), and St Davids (1363).[85]

Most of the evidence we have comes from post-Norman Wales, but in a period closer to that of our Ovid manuscript, the text entitled *De raris fabulis* (preserved in Oxford Bodleian 572, fol. 41v–47r (s. x^2)) contains a colloquy text designed to teach pupils Latin, and versions of such texts were prevalent

---

84. Thomson, "Cistercians and Schools in Late Medieval Wales"; cf. also Knight, "The Welsh Monasteries."

85. Orme, *Medieval Schools,* 346–72; cf. also id. "Schools and Schoolmasters."

in Anglo-Saxon England.[86] On the basis of its provenance and glossing, this particular text is thought to have originated in Wales but to have been taken to Cornwall. Colloquy texts can sometimes be glossed in the vernacular of choice, whether Old Welsh,[87] Old Cornish or Old English. The type of pedagogical background implied by *De raris fabulis* is elementary but not that elementary; it sets out to teach vocabulary and nominal declension, but at the same time presupposes a basic grasp of Latin grammar and syntax. It has been argued above that the prime function of the glossing on our Ovid text was to teach Latin verse. The Latin and Old Breton glossing on the text of Eutyches, *De uerbo*, which now forms the first part of the same manuscript as our text of Ovid (Bodleian Auct. Ff. 4. 32, fols. 2v–9v) was unsurprisingly related to teaching the Latin verb, and one of the most heavily glossed parts concerns the rules for forming denominative verbs. But other glossed texts, such as the Cambridge Juvencus (CUL Ff. 4. 42, s. ix–x) glossed in Old Welsh and Old Irish, or the Martianus Capella preserved in Cambridge, Corpus Christi College, 153 (s. ix²) and glossed in Old Welsh, seem to have more glosses which are concerned with explanation and exegesis than elementary language teaching, though, as noted above, such glossing may not be incompatible with language learning.[88] More generally, for pre-Norman Wales there is evidence for teachers in monasteries and earlier churches with their hereditary families (the family of Sulien, for example, being prominent through much of the twelfth century).[89] In other words, it is possible that what knowledge of Ovid there was might have been transmitted from the older houses rather than through the Cistercians. This is also consistent with the possibility suggested by Huws that some such churches in North Wales might have held on to Insular minuscule even into the thirteenth century and that the ca. 1250 date for Welsh vernacular MSS might be a result of their final abandonment of the old script (and thus the obsolescence of the books written in that script).[90]

From the eleventh century onwards, we begin to see indications of a different style of teaching and learning in the form of versions of the *Liber*

---

86. For editions of the text, see *Early Scholastic Colloquies* (ed. Stevenson), 1–11; *De raris fabulis* (ed. and trans. Gwara (but note Lapidge's warning about this edition in Lapidge, "Colloquial Latin," 410, n. 7)); for discussion of this text, see Gwara, *Education in Wales and Cornwall*; Russell, "An habes linguam Latinam?," 200–204. For colloquy texts more generally, *Latin Colloquies* (ed. Gwara); Gwara and Porter, *Anglo-Saxon Conversations*; and Lapidge, "Colloquial Latin"; Gwara, "Anglo-Saxon Schoolbooks." See above, 10–12.

87. In addition to the Old Welsh glosses in *De raris fabulis* noted above, there is one Old Welsh gloss, **tuic** gl. *curbanam* in the colloquy entitled *Colloquia Hisperica*; see *Early Scholastic Colloquies* (ed. Stevenson), 16 (l. 21); *Latin Colloquies* (ed. Gwara), 105 (l. 178).

88. See 8–12 above; cf. also Russell, "Teaching between the Lines," 135–40.

89. Charles-Edwards, *Wales and the Britons*, 640–43.

90. Huws, *Medieval Welsh Manuscripts*, 1–14.

Catonianus, a compilation of classical texts which formed the basis of the syllabus.[91] As Hexter has observed,

> Study of the *auctores* is undeniably central to the history of Latin in the Middle Ages—both language and literature, because the medium itself was learned in schools. It is evident that the authors with whom a schoolboy would become familiar and the means by which these authors were presented would have had a profound effect on his literary tastes, attitudes, and values for the rest of his life. This was doubly true when the authors were read not only for literary culture but primarily (at first, at least) for instruction in grammar.[92]

The final sentence of this could be applied to the earlier period and to our Ovid manuscript, but as usual we know very little about the situation in Wales apart from the evidence for the existence of the schools noted above. The evidence for England, however, indicates that versions of the *Liber Catonianus* were in widespread use. Hunt has shown that, while the twelfth-century versions did not contain any Ovid, by the thirteenth century the elegies of Maximianus were beginning to be replaced by Ovid's *Remedia amoris* on the grounds that "it was less likely to cause harm to the minds of boys."[93] That said, Alexander Nequam, writing in the late twelfth and early thirteenth century, was not even sure about Ovid's amatory works as teaching texts:

> Elegias Nasonis et Ovidium Metamorfosos audiat, sed et precipue libellum De remedio amoris familiarem habeat. Placuit tamen viris autenticis carmina amatoria cum satiris subducenda esse a manibus adolescentium.[94]

As with the earlier sections of this discussion, the real question is to what extent we might extrapolate from the English evidence for Wales. While we might be confident that such texts were available in the marcher lordships between England and Wales and in south Wales in the thirteenth century, what was to hand in the (mainly monastic) schoolrooms of Wales is less clear the further one goes west and north, and the further one goes back in time. It is likely that such texts were available in St Davids and perhaps some of

---

91. For a general discussion, see Orme, *Medieval Schools,* 98–105; for a far more detailed discussion relating to England, see Hunt, *Teaching and Learning,* I.59–79.

92. Hexter, "*Latinitas* in the Middle Ages," 76.

93. Hunt, *Teaching and Learning,* I.70; on the complications of later versions of *Liber Catonianus,* see ibid., 70–79. On the *Remedia,* see Pellegrin, "Les 'Remedia amoris' d'Ovide."

94. Hunt, *Teaching and Learning,* I.269–70: "Let him hear Ovid's *Elegies* and *Metamorphoses,* but especially let him be familiar with the little book of *The Remedy of Love.* It has seemed right to men of authority, however, that the amatory songs and satires should be withdrawn from the hands of adolescents" (trans. Orme, *Medieval Schools,* 97).

the Cistercian monasteries if they were engaged in elementary education. However, in contrast to the previous sections of this chapter, there is a further point which might give us greater confidence that such teaching texts were to be had in Wales: the first text in the *Liber Catonianus* (and the one from which its name derives) was the third- or fourth-century *Disticha Catonis*. From about 1300 onwards several versions of this text survive translated into Middle Welsh; the fact that there was a vernacular translation strongly suggests that it was a well-known text. At this period it seems to be rare to find the *Disticha Catonis* travelling by itself, and so it is not unreasonable to think that the other texts of the *Liber Catonianus* might have been circulating in Wales as well, including Ovid's *Remedia amoris*.

Preliminary Conclusions

Consideration of the survival of books and manuscripts in Wales in the centuries between 900 and 1400 has revealed little evidence for texts of Ovid, or indeed any other classical author. Extrapolation from the more substantial evidence in England has only a limited usefulness. From the twelfth century Welsh monasteries were predominantly Cistercian and, as far as we can tell from the surviving library catalogues from Cistercian houses in England, the bookshelves of Cistercian libraries seem to have been particularly bare in regard to such works. On the other hand, snapshots provided by authors working in the period of what they knew and had read indicate that they did have some access to classical texts, especially in places such as Llanbadarn or St David's. Furthermore, it is important to emphasize that the absence of evidence relates to texts of all kinds, not just classical texts and not just Ovid. When we turn to lower-level educational practice in Wales, the evidence is almost as thin (and we are just as reliant on extrapolation from the English evidence), but there are some tantalizing hints. It is clear from England that *Liber Catonianus*, for all its shifting form and content, was the set text of preference. The fact that a Welsh version of the *Disticha Catonis* is attested from around 1300 is highly suggestive. It is possible, then, that especially in the March, and perhaps further west and north, versions of the *Liber Catonianus* were also in use from the late thirteenth century onwards, and they may have contained copies of *Remedia amoris*. In other words, it is thinkable that the knowledge that the *cywyddwyr* display of the name *Ofydd* and some minimal other details may derive from their school education and not from some higher-level perusal of surviving manuscripts of Ovid's poetry. Another reason why the latter is less likely is that (even if we set aside the lack of manuscripts) the common form in which texts of Ovid survive in England is the

Ovidius magnus. If such texts had survived in Wales, there would be no good reason why Welsh poets would be fixated on Ovid as a love poet rather than as, for example, the composer of the *Metamorphoses,* a work which would have accorded well with accounts of shape-shifting and the like in native Welsh tales.[95] For the *cywyddwyr, Ofydd* is pre-eminently associated with love and love poetry, and it might make sense if their experience of Ovid was restricted to the *Remedia.*

FFERYLL, DWNED, AND ARGUMENTS BY ANALOGY

We may return to the question of what *Ofydd* actually meant when used in the poetry of the fourteenth and fifteenth centuries. It is clearly extremely difficult to take specific examples and come to a clear decision that in one case it refers to Ovid and in another to "love poetry" generally. One avenue is still to be explored and this involves an argument from analogy. The use of *Ofydd* to refer to love poetry is similar to the kind of semantic shift we are familiar with in the modern world in terms like *Hoover* or *biro.* There are two stages in the semantic development: first, an item is named after a person closely associated with it (in these examples usually the inventor); second, all similar items are so named whether made by the same person or company or not and whether made in the same way or not as long as they perform the same function. The semantics of personal names are notoriously problematic; at one level it can be claimed that they mean nothing but are simply designators and as such can be distinguished from nicknames which do have some semantic content (though sometimes distorted from the norm[96]); on the other hand, they can acquire a more general connotation, such as describing someone as a "right Charlie."[97] Names of manufactured objects named after their inventor are more like the latter than the former. Following this argument in the case of *Ofydd* it might be claimed that, in addition to instances where it designates the poet directly, it refers in some cases to love poetry composed by Ovid but in others to love poetry unconnected to Ovid; the case, discussed above, of *Llyfr Ofydd* being used as a title for extracts translated from a bestiary is striking.[98] This would be difficult to demonstrate in almost all cases, but the semantic shift is thinkable. There are two other examples in medieval Welsh

---

95. The punitive nature of shape-shifting in some tales, e.g *Math, Culhwch,* etc. might fit the Ovidian pattern but is too common to pursue as evidence for Ovid; cf. also Rachel Bromwich's suggestion that there were echoes of the Philomela episode from Ovid, *Metamorphoses,* Book 6, in the poetry of Dafydd ap Gwilym (*Aspects,* 117).

96. For example, someone called Curly may be completely bald, a Lofty very short.

97. See Russell, "Patterns of Hypocorism," 238–39.

98. See above, 207–8.

which we might use to test these possibilities which have not previously been drawn into the ambit of this argument, and these involve *Fferyll(t)* "Virgil" and *Dwned* "Donatus."[99]

Fferyll(t) "Virgil"

The name *Fferyll(t)* is a borrowing into Welsh of Latin *Vergilius*.[100] An early borrowing of a /wergilius/ would explain the *–yll* < *-ilius* (cf. *Ebryll* "April" from *Aprili(u)s*, etc.), but we would expect the first syllable to have produced **Gweryll*.[101] But *Fferyll(t)* seems to have been borrowed from a form pronounced with initial /v/- which was devoiced to /f/-. Now initial consonants in Welsh are subject to lenition in certain grammatical environments, but /f/- did not take part in the mutation system. A borrowed initial /v/- could only have been perceived as lenited and so a delenited version had to be created; it could be perceived as the lenited variant of /b/- and /m/- and thus *verbum* was borrowed as *berf* but English *velvet* as *melfed*; Middle Welsh *bilaen* and *milaen* both from *villein*.[102] But there seems to have been some secondary development that allowed a borrowed initial /v/- to be treated as /f/- which stood outside the alternations associated with the mutations. Parallel examples are hard to come by, but it is possible that *Ffraid* from Irish *Brigid* (in a Latin form *Brigida*) is one: in place names we might expect the /b/- to have lenited to /v/- before *llan* "church" and other feminine nouns, and it may be that the /f/- of *Ffraid* might the outcome of a similar reanalysis to that proposed for *Fferyll*. The upshot is that *Fferyll* seems to display both early and late features; it therefore may be a secondary modification of an original **Gweryll* under the influence of the later forms pronounced with /v/-. As with *Ofydd*, then, the form of the name seems secondary and maybe for the same reasons, learned influence and perhaps the written form of the name.

Two chronologically distinct Virgilian personae are found in medieval Welsh literary sources.[103] First, the classical poet, who was as much associated with the *Eclogues* and *Georgics* as with the *Aeneid*, figures in a number of

---

99. For a brief attempt to consider *Dwned* alongside *Fferyll*, see Chotzen, *Recherches*, 144.

100. On the variant with *-t*, cf. *bwyall/bwyallt* "axe," *deall/deallt* "understand" (cf. especially *dealltwriaeth* "understanding"); they may well have arisen from hypercorrection from cases where the *-llt* is historical. Early examples include: OW *guell* (for *guellt* "pasture") (*The Text of the Book of Llan Dâv* (ed. Evans and Rhys), 120.19); the place name, *Buell* (rhyming with *guell* "better") usually spelt *Buellt* in in a poem entitled *Mawl Hywel ap Goronwy* "Praise Poem for Hywel ap Goronwy" (CBT I.1.19).

101. On the chronology of *-ilius* > *-yll*, see Schrijver, *Studies*, 321–24.

102. Cf. also *bogal*, a late borrowing of Latin *vocālis*, late because it did not take part in the regular change of *-/aːlis/* to *-awl*; for these developments, see Lewis, *Elfen Ladin*, 16.

103. Appendix 2 below contains a full list of occurrences.

Welsh translations of Latin texts. For example, the Middle Welsh translation of the *Disticha Catonis*, which was discussed above in relation to Ovid, refers to Virgil in the context of learning how to farm:[104] *Or mynny wybot ardymhereu tir ae diwyllodraeth, dysc llyfyr Fferyll yr hwnn a elwir Vyrgil* "If you wish to know how to regulate the land and to cultivate it, learn the book of Fferyll(t), who is called Virgil" (rendering *Telluris si forte velis cognoscere cultus, Virgilium legito*).[105] Virgil the poet is also invoked at times of lament and mourning with the refrain along the lines of "not even Virgil could relate our grief"—some of the various distraught obituaries of the Lord Rhys in 1197 preserved in *Brut y Tywysogion*, the Welsh versions of the chronicles, refer to Virgil alongside Statius as the two Roman authors who would not be able to record the depth of grief and lamentation at his death:[106] for example, the *Red Book of Hergest* (Oxford, Jesus College MS 111) version has *hyt na allei ystoriaeu Ystas ystoriawr na chath[l]eu Feryll vard menegi y veint gwynuan a dolur thrueni a doeth y holl genedyl y Brytanyeit* "that neither the histories of Statius, the historian, nor the songs of Virgil, the poet, could tell how great a lamentation and grief and misery came to the whole race of the Britons."[107] This renders a rather more oblique reference to Virgil in the Latin of the *Cronica de Wallia: Tanti uiri probitates quas ille magnanimus historiographus Thebanus, si temporis uicissitudo concessissit, Tebaide sopita pertractante, gauderet, uerum ille historiographus Troianus poetarum nobilissimus, si misera fata dedissent, grandiloquo stilo in longum diffunderet euum* "The honesty of such a man, which that great-hearted Theban historiographer would have celebrated, as the *Thebaid* relates things past, if the vicissitudes of time had granted it; then that Trojan historian, most noble of poets, if the wretched fates had allowed, would have long praised it with his eloquent pen."[108] The association of Virgil with Troy might help to explain why the student consulting *Disticha Catonis* is advised to consult Lucan over battles and warfare.[109] A decade or so later the Welsh translator of the life of Gruffudd ap Cynan recalled the death of Gellan, Gruffudd's chief poet, at the battle of Aberlleiniog in similar terms: *Mivi a gyuadeuaf nas dichonaf vi, ac nas dichonvn, pei bedun kyn huotlet a Thullius vard ym pros ac a Maro vard en traethaut*

---

104. For discussion in relation to Ovid, see 203.

105. Williams, "Testunau," 22; *Disticha Catonis* (ed. Boas), 90. It is striking that, when the same text asks about war and fighting they are directed to Lucan: *Or mynny wybot neu adnabot ymladeu gwyr Rufein neu wyr Punic, keis y llyfr a elwir Lucan* "If you wish to know about, or be familiar with, the battles of the Romans or Carthaginians, seek out the book called Lucan" (rendering Latin *Si Romana cupis et Punica noscere bella, Lucanum quaeras, qui Martis proelia dixit*) (Williams, "Testunau," 22; *Disticha Catonis* (ed. Boas), 90).

106. For a more detailed discussion of the Latin literature occasioned by the death of the Lord Rhys than is possible here, see Russell, "'Go and look in the Latin books,'" 215–30.

107. *ByT* (RB) 178.7–10.

108. Jones, "'Cronica de Wallia,'" 31 (my translation).

109. *Disticha Catonis* (ed. Boas), 90.

mydyr "I admit that I cannot, nor could not, do it (sc. relate the deeds of Gruffudd as well as Gellan) were I as eloquent as the bard Tullius in prose, and the bard Maro in verse."[110] In this case the translation (which was composed some half a century before 1197) mentions Homer rather than Virgil. The translator may have misread *Homerum* as *Maronem*; or alternatively, he anticipated that his audience would be more familiar with Virgil than with Homer. If so, it does at least suggest that Virgil was the expected point of reference for such laments.[111]

By contrast, most references to Virgil/Fferyll in medieval Wales portray him in the conventional medieval persona of magician, necromancer, and alchemist, capable of using his magical powers in particular to produce great buildings.[112] The conduit seems to be the idea that his fourth *Eclogue* prophesied the birth of Christ, and references to this are attested in Welsh in both prose and verse. The BL Cotton Cleopatra B.v (ca. 1320) version of *Brut y Brenhinedd* (the Welsh translation of Geoffrey of Monmouth's *Historia Regum*) refers to the fourth *Eclogue* in the context of Christ's birth in a section which was added to Geoffrey's original text: *y nawuet ulwydyn y dywat Fferyll am gnawdoliaeth Christ* "the ninth year Virgil spoke of the incarnation of Christ."[113] That the prophecy was a familiar part of Virgil's medieval persona is indicated by its appearance in a poem, *Kat Godeu* (The Battle of the Trees), which ends with the lines, *Eurem yn euryll / mi hud wyf berthyll / ac ydwyf drythyll / o erymes Fferyll* "[Like] a magnificent jewel in a gold ornament, thus I am resplendent, and I am exhilarated by the prophecy of Virgil." Marged Haycock has argued that these concluding lines show Taliesin, in whose voice the poem is delivered, making claims to be the Welsh Virgil since (as suggested by Wace) he too can prophesy the birth of Christ.[114]

There seems to have been a particularly south-Italian preoccupation with the talismanic qualities of objects associated with Virgil which are probably related to the claim that Virgil was buried in Naples.[115] But in addition to this, his fame seems in part to have spread through the narrative of the *Seven Sages of Rome* and especially his reputation as a magical builder. The earliest reference to Virgil in this context in Welsh is indeed in *Saith Doethion*

---

110. *HGK* 21.19–20; *MPW* 74.2–5.

111. *VGC* §23/17.

112. For the medieval Virgil, see Comparetti, *Virgil in the Middle Ages*; Rand, "The Medieval Virgil" (and other essays in the same volume of *Studi Medievali*); Spargo, *Virgil the Necromancer*; Williams and Pattie, *Virgil*; Ziolkowski and Putnam, *The Virgilian Tradition*; and particularly useful on the Welsh connections, Wood, "Virgil and Taliesin."

113. *ByT* (Cleo), 80.11. This version of *Brut y Brenhinedd* is a very much shortened and re-worked version; see Roberts, "*Ystoriaeu Brenhinedd Ynys Brydeyn*."

114. *Legendary Poems* (ed. Haycock), 5.246–49 (and discussion at 173, and the notes on 238–39); for Wace, see in particular, 238–39; see also Wood, "Virgil and Taliesin."

115. Cf. Comparetti, *Virgil in the Middle Ages*, 258, 268, 293–94, 296, 303.

Rhufain, a Middle Welsh version of the *Seven Sages* narrative, where Virgil is depicted setting up a magic tower and mirror by means of which the emperor could watch over all the provinces of his empire: *"Fferyll," heb hi, "a ossodes colofyn ymperued Rufein ac ar benn y golofyn drych o geluydyt ingyrmars"* "'Virgil' she said, 'set up a column in the middle of Rome and on top of the column a mirror with necromantic arts.'"[116] But again, as with the concept of Virgil as prophet, we see this narrative sufficiently embedded to appear in verse as well and used as a measure against which to gauge the quality of a building: for example, the fourteenth-century poet Prydydd Breuan compares the building skills of Maredudd of Ynys Derllys to those of Virgil: *Mawr adail cynhail, cynnydd Fferyll* "He builds a great building, with the same success as Virgil."[117] Similarly, in a poem closely dated to 1468–69, Guto'r Glyn compares the *plas* of Sir Richard Herbert at Coldbrook to the works of Virgil: *gwaith Fferyll ar gestyll gynt* "the way Virgil once worked on castles."[118]

The second aspect of the medieval Fferyll has to do more directly with magic. In the story of Taliesin, *Chwedl/Hanes Taliesin*, preserved in an early seventeenth-century manuscript, the cauldron of inspiration is cooked up by Ceridwen using a Virgilian recipe book: *Ag yna ordeiniodd hi drwy gelfyddyd llyfrau Pheryllt i ferwi pair o awen a gwybodau oi map* "She arranged through the art of the books of Virgil to boil up a cauldron of inspiration and knowledge for her son."[119] Elsewhere, in verse we find references to *kelvydyt Fferyll* "the art of Virgil" and to being a *car i Fferyll* "a friend of Virgil." These are presumably intended to indicate an association with magic and alchemy.[120] It is less clear what *ffeiriau Fferyll* "the fairs of Virgil" refer to, but it may have to do with fairs where magical tricks were performed.[121]

These references to Fferyll are to be seen in the broader context of other characters with magical skills in medieval Welsh literature, such as Taliesin and Myrddin. The association between Fferyll and Taliesin has been discussed by Juliette Wood who provides a useful compilation and discussion of references to Fferyll in Welsh.[122] She considers Fferyll mainly in conjunction with Taliesin. However, aspects of the depiction of Fferyll's art are not dissimilar to some of the general all-purpose features of medieval magicians: Fferyll as

---

116. *SDR* 480; cf. also the Welsh version of the Grail legend: *pan wnaeth Fferyll y castell hwnnw drwy y gelvydyt ae synnwyr* "when Feryll made that castle through his art and cleverness" (*SG* 327.39–328.2).

117. *GPB* 1.22.

118. *GGG* XLIX.22; the translation is from the online edition of his works at http://www .gutorglyn.net/gutorglyn/poem/?poem=022&first-line=022 (consulted 18 Dec 2013)

119. *YT* 133.

120. *GDG* 84.58 (= *CDG* 135.56); *GTA* 255.64 (cf. *GTA* 400.35). The modern use of *fferyllfa* to refer to a "pharmacy" is a modern continuation of this usage.

121. *GDG* 32.32 (= *CDG* 134.32).

122. Wood, "Virgil and Taliesin," 91–95.

magical builder is framed in similar terms to Merlinus in Geoffrey's *Historia regum* who is depicted as building Stonehenge.[123] Likewise the magical functions of the Welsh Myrddin and Taliesin are strikingly similar in early Welsh literature but gradually separate out into separate "brands," a prophetic Myrddin and an all-knowing, all-too-clever Taliesin. On the other hand, Fferyll, arguably a latecomer to this party, is depicted much more as a magician and alchemist. As is conventional, the entry on *fferyll(t)* in *Geiriadur Prifysgol* follows the analysis of the editors of the texts it cites and thus notes the earliest usage as a common noun, "chemist, druggist, alchemist, magician" in the seventeenth-century lexicographers, with a similar range of senses in its adjectival and abstract derivatives.[124] By implication, therefore, earlier attestations are assumed to be of the personal name. However, closer examination of the examples from the fourteenth century onwards suggests that, as with *Ofydd,* we should not always assume that *Fferyll* refers to the individual otherwise known as "Virgil" but rather in some instances it is easy to replace the poet, the medieval magician, or alchemist with a more abstract term such as "magic" or "alchemy"; thus, instances such as *keluydyt Fferyll* could simply be understood as "the art of magic /alchemy." If so, we have at least some parallel support for treating *ofydd* as a common noun.

Dwned "Donatus"

A similar argument can be made for *Dwned*, although in this case the argument has a broader base taking in Middle English as well. Latin *Dōnātus* was borrowed directly as Welsh *Dunawd*, Old/Middle Welsh *Dunaut*, but Welsh *Dwned* was borrowed from Middle English *Donet,* itself borrowed from *Dōnātus*.[125] While *Dunawd* is preserved only as a personal name,[126] our concern is with *Dwned*, which means both "a book of grammar" (though not necessarily the grammar of Donatus) and then more generally in the later period "talk, chatter, gossip."[127] The development of this word in English, before it was borrowed, and subsequently in Welsh is of particular interest for our purposes. Essentially, the name of the grammarian was used to refer to his grammar, the *Ars grammatica,* and especially the *Ars minor* dealing with parts of speech. Donatus became the best known grammarian in the early medieval period and in the insular world

---

123. *HRB* VIII.128–30.

124. *GPC*, s.v. *fferyll.*

125. Parry-Williams, *English Element in Welsh,* 108.

126. For example, Bede's *Dinoot* (*Historia Ecclesiastica* (ed. Colgrave and Mynors), II.ii); [D]*unaut mab Pappo* in the Welsh genealogies (*Early Welsh Genealogical Tracts,* ed. Bartrum, 11, etc.); Parsons, *Martyrs and Memorials,* 74–75.

127. See *GPC*, s.v. *dwned.*

his works were the basis of the development of the more elementary grammars for teaching non-native speakers and learners of Latin.[128] The success of *Ars minor* also ensured that reflexes of *Donatus* shifted to become the standard term for elementary grammars; for example, in *De raris fabulis, Donaticus* is used to refer generally to a grammar book.[129] The usage was also then extended to refer to grammars (elementary or otherwise) of languages other than Latin, thus Uc Faidit's *Donatz proensals,* a grammar of Provençal composed in Italy ca. 1240.[130] This usage is also found in Wales in the fifteenth century: the grammar associated with the poet Gutun Owain begins *Llyma Gyfrinach Beirdd Ynys Brydain, yr hwnn a elwir y Dwned ynghymraeg* "Here begins the secret of the bards of the Island of Britain which is called the *Dwned* in Welsh."[131] A further development in English was the spread of the term to refer to an elementary treatise or primer on any subject: thus, Pecock, "is before said in þe folewer to þe donet" and "which dialog is, as it were, a donet or a key to be learned afore þis book."[132] In Langland we see a further extension where it refers to an apprentice draper learning the rudiments of his trade: *Thanne drouȝ I me among drapiers my Donet to lerne, to drawe þe liser along—þe lenger it semede.*[133]

In Welsh, although references to *Dwned/dwned* are more restricted, it is assumed that it refers to grammar or to a grammar book.[134] Lews Glyn Cothi used it on several occasions as a term of praise: *Y dyn a wypo Dwned—a rhywlys / a rhoi yn felys yr hen foled / doed i Gil-y-Sant, dyweded—odlau / ac aur a bwydau nac arbeded* "Whoever might know Dwned and the rules and how to provide the old praise sweetly, let him come to Gil-y-Sant; let him utter *odlau* and let him not stint himself in gold and food."[135] Here it seems to be referring to knowing

---

128. Law, *Insular Latin Grammarians,* 14–16; even by the time of Gregory, *Donatus* was being used as a term for "grammar."

129. In the context of elementary Latin learning, it makes no sense to think that it refers to the work of Donatus himself. For this passage and discussion of the text, see above 58n136; cf. also Russell, "Teaching between the Lines," 138–39.

130. *Donatz proensal* (ed. Marshall). Cf. also a similar extension of the use of the names of other grammarians: cf., for example, Varro is used as a mode of reference to a word-list: Capis, *Varon Milanes* (word list and etymological dictionary); and Priscian is used to refer to a manual of pronunciation: Biffi, *Prissian de Milan* (pronunciation guide) (both composed in the sixteenth century and printed together in 1606). On the use of "Donatus" to refer to grammars of vernacular languages, see Ciccolella, *Donati Greci,* 44–46.

131. *GP* 67 (note that the last phrase is printed as *yng* [*Ng*]*hymraeg* in this edition); this version of *GP* is a relatively late reworking of earlier versions of the bardic grammars preserved in Peniarth 20 and the *Red Book of Hergest* (Oxford, Jesus College 111), for editions of which see *GP*.

132. Pecock, *The Rule of Christian Religion* (ed. Greet), 133, 230.

133. Langland, *Piers Plowman* (ed. Schmidt), I.204–7.

134. Cf. Johnston, *Llên yr Uchelwyr,* 27. Note that the suggested example in the work of Cynddelw *ym pryssur llauur llyuyrdoneit* "in the rush of working in grammar books" (*CBT* IV (Cynddelw Brydydd Mawr II) 16.143) where *-doneit,* though confirmed by rhyme, may better be understood as "books of donation."

135. *GLGC* 69.21–24. For the other examples, see the Appendix (234–35 below).

how to compose and perform praise poetry, as in Gutun Owain's grammar, rather than precisely to grammar. Similarly Tudur Aled in his *marwnad* "death poem" for Dafydd ab Edmwnd clearly used *dwned* to refer to poetical expertise: *Llaw Dduw a fu'n lladd awen / lladd enaid holl ddwned hen* "The hand of God has killed inspiration by killing the whole soul of the old Dwned";[136] and later in the same poem returned to the theme: *Dy ddwned oedd o'i enau* "Your Dwned was from his mouth."[137] A particularly striking example illustrating the issues we are concerned with occurs at an earlier date in the work of Dafydd ap Gwilym and is worth considering in greater detail. An *awdl* to his uncle, Llywelyn, dated to the 1330s and thus providing the earliest attested example of the use of *dwned* in Welsh, opens as follows:[138]

> Llyfr dwned Dyfed dyfyn—ar windai
>   i randir Llywelyn
> Llannerch, aed annerch pob dyn,
> Lle twymlys llu, at Emlyn.[139]

A literal translation runs as follows: "The grammar book of Dyfed (i.e. Llywelyn) invites to wine houses in the district of Llywelyn—a grove (let greeting of every person go out), a place of a warm court for a host—to Emlyn."[140] Opinions, however, have diverged over the sense of the opening phrase. Bromwich took it as referring to Dafydd's uncle Llywelyn and ties its sentiment to other references in another poem, a *marwnad* "death poem" for his uncle, in which he refers to him as *prydydd ac ieithydd* "poet and linguist" and *ys difai a'm dysgud* "faultlessly did you teach me."[141] She argues that his uncle was not only his poetical teacher but in fact educated him more broadly, "a literary intermediary introducing his nephew to literary influences which originated far beyond the borders of Wales."[142] However, other interpretations have been canvassed: Thomas Parry suggested that *llyfr Dwned* here could be understood as simply meaning "custom, usage"; thus, "The custom of Dyfed is to invite . . ." or "This is how things are done in Dyfed, inviting . . ."[143] The poem would then have less to do with Dafydd's education and more with

---

136. *GTA* LXX.1–2.

137. *GTA* LXX.41.

138. For the dating, see *CDG*, 595.

139. *GDG* 12.1 (= *CDG* 5.1).

140. Cf. the translation of *CDG* 5.1–4 at http://www.dafyddapgwilym.net/ (consulted 9 July 2014).

141. Bromwich, *Aspects*, 14; *GDG* 13.12 (= *CDG* 6.12) and *GDG* 13.18 (= *CDG* 6.22), respectively.

142. Bromwich, *Aspects*, 14; cf. also 105 where it is also suggested that Dafydd may have been familiar with the bardic grammars.

143. Parry, *GDG* 12.1n. The translations are my own. Note that *dyfyn* can be construed either as a third sg. present (as in the former rendering) or as the verbal noun (as in the latter).

conventional praise of Llywelyn's generosity. Parry's preference is clearly for this latter interpretation: "efallai mai hwn yw'r dehongliad gorau."[144] Another possibility is simply to interpret *llyfr Dwned* here as something like "authority" without needing to be more specific.[145] If one of the latter readings is followed, then already by the first half of the thirteenth century it was possible to use *llyfr Dwned* in this more abstract sense.

A corollary of this argument is that in the above discussion mention of *llyfr X* "the book of X"—with its suggestion of the reality of a book, of a text which might be read or consulted—has been taken as more solid evidence of a specific reference to a poet's work than a plain reference to, for example, *Ofydd*; this is how *Llyfr Ofydd* has been implicitly (and sometimes explicitly) read. But, in the light of the way *Fferyll* and *Dwned* can be read, and especially how *llyfr Fferyll* and *llyfr Dwned* can be understood, it perhaps may be less useful, and more misleading, to think of *llyfr* as text; it seems much more likely that we should read it as "introductory guide, text book" to some more generic activity, such as language (Dwned), magic (Fferyll) and love (Ofydd).

CONCLUSION

The commentaries to the editions of Dafydd ap Gwilym and the other *cywyddwyr* are littered with short notes on the works of Ovid whenever a reference of *Ofydd* is encountered, and speculation has then followed as to which works might have been known and how—whether directly or indirectly through French or English reworkings. While it has been usually acknowledged in the scholarship that some of the references to *Ofydd* are probably non-specific, the default has been to assume specificity. In the latter part of this chapter I have attempted to reach out to other analogical evidence, in the form of the usage of *Fferyll* and *Dwned,* to suggest that the default reading of *(Llyfr) Ofydd* should probably be the generic one, unless there are particular reasons for a more specific reading.

Furthermore, in the middle part of this chapter it has been argued that there is little or no evidence that the poets had any direct access to texts of Ovid. At best, they may have encountered him in their schoolroom education as part of the *Liber Catonianus,* and then perhaps only in the form of *Remedia amoris.* Given the difficulty of pinning down clear and unambiguous references to the works of Ovid, it seems most likely that their use of *Ofydd* as a point of reference to love poetry (and only love poetry) was more

---

144. "Perhaps this is the best interpretation" (*GDG* 12.1n).
145. I am grateful to Barry Lewis for suggesting this.

generic than specific, reaching back into hazy recollections of the school-room. In terms of transmission, translation, and dissemination, the argument presented here replaces specific claims about Ovidian texts in Wales with a more general claim about the absorption of Ovidian ideals into Wales as into England, France, and Western Europe. It thus strengthens the arguments that medieval Wales was more, rather than less, like its neighbours.

APPENDICES

The following collection of references is as complete as possible; further examples may emerge in forthcoming editions in the series of texts of the Cywyddwyr, Cyfres Beirdd yr Uchelwyr. The citations are listed in an approximate chronological order of composition.

1. *Ofydd*

Prose

Williams, "Testunau," 22 (translation of *Disticha Catonis* (earliest MS ca. 1300)): *Os da gennyt dyscu garu ne ordderchu, keis lyfr ofydd yr hwn a elwit naset.* "If you want to learn how to love or be a lover, seek out the book of Ovid, who was called Naso."

Verse

CBT II (Owein Cyfeiliog) 15.17: *boen Ouyt gennad* "messenger of Ovid's pain."

CBT II (Hywel ab Owain Gwynedd) 6.40: *Ked bwyf i cariadavg certed Ouyt* "though I be a lover in the manner of Ovid."

CBT VII (Iorwerth Fychan) 30.63: *Ys mawr vy angof na bvm Ouyd* "Great is my oblivion (sc. that I have fallen into) that I was not Ovid."

GDG 6.16 (= CDG 12.16): *araith Ofydd* (CDG *euriaith*) "Ovid's (fine) language."[146]

GDG 6.23 (= CDG 12.23): *Ofydd cad* (CDG *faedd cad*) "Ovid/boar of battle."

GDG 22.3 (= CDG 60.3): *dan gyrs Ofydd* "under the branches of Ovid."

GDG 24.29 (= CDG 34.29): *Dyn Ofydd* "Ovid's man."

GDG 28.21 (= CDG 159.21): *prydydd cerdd Ofydd ddifai* "poet of Ovid's faultless song."

GDG 31.60 (= CDG 19.58): *digrifaf dyn deigr Ofydd* "most pleasant man of Ovid's tears."

GDG 35.43 (= CDG 106.43): *Ni byd dy Ofydd difai . . .* "Your faultless Ovid will never be . . ."

GDG 50.1 (= CDG 95.1): *Salm i'm cof o lyfr Ofydd* "I have a psalm in my memory from Ovid's book."

GDG 58.20 (= CDG 72.20): *Nid gwas . . . llwfr ar waith llyfr Ofydd* "I'm no coward at the work of Ovid's book."

GDG 70.9 (= CDG 58.7): *ni lefys dyn ail (GDG hael) Ofydd* "a man of Ovid's nature (or 'of generous Ovid') will not venture."

GDG 83.39–42 (= CDG 96.39–42): *Nid oes dwyn na dwys dyno . . . nas medrwyf . . . heb y llyfr hoywbwyll Ofydd* "There is no hillock nor thickset meadow which I do not make for . . . without the book of lively-minded Ovid" (my translation).

---

146. Unless otherwise indicated, translations of the works of Dafydd ap Gwilym are from http://www.dafyddapgwilym.net/ and therefore follow the CDG readings where there is a difference. Other translations are my own unless the edition contains a translation or are otherwise indicated.

GDG 116.34 (= *CDG* 46.30): *dull Ofydd* "Ovid's method."

GDG 143.51 (= *CDG* 71.51): *ciliawdr nid wyf, wyf Ofydd* "I am not a retreater; I am Ovid."

GDG 148.8 (= *CDG* 24.8): *cywydd gwiw Ofydd* "a worthy love poem."[147]

GIG XXII.43: *Prifeistr cywydd Ofydd oedd* "He was the master of Ovid's verse" (n.b. no MS authority for *primas*).

GSRh 11.155: *Salm o hen gof llyfr Ofydd* "the book of Ovid is a song of ancient memory" (cf. *GDG* 50.1 (= *CDG* 95.1) above).

GRhGE 6.35: *Pynciau cof o lyfr Ofydd* "memory of the matter of the book of Ovid."

GLlGMH 11.7: *deugur Ofydd* "the double pang of Ovid" (cf. *DGA* 1.7).

GLlGMH 12.53: *sathr Ofydd serch* "trampling the love of Ovid."

GIRh 2.1: *Da yw 'nghof am lyfr Ofydd* "My memory is good about the book of Ovid."

GIRh 2.27: *Gleiniau ofydd o ruddaur* "gems of love of red-gold."

GDB 14.5 (Llywelyn ab y Moel): *iaith Ofydd iawn fu bennaeth cerdd* "the language of Ovid he was properly the head of song" (but most MSS read *dofydd*).

GDB 15.42 (Llywelyn ab y Moel): *air ofydd* "the word of Ovid" (cf. Rhys Goch (*IGE* 158.7)).

GGM 3.65–6: *Ofydd drosof oedd draserch | fryd Sylus wyf* "An Ovid with the attitude of Sylus am I—there was excessive love over me."

GDE 5.77: *Ni allaf rif yn llyfr Ofydd* "I cannot reckon in the book of Ovid."

GDE 15.24: *Dafydd oedd Ofydd* "Dafydd was Ovid."

GMRh 3.30: *Digrifion diagr Ofydd* "the pleasant things of fair Ovid."

GILlF 2.25: *Llefain am fantell Ofydd* "wailing over the mantle of Ovid."

GILlF 5.8: *Llafur Ieuan, llyfr Ofydd* "the work of John, the book of Ovid."

GLlG 14.1: *Dafydd Llwyd, Ofydd y llu* "Dafydd Llwyd, the Ovid of the host" (= *GDLlF* 72.1).

GLl 5.6: *lifreifardd ar lyfr Ofydd* "a liveried poet of the book of Ovid."

GLl 7.63: *Iefainc wyf ar fainc Ofydd* "I am a youth on the bench of Ovid."

GRB 21.37: *Hen Ifor a hŷn oedd Ofydd* "Ifor was old, and Ovid was older."

GGG XIII.53–4: *A llys ar ei lled y lleddir lludded, a lle afrifed, a llyfr Ofydd* "And a court in all its breadth where tiredness is destroyed, and an immeasurable place, and a book of Ovid."

GDLlF 94.1: *Dafydd, llew Ofydd, Llwyd* "David, lion of Ovid, Llwyd."

GDLlF 97.65: *Aeth i nef weithian Ofydd* "Ovid has gone to heaven now."

GDLlF 98.77: *Aeth Ofydd o Fathafarn* "Ovid went from Mathafarn."

DN XVIII.1: *Eirchiad wyf, archiad Ofydd* "A petitioner am I, a petition for Ovid."

GHD II.502: *Mae ynof gariad Ofydd* "Love of Ovid is in me (or 'Love like Ovid's is in me')."

ID VIII.17–18: *Tro a gaiff mewn tyrau gwydd | ai law vryviau llyfr Ofydd* "He takes a turn in the towers of a wood with writs of the book of Ovid in his hand."

CYSDT 11.57–8: *Yn ifanc ni wnai Ofyd ogan i ferch (gwyn ei fyd!)* "As a lad Ovid did not used to slander a girl (bless him!)."[148]

CYSDT 12.71: *Na'm tw' Ofydd na'm tafod* "Neither is my achievement nor my tongue that of Ovid."

---

147. Cf. *GDG* 96.39b (= *CDG* 100.39): *cyfraith serch y sy'n erchi* "the law of love which asks."

148. Note that it is spelt here with -/d/ to rhyme with *fyd* (*CYSDT* 11.57n.); for discussion, see above, 205.

GSH At. ii.4: *Gwyddost, Cadi, . . . Lyfr Ofydd* "You know, Cadi, . . . a book of Ovid (sc. an authority on love)?"

GLM 54.21 *Pa wyr—Ofid—lle prifiwyd?* "Who knows? Where Ovid (or 'love') was put to the test."[149]

GLM 107.13: *yn fardd Ofydd* "as the poet Ovid."

GLM At.ii.1: *Dyn wyf ym mhurdan Ofydd* "I am a person in the purgatory of Ovid" (= TA CXXII. 1).

GSDT 3.8: *Plas Ofydd fel Plas Ifor* "Plas Ofydd like Plas Ifor (sc. Hael)."

GST I 200.27: *Dugum gof o lyfr Ovydd* "I took my recollection from the book of Ovid."

Offyddiaeth (or *ofyddiaeth*)

GDG 14.22 (= *CDG* 7.22): *gwir ofyddiaeth* "true lovemaking."

GDG 20.60 (= *CDG* 22.60): *gwawd graffaf . . . gwaethwaeth heb ofyddiaeth Ofydd* "the most assured verse . . . will decline without Ovid's art."

2. *Fferyll(t)*

Prose

ByT (Cleo), 80.11: *Y nawuet ulwydyn y dywat Fferyll am gnawdoliaeth Christ* "The ninth year Virgil spoke of the incarnation of Christ."

ByT (RB) 178.8: *hyt na allei ystoriaeu Ystas ystoriawr na chath[l]eu Fferyll vard . . .* "that neither the histories of Statius the historian nor the songs of Virgil the poet could . . ."

HGK 21.19–20: *pei bedun kyn huotlet a Thullius vard ym prol [pros] ac a Maro vard en traethaut mydyr* "were I as eloquent as the bard Tullius in prose, and the bard Maro in verse."[150]

Williams, "Testunau," 22 (translation of *Disticha Catonis* (earliest MS ca. 1300)): *Or mynny wybot ardymhereu tir ae diwyllodraeth, dysc llyfyr Fferyll yr hwnn a elwir Vyrgil* "If you wish to know how to regulate the land and to cultivate it, learn the book of Fferyll(t), who is called Virgil."

SDR 480: *"Fferyll,"* heb hi, *"a ossodes colofyn ymperued Rufein ac ar benn y golofyn drych o geluydyt ignyrmars"* "'Virgil,' she said, 'set up a column in the middle of Rome and on top of the column a mirror with necromantic arts.'"

SG 327.39–328.2: *yn y castell troedic yr hwnn y mae Iosep yn hyspyssu pan wnaeth fferyll y castell hwnnw drwy y gelvydyt ae synnwyr . . .* "in the turning castle which Joseph declares that, when Virgil made that castle through his art and cleverness . . ."

YT 133: *Ag yna ordeiniodd hi drwy gelfyddyd llyfrau Pheryllt i ferwi pair o awen a gwybodau oi map* "she arranged through the art of the books of Virgil to boil a cauldron of inspiration and knowledge for her son."

---

149. On the spelling *Ofid,* see above, 205.

150. cf. *VGC* §23/7 where Homer, not Virgil, is mentioned.

Verse

Cad Goddeu (LPBT 5.249): *o erymes Fferyll* "by the prophecy of Virgil."

GDG 32.32 (= CDG 134.32): *drychau o ffeiriau Fferyllt* "mirrors from Virgil's merchandise."[151]

GDG 84.58 (= CDG 135.56): *o ffyrf gelvydyt Fferyll* "is shaped by Virgil's mighty art."

IGE[2] XC.26 (Siôn Cent): *saith ddysg Fferyll* "the seven lessons of Virgil."

GPB 1.22: *mawr adail cynhail, cynnydd Fferyll* "he maintains a great building, with the same success as Virgil."

IGE[1] XXVIII.36 (Ieuan ap Rhydderch):[152] *mentyll tai Fferyll* "mist of the houses of Virgil."

GGG XLIX.22: *gwaith Fferyll ar gestyll gynt* "the work of Virgil on castles of old."

GIF 27.11–12: *Gwal i feirdd fu gelfyddyd | Fferyll fwy bo ffair holl fyd* "The art of Virgil was a wall for poets greater than a fair of the whole world."

GTA LXIII.64–5 (also CII.35): *câr i Fferyll* "a friend of Virgil."

3. Dwned

Prose

GP 67 (Gutun Owain's grammar): *Llyma Gyfrinach Beirdd Ynys Brydain, yr hwnn a elwir y Dwned yng [Ng]hymraeg* "Here is the Secret of the Poets of the Island of Britain, which is called in Welsh *Dwned*."

Verse[153]

GDG 12.1 (= CDG 5.1):

> *Llyfr dwned Dyfed dyfyn ar windai*
> > *i randir Llywelyn*
> *Llanerch, aed annerch pob dyn,*
> > *Lle twymlys llu, at Emlyn.*[154]

GLGC 69.21–4: *Y dyn a wypo Dwned—a rhywlys | a rhoi yn felys yr hen foled | doed i Gil-y-Sant, dyweded—odlau | ac aur a bwydau nac arbeded* "Whoever might know Dwned and the rules and how to provide the old praise sweetly, let him come to Gil-y-Sant; let him utter *odlau*, and let him not stint himself in gold and food."

---

151. Cf. the note at CDG 134.32n: "deellir yr enw hwn hefyd fel cyfeiriad at 'grefftwr celfydd, gof haearn, metelydd'" [this name is also understood as referring to "a skilled craftsman, a blacksmith, a metalworker"].

152. This poem is not included in GIRh.

153. On the suggested example in the work of Cynddelw Brydydd Mawr, see above, n. 134.

154. For possible translations, see above, 228-29.

GLGC 197.21–2: *Ar lyfr Dwned Maredudd / wedy'i wisgo y dysgodd* "He learned from the Dwned book of Maredudd so dressed."

GLGC 159.63: *Da ynn fal Dwned* "It is good for us like Dwned."

GTA IX.88: *Cyfion d'enwi cefn y Dwned* "Proper is your naming as the upholder of the Dwned."

GTA XXX.47: *Dyn at wraidd y Dwned draw* "a person at the root of Dwned yonder."

GTA LXX.1–2: *Llaw Dduw a fu'n lladd awen / lladd enaid holl ddwned hen* "The hand of God has killed inspiration by killing the whole soul of the old Dwned."

GTA LXX.41: *Dy ddwned oedd o'i enau* "Your Dwned was from his mouth."

BIBLIOGRAPHY

EDITIONS OF OVID CONSULTED (LISTED IN CHRONOLOGICAL ORDER)

[*Publii Ovidii Nasonis Opera omnia*]. Edited by Jacobus Rubeus. Venice, before 1474.

Opera P. Ovidii Nasonis. Edited by Bonus Accursius and Valerius Superchius. Venice, 1489.

Ovidius De arte amandi et de remedio amoris cum commento Bartholomei Merulae. Venice, 1494.

Publii Ovidii Nasonis Heroidum epistolae. Auli Sabini, epistolae tres, P. O. N. Elegiarum libri tres. De arte amandi libri tres. . . . Venice, 1503.

P. Ouidii Nasonis uita per Aldum ex ipsius libris excerpta. Heroidum epistolae. Amorvm libri III. De arte amandi libri III. . . . Venice, 1515.

P. Ovidii Nasonis Amatoria, Heroidum epistolae. . . . Paris, 1529.

P. Ouidii Nasonis uita per Aldvm ex ipsius libris excerpta. Heroidvm epistolae. Amorvm lib. III. De arte amandi lib. III. . . . Venice, 1533.

P. Ovidii Nasonis Opera omnia in tres tomos distributa. Edited by Gregorius Bersman. 3 vols. Heidelberg [?], 1582.

Pub. Ovidii Nasonis Opera. Edited by Danielis Heinsius. 3 vols. Leiden, 1629.

P. Ovidii Nasonis Operum editio Nova. Edited by Nicolaus Heinsius. 3 vols. Amsterdam, 1661.

Publii Ovidii Nasonis Opera omnia in tres tomos divisa. Edited by Nicolaus Heinsius and Cornelius Schrevelius. Leiden, 1662.

P. Ovidii Nasonis Operum editio nova. Edited by Nicolaus Heinsius. 2 vols. Amsterdam, 1664.

Publii Ovidii Nasonis Opera omnia IV voluminibus comprehensa cum integris Jacobi Micylli, Herculis Ciofani et Danielis Heinsii notis et Nicolai Heinsii curis secundis. Edited by Petrus Burman. 4 vols. Amsterdam, 1727.

Publii Ovidii Nasonis Opera omnia in tres tomos divisa cum integris Nicolai Heinsii, D. F. lectissimis variorum notis. Edited by Borchardus Cnippingius. 3 vols. Leiden, 1760.

P. Ovidii Nasonis Opera e textu Burmanni cum notis Bentleii hactenus ineditis, nec non Harlesii, Gierigii, Burmanni, Lemairii. 5 vols. Oxford, 1825.

P. Ovidius Naso. Edited by Rudolf Merkel. Leipzig, 1852.

P. Ovidius Naso. Edited by Rudolf Merkel. Rev. ed. by Rudolf Ehwald. Leipzig, 1891.

P. Ovidi Nasonis De arte amatoria libri tres. Edited by Paul Brandt. Leipzig, 1902.

Artis amatoriae libri tres. Edited by Concetto Marchesi. Turin, 1918.

Ovide, L'art d'aimer. Edited and translated by Henri Bornecque. 1st ed. Paris, 1924.

Ovid II: The Art of Love and Other Poems. Edited and translated by John H. Mozley. Cambridge, Mass., 1929.

P. Ovidi Nasonis Amores; Medicamina faciei femineae; Ars amatoria; Remedia amoris. Edited by Edward J. Kenney. 1st ed. Oxford, 1961.

Ars amatoria. Edited and translated by Friedrich W. Lenz. Schrift und Quellen der alten Welt 25. Berlin, 1969.

Ovid: Ars Amatoria Book I. Edited by Adrian S. Hollis. Oxford, 1974.

Ovid II: the Art of Love, and Other Poems. Edited and translated by John H. Mozley and G. P Goold. 2nd ed. Cambridge, Mass., 1979.

Ovidio, L'arte di amare. Edited by Emilio Pianezzola. Milan, 1991.

P. Ovidi Nasonis Amores, Medicamina faciei femineae; Ars amatoria; Remedia Amoris. Edited by Edward J. Kenney, 2nd ed. Oxford, 1994.

P. Ovidio, Obra amatoria II: El arte de amar. Edited and translated by Antonio Ramírez de Verger and Francisco Socas. Madrid, 1995.

P. Ovidius Naso. Carmina amatoria: Amores, Medicamina faciei femineae, Ars amatoria, Remedia amoris. Edited by Antonio Ramírez de Verger. Leipzig, 2003.

Ovid, Ars Amatoria, Book 3. Edited by Roy Gibson. Cambridge Classial Texts and Commentaries 40. Cambridge, 2003.

Ovide, L'art d'aimer. Edited and translated Henri Bornecque. 8th ed. Paris, 2010.

OTHER PRIMARY TEXTS

XII Facsimiles from Latin MSS. in the Bodleian Library. Edited by Robinson Ellis. Oxford, 1885.

XX Facsimiles from Latin MSS. in the Bodleian Library. Edited by Robinson Ellis. Oxford, 1891.

Accessus ad auctores, Bernard d'Utrecht, Conrad d'Hirsau, Dialogus super auctores. Edited by R. B. C. Huygens. Leyden, 1970.

Adversariorum Libri IV: numquam antea editi in quibus plurima veterum auctorum . . . ejusdem notae ad Catullum et Propertium curante Petro Burmanno, juniore . . . qui prefationem & commentarium de Vita Nicolai Heinsii adjecit. Edited by Petrus Burman. 4 vols. Harlingen, 1742.

Dialogo sugli autori, Corrado di Hirsau. Edited and translated by Roberta Marchionni. Annali dell'Università di Napoli "L'Orientale," sezione filologico-lettteraria12. Pisa, 2008.

Die altenglische Version des Halitgar'schen Bussbuches (sog. Poenitentiale Pseudo-Egberti). Edited by Josef Raith. Bibliothek der angelsächsischen Prosa XIII. Hamburg, 1933.

The Ancient Laws and Institutes of England. Edited and translated by Benjamin Thorpe. 2 vols. London, 1840.

Annales Cambriae. Edited by J. W. ab Ithel. London, 1860.

Appendix Probi. "A New Text of the *Appendix Probi*." Edited by Jonathan G. F. Powell. *Classical Quarterly* 57 (2007): 687–700, at 695–700.

Bede, *Historia ecclesiastica*. Edited and translated by Bertram Colgrave and Roger Mynors. Oxford Medieval Texts. Oxford, 1969.

Brut y Brenhinedd: Cotton Cleopatra Version. Edited by J. Jay Parry. Cambridge, Mass., 1937.

Brut y Tywysogyon or the Chronicle of the Princes, Red Book of Hergest Version. Edited and translated by Thomas Jones. Cardiff, 1955.

Brut y Tywysogyon, Peniarth MS. 20. Edited by Thomas Jones. Cardiff, 1941. In *Brut y Tywysogyon or the Chronicle of the Princes, Peniarth MS. 20 Version*. Translated by Thomas Jones. Cardiff, 1952.

Cardiff Records, Being Materials for a History of the Country Borough from the Earliest Times. Edited by John H. Matthews. 6 vols. Cardiff 1898–1911.

Casgliad o Waith Ieuan Deulwyn. Edited by Ifor Williams. Bangor, 1909.

Catalogue général des manuscrits des bibliothèques publiques de France, Départements, XIII. Paris, 1891.

Cerddi Dafydd ap Gwilym. Edited by Dafydd Johnston et al. Cardiff, 2010; English translations can be found in the online version http://www.dafyddapgwilym.net/.

Chwedlau Seith Doethon Rufein. Edited by Henry Lewis. Cardiff, 1958.

The Correspondence of James Ussher 1600-1656. Edited by Elizabethanne Boran. 3 vols. Dublin, 2015.

Cywyddau Iolo Goch ac Eraill. Edited by Henry Lewis, Thomas Roberts, and Ifor Williams. 1st ed. Bangor, 1925.

Cywyddau Iolo Goch ac Eraill. Edited by Henry Lewis, Thomas Roberts, and Ifor Williams. 2nd ed. Cardiff, 1937.

Cywyddau Ymryson Syr Dafydd Trefor. Edited by Rhiannon Ifans. Aberystwyth, 2013.

De raris fabulis, "On Uncommon Tales": A Glossed Latin Colloquy-Text from a Tenth-Century Cornish Manuscript. Edited by Scott Gwara. Basic Texts for Brittonic History 4. Cambridge, 2004.

Dictionary of the Irish Language based mainly on Old and Middle Irish Materials. Edited by Gordon Quin et al. Dublin, 1913–76; revised edition: http://edil.qub.ac.uk /dictionary/search.php.

The Dictionary of Medieval Latin from British Sources. Edited by R. E. Latham et al. Oxford, 1975–2013.

A Dictionary of the Old Irish Glosses. Edited by David Stifter and Aaron Griffith: http:// www.univie.ac.at/indogermanistik/milan_glosses.htm.

Disticha Catonis. Edited by Marcus Boas. Amsterdam, 1952.

The Donatz Proensals of Uc Faidit. Edited by J. H. Marshall. London, 1969.

Early Manuscripts at Oxford University: http://image.ox.ac.uk/.

Early Scholastic Colloquies. Edited by William H. Stevenson. Oxford, 1929.

Early Welsh Genealogical Tracts. Edited by Peter C. Bartrum, Peter C. Cardiff, 1966.

Egbert of Liège. The Well-Laden Ship. Edited by Robert G. Babcock. Dumbarton Oaks Medieval Library 25. Cambridge, Mass., 2013.

English Benedictine Libraries. The Shorter Catalogues. Edited by Richard Sharpe, J. P. Carley, Rodney M. Thomson, Andrew G. Watson. CBMLC 3. London, 1996.

The Etymologies of Isidore of Seville., Ttranslated by. Stephen A. Barney, W. J. Lewis, J. A. Beach, and Oliver Berghof. Cambridge, 2006.

The Friars' Libraries. Edited by K. W. Humphries, CBMLC 1. London, 1990.

Geiriadur Prifysgol Cymru, 1st ed. Edited by R. J. Thomas et al. Cardiff, 1953–2002. 2nd ed. Edited by Gareth Bevan et al. Cardiff, 2003–; online edition, Cardiff, 2014: http://www.geiriadur.ac.uk/.

Geoffrey of Monmouth, The History of the Kings of Britain. *An Edition and Translation of "De gestis Britonum"* [Historia Regum Britanniae]. Edited by Michael D. Reeve. Translated by Neil Wright. Woodbridge, 2007.

Glossae divinae historiae. The Biblical Glosses of John Scottus Eriugena. Edited by John J. Contreni and Pádraig P. Ó Néill. Florence, 1997.

Gramadegau'r Penceirddiaid. Edited by G. J. Williams and E. J. Jones. Cardiff, 1934.

Grammatici Latini. Edited by Heinrich Keil. 8 vols. Leipzig, 1857 (repr. Hildesheim, 1961).

Gwaith Bleddyn Fardd a Beirdd Eraill Ail Hanner y Drydedd Ganrif ar Ddeg. Edited by Rhian M. Andrews et al., CBT VII. Cardiff, 1996.

Gwaith Cynddelw Brydydd Mawr II. Edited by Nerys Ann Jones and Ann Parry Owen, CBT IV. Cardiff, 1995.

Gwaith Dafydd ap Gwilym. Edited by Thomas Parry. 3rd ed. Cardiff, 1979.

Gwaith Dafydd Bach ap Madog Wladaidd "Sypyn Cyfeiliog" a Llywelyn ab y Moel. Edited by R. Iestyn Daniel. Aberystywyth, 1998.

Gwaith Dafydd Epynt. Edited by Owen Thomas. Aberystwyth, 2002.

Gwaith Dafydd Llwyd o Fathafarn. Edited by W. L. Richards. Cardiff, 1964.

Gwaith Guto'r Glyn. Edited by J. Ll. Willams and Ifor Williams. Cardiff, 1961.

Gwaith Gwerful Mechain ac Eraill. Edited by Nerys Ann Howells. Aberystwyth, 2001.

Gwaith Hywel Dafi. Edited by Cynfael Lake. 2 vols. Aberystwyth, 2015.

Gwaith Ieuan ap Llywelyn Fychan, Ieuan Llwyd Brydydd a Lewys Aled. Edited by M. Paul Bryant-Quinn. Aberystwyth, 2003.

Gwaith Ieuan ap Rhydderch. Edited by R. Iestyn Daniel. Aberystwyth, 2003.

Gwaith Iolo Goch. Edited by Dafydd Johnston. Cardiff, 1988.

Gwaith Iorwerth Fynglwyd. Edited by Howell Ll. Jones and Eurys I. Rowlands. Cardiff, 1975.

Gwaith Lewys Glyn Cothi. Edited by Dafydd Johnston. Cardiff, 1995.

Gwaith Lewys Morgannwg. Edited by A. Cynfael Lake. 2 vols. Aberystwyth, 2004.

Gwaith Llawdden. Edited by R. Iestyn Daniel. Aberystwyth, 2006.

Gwaith Llywelyn ap Gutun. Edited by R. Iestyn Daniel. Aberystwyth, 2007.

Gwaith Llywelyn Fardd I ac Eraill o Feirdd y Ddeuddegfed Ganrif. Edited by Kathryn A. Bramley et al., CBT II. Cardiff, 1994.

Gwaith Llywelyn Goch ap Meurig Hen. Edited by Dafydd Johnston. Aberystwyth, 1998.

Gwaith Maredudd ap Rhys a'i Gyfoedion. Edited by Enid Roberts. Aberystwyth, 2003.

Gwaith Meilyr Brydydd a'i Ddisgynyddion. Edited by J. E. Caerwyn Williams et al. CBT I. Cardiff, 1994.

Gwaith Prydydd Breuan a Cherddi Dychan Eraill o Lyfr Coch Hergest. Edited by Huw Meirion Edwards. Aberystwyth, 2000.

Gwaith Rhys Brydydd a Rhisiart ap Rhys. Edited by John Morgan Williams and Eurus I. Rowlands. Cardiff, 1976.

Gwaith Rhys Goch Eryri. Edited by Dylan Foster Evans. Aberystwyth, 2007.

Gwaith Sefnyn, Rhisierdyn, Gruffudd Fychan ap Gruffudd ab Ednyfed a Llywarch Bentwrch. Edited by Nerys Ann Jones and Erwain Haf Rheinallt. Aberystwyth, 1995.

Gwaith Siôn ap Hywel ap Llywelyn Fychan. Edited by A. Cynfael Lake. Aberystwyth, 1999.

Gwaith Siôn Tudur. Edited by Enid Roberts. 2 vols. Cardiff, 1980.

Gwaith Syr Dafydd Trefor. Edited by Rhiannon Ifans. Aberystwyth, 2005.

Gwaith Tudur Aled. Edited by T. G. Jones. 2 vols. Cardiff, 1926.

Henry of Kirkstede, Catalogus de Libris Autenticis et Apocrifis. Edited by Richard H. Rouse and Mary A. Rouse, CBMLC 11. London, 2004.

Historia Gruffud vab Kenan. Edited by D. Simon Evans. Cardiff, 1977.

Isidore, *Etymologiae: Isidori Hispalensis Episcopi Etymologiarum sive Originum Libri XX.* Edited by J. M. Lindsay. 2 vols. Oxford, 1911.

Juvencus codex Cantabrigiensis Ff.4.22. A Ninth-Century Manuscript Glossed in Welsh, Irish and Latin. Facsimile. Edited by Helen McKee. Aberystwyth, 2000.

Langland, William. *Piers Plowman. A Parallel-Text Edition of the A, B, C and Z Versions*. Edited by A. V. C. Schmidt. 2 vols. Kalamazoo, 1995–2008.

Latin Colloquies from Pre-conquest Britain. Edited by Scott Gwara. Toronto Medieval Latin Texts 22. Toronto, 1996.

The Latin Texts of the Welsh Laws. Edited by Hywel D. Emanuel. Cardiff, 1967.

The Legendary Poems from the Book of Taliesin. Edited by and tr. Marged Haycock. Aberystwyth, 2007; 2nd ed. 2015.

"Letter I: Mr. Edward Llwyd to Mr. Humphrey Wanley," ed. anon. *The Cambro-Briton* 1 (1819–20): 14–17.

The Libraries of the Augustinian Canons. Edited by Theresa Webber and Andrew G. Watson, CBMLC 6. London, 1998.

The Libraries of the Cistercians, Gilbertines and Premonstratensians. Edited by David N. Bell, CBMLC 2. London, 1992.

The Libraries of Collegiate Churches. Edited by James M. W. Willoughby. 2 vols. CBMLC 15. London, 2013.

The Life of the Most Reverend Father in God, James Ussher, Late Lord Arch-bishop of Armagh, Primate and Metropolitan of all Ireland. With a Collection of Three Hundred Letters. Edited by Richard Parr. London, 1686.

A Medieval Prince of Wales. The Life of Gruffudd ap Cynan. Translated by D. Simon Evans. Felinfach, 1990 (English translation of *HGK*).

L'oeuvre poétique de Gutun Owain. Edited by Edouard Bachellery. Paris, 1950–51.

The New Palaeographical Society. Facsimiles of Ancient Manuscripts, etc. Edited by Edward Maunde Thompson, George F. Warner, Frederic G. Kenyon, and Julius P. Gilson. 1st series, vol. I. London, 1903–12.

The Old English Finding of the True Cross. Edited and translated by Mary-Catherine Bodden. Cambridge, 1987.

Ovid, "Ars amatoria," Book 3. Edited by Roy K. Gibson. Cambridge, 2003.

Oxford Dictionary of National Biography. Edited by H. C. G. Matthew, Brian Harrison et al. Oxford, 2004; online edition, Oxford, 2014: http://www.oxforddnb.com/.

Paléographie des classiques latins. Edited by Émile Chatelain. 2 vols. Paris, 1884–1900.

The Patrician Texts in the Book of Armagh. Edited by Ludwig Bieler. Scriptores Latini Hiberniae X. Dublin, 1979.

Pecock, Reginald. *The Rule of Christian Religion. The Reuele of Crysten Religioun.* Edited by William C. Greet, Early English Texts Society 171. London, 1927 (repr. 1987).

Peterborough Abbey. Edited by Karsten Friis-Jensen and James M. W. Willoughby, CBMLC 8. London, 2001.

The Poetical Works of Dafydd Nanmor. Edited by Thomas Roberts and Ifor Williams. Cardiff, 1923.

The Prologues to the Medieval Welsh Lawbooks. Edited by Paul Russell. Cambridge, 2004.

Psalterium Suthantoniense. Edited by Pádraig P. Ó Néill. Corpus Christianorum Continuatio Medievalis 240. Turmhout, 2012.

Registrum Anglie de libris doctorum et auctorum veterum. Edited by Richard H. Rouse and Mary A. Rouse, CBMLC 2. London, 1991.

St. Augustine's Abbey, Canterbury. Edited by Bruce Barker-Benfield. 3 vols, CBMLC 13. London, 2008.

Saint Dunstan's Classbook from Glastonbury. Codex biblioth. Bodeianae Oxon. Auct. F.4.32. Edited by Richard W. Hunt, Umbrae Codicum Occidentalium 4. Amsterdam, 1961.

St Gall Priscian glosses. Edited by Rijcklof Hofman and Pádraic Moran: http://www .stgallpriscian.ie/.

Y Seint Greal, being the Adventures of King Arthur's Knights of the Round Table, in the Quest of the Holy Greal, and on Other Occasions. Edited by R. Williams. London, 1876. Reprinted by Pwllheli, 1987.

Selections from Dafydd ap Gwilym: Apocrypha. Edited by Helen Fulton. Llandysul, 1996.

Specimens of Latin Palaeography from MSS. in the Bodleian Library. Edited by Robinson Ellis. Oxford, 1903.

Sylloges Epistolarum a Viris Illustribus Scriptarum Tomi Quinque. Edited by Petrus Burman. 5 vols. Leiden, 1727.

The Text of the Book of Llan Dâv. Edited by J. Gwenogvryn Evans and John Rhys. Oxford, 1893.

Thesaurus Palaeohibernicus. A Collection of Old Irish Glosses, Scholia, Prose and Verse. Edited by Whitley Stokes and John Strachan. 2 vols. Cambridge, 1901–3.

Vita Griffini filii Conani. The Medieval Latin Life of Gruffudd ap Cynan. Edited by Paul Russell. Cardiff, 2005.

Walter Map, *De nugis curialium: Courtiers' Trifles*. Edited by Montague R. James (rev. Christopher N. L. Brooke and Roger A. B. Mynors). Oxford, 1983.

A Welsh Bestiary of Love. Edited by Graham C. G. Thomas. Dublin, 1988.

Ystoria Taliesin. Edited by Patrick K. Ford. Berkeley, 1992.

SECONDARY LITERATURE

Alcamesi, Filippa. "Remigius' Commentary on *Disticha Catonis* in Anglo-Saxon Manuscripts." In *Form and Content of Instruction in Anglo-Saxon England in the Light of Contemporary Manuscript Evidence*, edited by Patrizia Lendinara, 143–86. Turnhout, 2007.

Alexander, Jonathan J. G. *Insular Manuscripts, 6th to 9th Century. A Survey of Manuscripts Illuminated in the British Isles* 1. London, 1978.

Alton, E. H. "The Medieval Commentators on Ovid's *Fasti*." *Hermathena* 20 (1926): 119–51.

Alton, Ernest H. and Donald E. Wormell. "Ovid in the Medieval Schoolroom." *Hermathena* 94 (1960): 21–38; 95 (1961): 67–82.

Bauer, Bernhard. "Parallel Old Irish and Old Breton Glosses on Priscian's *Institutiones Grammaticae*." In *Linguistics and Philological Studies in Early Irish*. Edited by E. R. Roma and D. Stifter. Lampeter, 2009. 31–52.

Bernard, Michael, Humphrey Wanley, and Michael Burghers. *Catalogi Librorum Manuscriptorum Angliae et Hiberniae in Unum Collecti.* Oxford, 1697.

Bieler, Ludwig. "Nachaugustische nichtchristliche Dichter." *Lustrum* 2 (1957): 207–93.

Biffi, Giovanni Ambrogio. *Prissian de Milan de la Parnonzia Milanesa.* Milan, 1606.

Binns, James W. (ed.). *Ovid.* London, 1973.

Bischoff, Bernhard. *Manuscripts and Libraries in the Age of Charlemagne.* Translated by Michael M. Gorman. Cambridge, 1994.

Bischoff, Bernhard. "Benedictine Monasteries and the Survival of Classical Literature." In *Manuscripts and Libraries.* Translated by Michael M. Gorman. 134–60.

———. Bischoff, Bernhard. "Libraries and Schools in the Carolingian Revival of Learning." In *Manuscripts and Libraries.* Translated by Michael M. Gorman. 93–114.

Bishop, T. Alan M. "The Corpus Martianus Capella." *Transactions of the Cambridge Bibliographical Society* 4 (1964–8): 257–71.

Black, Robert. "Teaching Techniques: the Evidence of Manuscript Schoolbooks Produced in Tuscany." In *The Classics in the Medieval and Renaissance Classroom,* edited by Juanita Feros Ruys, John O. Ward, and Melanie Heyworth, 245–65.

Blair, Ann M. "Lectures on Ovid's *Metamorphoses:* the Class Notes of a Sixteenth-Century Paris Schoolboy." *Princeton University Library Chronicle* 5 (1989): 116–44.

Blok, Frans Felix. *Nicolaas Heinsius in dienst van Christiana van Zweden.* Delft, 1949.

Blom, Alderik. *Glossing the Psalms: The Emergence of the Written Vernaculars in Western Europe from the Seventh to the Twelfth Centuries.* Berlin / New York, 2017.

Bodden, Mary-Catherine. "A Study of the Anglo-Saxon Classbook Bodley, Auct. F.4.32, along with a Close Study of Its Second Gathering, an 11th-century Old English Homily on the Finding of the True Cross." Unpublished University of Toronto PhD thesis. Toronto, 1979.

Boese, Helmut. "Zu den Ovidkollationen des N. Heinsius." *Philologus* 106 (1962): 155–73.

Boutemy, André. "Un manuscrit inconnu de l'*Ars amatoria* au British Museum." *Revue des Études Latines* 14 (1936): 271–73.

Boutemy, André. "Une copie de l'*Ars amatoria* au British Museum." *Revue des Études Latines* 15 (1937): 92–102.

Boyd, Barbara W. (ed.). *Brill's Companion to Ovid.* Leiden, 2002.

Boyle, Elizabeth, and Paul Russell, eds. *The Tripartite Life of Whitley Stokes (1830-1909).* Dublin, 2011.

Bradshaw, Henry. *Collected Papers of Henry Bradshaw.* Edited by F. Jenkinson. Cambridge, 1889.

Breen, Aidan. "The Liturgical Material in MS Oxford, Bodleian Library, Auct. F.4.32." *Archiv für Liturgiewissenschaft* 34 (1992): 121–53.

Bromwich, Rachel. *Aspects of the poetry of Dafydd ap Gwilym.* Cardiff, 1986.

Bronner, Dagmar. *Verzeichnis altirischer Quellen. Vorläufige Version.* Marburg, 2013.

Budny, Mildred. "'St Dunstan's Classbook' and Its Frontispiece: Dunstan's Portrait and Autograph." In *St Dunstan. His Life, Times and Cult,* edited by N. Ramsay, M. Sparks and T. Tatton-Brown, 103–42. Woodbridge, 1992.

Cappelli, Adriano. "Angelo Decembrio." *Archivio Storico Lombardo* 19 (1892): 110–17.

Capis, Giovanni. *Varon Milanes de la lengua de Milan.* Milan, 1606.

Charles-Edwards, Thomas M. "*Gorsedd, dadl,* and *llys:* Assemblies and Courts in Medieval Wales." In *Assembly Places and Practices in Medieval Europe,* edited by Aliki Pantos and Sarah Semple, 95–105. Dublin, 2004.

——. "*Nei, Keifn,* and *Kefynderw.*" *BBCS* 25 (1973–74), 386–88.

——. "Some Celtic Kinship Terms." *BBCS* 24 (1971): 106–22.

——. "The Use of the Book in Wales, ca. 400–1100." In *The Book in Britain I,* edited by Richard Gameson, 389–405.

——. *Wales and the Britons 350–1064.* Oxford, 2013.

Charles-Edwards, Thomas M., and Paul Russell. "The Hendregadredd Manuscript and the Orthography and Phonology of Welsh in the Early Thirteenth Century." *NLWJ,* 28 (1993–94), 419–62.

Chotzen, Theodor M. *Recherches sur la poésie de Dafydd ap Gwilym, barde gallois du XIV siècle.* Amsterdam, 1927.

Ciccolella, Federica. *Donati Graeci: Learning Greek in the Renaissance.* Columbia Studies in the Classical Tradition 32. Leiden, 2008.

Clark, James G. "Introduction." In *Ovid in the Middle Ages,* edited by Clark et al., 1–25.

——. "Ovid in the Monasteries: the Evidence from Late Medieval England." In *Ovid in the Middle Ages,* edited by Clark et al., 177–96.

Clark, James G., Frank T. Coulson, Kathryn L. McKinley, eds. *Ovid in the Middle Ages.* Cambridge, 2011.

Comparetti, Domenico. *Virgil in the Middle Ages.* Translated by E. F. M. Benecke. London, 1895.

Conway, Gillian. "Towards a Cultural Context for the Eleventh-Century Llanbadarn Manuscripts." *Ceredigion* 13 (1997): 9–28.

Coulson, Frank T. "Addenda et Corrigenda to *Incipitarium Ovidianum.*" *Journal of Medieval Latin* 12 (2002): 154–80.

——. "Ovid's *Metamorphoses* in the School Tradition of France, 1180–1400: Texts, Manuscript Traditions, Manuscript Settings." In *Ovid in the Middle Ages,* edited by Clark et al., 26–47.

——. "The Vulgate Commentary on Ovid's Metamorphoses." *Mediaevalia* 13 (1989) [*Ovid in Medieval Culture,* special issue. Edited by M. R. Desmond]: 29–62.

Coulson, Frank T., and Bruno Roy. *Incipitarium Ovidianum: A Finding Guide for Texts related to the Study of Ovid in the Middle Ages and Renaissance.* Turnhout, 2000.

Cowley, Frederick G. *The Monastic Order in South Wales, 1066–1349.* Cardiff, 1977.

Crick, Julia. "The Power and the Glory: Conquest and Cosmology in Edwardian Wales." In *Textual Cultures: Cultural Texts,* edited by Orietta Da Rold and Elaine Treharne, 21–42. Woodbridge, 2010.

Derolez, René. *Runica manuscripta. The English Tradition.* Brugge, 1954.

Dimmick, Jeremy. "Ovid in the Middle Ages: Authority and Poetry." In *Cambridge Companion to Ovid,* edited by Philip Hardie, 264–87.

Draak, Martje. "Construe Marks in Hiberno-Latin Manuscripts." *Mededelingen der koninklijke Nederlandse Akademie van Wetenschappen, Afdeling Letterkunde,* 20 (1957): 261–82 (also issued separately, Amsterdam, 1957).

——. "The Higher Teaching of Latin Grammar in Ireland During the Ninth Century." *Mededelingen der koninklijke Nederlandse Akademie van Wetenschappen, Afdeling Letterkunde,* 30 (1967): 109–44 (also issued separately, Amsterdam, 1967).

Dumville, David N. "A *Thesaurus Palaeoanglicus?* The Celtic Experience." In *Anglo-Saxon Glossography. Papers read at the International Conference held in the Koninklijke Academie voor Wetenschappen Letteren en Schone Kunsten van België, Brussels, 8 and 9 September 1986,* edited by René Derolez, 61–76. Brussels, 1992.

Dumville, David N. "An Irish Idiom Latinised." *Éigse* 16 (1975–76): 183–86.

———. "Notes on Celtic Latin." *BBCS* 30 (1982–83): 283–88.

Ebel, Hermann. "Miscellanea: (9) Zur *Grammatica Celtica.*" *Beiträge zur vergleichende Sprachforschung* 8 (1876): 371–75.

Edwards, Huw Meirion. *Dafydd ap Gwilym: Influences and Analogues.* Oxford, 1996.

Edwards, Nancy. "The Decoration of the Earliest Welsh Manuscripts." In *The Book in Britain I,* edited by RichardGameson, 244–48.

Ellis, Robinson. "De *Artis amatoriae* Ovidianae codice Oxoniensi." *Hermes* 15 (1880): 425–32.

Engelbrecht, Wilken. (ed.). *Filologie in de Dertiende Eeuw: De Bursarii super Ovidius van Magister Williem van Orléans (fl. 1200 AD).* Olomouc, 2003.

Engelbrecht, Wilken. "'Carmina Pieridum multo vigilata labore / exponi, nulla certius urbe reor': Orléans and the Reception of Ovid in the *Aetas Ovidiana* in School Commentaries." *Mittellateinisches Jahrbuch* 4 (2006): 209–26.

Engelbrecht, Wilken. "Fulco, Arnulf, and William: Twelfth-Century Views on Ovid in Orléans." *Journal of Medieval Latin* 18 (2008): 52–73.

Evans, D. Simon. *A Grammar of Middle Welsh.* Dublin, 1964.

Evans, Nicholas. "Royal Succession and Kingship among the Picts." *Innes Review* 59 (2008): 1–48.

Falileyev, Alexander. *An Etymological Glossary of Old Welsh.* Tübingen, 2000.

Falileyev, Alexander (with Hildegard Tristram and Yves Le Berre). *Le Vieux-Gallois.* Potsdam, 2008.

Falileyev, Alexander. Llawlyfr Hen Gymraeg. Aberystwyth, 2016 (online at https://llyfrgell .porth.ac.uk/view2.aspx?id=1411~4h~GDh5Q67L (consulted 27 September 2016)).

Fleuriot, Léon, and Claude Evans. A Dictionary of Old Breton / Dictionnaire du Vieux Breton: Historical and Comparative. 2 vols. Toronto, 1985. Reprinted and updated version of Léon Fleuriot, Dictionnaire des gloses en vieux breton. Paris, 1964.

Friedlein, Gottfried. "Der Calculus des Victorius." *Zeitschrift für Mathematik und Physik* 16 (1871): 42–79.

Friedlein, Gottfried. "Victori calculus e codice Vaticano editus," *Bulletino di bibliografia e di storia delle scienze matematiche e fisiche* 4 (1871): 443–63.

Fulton, Helen. *Dafydd ap Gwilym and His European Context.* Cardiff, 1989.

Fyler, John M. "The Medieval Ovid." In *A Companion to Ovid,* edited by Knox, 411–22.

Gameson, Richard. "Book Decoration in England, ca. 871–ca. 1100." In *The Book in Britain I,* edited by Richard Gameson, 249–93.

———. "From Vindolanda to Domesday: The Book in Britain from the Romans to the Normans." In *The Book in Britain,* edited by Richard Gameson, 1–9.

———. *The Manuscripts of Early Norman England (ca. 1066–1130).* Oxford, 1999.

Gameson, Richard, ed. *The Book in Britain, Volume I, ca. 400–1100.* Cambridge, 2012.

Ganz, David. "Anglo-Saxon England." In *The Cambridge History of Libraries in Britain and Ireland I,* edited by Elisabeth Leedham-Green and Teresa Webber, 91–108.

———. "Conclusion: Visions of Carolingian Education, Past, Present, Future." In *"The Gentle Voices of Teachers,"* edited by Sullivan, 261–83.

Gneuss, Helmut. "Dunstan und Hrabanus Maurus. Zur HS. Bodleian Auctarium F.4.32." *Anglia* 96 (1978): 136–48.

Gneuss, Helmut, and Michael Lapidge. *Anglo-Saxon Manuscripts. A Bibliographical Handlist of Manuscripts and Manuscript Fragments Written or Owned in England up to 1100.* Toronto, 2014.

Goold, G. P. "*Amatoria critica.*" *Harvard Studies in Classical Philology* 69 (1965): 1–107.

Graham, Timothy. "The Poetic, Scribal, and Artistic Work of Ieuan ap Sulien in Corpus Christi College, Cambridge, MS 199: Addenda and Assessment." *NLWJ* 29 (1995–96): 241–56.

Green, Peter. *Ovid. The Erotic Poems.* London, 1982.

Gunther, Robert T., ed. *Early Science in Oxford, Vol. XIV: Life and Letters of Edward Lhuyd.* Oxford, 1945.

Gwara, Scott. "Anglo-Saxon Schoolbooks." In *The Book in Britain I,* edited by Richard Gameson, 507–24.

———. *Education in Wales and Cornwall in the Ninth and Tenth Centuries: Understanding "De raris fabulis."* Cambridge, 2004.

Gwara, Scott and David W. Porter, eds. *Anglo-Saxon Conversations: The Colloquies of Aelfric Bata.* Woodbridge, 1997.

Hablitzel, Hans, and David Stifter, eds. *Johann Kaspar Zeuss im kultur- und sprachwissenschaftlichen Kontext (19. bis 21. Jahrhundert): Kronach 21.-23.7.2006.* Keltische Forschungen 2. Wien, 2007.

Hardie, Philip, ed. *The Cambridge Companion to Ovid.* Cambridge, 2002.

Harvey, Anthony. "The Cambridge Juvencus Glosses—Evidence of Hiberno-Welsh Interaction." In *Proceedings of the Eighth International Symposium on Language Contact in Europe, Douglas, Isle of Man, 1988,* edited by P. Sture Ureland and George Broderick, 181–98. Tübingen, 1991.

Harvey, Anthony. "Cambro-Romance? Celtic Britain's Counterpart to Hiberno-Latin." In *Culture and Tradition in Medieval Ireland. Festschrift for Dáibhí Ó Cróinín,* edited by J. Bisagni and P. Moran, 179–202. Turnhout, 2015.

Haycock, Marged, ed. and trans. *Blodeugerdd Barddas o Ganu Crefyddol Cynnar.* Llandybïe.

Hegarty, A. J. 'Langbaine, Gerard (1608/9–1658).' In *ODNB, s.n.*

Henley, Georgia. "Quotation, Revision, and Narrative Structure in Giraldus Cambrensis's *Itinerarium Kambriae.*" *Journal of Medieval Latin* 24 (2014): 1–52.

———. "Rhetoric, Translation and Historiography: The Literary Qualities of *Brut y Tywysogion.*" *Quaestio Insularis* 13 (2012): 94–123.

———. "Through the Ethnographer's Eyes: Rhetoric and Ethnicity, and Quotation in the Welsh and Irish Works of Gerald of Wales." In *Rhetoric and Reality: Essays in Honor of Daniel F. Melia,* edited by Georgia Henley and Paul Russell, CSANA Yearbook 11–12, 63–74. Colgate, 2014.

Herman, József. *Vulgar Latin.* Translated by Roger Wright. Pennsylvania, 2000.

Herren, Michael. "Latin and the Vernacular Languages." In *Medieval Latin: An Introduction and Bibliography,* edited by F. A. C. Mantello and A. G. Rigg, 122–29. Washington, 1996.

Hersart de la Villemarqué, Théodore. "Rapport . . . sur une mission littéraire accompli en Angleterre—Seconde partie. Notices des principaux manuscrits d'Angleterre concernant la langue, la littérature et l'histoire des anciens Bretons." *Archives des missions scientifiques et littéraires* 5 (1856): 234–72.

Hexter, Ralph J. "*Latinitas* in the Middle Ages: Horizons and Perspectives." *Helios* 14 (1987): 69–92.

———. "Medieval Articulations of Ovid's Metamorphoses: from Lactantian Segmentation to Arnulfian Allegory." *Mediaevalia* 13 (1989) [*Ovid in Medieval Culture,* special issue. Edited by M. R. Desmond]: 63–82.

——. *Ovid and Medieval Schooling: Studies in Medieval School Commentaries on Ovid's "Ars amatoria," "Epistulae ex ponto," and "Epistulae heroidum."* Münchener Beiträge zur Mediävistik und Renaissance-Forschung 38. Munich, 1986.

——. "Ovid in the Middle Ages: Exile, Mythographer, Lover." In *Brill's Companion to Ovid,* edited by Boyd, 413–42.

——. "Ovid's Transformation in Medieval France, ca. 1100—i. 1350." In *Metamorphosis: the Changing Face of Ovid in Medieval and Early-Medieval Europe,* edited by A. Keith and S. Rupp, 33–60. Toronto, 2007.

——. "Sex Education: Ovidian Erotodidactic in the Classroom." In *The Art of Love. Bimillennial Essays on Ovid's Ars Amatoria and Remedia Amoris,* edited by Roy Gibson, S. Green, A. Sharrock, 298–317. Oxford, 2006.

Heyworth, P. L., ed. *Letters of Humphrey Wanley, Palaeographer, Anglo-Saxonist, Librarian, 1672-1726.* Oxford, 1989.

Hofman, Rijklof. *The Sankt Gall Priscian Commentary. Part 1.* 2 vols. Münster, 1996.

Hollis, Adrian S., ed. *Ovid: Ars Amatoria Book I.* Oxford, 1974.

Homburger, Otto S. *Die illustrierten Handschriften der Burgerbibliothek Bern: die vorkarolingischen und karolingischen Handschriften.* Bern, 1962.

Howlett, David. "Rhigyfarch ap Sulien and Ieuan ap Sulien." In *The Book in Britain I,* edited by Richard Gameson, 701–5.

Hunt, Tony. *Teaching and Learning in Thirteenth-Century England.* 3 vols. Cambridge, 1991.

Huws, Daniel. *Medieval Welsh Manuscripts.* Cardiff/Aberystwyth, 2000.

——. "Vernacular Literature and Its Readership: Welsh." In *The Book in Britain II,* edited by Morgan and Thomson, 390–96.

Irvine, Martin. *The Making of Textual Culture. "Grammatica" and Literary Theory 350-1100.* Cambridge, 1994.

Isaac, Graham. *The Verb in the Book of Aneirin. Studies in Syntax, Morphology and Etymology.* Tübingen, 1996.

Jackson, Kenneth H., *Language and History in Early Britain.* Edinburgh, 1953.

Jacobs, Nicolas. "Irish Influence on Mediaeval Welsh Vocabulary: The Case of the Gnomic Poems." In *Ilteangach, Ilseiftiúil. Féilsgribhinn in Ómós do Nicholas Williams. A Festschrift for Nicholas Williams,* edited by L. Mac Amhlaigh and B. Ó Curnáin, 97–120. Dublin, 2013.

James, Montague R. *A Descriptive Catalogue. The Manuscripts in the Library at Lambeth Palace.* Cambridge, 1930–32.

Jenkins, Dafydd, and Morfydd E. Owen. "The Welsh Marginalia in the Lichfield Gospels." *CMCS* 5 (1983): 37–66; 7 (1984): 91–120.

Jeudy, Colette. "Les manuscrits de L'*Ars de verbo* d'Eutyches et le commentaire de Rémi d'Auxerre." In *Études de civilisation médiévale (ix-xii siècles). Mélanges offerts à Edmond-René Labande,* 421–36. Poitiers, 1974.

Johnston, Dafydd. *Llên yr Uchelwyr. Hanes Beirniadol Llenyddiaeth Gymraeg 1300-1525.* Cardiff, 2005.

Jones, Mari. "Byd y Beirdd, sef Ymchwiliad i Amgylchfyd a Diddordebau Beirdd yr Uchelwyr yn y Bedwaredd Ganrif ar Ddeg a'r Bymthegfed Ganrif." Unpublished University of Wales MA dissertation. Bangor, 1983.

Jones, Thomas, ed. "*Cronica de Wallia* and Other Documents from Exeter Cathedral Library MS. 3514." *BBCS* 12 (1946): 27–44.

Kavanagh, Séamus. *A Lexicon of the Old Irish Glosses in the Würzburg Manuscript of the Epistles of St. Paul.* Edited by Dagmar Wodtko. Vienna, 2001.

Kenney, Edward J. *The Classical Text: Aspects of Editing in the Age of the Printed Book.* Berkeley, 1974.

———. "First Thoughts on the Hamiltonensis." *Classical Quarterly,* NS 16 (1966): 267–70.

———. "The Manuscript Tradition of Ovid's *Amores, Ars Amatoria,* and *Remedia Amoris.*" *Classical Quarterly,* NS 12 (1962): 1–31.

———. "Notes on Ovid: II." *Classical Quarterly,* NS 9 (1959): 240–60.

———. "Ovid, *Ars Amatoria* i.147." *Classical Review,* NS 3 (1953): 7–10.

Ker, Neil R. *Catalogue of Manuscripts Containing Anglo-Saxon.* Oxford 1957.

———. *Medieval Libraries of Great Britain: A List of Surviving Books,* 2nd ed. London, 1964.

Kitson, Peter. "Old English Literacy and the Provenance of Welsh *y*." In *Yr Hen Iaith,* edited by Paul Russell, 49–65. Aberystwyth, 2003.

Knappe, Gabrielle. "Manuscript Evidence of the Teaching of the Language Arts in Late Anglo-Saxon and Early Norman England, with Particular Regard to the the the Role of Classics." In *The Classics in the Medieval and Renaissance Classroom,* edited by Juanita Feros Ruys, John O. Ward, and Melanie Heyworth, 23–60.

Knight, L. Stanley. "The Welsh Monasteries and their Claims for Doing the Education of Later Medieval Wales." *Archaeologia Cambrensis,* 20, 6th ser. (1920): 257–75.

Knox, Peter E., ed. *A Companion to Ovid.* Oxford, 2009.

Koch, John T. "*Ériu, Alba,* and *Letha:* When was a Language Ancestral to Gaelic First Spoken in Ireland?" *Emania* 9 (1991): 17–27.

———. "New Thoughts on *Albion, Iernē* and the Pretanic Isles." *Proceedings of the Harvard Celtic Colloquium* 6 (1986): 1–28.

Korhammer, Michael. "Mittelalterliche Konstruktionshilfen und altenglische Wortstellung." *Scriptorium,* 34 (1980): 18–58.

Lambert, Pierre-Yves. "'Fraudatiuus': une denomination ancienne du 'datiuus incommodi' dans le monde celtique." *Revue de Philologie* 57 (1983): 39–45.

———. "Gloses en vieux-breton: 1–5." *Études celtiques* 26 (1989): 81–93.

———. "Gloses en vieux-breton: 6–9." *Études celtiques* 27 (1990): 337–61.

———. "La situation linguistique de la Bretagne dans le haut moyen age." *La Bretagne linguistique,* 5 (1988–89): 139–51.

———. "La typologie des gloses en vieux-breton." *Britannia Monastica* 1 (1990): 13–21.

———. "Les commentaires celtiques à Bède le vénérable, I." *Études celtiques* 20 (1983): 119–143.

———. "Les commentaires celtiques à Bède le vénérable, II." *Études celtiques* 21 (1984): 185–206.

———. "Les gloses du manuscript BN Lat. 10290." *Études celtiques* 19 (1982): 173–213.

———. "Les gloses en vieux-breton aux écrits scientifiques de Bède, dans le manuscrit Angers 477." In *Bède le Vénérable entre Tradition et Postérité,* edited by S. Lebecq, M. Perrin, and O. Szerwiniack, 309–19. Lille, 2005.

———. "Les gloses grammaticales brittoniques." *Études celtiques* 24 (1987): 285–308.

———. "Notes sur quelques gloses à Priscien." In *A Companion in Linguistics. A Festschrift for Anders Ahlqvist on the Occasion of his Sixtieth Birthday,* edited by B. Smelik, R. Hofman, et al., 36–48. Nijmegen, 2005.

———. "Old Irish *gláosnáthe* 'linea, norma.'" *Celtica* 21 (1990): 235–39.

———. "The Old Welsh Glosses on Weights and Measures." In *Yr Hen Iaith. Studies in Early Welsh,* edited by Paul Russell, 103–34. Aberystwyth, 2003.

——. "Rencontres culturelles entre Irlandais et Bretons aux IXe et Xe siècles: le témoignage des gloses." In *Irlande et Bretagne. Vingt siècles d'Histoire*, edited by C. Laurent and H. Davis, 96–107. Rennes 1994.

——. "'Thirty' and 'Sixty' in Brittonic." *CMCS* 8 (1984): 29–43.

——. "Vieux-gallois *nou, nom, inno.*" *BBCS* 20 (1982-83): 20–29.

Lapidge, Michael. *The Anglo-Saxon Library*. Oxford, 2006.

——. "Colloquial Latin in the Insular Latin Scholastic *Colloquia?*" In *Colloquial and Literary Latin*, edited by Eleanor Dickey and Anna Chahoud, 406–18. Cambridge, 2010.

——. "Latin Learning in Dark Age Wales: Some Prolegomena." In *Proceedings of the Seventh International Congress of Celtic Studies, Oxford 1983*, edited by D. Ellis Evans, John G. Griffith, Eric M. Jope, 91–107. Oxford, 1986.

——. "The Study of Latin Texts in Anglo-Saxon England: I. The Evidence of Latin Glosses." In *Latin and the Vernacular Languages in Early Medieval Britain*, edited by Nicholas Brooks, 99–140. Leicester, 1982.

——. "The Welsh-Latin Poetry of Sulien's Family." *Studia Celtica* 8–9 (1973–74): 68–106.

Law, Vivian. *The Insular Latin Grammarians*. Woodbridge, 1982.

Lawrence, Anne. "English Cistercian Manuscripts of the Twelfth Century." In *Cistercian Art and Architecture in the British Isles*, edited by Christopher Norton and David Park, 284–98. Cambridge, 1956.

Leedham-Green, Elisabeth, and Teresa Webber, eds. *The Cambridge History of Libraries in Britain and Ireland. Volume I to 1640.* Cambridge, 2006.

Leitschuh, Friedrich, and Hans Fischer. *Katalog der Handschriften der königlichen Bibliothek zu Bamberg.* 3 vols. Bamberg, 1887–1912; repr. 1966.

Lemmen, Karianne. "The Old Welsh Glosses in Martianus Capella Revised and Rearranged with Newly Found Glosses." Unpublished Utrecht University thesis. Utrecht, 2006.

Lendinara, Patrizia. "Instructional Manuscripts in England: the tenth- and eleventh-century codices and the early Norman ones." In *Form and Content of Instruction in Anglo-Saxon England in the Light of Contemporary Manuscript Evidence*, edited by Patrizia Lendinara, 59–113. Turnhout, 2007.

Lenz, Friedrich W. "Die Wiedergewinnung der von Heinsius benutzten Ovidhandschriften in den letsten fünfzig Jahren." *Eranos* 51 (1953): 66–88.

Lewis, Barry. "Bardd Natur yn Darllen Bardd y Ddinas? Dafydd ap Gwilym, 'Y don ar Ddyfi,' ac Ofydd, *Amores*, III.6." *Llên Cymru* 31 (2008): 1–22.

Lewis, Henry. *Yr Elfen Lain in yr Iaith Gymraeg*. Cardiff, 1943.

——. "Glosau Rhydychen," *BBCS* 3 (1926–27): 1–4.

——. "Nodiadau Cymysg." *BBCS* 11 (1941–44): 77–85.

——. "Nodiadau Cymysg." *BBCS* 14 (1949–50): 193–204.

Lewis, Henry, and Holger Pedersen. *A Concise Comparative Celtic Grammar.* 2nd ed. Göttingen, 1961.

Lewis, J. M. and David H. Williams. *The White Monks in Wales.* Cardiff, 1976.

Lewis, Meinir. "Disgrifiad o Orgraff Hen Gymraeg gan ei Chymharu ag Orgraff Hen Wyddeleg." Unpublished University of Wales M. A. dissertation. Aberystwyth, 1961.

Lhuyd, Edward. *Archaeologia Britannica.* Oxford, 1707.

Lindsay, W. M. *Notae Latinae: an Account of the Abbreviations in Latin MSS. of the Early Minuscule Period (ca. 700–850).* Cambridge, 1915.

Lindsay, W. M. *Early Welsh* Script. Oxford, 1912.

Lloyd-Jones, John. "Nodiadau ar Eiriau." *BBCS* 15 (1952–53): 194–203.

Lloyd-Morgan, Ceridwen. "The Book in Fifteenth-Century Wales." *Poetica* 60 (2004): 1–13.

———. "Manuscripts and the Monasteries." In *Monastic Wales. New Approaches,* edited by J. Burton and K. Stöber, 209–27. Cardiff, 2013.

———. "Medieval Manuscripts at the National Library of Wales." In *Sources, Exemplars, and Copy-Texts: Influence and Transmission,* edited by William Marx. *Trivium* 31 (1999): 1–12.

Loew, E. Avery. *The Beneventan Script: A History of the South Italian Minuscule,* Sussidi Eruditi 33 and 34, rev. ed. Rome, 1980.

Löfstedt, Bengt. "*Fregit bellum ante Cassibellaunum.*" *Éigse,* 18 (1980–81): 181.

Loomis, Richard Morgan. *Dafydd ap Gwilym. The Poems.* Binghampton, 1982.

Loth, Joseph. *Vocabulaire vieux-breton.* Paris, 1884; repr. Geneva, 1982.

Love, Rosalind. "The Library of the Venerable Bede." In *The Book in Britain I,* edited by Richard Gameson, 606–32.

Madan, Falconer, and Herbert H. E. Craster. *A Summary Catalogue of Western Manuscripts in the Bodleian Library at Oxford.* 7 vols. Oxford, 1895–1953.

Maltby, Robert. *A Lexicon of Ancient Latin Etymologies.* Leeds, 1991.

Marx, William. "Middle English Texts in Welsh Contexts." In *Authority and Subjugation in Writing of Medieval Wales,* edited by Ruth Kennedy and Simon Meecham-Jones, 13–26. London and New York, 2008.

Matonis, Ann. "The Rhetorical Patterns in Marwnad Llywelyn ap Gruffudd by Gruffudd ab yr Ynad Coch." *Studia Celtica,* 14–15 (1979–80): 188–92.

McGregor, J. H. "Ovid at School: from the Ninth to the Fifteenth Century." *Classical Folia. Studies in the Christian Perpetuation of the Classics,* 32 (1978): 29–51.

McKee, Helen. *The Cambridge Juvencus Manuscript Glossed in Latin, Old Welsh and Old Irish. Text and Commentary.* Aberystwyth, 2000.

———. "The Circulation of Books between England and Celtic Realms." In *The Book in Britain I,* edited by Richard Gameson, 338–43.

———. "Scribes and Glosses from Dark Age Wales: the Cambridge Juvencus Manuscript." *CMCS* 39 (2000): 1–22.

———. "Script in Wales, Scotland and Cornwall." In *The Book in Britain I,* edited by Richard Gameson, 167–73.

McKie, David S. "Ovid's *Amores*: The Prime Sources for the Text." *Classical Quarterly* 36 (1986): 219–38.

McKinley, Kathryn L. "Manuscripts of Ovid in England, 1100–1500." *English Manuscript Studies, 1100–1700* 7 (1998): 41–86.

McKitterick, David. "Bradshaw, Henry (1831–1886)." In *ODNB, s.n.*

Morgan, Nigel, and Rodney M. Thomson, eds. *The Book in Britain II, 1100–1400.* Cambridge, 2008.

Munari, Franco. "Codici Heinsiani degli *Amores*." *Studi Italiani di Filologia Classica* 24 (1949): 161–65.

Munari, Franco. *Il codice Hamilton 471 di Ovidio* (Ars Amatoria, Remedia Amoris, Amores), Note e Discussioni Eruditi 9. Rome, 1965.

———. "Manoscritti Ovidiani di N. Heinsius." *Studi Italiani di Filologia Classica* 29 (1957): 98–114.

Munk Olsen, Birger. "Accessus to the Classical Poets in the Twelfth Century."
In *The Classics in the Medieval and Renaissance Classroom*, edited by Juanita Feros Ruys,
John O. Ward, and Melanie Heyworth, 131–44.

———. *L'étude des auteurs classiques latins aux XIe et XIIe siècles.* 4 vols. Paris 1982–2009.

———. "Ovide au Moyen-Age (du IXe et XIIe siècle)." In *Le strade del Testo*, edited by
G. Cavallo, 65–96. Bari, 1987. Reprinted in B. Munk Olsen, *La réception de la littérature
classique au Moyen Age (IXe–XIIe siècle).* Copenhagen, 1995. 71–94.

Mynors, Roger, and Rodney M. Thomson. *Catalogue of the Manuscripts of Hereford Cathe-
dral Library.* Cambridge, 1993.

Ó Cróinín, Dáibhí. "The Reception of Johann Kaspar Zeuss's *Grammatica Celtica* in Ire-
land and Britain, and on the Continent: Some New Evidence." In *Recht—Wirtschaft—
Kultur: Herausforderungen an Staat und Gesellschaft im Zeitalter der Globalisierung. Fest-
schrift für Hans Hablitzel zum 60. Gerburtstag*, edited by M. Wollenschläger, E. Kressel,
and J. Egger, 83–93. Berlin, 2005.

Ó Néill, Pádraig. "Celtic Britain in the Early Middle Ages." In *The Cambridge History
of Libraries in Britain and Ireland I*, edited by Elisabeth Leedham-Green and Teresa
Webber, 69–90.

O'Neill, Patrick. "Latin Learning at Winchester in the Early Eleventh Century: the Evi-
dence of the Lambeth Psalter." *Anglo-Saxon England* 20 (1991): 143–66.

Ogilvy, Jack D. A. *Books Known to the English.* Cambridge, Mass., 1967.

Orchard, Andrew. "Aldhelm's Library." In *The Book in Britain I*, edited by Richard Game-
son, 591–605.

Orme, Nicholas. "Schools and Schoolmasters (to ca. 1550)." In *The Cambridge History
of Libraries in Britain and Ireland I*, edited by Elisabeth Leedham-Green and Teresa
Webber, 420–34.

———. *Medieval Schools: from Roman Britain to Renaissance England.* New Haven, 2006.

Owen, Arthur E. B. "Henry Bradshaw and his Correspondents." *Transactions of the Cam-
bridge Bibliographical Society* 11 (1996–99): 480–97.

Pächt, Otto, and Jonathan J. G. Alexander *Illuminated Manuscripts in the Bodleian Library.*
3 vols. Oxford, 1966–73.

Parina, Elena. "On the Semantics of Adjectives in Old Welsh Glosses: *Dur* in Ovid 41b."
Journal of Celtic Linguistics 16 (2015): 1–39.

Parry, Thomas. "Dafydd ap Gwilym." *Yorkshire Celtic Studies* 5 (1945–52): 19–31.

Parry-Williams, Thomas H. *The English Element in Welsh: A Study of English Loanwords in
Welsh.* London, 1923.

Parsons, David. *Martyrs and Memorials. Merthyr Place-Names and the Church in Early Wales.*
Aberystwyth, 2013.

Patterson, Robert B. *The Scriptorium of Margam Abbey and the Scribes of Early Angevin
Glamorgan. Secretarial Administration in a Welsh Marcher Barony, ca. 1150–ca. 1225.*
Woodbridge, 2002.

Pedersen, Holger. *Vergleichende Grammatik der keltischen Sprachen.* 2 vols. Göttingen,
1909–13.

Pellegrin, Elisabeth. "Les *Remedia amoris* d'Ovide: texte scolaire médiévale." *Bibliothèque
de l'École des Chartes* 115 (1957): 172–79.

Philip, Ian. *The Bodleian Library in the Seventeenth and Eighteenth Centuries.* Oxford, 1983.

Porter, David W. "The Latin Syllabus in Anglo-Saxon Monastic Schools." *Neophilologus*
78 (1994): 463–82.

Pryce, Huw, ed. "Y Canu Lladin er Cof am yr Arglwydd Rhys." In *Yr Arglwydd Rhys*, edited by Huw Pryce and Nery Ann Jones, 212–23. Cardiff, 1996.

Rand, Edward K. "The Medieval Virgil." *Studi medievali* NS 5 (1932): 418–42.

Reeve, Michael D. "Heinsius' Manuscripts of Ovid." *Rheinisches Museum für Philologie* 117 (1974): 133–66.

———. "Heinsius' Manuscripts of Ovid: A Supplement." *Rheinisches Museum für Philologie* 119 (1976): 65–78.

———. "The Rediscovery of Classical Texts in the Renaissance." In Michael D. Reeve, *Manuscripts and Methods. Essays on Editing and Transmission*, 229–54. Rome, 2011. (Originally published in *Itinerari dei Testi Antichi*, edited by O. Pecere, 115–57. Rome, 1991.)

Reynolds, Leighton D., ed. *Texts and Transmission. A Survey of the Latin Classics*. Oxford, 1983.

Reynolds, Suzanne. *Medieval Reading: Grammar, Rhetoric, and the Classical Text*. Cambridge, 1996.

Rhŷs, John. "Die kymrischen Glossen zu Oxford." *Beiträge zur vergleichende Sprachforschung* 7 (1873): 228–39.

Riché, Pierre. *Écoles et enseignement dans le haut hoyen âge (fin du Vᵉ—milieu du XIᵉ siècle)*. 2nd ed. Paris, 1989.

Richmond, J. "Manuscript Traditions and the Transmission of Ovid's Works." In *Brill's Companion to Ovid*, edited by Barbara W. Boyd, 443–83.

Rickert, Margaret. *Painting in Britain: The Middle Ages*. London, 1954.

Rittmueller, Jean. "Construe Marks, a Contraction Mark, and an Embedded Old Irish Gloss in an Hiberno-Latin Homily on the Octave of Easter." In *Culture and Tradition in Medieval Ireland. Festschrift for Dáibhí Ó Cróinín*, edited by Jacopo Bisagni and Pádraic Moran, 537–76. Turnhout, 2015.

Robathan, Dorothy M. "Ovid in the Middle Ages." In *Ovid*, edited by J. W. Binns, 191–209.

Roberts, Brynley F. "The Discovery of Old Welsh." *Historiographia Linguistica*, 26 (1999): 1–21.

———. "Edward Lhuyd a Darganfod Hen Gymraeg." In *Hispano-Gallo-Brittonica. Essays in Honour of Professor D. Ellis Evans on the Occasion of his Sixty-Fifth Birthday*, edited by Joseph F. Eska, R. Geraint Gruffydd, and Nicolas Jacobs, 151–65. Cardiff, 1995.

———. "Translating Old Welsh: the First Attempts." *ZCP* 49–50 (1997): 760–77.

———. "*Ystoriaeu Brenhinedd Ynys Brydeyn*: A Fourteenth-Century Welsh Brut." In *Narrative in Celtic Tradition: Essays in Honour of Edgar M. Slotkin*, edited by Joseph F. Eska, 217–27. CSANA Yearbook 8–9. Colgate, 2011.

Robinson, Fred C. "Syntactical Glosses in Latin Manuscripts of Anglo-Saxon Provenance." *Speculum* 48 (1973): 443–75.

Rodway, Simon. *Dating Medieval Welsh Literature: Evidence from the Verbal System*. Aberystwyth, 2013.

Rooney, Catherine M. "The Manuscripts of the Works of Gerald of Wales." Unpublished University of Cambridge PhD Dissertation. Cambridge, 2005.

Russell, Paul. "*An habes linguam Latinam? Non tam bene sapio*: Views of Multilingualism from the Early Medieval West." In *Multilingualism in the Graeco-Roman Worlds*, edited by Alex Mullen and Patrick James, 193–224. Cambridge, 2012.

——. "Beyond Juvencus: An Irish Context for Some Old Welsh Glossing?" In *Culture and Tradition in Medieval Ireland. Festschrift for Dáibhí Ó Cróinín,* edited by Jacopo Bisagni and Pádraic Moran, 203–14. Turnhout, 2015.

——. *Celtic Word-Formation.* Dublin, 1990.

——. "'Go and Look in the Latin Books': Latin and the Vernacular in Medieval Wales." In *Latin in Medieval Britain,* edited by Richard Ashdowne and Carolinne White, 213–46. Proceedings of the British Academy. London, 2017.

——. "'Grilling in Calcutta': Stokes, Bradshaw and Old Welsh in Cambridge." In *The Tripartite Life of Whitley Stokes,* edited by Elizabeth Boyle and Paul Russell. 144–60.

——. *An Introduction to the Celtic Languages.* London, 1995.

——. "Patterns of Hypocorism in Early Irish Hagiography." In *Saints and Scholars. Studies in Irish Hagiography,* edited by John Carey, Máire Herbert, and P. Ó Riain, 237–49. Dublin, 2001.

——. "Recent Work in British Latin." *CMCS* 9 (1985): 19–29.

——. "Revisiting the 'Welsh Dictator' of the Old English Orosius." *Quaestio Insularis* 12 (2011): 31–62.

——. "*Rowynniauc, Rhufoniog:* the Orthography and Phonology of /μ/ in Early Welsh." In *Yr Hen Iaith,* edited by Paul Russell, 25–47. Aberystwyth, 2003.

——. "Teaching between the Lines: Grammar and *Grammatica* in the Classroom in Medieval Wales." In *Grammatica, Gramadach, Gramadeg: Vernacular Grammar and Grammarians in Medieval Ireland and Wales,* edited by Deborah Hayden and Paul Russell, 133–48. Amsterdam, 2016.

——. "'Verdunkelte Komposita' in Celtic," *Studia Celtica* 30 (1996): 113–25.

Ruys, Juanita Feros, John O. Ward, and Melanie Heyworth, eds. *The Classics in the Medieval and Renaissance Classroom. The Role of Ancient Texts in the Art Curriculum as Revealed by Surviving Manuscripts and Early Printed Books.* Disputatio 20. Turnhout, 2013.

Sarginson, Penelope J. "An Edition of the *Ars de Verbo* of Eutyches." Unpublished University of Cambridge PhD Dissertation. Cambridge, 2006.

Scappaticcio, Maria Chiara. "Il 'PHerc.' 817, Angelo Decembrio, Jean d'Armagnac." *Vichiana* (ser. 4) 1 (2008): 84–90.

Scarcia Piacentini, Paola. "Angelo Decembrio e la sua scrittura." *Scrittura e Civiltà* 4 (1980): 247–77.

Schad, Samantha. *A Lexicon of Latin Grammatical Terminology.* Pisa, 2007.

Schrijver, Peter. *Studies in British Celtic Historical Phonology.* Leiden Studies in Indo-European 5. Amsterdam, 1995.

Schwarz, A. "Glossen als Texte." *Beiträge zur Geschichte der deutschen Sprache und Literatur* 99 (1977): 25–36.

Sharpe, Richard. "In Quest of Pictish Manuscripts." *Innes Review,* 59 (2008): 145–67.

Sims-Williams, Patrick. "The Emergence of Old Welsh, Cornish and Breton Orthography, 600–800: The Evidence of Archaic Old Welsh." *BBCS,* 38 (1991): 20–86.

——. "The Uses of Writing in Early Medieval Wales." In *Literacy in Medieval Celtic Societies,* edited by Huw Pryce, 15–38. Cambridge, 1998.

Spargo, J. W. *Virgil the Necromancer: Studies in the Virgilian Legend.* Cambridge, Mass., 1934.

Stokes, Whitley. "Cambrica: 2. The Old-Welsh Glosses at Oxford." *TPhS* (1860–61): 232–88 (corr. 292–93).

——. "Die Glossen und Verse in dem Codex des Juvencus zu Cambridge." *Beiträge zur vergleichende Sprachforschung* 4 (1865): 385–423.

——. "The Old Welsh Glosses in Juvencus." *Beiträge zur vergleichende Sprachforschung* 7 (1873): 410–16.

——. "The Old-Welsh Glosses on Martianus Capella, with Some Notes on the Juvencus-Glosses." *Beiträge zur vergleichenden Sprachforschung* 7 (1871–73): 285–416.

——. Review of E. Schröder, *Zeuss, Johann Kaspar.* Sonderabdruck aus der *Allgemeinen Deutsche Biographie*, Band XLV (1899), *ZCP* 3 (1901): 199–202.

Sullivan, Richard, E., ed. *"The Gentle Voices of Teachers": Aspects of Learning in the Carolingian Age.* Columbus, 1995.

Tafel, Sigmund. "Die Überlieferungsgeschichte von Ovids *Carmina amatoria.* Verfolgt bis zum 11. Jahrhundert." Unpublished dissertation. Tübingen, 1910.

Tarrant, Richard J. "The *Narrationes* of Lactantius and the Transmission of Ovid's *Metamorphoses.*" In *Formative Stages of Classical Traditions: Latin Texts from Antiquity to the Renaissance: Proceedings of a Conference Held at Erice, 16–22 October 1993*, edited by O. Pecere and Michael D. Reeve, 83–115. Spoleto, 1995.

——. "Nicolaus Heinsius and the Rhetoric of Textual Criticism." In *Ovidian Transformations*, edited by Philip Hardie, A. Barchiesi, S. Hinds, 288–300. Cambridge, 1999.

——. "Ovid." In *Texts and Transmission*, edited by L. D. Reynolds, 257–84.

Thomson, D. "Cistercians and Schools in Late Medieval Wales." *CMCS* 3 (1982): 76–87.

Thomson, Rodney M. *A Descriptive Catalogue of the Medieval Manuscripts in Worcester Cathedral Library.* Woodbridge, 2001.

Thurneysen, Rudolf. *A Grammar of Old Irish.* 2nd ed. Revised and translated by Daniel A. Binchy and Osborn J. Bergin. Dublin, 1946.

——. "Notes sur quelques gloses galloises." *Revue celtique* 11 (1890): 203–6.

Väänänen, Veilo. *Introduction au latin vulgaire.* Paris, 1967.

Wanley, Humphrey. *Librorum vett. septentrionalium, qui in Angliae biblioth. extantium catalogus historico-criticus.* Oxford, 1705 [published as volume II of G. Hickes et al., *Antiquae literaturae septentrionalis libri duo.* Oxford, 1703–5].

Ward, John O. "The *Catena* Commentaries in the *Rhetoric* of Cicero and Their Implications for the Development of a Teaching Tradition in Rhetoric." *Studies in Medieval and Renaissance Teaching* 6.2 (1998): 79–95.

——. "The Classics in the Classroom." In *The Classics in the Medieval and Renaissance Classroom*, edited by Juanita Feros Ruys, John O. Ward, and Melanie Heyworth, 1–22.

——. "From Marginal Gloss to *Catena* Commentary; the Eleventh-Century Origins of a Rhetorical Teaching Tradition in the Medieval West." *Parergon (Text, Scribe, Artefact*, special issue. Edited by B. A. Masters) 13.2 (1996): 109–20.

Warntjes, Immo. "Irische Komputistik zwischen Isidor von Sevilla und Beda Venerabilis: Ursprung, karolingische Rezeption und generelle Forschungsperspektiven," *Viator* 42 (2011): 1–31.

——. *The Munich Computus: Text and Translation. Irish Computistics between Isidore of Seville and the Venerable Bede and Its Reception in Carolingian Times.* Sudhoffs Archiv. Zeitschrift für Wissensscahftgeschichte, Beiheft 59. Stuttgart, 2010.

Watkins, T. Arwyn. "Englynion y Juvencus." In *Bardos. Penodau ar y Traddodiad Barddol Cymreig a Cheltaidd Cyflwynedig i J. E. Caerwyn Williams*, edited by R. Geraint Gruffydd, 29–43. Cardiff, 1982.

Watson, Andrew G. "Thomas Allen of Oxford and his Manuscripts." In *Medieval Scribes, Manuscripts, and Libraries: Essays Presented to N. R. Ker.* London, 1978. 279–314. Reprinted in in *Medieval Manuscripts in Post-Medieval England.* Aldershot, 2004. VII).

Whitbread, Leslie G. "Conrad of Hirsau as Literary Critic." *Speculum* 47 (1972): 234–45.

Wieland, Gernot R. "The Glossed Manuscript: Classbook or Library Book?" *Anglo-Saxon England* 14 (1985): 153–73.

——. *The Latin Glosses on Arator and Prudentius in Cambridge University Library, MS Gg 5. 35.* Studies and Texts (Pontifical Institute of Mediaeval Studies, 61). Toronto, 1983.

——. "Latin Lemma–Latin Gloss: the Stepchild of Glossologists." *Mittellateinisches Jahrbuch* 19 (1984): 91–99.

Williams, David H. *The Welsh Cistercians.* 2 vols. Tenby, 1984.

Williams, Heather. "Dafydd ap Gwilym and the Debt to Europe." *Études celtiques* 34 (1998–2000): 185–213.

Williams, Ifor. "Glosau Rhydychen." *BBCS* 5 (1929–31): 1–8.

——. "Glosau Rhydychen a Chaergrawnt." *BBCS* 6 (1932–3): 112–15.

——. "Glosau Rhydychen: mesurau a phwysau." *BBCS* 5 (1929–31): 226–48; 13 (1948–50): 129.

——. "Naw Englyn y Juvencus." *BBCS* 6 (1933): 205–24, 13 (1948–50): 205.

——. "Notes on Nennius." *BBCS* 7 (1933–35): 380–83.

——. "Testunau." *BBCS* 2 (1923–24): 8–36.

——. "Testunau." *BBCS* 2 (1925): 8–48.

——. "Tri Englyn y Juvencus." *BBCS* 6 (1933): 101–10.

Williams, Ifor, ed. and trans. "The Juvencus Poems." In *The Beginnings of Welsh Poetry,* edited by Rachel Bromwich, 89–121. Cardiff, 1980 [Originally published as Williams, "Tri Englyn y Juvencus" and "Naw Englyn y Juvencus"].

Williams, J. E. Caerwyn. "Cerddi'r Gogynfeirdd i Wragedd a Merched, a'u Cefndir yng Nghymru a'r Cyfandir." *Llên Cymru* 13 (1974–81): 3–112.

Williams, J. E. Caerwyn. "Difod, Diw, Pyddiw." *BBCS* 23 (1969–70): 217–33.

Williams, Robert D. and Thomas S. Pattie. *Virgil. His Poetry Through the Ages.* London, 1982.

Winter, Ursula. *Die Europäischen Handschriften der Bibliothek Diez: Teil 1. Die Manuscripta Dieziana B Santeniana; Teil 2. Die Libri Impressi cum Notis Manuscriptis.* 2 vols. Leipzig, 1986.

Wood, Juliette. "Virgil and Taliesin: The Concept of the Magician in Medieval Folklore." *Folklore* 94 (1983): 91–104.

Woods, Marjorie C. *Classroom Commentaries: Teaching the* Poetria Nova *across Medieval and Renaissance Europe.* Columbus, OH, 2010.

Woods, Marjorie C., ed. and trans. *An Early Commentary on the "Poetria Nova" of Geoffrey of Vinsauf.* New York, 1985.

Wormald, Francis. "Decorated Initials in English MSS. from A. D. 900–1100." *Archaeologia* 91 (1945): 107–35.

Wright, Neil. "Geoffrey of Monmouth and Bede." *Arthurian Literature* 6 (1986): 25–59.

——. "Geoffrey of Monmouth and Gildas." *Arthurian Literature* 2 (1982): 1–40.

——. "Geoffrey of Monmouth and Gildas Revisited." *Arthurian Literature* 4 (1984): 155–63.

Zeiser, Sarah E. "Latinity, Manuscripts, and the Rhetoric of Conquest in Late-Eleventh Century Wales." Unpublished Harvard PhD dissertation. Cambridge, Mass., 2012.

Zeuss, Johann Kaspar. *Grammatica Celtica.* 1st ed. Leipzig, 1853.

——. *Grammatica Celtica,* 2nd ed. Edited by Hermann Ebel. Berlin, 1871.

Ziolkowski, Jan M. "University and Monastic Texts: Latin Poetry, Satire, Fables and Grammar." In *The Book in Britain II,* ed. Morgan and Thomson. 229–44.

Ziolkowski, Jan M., and Michael C. J. Putnam (ed.). *The Virgilian Tradition: The First Fifteen Hundred Years.* New Haven, Conn., 2008.

INDEX OF GLOSSES IN TEXTUAL ORDER

Old Welsh glosses are in **bold**. All references are to the line numbers of the edition.

ALPHABETICAL INDEX OF GLOSSES

The longer glosses are alphabetized under the first word. In addition the separate elements of the longer glosses are alphabetized individually with * indicating that the headword is part of a longer gloss. Old Welsh glosses are in **bold**. All references are to the line numbers of the edition.

a (voc. particle)	31*, 32*
a domina	375
a hir etem	32
a mein funiou	31
a te	71, 138, 142
a(b) (prep.)	18 (r.m.)*, 52*, 71*, 98*, 99*, 138*, 142*, 184* (r.m.), 225*, 324*
ab alis	99
ab ioue	324
abiunt	240
ablatiuus	11, 54, 81, 85, 154, 164, 206, 215, 231, 237, 310, 336, 368, 374
achiles	13, 14, 16, 17*, 18 (r.m.)*
achmonou	332*
ad	99*, 330
ad sspectandos alios	99
adepiscaris	356*
adriaticum	173*
adriaticum et tuscium	173
adsumpta	40
aduerbum	89, 635
aduerte	267
aedes	105
aedificauit	60* (into r.m.), 101*
aegypti	73*

bellum tuum	212
bestiae	224* (r.m.)
bleuporthetic	77*
boi	150*
bonus	146*
bonum	141*
bronnbreithet	271*
buch	77
budicaul	211

caiauc	167*
caitoir	332*
caldaicis	226
cant	102*
captiuos	215
cared	138
carmen	2*
carmine	206
cecinet	271*
cecinet bronnbreithet	271
ceenn	251*
cein	180*
ceintiru	73*
celat	276
cemmein	107*
cessar	202, 204*
cesarem	181
cessaris	193
cessari	203
cessaribus	184* (r.m.)
cessar deus octauianus	204
cilchetou	103*
citharistae	11
citius	317*
ciuitas	225*, 255*, 259
ciuitatis	60 (into r.m.)
ciuitas in italia	255
ciuitas quae a danio fabricata	225
clamoris	113
claritas	72
cloriou	71*
cogitant	110
coilou	191*
colorem	250*
com	188
concaua	255
concubina	365

feret	199
fieri	184* (r.m.)
fili aegypti	73
filia	331*
filiae	74*
filiae danai filius beli	74
filius	74*, 165*, 337* (r.m.)
fili	73*
filiorum	336
finem	281* (r.m.) (*bis*)
flos	96*
flos uel proprium	96
fluminis	60 (into r.m.)
fluuius	223* (l.m.)
forma	224* (r.m.)
formam	307* (r.m.)
forma bestiae; tigris de nomine bestiae uelocis quae dicitur tigris	224 (r.m.)
forum	foro 83*
fora	81 (*bis*)
frangere	200*
frangere bellum ante se	200
frigea	625
fronte	309* (r.m.)
fugam	209*
funiou	31*
furio	119

garr	32*
genetiuus	29
gladio	74*
graecia	54
graecos	13
grudou	129
guarai	106
guaroimaou	89
guaroiou	133
guas	309*
guas marchauc	309
gubernatoris	6
guiannuin	271*
guis	214*
gulan	251
guobri	234
guobriach (comp.)	65
guodemisauch	180*
guoguith	302

pu	120
puella	43, 123, 128, 218, 221, 234
puellam	127*, 367
puellas	78, 126, 623
puellarum	159
puellis	134, 218, 639
pui	305

quae	225*, 335* (into r.m.)
quae dicitur	224* (r.m.)
quaeras	43*
quam	60 (into r.m.), 342
quando	250*
quando fuerint	249
quando fuerint conuiuium et ignis unum colorem habent mulieres omnes	250
quando	249*
quasi	139*
quasi dominae	139
qui	101*, 170*, 240*, 337* (r.m.)
quibus	79*
qui ante fuit	240
qui poscit	170
quia	130*, 173, 187* (into r.m.), 241*
quia sagaciores sunt quam quomodo fuerunt	241
quis	79, 158
quod	238*
quomodo	241*

referes	221
regionis	57*
regis	649*
renouat	628
repleta	80*
repleta est	80
responsa	345
retia	270
rex	101*
rex qui aedificauit romam	101
ringuedaulion	137
roga	148
rogare	37*
rogare usque dun inuenies	37
roma	56
romam	101*
romano	1

taurum	293, 315
tauro	322
teg	214*
teg guis	214
tellure	107
tergum	157*
termisceticion	101
terrarum	194
tiberis	60 (into r.m.)
tigris	224* (r.m.)
tinetic	251*
tinguit	235
tiphis	18 (r.m.)*
tirinthio	187* (into r.m.)
titiones	22
tolle	389
tra	182
tristis	123
triumphales	184* (r.m.)
troi	138*
troi enmeituou	138
troia	364
troiae	333
troiano	54
troianos	13*, 363
tu	370*
te	52*, 71*, 138*, 142*, 372
tibi	309
tu ipsa	370
tunc	87, 106, 155, 178, 233, 636, 649
tuscium	173*
tuscois	111*
tuum	212*

---

uacca	279, 314, 324
uaccam	317, 318, 325
ubique	41
uel	96*, 102*, 146* (*bis*), 186*, 356*
uel bonus uel malus	146
uelocis	224* (r.m.)
ueloces	3*
uenus	18 (r.m.)*, 30, 60, 69
ueneris	80*, 165*
ueneris amoris	80
uettes	190
uia	40
uim	130*, 141*

INDEX OF MANUSCRIPTS CITED

All references are to page numbers.

GENERAL INDEX

References to manuscripts, text, and glosses are to be found in the other indices. All references below are to page numbers.

TEXT AND CONTEXT

Frank Coulson, Series Editor

Text and Context is devoted to the study of manuscripts and manuscript culture from late antiquity to the Renaissance. Works published in the series encompass all aspects of manuscript production, including the material culture of the codex, editions of new texts, manuscript catalogs, as well as more theoretical studies. The series covers vernacular as well as Latin manuscripts.

CPSIA information can be obtained
at www.ICGtesting.com
Printed in the USA
LVHW102117030423
743296LV00006B/42